Fragments Of A Faith Forgotten: Some Short Sketches Among The Gnostics, Mainly Of The First Two Centuries. A Contribution To The Study Of Christian Origins Based On The Most Recently Recovered Materials

George Robert Stow Mead

Nabu Public Domain Reprints:

You are holding a reproduction of an original work published before 1923 that is in the public domain in the United States of America, and possibly other countries. You may freely copy and distribute this work as no entity (individual or corporate) has a copyright on the body of the work. This book may contain prior copyright references, and library stamps (as most of these works were scanned from library copies). These have been scanned and retained as part of the historical artifact.

This book may have occasional imperfections such as missing or blurred pages, poor pictures, errant marks, etc. that were either part of the original artifact, or were introduced by the scanning process. We believe this work is culturally important, and despite the imperfections, have elected to bring it back into print as part of our continuing commitment to the preservation of printed works worldwide. We appreciate your understanding of the imperfections in the preservation process, and hope you enjoy this valuable book.

PREFACE TO THE SECOND EDITION.

THE second edition is practically a reprint of the first. I have removed or altered a few words and phrases, have added the newest-found Oxyrhynchus *logoi*, endeavoured to bring the bibliography up-to-date, and appended an index.

G. R. S. M.

CHELSEA, 1906.

PREFACE TO THE FIRST EDITION.

SOME years ago I published in magazine-form a series of short sketches, entitled *Amongst the Gnostics of the First Two Centuries*, drawn from the polemical writings of the Church Fathers. I have since then been asked repeatedly to rescue them from the oblivion of the back-numbers of a Review, and publish them apart. This I was for long unwilling to do because I had planned a large work, to comprise a number of volumes, and to be called *Round the Cradle of Christendom*, the materials of which I was collecting and gradually publishing in magazine articles, with the intention of gathering them all finally together, revising, and printing them in book-form. This, however, would have meant the work of many years, work that might never be completed (for no man can count on the future), and which would, therefore, have remained in the form of an apparently disconnected mass of articles, without plan or purpose. I have, therefore, decided to publish a pioneer sketch —a programme as it were—the outlines of which I hope to fill in with more detailed work in a series of volumes, small or large as the importance of the various subjects demands.

The second of the three main divisions of the present volume, then, consists, for the most part, of matter already published; it has, however, been throughout carefully revised. For the rest, I have endeavoured to give the reader a bird's-eye view of the whole field of early Gnosticism. I have, therefore, added to the above-mentioned articles the main material to be derived from the Uncanonical Acts and the Coptic Gnostic works, and have prefaced the whole with a general introduction, dealing mainly with the background of the Gnosis. To all of this I have appended a short conclusion and some bibliographical indications to help the student. The treatment of the subject is, therefore, new, in that no one has previously attempted to bring the whole of these materials together.

These sketches are not, however, primarily intended for the student, but are written for the general reader. I have throughout endeavoured my best to keep the interests of the latter always in view, though I hope at the same time to have given the student the assurance that the best authorities have been invariably consulted. I have, therefore, on the one hand, explained many things with which the scholar is generally supposed to be already familiar, and, on the other, have strenuously resisted the temptation to learned annotation, to which the subject readily lends itself in every paragraph, but which would swell this volume to ten times its present size. I have, then, written so that the man of one language only may read from the first to the last page, without being forced to regret his ignorance of other tongues; for I believe that the subject is of profoundly human interest, and not one of merely academical importance. It is true that the difficulty of the subject is at times so great that even with the best will in the world I have entirely failed to make the matter clear; but this is also true of every other writer in the field. The nature of these sketches, however, is such that if one paragraph deals with a subject which is beyond our comprehension, another is simple enough for all to understand; so that when the general reader comes to a difficult passage he need not lose courage, thinking that greater difficulty is to follow, for it frequently happens that just the opposite is the case.

Above all things I would have it understood that whatever views I have expressed in these pages, they are all purely tentative; my main object has been to hand on what the earliest Christian philosophers and teachers wrote and thought. They seem to me to have written many beautiful things, and I, for my part, have learned through them to sense the work of the Great Master in a totally new light.

G. R. S. M.

LONDON, 1900.

SYNOPSIS OF CONTENTS.

	PAGE
INTRODUCTION	1—153
PROLEGOMENA	3—28
The Creed of Christendom	3
The New Era Two Thousands Years ago	4
The New Hope of To-day	5
Our Present Task	5
The One Religion	6
The Sunshine of its Doctrine	7
The Comparative Science of Religion ...	8
The True Scholar of Religion	9
The Just Method of Comparison ...	9
The Analysis of Religion	10
The Beginnings of Christianity ...	11
The First Two Centuries	12
The "Higher Criticism"	14
"Providentissimus Deus"	14
Its Immediate Result	16
The Force of Reaction	17
The Force of Progress	18
The Nature of Criticism	18
The Resultant	19

	PAGE
Nineteen Centuries Ago and Now	21
The Return of Souls	23
The Conditions of the Comparison	23
The Intensified Present	24
Occident and Orient	25
The Reconciliation of Science and Theology	25
The Coming and Going of Souls	26
The Birth and Death of Races	27
The Manhood of the Western World	28

SOME ROUGH OUTLINES OF THE BACKGROUND OF THE GNOSIS ... 29—120

PRELIMINARY CONSIDERATIONS ... 29—36

The Greatest Story in the World	29
The Need of a Background	30
The Main Means to a Recovery of the Outlines	30
The Gnostic Schools	32
Where to look for their Origins	32
The Nature of the Field to be Surveyed	33
The Soil of the Field	34
Three Mother Streams	35

GREECE ... 36—57

The Greece of 600 B.C.	36
The Precursors of Pythagoras	37
The Orphic Tradition	39
Primitive Hellas	39
The Wavelets of Aryan Immigration	41
The Orphic Line	42
The Greece of "Homer"	43
"Orpheus" returns to Greece	44
The Mysteries	46
Their Corruption	47
The Reason of it	47

SYNOPSIS OF CONTENTS.

xiii.

	PAGE
The Various Traditions	48
The Political Mysteries	49
The Private Mysteries	49
The Orphic Communities	50
The Philosophic Mysteries	51
Pythagoras and Plato	51
Aristotle and Scepticism	53
East and West	54
Rome	55
The Mysteries of Mithras	55

EGYPT ... 57—65

The Wisdom of Egypt	57
The Blendings of Tradition	58
The Mystic Communities	60
The Therapeuts	60
The Earliest Christians of Eusebius	61
The Pseudo-Philo Theory	62
Its Death-blow	63
An Interesting Question of Date	64
The Title and Context	65

PHILO ON THE CONTEMPLATIVE LIFE ... 66—86

The Essæans	66
The Name Therapeut	66
Their Abandonment of the World	67
Their Retreats	68
The Mareōtic Colony	69
Their Dwellings	69
The Original Meaning of the Term Monastery	70
Their Prayers and Exercises	70
The Nature of their Books	71
Their Mode of Meeting	71
The Sanctuary	72
Their Rule	72

xiv.   FRAGMENTS OF A FAITH FORGOTTEN.

	PAGE
Fasting	73
The Seventh-day Common Meal	73
Housing and Clothing	73
Their Sacred Feasts	74
The Banquet on the Fiftieth Day	75
Seniority	75
The Women Disciples	75
The Plain Couches	76
The Servers	76
The Frugal Fare	77
The President	78
The Instruction	78
The Interpretation of Scripture	79
The Singing of Hymns	79
Bread and Salt	80
The Sacred Dancing	80
The Morning Prayer	82
A Note on the Sacred Numbers	82
Philo's Connection with the Therapeuts	84
The Lay Disciples	85
The Variety of Communities	85
JEWRY	86—95
The Influence of Babylon	86
The Writing of Scripture-history	88
The Mythology of History	88
Honest Self-delusion	90
The Spiritualizing of Judaism	91
Zealotism	91
Pharisaism	92
The Chassidim and Essenes	93
The Inner Schools	94
ALEXANDRIA	95—120
A Bird's-eye View of the City	96

	PAGE
The Populace	100
The Library	102
The Museum	106
The Schools of the Sophists	109
The Dawn-land	110
The New Religion	113
Jewish and Christian Schools	116

GENERAL AND GNOSTIC CHRISTIANITY 121—153

THE EVOLUTION OF CATHOLIC CHRISTIANITY ... 121—125

The Canon	121
The Gospels	122
The Letters of Paul	123
The Gentilization of Christianity	124

THE EBIONITES ... 126—130

The Nazoræans	126
The Poor Men	127
The Ebionite Tradition of Jesus	128

THE ESSENES ... 131—136

Their Manner of Life	132
The Degrees of Holiness	133
Points of Contact with Christianity	134

THE TENDENCIES OF GNOSTICISM ... 136—142

The "Secularizing" of Christianity	136
Yahweh not "the Father" of Jesus	138
The Inner Teaching	138
Various Classes of Souls	139
The Person of Jesus	140
The Main Doctrines	141

THE LITERATURE AND SOURCES OF GNOSTICISM. 143—153

Literature	143
Indirect Sources	146
Direct Sources	151

xvi.   FRAGMENTS OF A FAITH FORGOTTEN.

	PAGE
THE GNOSIS ACCORDING TO ITS FOES	155—449
SOME GNOSTIC FRAGMENTS RECOVERED FROM THE POLEMICAL WRITINGS OF THE CHURCH FATHERS	157—414
No Classification possible	157
THE "SIMONIANS"	160—161
The Origin of the Name	160
DOSITHEUS	162—164
A Follower of John the Baptist	162
The Pre-Christian Gnosis	163
"SIMON MAGUS"	164—174
The Ebionite "Simon"	165
The "Simonian" Literature	167
The "Simonian" System of Irenæus	168
The Great Announcement	170
The Hidden Fire	171
The Fire Tree	172
The Æons	173
MENANDER	175—177
His Date	175
His Doctrines	175
A Link with Zoroastrianism	177
SATURNINUS	177—180
The Chain of Teachers	177
Asceticism	178
Summary of Doctrines	178
The Making of Man	180
THE "OPHITES"	181—188
The Obscurity of the Subject	181

The Term "Ophite"	182
The Serpent Symbol	183
The Myth of the Going-forth	186
Pseudo-philology	187
An Anonymous System from Irenæus	188—193
The Spiritual Creation	188
Yahweh Ialdabaōth	189
O. T. Exegesis	189
Christology	191
Jesus	191
An Early "Ophite" System	193—197
Justinus	193
The Book of Baruch	194
Baruch	196
Christology	197
The Naasseni	198—206
Their Literature	198
Their Mystical Exegesis	199
The Assyrian Mysteries	200
The Egyptian	201
The Greek	201
The Samothracian	202
The Phrygian	202
The Mysteries of the Great Mother	203
The Fragment of a Hymn	205
The Peratæ	206—212
The Source of their Tradition	206
The Three Worlds	207
A Direct Quotation	208
The Meaning of the Name	209
Psychological Physiology	210
The Lost Books of Hippolytus	212

xviii. FRAGMENTS OF A FAITH FORGOTTEN.

	PAGE
THE SETHIANS	213—216
Seth	213
An Outline of their System	214
The Mysteries	215
THE DOCETÆ	217—221
God	218
The Æons	218
Cosmos and Man	219
The Saviour	220
MONOÏMUS	222—223
Number Theories	222
How to Seek after God	223
THE SO-CALLED CAINITES	224—229
The Obscurity of the Subject	224
The Enemies of Yahweh the Friends of God	225
Judas	226
A Scrap of History	228
THE CARPOCRATIANS	229—233
Their Idea of Jesus	230
Reincarnation	231
"EPIPHANES"	233—236
The Moon-god	234
Communism	234
The Monadic Gnosis	236
CERINTHUS	237—238
The Scape-Goat for the "Pillar-Apostles"	237
The Over-Writer of the Apocalypse ...	238
NICOLAUS	239—240
"Which Things I hate"	239
CERDO	240—241
The Master of Marcion	240

MARCION	241—249
The Spread of Marcionism	241
The "Higher Criticism"	242
The Gospel of Paul	244
Eznik	246
A Marcionite System	247
The Title Chrēstos	249
APELLES	250—252
His Wide Tolerance	250
Philumēnē	250
Her Visions	251
THE BASILIDIAN GNOSIS	253—284
Basilides and his Writings	253
Our Sources of Information	255
The Divinity beyond Being	256
Universality beyond Being	257
Ex Nihilo	259
The Sonship	260
The Holy Spirit	261
The Great Ruler	262
The Ætherial Creation	263
The Sub-lunary Spaces	264
Soteriology	265
The Mystic Gospel	267
The Sons of God	268
The Final Consummation	270
Jesus	272
Karman and Reincarnation	274
The Theory of "Appendages"	276
Moral Responsibility	277
A Trace of Zoroastrianism	278
The Spurious System	280
Abrasax	282

xx.   FRAGMENTS OF A FAITH FORGOTTEN.

	PAGE
THE VALENTINIAN MOVEMENT	284—293
The "Great Unknown" of Gnosticism	284
"They of Valentinus"	285
The So-called Eastern and Western Schools	287
The Leaders of the Movement	287
The Syntheticizing of the Gnosis	289
Sources of Information	291
VALENTINUS	294—311
Biography	294
Date	296
Writings	297
The Fragments that Remain	298
Concerning the Creation of the First Race of Mankind	299
On the Pure in Heart	300
Concerning One of the Powers of the Perfect Man	302
Ye are Sons of God	303
The Face of God	303
Concerning the People of the Beloved	305
The Galilæans	306
The Wisdom of the "Little One"	306
The Chain of Being	307
The Ariadne's Thread out of the Maze	309
SOME OUTLINES OF ÆONOLOGY	311—335
Towards the Great Silence	311
The Depth beyond Being	312
The Æon World	313
The Platonic Solids	314
A Living Symbolism	316
The "Fourth Dimension"	318
The Eternal Atom	320
The Law of Syzygy	321

SYNOPSIS OF CONTENTS.

The Law of Differentiation	322
The Three and the Seven	323
The Twelve and Ten	323
The Dodecahedron	325
The Decad	326
Chaos	328
Theos	329
Cosmos	331
Mythology	332
The Sophia-Mythus	333
The Mother of Many Names	334
HIPPOLYTUS' ACCOUNT OF ONE OF THE VARIANTS OF THE SOPHIA-MYTHUS	335—357
The Father of All	335
The Parents of the Æons	336
The Names of the Æons	338
The World-Mother	339
The Abortion	340
The Term "Only-begotten"	341
The Cross	342
The Last Limit	343
The Mystic or Cosmic Jesus	345
The Grief of Sophia	346
The Sensible World	347
Its Demiurge	348
"Words" or Minds	351
Souls	351
Bodies	352
The New Man	353
The Mystic Body of the Christ	354
Soteriology	355
THE NUMBER-SYMBOLISM OF MARCUS	358—382
Sources	358

	PAGE
Number-letters	359
Kabalism	361
The Great Name	363
The Echo of the Name	365
The Symbolic Body of the Man of Truth	366
The Numbers	369
Gospel Exegesis	370
The Creation of the Sensible World	372
The Tetraktys	373
Theological Arithmetic	375
Jesus the Master	376
The "Moving Image of Eternity"	378
From the Marcosian Ritual	380
PTOLEMY	383—390
The Letter to Flora	383
The "Higher Criticism"	385
The Source of Moses' Inspiration	387
The Proem to the Fourth Gospel	388
HERACLEON	391—392
His Commentary on the Fourth Gospel	391
BARDESANES	392—405
Biography	392
Writings	393
Indirect Sources	395
From His Hymns	396
The Book of the Laws of Countries	398
Karman	399
Fortune and Nature	400
The Right and Left	401
The Hymn of the Soul	403
THE HYMN OF THE ROBE OF GLORY	406—414

	PAGE
SOME TRACES OF THE GNOSIS IN THE UNCANONICAL ACTS	415—449
FOREWORD	415—418
The Gnostic Acts	415
Catholic Over-Working	416
Early Collectors	417
FROM THE ACTS OF THOMAS	419—426
A Hymn to Wisdom	419
Its Meaning	421
Two Sacramental Invocations	422
A Note thereon	423
The Palace that Thomas built	424
FROM THE ACTS OF JOHN	426—444
A Recently-published Fragment	426
The Rationale of Docetism	426
The Evolution of Tradition	427
Mystic Stories of Jesus	428
The Christ speaks with Jesus	429
An Early Form of One of the Great Miracles	430
A Ritual from the Mysteries	431
The Doxology	434
The Mystery of the Cross	435
The Interpretation thereof	437
The Initiation of the Cross	438
The Higher and Lower Selves	439
A Prayer of Praise to Christ	440
John's Farewell Address to his Community	441
John's Last Prayer	442
The Story of John and the Bugs	443
FROM THE ACTS OF ANDREW	445—446
Address to the Cross	445

xxiv. FRAGMENTS OF A FAITH FORGOTTEN.

	PAGE
FROM THE TRAVELS OF PETER	446—449
The Descent of Man	446
The Mystic Redemption through the Cross	447
Afterword	449

THE GNOSIS ACCORDING TO ITS FRIENDS ... ... 451—602

SOME GREEK ORIGINAL WORKS IN COPTIC TRANSLATION ... 453—592

THE ASKEW AND BRUCE CODICES ...	... 453—458
The Askew Codex	453
The Bruce Codex	454
Translations	455
The Difficulty of the Subject	456
Programme	457

SUMMARY OF THE CONTENTS OF THE SO-CALLED PISTIS SOPHIA TREATISE ...	... 459—506
The Teaching of the Eleven Years ...	459
The Mystic Transfiguration and Ascent in the Twelfth Year	459
The Master Returns to His Disciples ...	460
The Mystic Incarnation of the Twelve ...	460
That the Soul of Elias is Born in John the Baptist	461
Of His Own Incarnation	461
Concerning the Robe of Glory	461
The Hymn of Welcome "Come unto Us"	462
The Three Vestures of Light	463
The Journey into the Height	464
The Master Robs the Æons of a Third of Their Light	465
The Questions of Mary	466
Why the Rulers have been Robbed ...	466

SYNOPSIS OF CONTENTS.

	PAGE
The Shortening of the Times	468
The Heaven-journey Continued	468
The Myth of Pistis Sophia	469
The Enmity of Arrogant	469
The Fall into Matter	470
The Descent of the Soul	471
Its Repentance and Redemption	471
The Degrees of Purification	472
The Light-crown	473
The Final Victory	473
An Otherwise-unknown Story of the Infancy	474
Of the Glory of them of the Thirteenth Æon	476
The Scale of Light	477
The Perfect shall be Higher than the Emanations of Light in the Kingdom	477
The "Last" shall be "First"	478
The Three Supernal Spaces of the Light	478
The Inheritance of Light	479
The Mystery of the First Mystery	479
The Gnosis of Jesus, the Mystery of the Ineffable	479
The Disciples lose Courage in Amazement at the Glories of the Gnosis	480
The Highest Mystery is the Simplest of them All	481
Concerning the One Word of the Ineffable	481
The Glory of Him who Receiveth the Mystery	483
Of the Thrones in the Light-kingdom	484
There are Other Logoi	484
The Degrees of the Mysteries	484
The Boons they Grant	485
The Limbs of the Ineffable	485
The Thousand Years of Light	486
The Books of Ieou	487

xxvi. FRAGMENTS OF A FAITH FORGOTTEN.

	PAGE
Ye are Gods	487
Of Souls in Incarnation	488
The Preaching of the Mysteries	489
The Burden of the Preaching	489
The Boundary Marks of the Paths of the Mysteries	490
The After-death State of the Uninitiated Righteous	490
Of those who Repent and again Fall Back	491
The Added Glories of the Saviours of Souls	492
Concerning the Irreconcilables	492
Of the Infinite Compassion of the Divine	493
Of Those who Mimic the Mysteries	493
Can the Pains of Martyrdom be Avoided	494
The Mystery of the Resurrection of the Dead	494
The Transport of the Disciples	495
That this Mystery is to be Kept Secret	495
The Constitution of Man	496
The Evil Desire which Constraineth a Man to Sin	497
The After-death State of the Sinner	497
And of the Initiated Righteous	498
"Agree with Thine Enemy"	499
The Stamping of the Sins on the Souls	499
The Burning up of the Sins by the Fires of the Baptism-Mysteries	500
The Infinite Forgiveness of Sins	501
But Delay Not to Repent	502
For at a Certain Time the Gates of the Light will be Shut	502
"I know not whence ye are"	503
The Dragon of Outer Darkness	503
The Draught of Oblivion	504

SYNOPSIS OF CONTENTS.

	PAGE
The Parents we are to Leave	504
The Books of Ieou Again	505
The Christ the First of this Humanity to Enter the Light	506
'Tis He Who Holds the Keys of the Mysteries	506
SUMMARY OF THE EXTRACTS FROM THE BOOKS OF THE SAVIOUR	507—517
The Immanent Limbs of the Ineffable	507
The Christ is the Ineffable	507
The Gnosis of the Christ	508
The Initiation of the Disciples on the Mount	508
The First Veil is Drawn Aside	509
They Enter the Way of the Midst	510
The Ordering of the Fate-sphere is Described	510
All Mysteries up to the Light-treasure are Promised them	511
The Punishments of the Ways of the Midst	512
The Duration of the Punishments	512
The Disciples Pray for Mercy to Sinners	513
They Enter an Atmosphere of Exceeding Great Light	514
The Vision of the Baptism-Mysteries	514
They Return to Earth	515
The Celebration of the Mystic Eucharist	515
The Mysteries that are to be Revealed	515
The Punishment of Sinners in the Lower Regions and the Evil Bodies they Receive when Reborn	516
The Cup of Wisdom	516
The Note of a Scribe	517
SUMMARY OF THE FRAGMENTS OF THE BOOK OF THE GREAT LOGOS ACCORDING TO THE MYSTERY	518—546

xxviii. FRAGMENTS OF A FAITH FORGOTTEN.

	PAGE
The Book of the Gnoses of the Invisible God	518
The Hidden Wisdom	518
A Dark Saying is Explained	519
The Flesh of Ignorance	520
The Mysteries of the Treasure of Light	520
To be Revealed to the Worthy Alone	521
The Lesser Mysteries	522
The Good Commandments	522
The Greater Mysteries	523
The Powers they Confer	523
The Mystic Rite of the Baptism of the Water of Life	524
The Baptism of Fire	526
The Baptism of the Holy Spirit	526
The Mystery of Withdrawing the Evil of the Rulers	527
The Powers the Lesser Mysteries Confer	527
The Mystery of the Forgiveness of Sins	528
The Powers it Confers	528
The Ordering of the Light-treasures	529
The Great Light	529
Invocation to the True God	530
Invocation to the Unapproachable	531
The Mystery of the Twelve Æons	531
The Thirteenth Æon	532
The Fourteenth Æon	532
The Three Great Rulers	532
Concerning Ieou the Emanator of the Middle Light-world	533
The Tetragrammaton	534
The Type of the Treasures	535
The Type of the True God Ieou	535
The Mystic Diagrams	536
Cosmic Embryology	536

SYNOPSIS OF CONTENTS.   xxix.

	PAGE
The Seal on the Forehead of Ieou	537
General Characteristics of the Diagrams	537
The Twelve the Order of Jesus	538
Hymn to the First Mystery sung in the Thirteen Æons	539
The Thirteenth Æon	539
The Sixty Treasures	540
The Little Idea	541
The Name of the Great Power	542
Hymn to the Unapproachable God sung in the Seventh Treasure	543
The Great Logoi according to the Mystery	544
The Universal Idea	545
Hymn to the [?First] Mystery	545
The Way of the Midst	546

SELECTIONS FROM THE UNTITLED APOCALYPSE OF THE CODEX BRUCIANUS... ... 547—566

The First Being	547
The Second Being	547
The Supernal Cross	548
The Twelve Depths	548
The Primal Source	549
The Unmanifested	550
The Manifested, the Plērōma	550
Three-faced and Two-faced Space	551
The View of the Commentator	552
Marsanēs, Nicotheus, and Phōsilampēs	553
The Creative Logos	553
The Descent of the Light-spark	554
The Spiritual Atom	554
Hymn to the Logos	555
The Christ	555
The Glorified of the Logos	556

XXX. FRAGMENTS OF A FAITH FORGOTTEN.

	PAGE
The At-one-ment	556
Soteriology	557
The Ineffable Vesture	557
The Purification of the Lower Nature	558
The World-Saviour	558
The Promise	559
The Powers of the Light-vesture	559
The Mothers of Men	560
The Song of Praise of the Mother Above	561
The Hidden Worlds	561
The Man	562
The Lord of Splendour	562
His Promise to Them who Believe	563
The Prayer of the Earth-born	564
The Powers of Discrimination are Given them	564
The Ladder of Purification	565
The Son of God	565
Hymn to the Light	566
NOTES ON THE CONTENTS OF THE BRUCE AND ASKEW CODICES	567—578
The Kinship of the Titled Treatises	567
Date	568
Authorship	568
The Titles	569
The Books of Ieou	569
The Probable Author	570
The Obscurity of the Subject	570
The Original Pistis Sophia Treatise	572
The Coptic Translation	572
The Books of the Saviour	573
The Copyist	573
The Scheme Pre-supposed in these Treatises	574

SYNOPSIS OF CONTENTS. xxxi.

	PAGE
An Appreciation of the Untitled Treatise	576
Not to be Attributed to a Single Author	577
Its Apocalyptic Basis...	577
The Over-working	578

THE AKHMĪM CODEX ... 579—592

The MS. and its Contents	579
The Gospel of Mary	580
The Wisdom of Jesus Christ	582
Irenæus quotes from The Gospel of Mary	582
An Examination of his Statements	583
The Father	583
The Mother	584
The Pentad	584
The Decad	586
The Christ	587
The Egyptian Origin of the Treatise	588
The Opinion of Harnack	589
The Importance of the MS.	591

SOME FORGOTTEN SAYINGS ... 593—602

Rejected Logoi	593
The Oxyrhynchus Papyri	600

CONCLUSION ... 603—633

AFTERWORD ... 605—607

BIBLIOGRAPHIES ... 608—633

GENERAL BIBLIOGRAPHY ... 609—623

Early Works	609
Critical Studies prior to 1851	610
Works subsequent to the Publication of the Philosophumena in 1851	613

xxxii. FRAGMENTS OF A FAITH FORGOTTEN.

	PAGE
THE COPTIC GNOSTIC WORKS	624—627
REVIEWS AND ARTICLES IN ENGLISH AND AMERICAN PERIODICALS	628—630
UNCANONICAL ACTS	630
GNOSTIC (?) GEMS AND ABRAXAS-STUDIES	631
GNOSTIC WORKS MENTIONED BY ANCIENT WRITERS	331
THE MOST RECENT TEXTS OF THE HÆRESIOLOGICAL CHURCH FATHERS AND THEIR ENGLISH TRANSLATIONS	631—633

INDEX.

A

Abdias, 418.
Aberamenthō, 514, 519.
Abiram, 226.
Abortion, 225, 269, 329, 340, 356.
Aboulfatah, 162, 163.
Abrasax, 280, 281, 282, 283.
Abyss, 188, 308, 312.
Accretions, 276.
Acembes, 208.
Achamōth, 334.
Acts, Gnostic, 153, 415.
Acts, Leucian, 417.
Acts of Apostles, 128, 568.
Acts of Andrew, 445.
Acts of John, 426, 434, 443, 445.
Acts of Peter, 152, 417, 580.
Acts of Thomas, 403, 419, 422, 424.
Adam, 189, 190, 247, 299, 446, 447, 551; sons of, 599.
Adam, Book of, 126.
Adamant, 277, 406, 413.
Adamas, 465, 474, 510, 512; Sabaōth, 521, 527.
Adembes, 208.
Adityās, 327.
Æon, 207; divine, 390; fourteenth, 532; incorruptible, 191; living, 311, 329, 344, 365; perfect, 218; of æons, 203; of night, 208; thirteenth, 325, 466, 468, 476, 511, 515, 520, 522, 528, 531, 532, 539.

Æons, 173, 218, 313; names of, 338; parents of, 336; seat of, 440; ten, 337; treasures of, 192; triacontad of, 341; twelve, 337, 465, 511, 531.
Æon-world, 313.
Ætherial, creation, 263; Jesus, 565.
Æthers, 208.
After-death state, 490, 497, 516.
Agapē, 235, 423.
Agathōpus, 302.
Agrapha, 412, 593.
"Agree with thine adversary," 231, 499.
Agrippa Castor, 147, 278.
Ahuramazda, 177.
Ākāsha, 204.
Akhmīm Codex, 152, 579.
Alexander, 39, 97, 99, 279, 357.
Alexandria, 24, 53, 60, 69, 91, 95, 295.
All-Father, 41, 385, 549, 583.
All-Mother, 334, 375.
"All things depending," 307.
Allegories, 71, 79.
Alone-begotten, 218, 341, 388, 390, 553, 554, 555, 586.
Alone-born, 551.
Alpha, 530.
Anāgāmin, 370.
Ananias, 580.
Anatolic, 287, 288, 354.
Anaxagoras, 68.
Anaximander, 37.
Ancestral heart, 301.

Ancient, of days, 348; of eternity, 397.
Andrew, 445, 487, 581.
Ani, 393.
Announcement, Great, 165, 167, 170, 173, 174.
Antioch, 175, 178, 288.
Antitheses, 226.
Ambrose, 64.
Amen, 365, 431; first, 527.
Amens, seven, 529; three, 523, 528.
Amru, 106.
Amshaspends, 177, 339.
Apelles, 250.
Aphrĕdōn, 551.
Aphrodite, 511, 512.
Apocalypse, untitled, 547.
Apocalypses, 94.
Apocrypha, 94.
Apollonius of Tyana, 55.
Apology, 381, 439, 483, 486, 499, 527, 600.
Appendages, 276, 277, 301.
Appended Soul, On an, 277.
Apostle, The, 245.
Arahat, 371.
Ararad, 505.
Archimedes, 108.
Ardesianes, 355.
Arēs, 510.
Arian, 261.
Arithmetic, 223, 335, 375.
Aristobulus, 117.
Aristophanes, 109.
Aristotle, 53, 104, 107.
Arrogant, 468, 469, 470.
Ascension of plērōma, 478.
Asceticism, 178, 184, 248, 274.
Askew Codex, 151, 343, 423, 453, 529.
As Others saw Him, 412, 594.
Astrology, 207, 209, 283, 397.
Athos, Mount, 212, 273.
Atlantic Island, 39, 40.
Atom, 222, 223, 316, 318, 319, 320, 331, 554.

At-one-ment, 389, 556.
Attalus, 104.
Augustine, 251.
Augustus, birthday of, 3.
Authentic, 304, 365, 504, 509, 512, 541, 542.
Axionicus, 288, 355.

B

Babe, 274, 307.
Babel, 407, 410, 411.
Babylon, 86, 89, 204.
Bacchi, 10.
Bacchic mysteries, 67, 81.
Bacchus, 534.
Balance, 512.
Baptism, 176, 238, 377; mysteries of, 499, 533, (vision of) 514, (fires of) 500; myth of dove, 371; of fire, 522, 526; of incense, 515; of Jesus, 278; of Holy Spirit, 515, 522, 526; of midst, 511; of right, 511; of water, 515, 522, (of life) 524.
Baptismal consecration, 380.
Barbĕlō, 178, 334, 514, 515, 531, 583, 584, 585, 586.
Barbĕlō-Gnostics, 167, 568, 583, 589.
Barcabbas and Barcoph, 278.
Bardesanes, 288, 355, 392, 414, 420.
Bardesanites, 395.
Bar-Manu, 393.
Baruch, Book of, 193, 196.
Basilides, 253.
Basilisk, 474.
Baur, 166.
Beelzeboul, 349, 350.
Beloved, people of, 305.
Be-with-us, day, 343.
Bird, great, 473.
Birth, new, 203; of Horus, 60; second, 191, 519; of spiritual man, 60.

INDEX.

Births of joy, 550; of matter, 563.
Bitter, 215, 598.
Blossoms, 442.
Body, 496.
Book of Adam, 126.
Book of Baruch, 193.
Book of the Dead, 301, 343.
Book of Gnoses of Invisible God, 518.
Book of Great Logos according to the Mystery, 152, 455, 457, 567.
Book of Laws of Countries, 394, 398.
Books of Ieou, 455, 487, 505, 533, 569.
Books of the Saviour, 151, 374, 507, 546, 567, 573.
Bosom, Abraham's, 351.
Boundary (*see* Limit) 307, 342, 343; great, 313, 379; highest, 313.
Brahmarandhra, 205.
Brain, 211.
Breath, great, 330; of their mouths, 467.
Bridal chamber, 419, 421.
Brooke, 391.
Brothel, 169.
Brother, Jesus my, 475; Paul our, 568.
Bruchion, 98, 100, 103, 105.
Bubastis, 512.
Buddha, 7, 37.
Bugs, story of John and the, 443.
Burton, 145.
Bythus, 312, 321, 323, 325, 327.

C

Caduceus, 185.
Cain, 190, 224, 226.
Cainites, 198, 224.
Called, 47, 199.
Calligraphists, 103.
Callimachus, 109.
Canon, 121, 241, 243.
Canopus, 97, 103.
Capernaum, 244.
Capparatea, 175.
Caracalla, 393.
Caravanserai (*see* Inn), 301, 443.
Carpocrates, 229.
Cave, 435.
"Cease not to seek," 489.
Cecrops, 41.
Celbes, 208.
Celsus, 150, 183, 233, 589.
Cerdo, 240.
Cerebellum, 211.
Cerinthus, 237.
Chaldæan, influence on Jewry, 93; logia, 172; mysteries, 51, 58, 89; star-cult, 206; tradition, 43, 94.
Chaos, 188, 208, 328, 469, 470, 471, 497; child of, 189.
Charinus, Lucius, 417.
Charis, 588, 595.
Charismatic, 124.
Chassidim, 93, 94.
Child, little, 406; of chaos, 189; of the child, 523, 528.
Children, little, 598; of life, 303; of the fulness, 524; of light, 521; of true mind, 519.
Chiliasm, 124.
Choïc, 199.
Chōrizantes, 104.
Chosen, of God, 90, 92; people, 87, 128.
Chrēstos, 249.
Chrism, 205, 382, 515, 522.
Christ, 227, 273, 327, 378, 448, 542, 556, 586, 587; a, 484; above, 190; and Holy Spirit, 341; distinguished from Jesus, 427; historic gnosis of, 508; invocation to, 380; is the word, 448; Jesus, 368; mystic body of, 354; name of, 422; the, 507, 555; the great master, 430.

Christliche Welt, Die, 4.
Christs, 176, 343, 595, 599.
Circuits (Tours), 446.
City, 419, 421, 547, 557, 566, 602.
Citizens of heaven, 82.
Claps of hands, 79.
Claudius, 109.
Clay, 208, 351.
Clement of Alexandria, 119, 148, 418.
Clementine literature, pseudo, 162, 164, 166.
Cleobius, 164.
Cleopatra, 98, 99, 106, 110.
Closet, 70.
Coats of skin, 190.
Codex, Akhmīm, 152, 579; Askew, 151, 343, 423, 453, 529; Brucianus, 151, 192, 213, 303, 312, 374, 382, 421, 454, 515, 529, 591.
"Come unto us," 409, 462; day of, 343.
Commandments, good, 522.
Commodus, 250.
Common fruit, 331, 345, 346, 349, 351, 352.
Communism, 234.
Communities, 30; mystic, 60; Orphic, 50; variety of, 85.
Community, Mareotic, 85; of friends, 305.
Compendium, 148; of Hippolytus, 14, 149; of Justin, 178; of Theodoret, 150.
Conception, 169, 173.
Concerning Fate, 394.
Concerning the Offspring of Mary, 198.
Confucius, 37.
Conglomeration of seed-mixture, 262, 265, 272, 276.
Consummation, final, 270; of first mystery, 503; gnostic, 405.

Conversion, 448, 449; of spheres, 465, 466, 467.
Conybeare, 61.
Coran, 226.
Corners, four, 525, 542.
Corybantic mysteries, 67.
Counterfeit spirit, 276, 471, 496, 498, 499, 500, 504, 505.
Couch, 433; couches, 76.
Cratylus, 200.
Critias, 39.
Cross, 221, 330, 342, 343, 352, 371, 445, 446, 447, 548, 550, 559; address to, 445; bush of, 435; initiation of the, 438; mystery of, 435; of light, 435; redemption of, 447; of wood, 436; salvation of, 229; supernal, 548.
Crotona, 50.
Crucified in space, 330.
Crucifixion, 227.
Crucify the world, 303, 518.
Cube, 222, 317, 324.
Cumont, 279.
Cup, of life-giving water, 215; of wisdom, 516.
Cureton, 394.
Cyprus, 296.
Cyrus, 89.

D

Dæmonian hierarchies, 512; powers, 190.
Dæmons, 59, 301.
Daevos, 59.
Daisan, 392.
Dance, 80, 433, 437; circular, 195; of initiation, 431.
Daniel, Book of, 25.
Darkness, 188, 390; dragon of, 490, 492, 503; outer, 490, 503, 546.
Darkness, The Light and the, 394.
Dathan, 226.
Daveithe, 588.

INDEX.   xxxvii.

David, 588.
Day Be-with-us, 343; great, 462; of light, 487; of perfect forms, 349; sixth, 371.
Dead, 203; prayers for, 381, 494; resurrection of, 494, 495; raised him from, 354; rise from, 176.
Death, face of, 304.
Decad, 82, 323, 324, 326, 378, 551, 586.
Decans, 510, 539.
Deficiency, 225, 265, 328, 343, 379.
De Legatione, 65.
Delights of world, 496.
Demiurge (*see* Workman), 180, 262, 264, 307, 348, 349, 355, 372, 381, 533.
Democritus, 68.
Depth, 313, 352, 547; beyond being, 312; unutterable, 188.
Depths, twelve, 548.
Desert, 186.
Destiny, 496, 497, 498.
Destruction of False Doctrines, 246.
Deucalion, flood of, 40.
Devas, 59, 363.
Devī, 363.
Diabolus, 232, 349, 350, 384.
Diagram of man of truth, 367; of Ophites, 589.
Diagrams, 536, 537.
Dialogues against the Marcionites, 394.
Diaspora or Dispersion, 91, 135, 361.
Didascaleion, 119, 120.
Dionysus, 42, 49.
Docetism, 217, 302, 328, 426, 427.
Dodecad, 323, 324, 432, 536, 551.
Dodecahedron, 209, 222, 317, 325; rhombic, 325.
Döllinger, 64.

Door, 433, 436.
Dositheus, 162.
Dove, 377, 423, 424, 459; baptism-myth of, 371; father in form of, 238, 278, 354, 515.
Dragon, great, 490; of darkness, 490, 492, 503, 510.
Dry, shame of, 424.
Dwarf, 439, 598.

E

Eagle, 262, 410.
Earth, most beautiful, 194.
Ebion, 127, 237.
Ebionism, 126, 165, 226, 237.
Echo, 365, 373.
Economy, 373, 378.
Eden, 194, 204, 334.
Edessa, 392.
Egg, 185, 214, 320, 331.
Egypt, 407, 466; before flood, 40, 569; Persian conquest of, 59; plagues of, 222; the body, 186; wisdom of, 38, 57.
Egyptian, discipline, 237; mysteries, 51, 58.
Elect, 93, 199, 275, 303, 365, 468.
Eleleth, 588.
Element, scheme of the one, 367.
Eleven years, 459.
Eleusinia, 49, 50, 51, 202.
Eleutherus, 296.
Elias, soul of, 461; to come, 220.
Elkesai, 127.
Elohīm, 189, 190, 194.
Embryology, 281, 505, 536.
Encratism, 178.
Energies, 436.
Enformation according to substance, 329, 376; to knowledge, 329, 376.
Ennads, 551.

Ennœa, 321, 323, 325.
Enoch, 487, 505, 569.
Ephemereuts, 75.
Ephraim, 395.
Epiphanes, 127, 233.
Epiphanius, 150, 589.
Epiphany, 234.
Epopteia, 355.
Erani, 50.
Eratosthenes, 108.
Erectheus, 41.
Esau, 226.
Essenes, 66, 84, 93, 94, 101, 131, 162, 227, 279.
Eta, 532.
Euclid, 108, 314.
Eucharist, 248, 423, 515, 526.
Eudæmonistic eschatology, 142.
Eulogius, 306.
Eumenes, 104.
Euphrates, 204, 208.
Eusebius, 61, 62, 64, 150.
Eve, 189, 190, 247, 351.
"Except a man be born of water," 221.
Excommunication, 241, 295.
Exegetica, 254, 255, 274.
Ex Nihilo, 259.
Exodus (*see* Going-forth) myth, 186.
Exterior of exteriors, 462, 506.
Excerpts from Theodotus, 287, 292, 332, 356.
Ezekiel, vision of, 94.
Eznik, 246.

F

Face, 176, 303, 304, 422, 548.
Faces, authentic, 504.
Fall, into matter, 470; of Sophia, 305; of the soul, 334.
Fate, 395, 397.
Fate, Concerning, 394.
Fate-sphere, 209, 465, 477, 498, 505, 510.
Father, alone good, 301; "he who shall leave," 504, 509; language of my, 533; -mother, 336, 337, 338.
Fatherhood, 368.
Fatherhoods, sixty, 544.
Fear, 361; mystery of their, 546; of the Lord, 267, 348.
Fifteenth year of Cæsar, 278.
Fiftieth day, 74, 75.
Fifty, 82.
Fig-tree, 218.
Filioque, 261.
Fire, 171, 468, 490; at Alexandria, 105, 109; baptism of, 522, 526; finger of, 329; flower of, 172; hidden, 171; life-giving, 219; mist, 185; tree, 172.
Firmament, 262, 263, 266, 311, 464.
First, born, 560, (sons of Satan), 13, 32, 174; last shall be, 478; man, 188, 190, 191, 371, 417, 418, 498, 584, 585; statute, 463, 465; woman, 188.
Fish, 261, 270.
Five, books, 385; impressions, 529; limbs, 422, 423; supporters, 529; trees, 523, 529, 544; years' silence, 278, 282.
Flesh, of ignorance, 520; perfect, 582; of rulers, 468; of unrighteousness, 519; tongue of, 438, 552, 578; word made, 390.
Flood, 40, 505, 569.
Flora, Letter to, 383.
Foreknowledge, 585.
Forethought, 550, 585.
Forgiveness of sins, 501, 523, 527, 530, 531, 533.
Formlessness, 268, 270, 329.
"For this cause I bow my knees," 352.
Fortune, 398, 399, 400.

Forty-nine, 464, 465, 471, 506, 523.
Four, 374; great lights, 588; holy ones, 377; quarters, 509, 525, 542; primal passions, 346; supernal, 363.
Four Quarters of the World, 167.
Four and twenty invisibles, 476.
Four and twentieth mystery, 462.
Fourteenth æon, 532.
Fourth, dimension, 318; gospel, 260, 388, 391.
Freewill, 399.
Fruits of spirit, 338.

G

Gabriel, 377, 473.
Galileans, 306.
Galilee, 524, 582; mount of, 515.
Garment, one, 425; wedding, 405.
Gate, Canopic, 103; "I am the true," 202; of the heavens, 203; of the lord, 202; of truth, 204.
Gates, 538; of light, 502, 503; of the powerful, 333; of the treasure, 474.
Gazzah, 406.
Gennesaret, 430.
"Geometrizes, God," 314.
Gifts of spirit, 441.
Gitta, 164.
Glad tidings, 243, 256, 517.
Glaucias, 254.
Glorified of Logos, 556.
Glory, hymn of the robe of, 406, 419; king of, 421; robe of, 460, 461, 464, 520; vestures of, 472.
Gnosis, 266, 446; Basilidian, 254, 577, (ethical side of), 273; definition of, 32; glories of, 480; Jewish, 118; monadic, 236; outlines of background of, 94; pre-christian, 163, 183; supreme, 480; synthesizing of, 289, 295; Syrian, 177; of all the gnoses, 484; of Christ, 508; of gnosis of ineffable, 508; of Jesus, 479; of mystery of ineffable, 480; of plērōma, 481, 484, 503; of things that are, 32, 52.
"Gods, Ye are," 487.
Going-forth, myth of the, 185, 210.
Good, 67, 201; commandments, 522; deity, 195; God, 203, 243, 247, 441; land, 340; "Why callest thou me," 201.
Gorthæus, 164.
Gospel, 266, 268.
Gospel according to Egyptians, 198, 200, 233, 249.
Gospel according to Hebrews, 126.
Gospel according to Mary, 580.
Gospel according to Thomas, 198, 201.
Gospel of Eve, 198, 439.
Gospel of Judas, 226, 228.
Gospel of Mary, 152, 165, 199, 423.
Gospel of Paul, 244.
Gospel of Perfection, 198.
Gospel of Philip, 198, 439, 540.
Governors, 399, 401.
Grace, 390, 432, 434, 436, 440, 554, 555, 558.
Grasshoppers, 73.
Grätz, 342.
Great, bird, 473; body, 366; boundary, 313, 379; breath, 330; consummation, 421; day, 462; deep, 312; dragon, 490; elements, 188; firmament, 263, 311; harvest,

308; Iao, 529; ignorance, 270, 271; invisible, 532; invisible forefather, 469; Jordan, 202; just one, 532; king, 529; light, 474, 523, 529, 587; lights, 188; limit, 270, 272; logoi according to the mystery, 544; logos, 544; man himself, 529; master, 430; mercy, 270; mind, 205; mother, 191; name, 363, 514, 523, 542, 599; one, 378, 420; peace, 142; power, 164, 171, 173, 185, 543; receiver, 467; ruler, 262, 266, 267, 272; Sabaōth, 513, 529; sea, 40; silence, 311; soul, 467; supporters, 479; teacher, 5; thought, 173; unknown, 309; wedding feast, 397.
Greatness, 352, 363, 372, 423, 424, 440.
Greatnesses, 368, 537.
Grief, 346.
"Greeks are but children," 111.
Grenfell and Hunt, 600, 602.
Guardians, 523, 528, 538.

H

Hades, 447.
Hair of his head, 548.
Hanging on the tree, 343.
Harmogen, 588.
Harmony, 365, 436.
Harmozel, 588.
Harnack, 4, 144, 589.
Harpocratians, 233.
Harvest, great, 308.
Healers, 61, 442.
Heart, ancestral, 301; of eternities, 317; pure in, 300.
Heaven, citizens of, 82; journey, 468; kingdom of, 201, 202, 203, 514, 602; man from, 371; wars in, 208; world, 347.
Heavens, seven, 396.
Heavenly man, 201, 202, 222, 300, 329, 330, 344, 423, 439, 566.
Hebdomad, 264, 266, 268, 269, 271, 272, 273, 280, 307, 323, 333, 348, 349, 371.
Hegesippus, 164.
Hell, 247.
Helen, 43; myth of, 168.
Helena, 163, 168.
Hellenists, 117.
Hephæstus, 40.
Heracleon, 288, 391.
Hercules, 194, 196.
Heresies, On, 251.
Hermes, 57, 201, 222, 511; first, 570; thrice-greatest, 440; shepherd of, 438.
Hermetic schools, 57.
Herodotus, 40.
Hesiod, 38, 43.
Hesychius, 388.
Higher criticism, 14, 25, 242, 385; ego, 471; self, 433; selves, 421.
Hipparchus, 108, 211.
Hippolytus, 149, 212, 293, 590.
Hiranya-garbha, 320.
Historicized legends of initiation, 278.
Historicizing of mythology, 88.
Hittites, 101.
Holiness, degrees of, 133.
Holy, holy, holy, 554; of holies, 374, 551; one, 434; ones, 377; "Spirit shall come upon thee," 269; table, 80; women, 251.
Homer, 44.
Honestas, 55.
Hormuz, 339.
Horn, of plenty, 205, 222; one, 222.
Horos (Boundary), 308.

Horus, 233; birth of, 60.
Hort, 144, 250.
"Hour hath not yet come, My," 271.
"How hath the lord of the plērōma changed us," 464.
"How long shall I bear with you," 487.
Hyksōs, 58, 213.
Hylē, 139, 210, 246, 466, 471, 472, 474.
Hylics, 193.
Hymn, 431; Naassene, 205; of Jesus, 431; of praise, 462; of the powers, 464; of the robe of glory, 406, 419; of the soul, 403; of welcome "Come unto us," 462; to light, 566; to first mystery, 539, 545; to logos, 555; to unapproachable god, 543; to wisdom, 419.
Hymns, 394; against heresies, 395; of Bardaisan, 414, 420; of Ephraim, 395; Orphic, 45; penitential, 471; singing of, 79.
Hypatia, 96, 100.
Hyrcania, 412.
Hystera, 225.
Hysterēma, 225.
Hyssop, 73, 77, 80, 342.

I

"I am a wanderer," 220.
"I am that man," 483.
"I am that mystery," 502.
"I am the god of Abraham," 266.
"I am the true gate," 202.
"I am thou," 439, 598.
"I become what I will," 201.
"I came not to call the righteous," 490.
"I have recognised myself," 540; "my sin," 268.
"I have torn myself asunder," 488.
"I know myself," 382.
"I know thee who thou art," 440.
"I recognised myself," 600.
"I will go into that region," 470.
Iabe (Iave), 534.
Iabraōth, 510, 527, 540.
Iacchus (Yach), 534.
Ialdabaōth, 189, 191, 192, 470.
Iaō, 381, 509, 534; great, 529.
Ice, 490.
Icosahedron, 222, 317.
Idea, little, 537, 541, 543, 545.
Ideas, 334; greatnesses or, 537.
Idolatry, 247.
Idols, things sacrificed to, 239.
Idol-worship, 300.
Ieou, 465, 504, 505, 510, 512, 513, 524, 529, 533, 534, 535, 540, 544; books of, 455, 487, 505, 533, 569; seal on forehead of, 537, 538; first man, 498; type of true god, 535.
Ieous, 537, 544.
Iessæi, 126.
"If ye drink not my blood," 202.
"If ye make not right like as left," 448.
Ignorance, 377, 472; flesh of, 520; great, 270, 271; nature of, 520.
Illumination, 377.
Illusionists, 217.
Illusory, 427.
Image, 180, 304, 313, 349, 387, 424, 471, 547, 584; images, 305, 328.
Imaging forth, 172.
Immovables, 529.
Impassables, 529, 545, 555.
Impressions, five, 529.

"In the place where I shall be," 484.
Incense, baptism of, 515.
Incorruptible æon, 191; treasure of, 192; mystery-names, 511.
Incorruptibility, 440, 585.
India, 55.
Indian religion, 393.
Individuitatis, principium, 344.
Indivisible, 552, 554.
Indweller of light, 478.
Ineffable, 462, 463, 464, 486; chrism, 205; first mystery of, 479; gnosis of gnosis of, 508; limbs of the, 483, 485, 507; mysteries of vestures of, 501; mystery of, 481, 482, 494, 500, 507; name, 543; one word of, 481; space of, 477, 479; tongue of, 482; vesture, 557.
Ineffables, 566.
Infancy, story of, 412, 474.
Inheritance of light, 477, 478, 479, 483, 487.
Iniquity, seed of, 504; wrath of their, 512.
Initiation, 355, 370, 375, 380, 411, 423, 427, 462; ceremonies, 358; dance of, 431; grades of, 182; historicized legends of, 278; mountain of, 598; of the cross, 438; of the disciples, 508; robe of, 405.
Initiations, 382.
Inn, 352.
Intercourse, mystery of, 469, 510; with males, 501.
Interior of interiors, 460, 462, 464, 506.
Investiture, 462.
Ion, 41, 43.
Iōta, 222.
Irenæus, 147, 291, 582; unreliability of, 280.

Isidorus, 273, 277, 301, 306.
Isis, 201, 323.
Italic, 287, 354.
Ithyē, 403.

J

Jacob, 202, 225.
Jamblichus, 57, 58.
James, 580.
Jehovah, 534.
Jerome, 150.
Jerusalem, 557; above, 349, 351, 396, 421; below, 435, 447; celestial, 340; church of, 119; destruction of, 92.
Jesus, 186, 199, 204, 221, 272, 302, 375, 353, 368, 376, 378, 472, 543, 565; a shepherd boy, 197; the name a substitute, 368; baptism of, 278; Christ distinguished from, 427, cosmic, 345; Ebionite tradition of, 128; hymn of, 431; Mary, mother of, 474; my brother, 475; mysteries of, 532; our God, 442; person of, 140; portrait of, 233; son of Mary, 269; stories of, 428; the master, 376; mystery of gnosis of, 479; six-lettered name, 369; twin of, 424.
Jeû (*see* Ieou), 534.
John, 237, 580, 581; *Apocryphon of*, 152, 580; farewell address, 441; last prayer of, 442; the virgin, 484; the baptist, 162, 461.
Jonah myth, 447.
Jordan, 185, 186, 202, 204, 221.
Joseph, 475.
Josephus, 118.
Joshua, 186.
Joy, 419; births of, 550.
Judas, 224, 226.

Judas Thomas, 419, 424; *Acts of*, 403.
Julian, 97.
Just, god, 243, 384; one, great, 532.
Justin Martyr, 148, 178, 590.
Justinus, 193, 246.

K

Kabalism, 94, 133, 361.
Kalapataurōth, 505.
Karman, 232, 265, 274, 394, 397, 399.
Kenōma, 307, 313.
Kingdom, of heaven, 201, 602; of light, 481, 506; of heavens, 202, 203, (keys of), 514; of midst, 308; of mysteries, 491.
"Kin to me," 437.
"Knees, For this cause I bow my," 352.
Knowledge, "falsely so called," 384; motions of, 413; of supermundane things, 254, 255; tree of, 487, 505.
Knowledges, 413.
Kolarbasus, 127.
Köstlin, 574.
Krishna, 7.
Kronos, 510.
Kuṇḍalinī, 204.
Kushān, 406.

L

Lake Marœa, 69, 97.
Lamp, 433.
Land, milk and honey, 340; god-bearing, 555; good, 340; promised, 186; Siriadic, 58.
Laotze, 37.
"Last shall be first," 478.
Left, 334, 348, 436, 447, 448, 449, 465, 466, 477, 513, 515, 523, 528, 548.

Leibnitz, 320.
"Let there be light," 259.
Leucian Acts, 417, 426.
Levi, 581.
Library, of Alexandria, 96, 98, 102; of Aristotle, 104; of Persepolis, 279.
Life, 389, 564; breath, 320; children of, 303; divine, 372; everlasting, 585; face of, 304; father of, 404; giving fire, 219; giving water, 197; of the father, 518; spark, 180; tree of, 446, 487, 505; virgin of, 526; water of, 201, 565; word and, 374.
Light and the Darkness, 394.
Light, 320, 380, 387, 434, 446, 564; atmosphere of, 514; beams, 75; boundless, 509, 525; children of, 521; collector of, 467; cross of, 435; crown, 473; flames, 504; day of, 487; fluid, 189; gates of, 502, 503; great, 474, 523, 529, 587; hymn to, 566; image of, 471, 544; indweller of, 478; inheritance of, 477, 478, 479, 483, 487; kingdom of, 481, 484, 506; maiden, 397; mysteries 479; of the treasure, 512; overseer of, 465; power, 470, 473, 496, 505; ray, 216; realm, 460; receivers of, 491; robe, 382, 404, 460; seven virgins of, 525; sons of, 371, 511; spark, 179, 180, 189, 190, 303, 305, 329, 465, 548, 554, 562, 584, 586, 599; sparks, 214, 461, 600; sphere, 322; spirit, 586; stream, 473, 483; streams of, 504; three spaces of the, 478; third of their, 465; treasure, 466, 468, 523, 530; treasure of, 477, 478, 509, 511, 514,

520, 522, 525, 527; vesture, 191, 468, 559; vesture of, 460, 463, 483, 499; virgin of, 476, 491, 497, 498, 499, 517; water of pure, 584; world, 195, 311, 320, 322, 421, 459, 477, 540.
Lights, great, 188, 512, 588.
Limbs, 366, 437, 439, 445, 462, 482, 540, 547, 556, 600; five, 422, 423; of heavenly man, 566; of ineffable, 483, 485, 507.
Limit (*see* Boundary), great, 267, 270, 272, 343, 462, 463.
Limitary spirit, 262, 266, 267, 269, 272, 343.
Linus, 418, 446.
Lipsius, 150, 291, 415.
Little, child, 406; children, 598; idea, 537, 541, 543, 545; man, 439; midst, 531; one, 306; Sabaōth, 512, 516.
Liturgi, 539.
Living one, 380, 381, 382, 518, 520, 534, 554, 602.
Logia, Chaldæan, 172.
Logoi, or logia, 294, 484, 507, 508, 593; rejected, 593.
Logos (*see* Word), 56, 201, 207, 216, 330, 344, 368, 372, 373, 384, 388, 412, 433, 445, 535, 537, 544; creator, 553, 556; doctrine of, 58; glorified of, 556; great, 544; hymn to the, 555; mind-born, 566; Osiris the, 59; perfect man or, 215; second aspect of, 261.
Lot, 225.
Luminaries, 588.

M

Magdalene, 466, 484.
Magi, 271, 279.
Magic, 167, 175, 318, 466.
Magna Vorago, 331.
Magus, 167.
Mahā-pralaya, 270.
Maiden, 419, 421.
Maimonides, 143.
Mainandros, 177.
Maishān, 407, 411.
Male-female, 173, 174, 199, 200, 218.
Malice, mystery of, 522.
Man, 273, 422, 433, 438, 439, 446, 547, 548, 550, 559, 562, 566; Adam the, 551; and church, 323, 337, 374; constitution of, 496; descent of, 446; doctrine, 188; first, 188, 190, 191, 371, 498, 584, 585; from heaven, 371; heavenly, 201, 202, 222, 300, 329, 330, 344, 423, 439 (limbs of), 586; himself, great, 529; "I am that," 483; inner, 351, 352; last, 371; little and great, 439; new, 353; of truth, 366, 367; perfect, 427; perfected, 354; powers of, 302; second, 188; son of, 189, 199, 202, 378, 581; son of this, 222; sons of, 372; spiritual, 271; thy, 440; way of the first, 448; woman, 334, 584.
Mandaïtes, 126.
Manetho, 40, 569.
Manichæism, 392, 395, 416.
Mansel, 145.
Many, "called, few chosen," 47; "members, one body," 507; "thyrsus-bearers, few bacchi," 10.
Marcians, 177, 288.
Marcion, 25, 175, 240, 241.
Marcionite, antitheses, 226; churches 242; movement, 240.
Marcionites, Dialogues against the, 394.

Marcellina, 233.
Marcosian ritual, 380.
Marcosians, 288.
Marcus, 287, 590; number-symbolism of, 358.
Mareōtic community, 69, 85; lake, 69, 97.
Mariamne, 199.
Marriage, 273; sacred, 420.
Marsanēs, 553.
Martha, 589.
Martyrdom, 275; pains of, 494.
Martyrs, 249, 274; of Lyons, 292.
Mary, Concerning the Offspring of, 198.
Mary, Genealogy of, 589.
Mary, Gospel of, 152, 165, 199, 423.
Mary, Gospel according to, 580.
Mary, Questions of, 198, 454, 466.
Mary, Greater and Lesser Questions of, 199, 589.
Mary, 353, 461, 506, 511, 581, 589; the body, 269; Jesus, son of, 269; Magdalene, 466, 484; mother of Jesus, 474.
Masbotheus, 164.
Mathematicians, 207, 361.
Mathēsis, 294, 315.
Matrix, 334.
Matter, 466, 471, 554, 557, 558, 560, 576; births of, 563; fall into, 470; devour their own, 467; purgations of, 489; virgin of, 564.
Matthias, 254.
Max Müller, 8.
Māyā-vādins, 217.
Māyāvi-rūpa, 428.
Medulla, 211.
Melchizedec, 467, 512, 513, 526.
Members, 539, 550.
Memoirs of the Apostles, 162.
Menander, 175.

Mercury, rod of, 185.
Mercy, great, 270; perfect, 422, 423.
Merinthians, 237.
Metempsychosis, 219.
Metensomatosis, 220.
Metropolis of Alone-begotten, 553.
Michael, 473.
Middle space, 173, 188, 334, 348, 540.
Midst, 308, 333, 488, 516; baptism of, 511; earth becometh, 519; little, 531; way of, 490, 510, 511, 513, 514, 546.
Miltiades, 291.
Mind, 173, 185, 205, 334, 388, 518, 519, 551, 561.
Mind and truth, 323, 336.
Mineral nature of soul, 277.
Miriam, 81.
Mirror, 433.
Miscellanies, The, 287.
Mithras, 55, 56, 279.
Mixture, 488, 496.
Moist essence, 204, 208.
Mohammed, 7.
Monad, 67, 222, 318, 335, 373, 548, 549, 550, 551, 555, 557.
Monadic gnosis, 236.
Monadity, 374.
Monadology, 320.
Monastery, 70, 71.
Money-changers, 596.
Monoïmus, 222.
Montanist, 251.
Moon, 263, 473, 510.
Moses, 81, 185, 196, 222, 225, 266, 387; of Chorēnē, 393.
Mosheim, 234.
Mother, above, 191, 396, 561; breath, 330; mysteries of great, 203; of all, 169, 185; of compassion, 422; of many names, 334; of living, 334; of thirty names, 379; of

your mother, 382; shining, 334; virgin, 58.
Mount, 370, 429, 430, 435, 439, 508, 598; Athos, 212, 273; of Galilee, 515; of Olives, 435, 459.
Mountain, Secret Sermon on the, 440.
Mysteries, 46, 411, 431, 433; Assyrian, 200; Bacchic and Corybantic, 67; boundary marks of, 490; Chaldæan, 51, 58; degrees of, 484; Egyptian, 51, 58, 201; Eleusinian, 51; greater, 203, 522; Greek, 201; keys of, 506; kingdom of, 491; lesser, 203, 215, 522, 527; mimics of, 493; Mithriac, 55, 56, 279; of baptism, 499, 514, 533; of embryology, 281; of Jesus, 532; of Seth, 58; of sex, 184; of great mother, 203; Orphic, 51, 216; philosophic, 50, 51; Phrygian, 201, 202; preaching of, 489; private, 49; political, 49; ritual from, 431; Samothracian, 202; state, 49; Thracian, 202; twelve, 485.
Mystery, 356, 437; according to the, 152, 455, 457, 544, 567; cultus, 49; drama, 433; fires of baptism, 500; first, 459, 460, 461, 462, 463, 464, 465, 472, 473, 474, 477, 478, 479, 482, 493, 500, 502, 503, 506, 507, (hymn to) 539, 545, (mystery of) 479, (outer space of), 479; four-and-twentieth, 462; "I am that," 502; kept secret, 495; last, 462, 463; looking within, 486; myths, 191; names, 511; of breaking of seals, 498; of every nature, 447; of intercourse, 469, 510; of cross, 435; of forgiveness of sins, 523, 527, 530, 531, 533; of ineffable, 479, 480, 481, 482, 494, 500, 507; of light of thy father, 515; of resurrection of dead, 494, 495; of spiritual chrism, 522; of twelve æons, 531; of their fear, 546; of withdrawing evil, 522, 527; relative of the, 552; that was unknown, 269, 353; type of race, 471; world beyond, 462; 'twixt heaven and earth, 439; wisdom declared in, 268.
Myrrh, 420.
Myrtle, 420.
Mysticæ voces, 365.
Myth, Exodus, 185, 186, 210; Jonah, 447; of Helen, 168; of Pistis Sophia, 469; of Valentinus, 306.
Mythologizing of history, 88.
Mythology, 332.
Muesis, 355.
Mūlaprakṛiti, 258.

N

Naas, 196.
Naasseni, 198.
Naassene, document, 198; hymn, 205.
Nādi's, 597.
Nahashirama, 392.
Nail of discipline, 449.
Name, 300, 304, 377, 381, 440, 462, 516, 565; authentic, 541, 542; echo of, 365; great, 363, 514, 523, 542, 599; ineffable, 543; "Jesus" a substitute, 369; of Christ, 422; of great power, 542; of power, 282; of the father, 509; of truth, 380; six-lettered, 368.
Names, 374, 550; authentic,

365, 509, 512; imperishable, 545, 546; mother of many, 334, (of thirty), 379; of æons, 338.
Narrow place, 560, 564.
Nativity, 400, 402.
Nature, 399, 400; seven-robed, 210; upper, 437.
"Naught was," 257.
Nazaræan, 580.
Nazaræans, 126.
Neander, 144, 236.
Net, 440.
"Never grow old," 176.
Nicolaïtans, 213, 239.
Nicopolis, 100.
Nicotheus, 553.
Night, 208.
Nile, heavenly, 204.
Nine times greater, 476.
Ninefold, 548, 559.
Nineveh, 447.
Nirvāṇa, 142, 236, 474.
Nirvāṇic, atom, 319; ocean, 330.
Nitrian valley, 101.
Noah, 190.
Nochaïtæ, 198.
Noëtic world, 320.
Nomina barbara, 339.
No-number, 373, 374.
Norton, 145.
Noughtness, 373.
Nuhama, 392.
Number, letters, 359; nuptial, 83; of perfect souls, 467, 486, 502, 503; permutations, 375; symbolism, 358; theories, 222.
Numbers, 82, 516.

O

Oaths of secrecy, 416.
Oblivion, 496; draught of, 504, 516.
Ocean, 186, 202, 326, 330, 509, 545.
Octahedron, 222, 317, 324.
Ode to Sophia, 419.
Odes, of Basilides, 255; of Solomon, 470, 572.
Ogdoad, 266, 268, 269, 271, 280, 307, 322, 323, 324, 333, 344, 345, 349, 350, 376, 396, 432, 587.
Omar, 106.
Omega, 530, 532.
Omphalē, 197.
On an Appended Soul, 277.
On Heresies, 251.
On Justice, 234.
On the Soul, 251.
One, 67, 374; and all, 321; and only one, 486, 531, 556, 561, 562, 565; word, 482; garment, 425; great, 378, (just), 532; holy, 434; horn, 222; in a thousand, 282, 506; little, 306; living, 380, 381, 382, 518, 520, 534, 554, 602; virgin, 218; word, 481.
Oneness, 373.
Only-begotten, 341.
Onamacritus, 38.
"Open unto us," 503.
Ophiani, 183.
Ophites, 181, 193; diagram of, 589.
Ophitism, 158.
Orgeones, 50.
Origen, 149.
Ōroiael, 588.
Orpheus, 42, 44, 331.
Orphic, 49, 192; communities, 50, 54; hymns, 45; life, 50; line, 42; mysteries, 51, 216, 411; poems, 38; songs, 45; tradition, 39.
Osiris, 59, 201, 323, 438.
Osirified, 600.
Osymandyas, 103.
Outline of face, 548.
Outlines, The, 292.

Overseer, 547, 551; of light, 465.
Ovum, 331, 536.
Oxyrhynchus, 600.

P

Pallas Athene, 41.
Pantænus, 294.
Paradise, 189, 190, 247, 334, 396, 487, 505.
Paraphrase of Seth, 213.
Paraplēx, 513.
Parchment, 104.
Parents, of æons, 336; we are to leave, 504.
Parentless, 337, 524, 529.
Passion, 371, 378, 390, 434, 438, 446.
Passions, 346, 347.
"Pass-not," ring, 311.
Pastos, 421.
Paul, 176, 248, 252, 499; *Ascent of*, 226; *Apocalypse of*, 227; churches of, 165; gospel of, 244; letters of, 123; our brother, 568; *Vision of*, 227.
Pearl, 407, 440.
Pelasgi, 40.
Pentad, 423, 551, 584.
Pentateuch, 388.
Peratæ, 186, 198, 206.
Perfect, æon, 218; deity, 387; flesh, 582; freedom, 557; man, 215, 302, 354, 427; mercy, 422, 423; mind, 551; number of, 467, 486, 502, 503; triangle, 74, 82.
Perfection, god of, 495; *Gospel of*, 198; seal of, 423.
Pergamus, 105, 239.
Persepolis, 279.
Person, 210; of Jesus, 140.
Peter, 176, 501, 581; *Acts of*, 152, 417, 580; *Circuits of*, 164, 166; interpreter of, 254; *Martyrdom of*, 446.

Petro-Pauline controversy, 128, 166, 245.
Petro-Simonian controversy, 166.
Pharisaism, 92, 93.
Pharos, 97.
Pherecydes, 37.
Philaster, 150.
Philip, 466; *Gospel of*, 198, 439, 540.
Philo, 55, 117; and wisdom-lovers, 60, 84; autobiography, 84; *On the Contemplative Life*, 61; pseudo, 62.
Philosophumena, 273.
Philoxenus, 397.
Philumēnē, 250.
Phlium, 216.
Phōsilampēs, 553.
Phronesis, 588.
Phrygian mysteries, 201, 202.
Pineal gland, 211.
Pistis Sophia (Faith-Wisdom), 339, 468, 470, 565; myth of, 469.
Pistis Sophia, 151, 199, 208, 281, 283, 290, 297, 303, 312, 343, 374, 382, 397, 398, 405, 409, 412, 449, 454, 529, 538, 567, 571, 578, 591; system of, 192, 574; translation of, 456; treatise, original, 572.
Plagiarism by anticipation, 117.
Plagues of Egypt, 222.
Plain, cities of, 226; of truth, 230.
Plato, 39, 45, 49, 51, 53, 314.
Plato, Nuptial Number of, 83.
Platonic solids, 222, 314.
Plērōma, 207, 225, 311, 389, 461, 547, 550, 566; ascension of, 478; boundary of, 342; common fruit of, 331, 345, 346, 349, 351, 352; configuration of, 551; drama, 327; emanation of, 499, 505; gnosis of, 481, 484, 503; lord of, 464; lords of, 501; seed of, 377; sons of, 511.

Plērōmata, 305, 365.
Plough, 440.
Plutarch, 55, 56, 57.
Pneumatics, 139, 421, 468.
Point, 218.
Polarity, 321.
Polyhedra, 314.
Polyhedric origin of species, 322.
Poor men, 126, 127, 166, 227, 427.
Porphyry, 25, 393.
Portrait of Jesus, 233.
Poseidon, 40, 99.
Power, 547; above, 334, 447; boundless, 173; dæmonian, 190; demiurgic, 349, 372; great, 164, 171, 173, 185, 542, 543; name of, 282; of highest, 269, 353, 377; robe of, 343, 344; super-celestial, 381.
Powers, 462; cruel, crafty, 474; forty-nine, 516, 523; of perfect man, 302; song of the, 409, 464; triple, 468, 469.
Pralaya, 344.
Prayer, John's last, 442; morning, 82; of the earth-born, 564.
Prayers of Therapeuts, 70; for dead, 381, 494; sacramental, 422.
Pre-Christian gnosis, 163, 183.
Preuschen, 567.
Principalities, 436.
Proasteioi up to Æther, 209, 280.
Proclus, 314.
Proculus, 291.
Prodigal son, parable of, 405.
Prophets, schools of the, 86, 94.
Prouneikos, 334.
Providence, 274, 275.
"Providentissimus Deus," 14.
Pseudepigraphs, 85, 94.
Pseudo-Clementines, 162, 164, 166.

Ptolemæus, 288, 590; to Flora, 293.
Ptolemies, 57.
Ptolemy, 108, 383; I. (Soter), 98, 102, 104; II. (Philadelphus), 104, 116; III. (Euergetes), 105.
Pullulation, 259.
Purānas, 204.
Purgations of matter, 468, 488, 489.
Purgatorial spheres, 381.
Purification, degrees of, 472; ladder of, 565.
Puruṣha, 301.
"Put not off," 502.
Pythagoras, 37, 39, 45, 51, 314.
Pythagoræan communities, 50, 54; triangle, 82.
Pythagoræans, 51, 82, 84.

Q

Queen of East, 405, 411
Questions of Mary, 198, 199, 454, 466, 589.

R

Rabbis of south, 94.
Race, 69, 437, 447, 564; elect, 303; mystery type of, 471; of mind, 518; righteous, 519.
Ragadouah, 99.
Raguel, 588.
Reasonings, 250.
Rebirth, 205, 220, 230, 354, 371, 381, 407, 504, 548.
Receiver, great, 467.
Receivers, 486, 498, 499, 511, 521; of light, 491; of wrath, 491, 497.
"Recognised myself, I have," 540, 600.
Red Sea, 81, 186.

Redemption, 265, 381, 471; angelic, 380; of Sophia, 334; of cross, 447.
Reflections, self-born, 565.
Refutatorii Sermones, 167.
Regeneration, 371, 372, 376, 445.
Reign of 1000 years, 92.
Reincarnating entity, 301.
Reincarnation, 167, 192, 231, 232, 274, 276, 404, 516.
Relative of mystery, 552.
"Remedy of Soul," 103.
Reminiscence, 230, 236, 474.
Renunciation of world, 481, 485, 489.
"Repent, Delay not to," 502.
Repentance, 446, 449, 471; place of, 565; songs of, 470.
Repentances, 470, 471.
Resch, 412, 593.
Restitution of all things, 364.
Restoration, 265, 268, 270, 271, 273, 380.
Resurrection, 254, 404, 440, 548; of body, 176; of dead, 494, 495.
Rhacotis, 99, 100.
Rhapsodists, 38.
Rheinhardt, 579.
Rhodon, 250, 251.
Right, 264, 334, 348, 357, 401, 411, 436, 447, 448, 449, 465, 466, 477, 478, 483, 488, 511, 512, 548, 563.
"Right like as the left," 448.
Righteous, 490, 498, 519, 551.
Ritual, from mysteries, 431; Marcosian, 380.
Rivers of Eden, 194.
Robe, of glory, 460, 461, 464, 520, (hymn of), 406, 419; of initiation, 405; of power, 343, 344.
Rod, 201, 222; Moses' 222; of Mercury, 185.
Root, æons, 218; lower, 436; of deathlessness, 440; universal, 171.
Rudras, 327.
Ruler, 264, 439, 498; great, 262, 266, 267, 272.
Rulers, 230, 467, 469, 497, 498; evil of 526; flesh of the, 468; seventy-two evil, 522; three great, 532.

S

Sabaōth, Adamas, 521, 527; great, 513, 529; little, 512, 516.
Sacrifices, 93.
Sadducees, 163.
Saïs, 39.
Sakadagāmin, 370.
Salmon, 236, 246, 424, 443.
Salome, 233, 598.
Salt, 73, 77, 80, 440; bread and, 80; with, 425.
Samaritan Chronicle, 162.
Samō, 234.
Samothracian mysteries, 202.
Saṃsāra, 197, 303, 381.
Sarbûg, 407, 410.
Satan, 436; sons of, 13, 32, 174.
Saturninus, 177.
Saviour, 58, 207, 271, 273, 505; *Books of the*, 374, 454, 507, 546, 567, 573; first, 485; of truth, 381; words of, 385.
Saviours, 176; of souls, 492; twelve, 461; twin, 529.
Schmidt (Carl), 159, 538, 545, 552, 567, 574, 577, 579, 588.
Schwartze, 146, 281.
Seals, 214, 219, 317, 423, 498, 499, 537, 538.
Secularizing of Christianity, 136.
Secundus, 287, 357.
Seed-mixture, 263; conglomeration of the, 262, 265; of all universes, 258; of iniquity, 504; of plērōma, 377.

Selēnē, 163, 168.
Seniority, 75.
Septuagint, 104.
"Sepulchres, Ye are whitened," 203.
Serapeum, 97, 99, 105, 106.
Sermon on the Mountain, Secret, 440.
Serpent, 189, 206, 215; and egg, 185, 331; flying, 331; formed, 189, 190; legend, 167; rod, 185; symbol, 183.
Serpentine force, 185, 222.
Servant, dress of a, 215, 216; form of a, 247.
Servers, 76.
Seth (or Set), 58, 59, 213; mysteries of, 58, 59; *Paraphrase of*, 213.
Setheus, 213, 551, 553.
Sethians, 213.
Seven, 74, 82, 323, 422; amens, 529; Elohim, 190; heads, 474; heavens, 396; numbered greatness, 372; pillars, 333; robed Isis, 323, (nature), 201; spheres, 379, 396; stars, 398; times, 491; virgins of light, 525; voices, 516, 523, 524, 526, 529; women disciples, 582; years, 201.
Seventh day common meal, 73.
Seventy, 116, 375, 522.
Severians, 251.
Shakti, 363, 432, 595.
Shame, of the dry, 424; vesture of, 598.
Sheep, 270; lost, 169.
Sheol, 447.
Shepherd boy, Jesus a, 197.
Sibylline Oracles, 126.
Siddhis, 302.
Sigē, 327.
Silence, 173, 313, 336, 341, 377, 378, 423, 548, 564; great, 311; of five years, 278, 282.

Silences, 524, 529.
Simon, 583; Magus, 158, 164; of Cyrene, 283.
Simonian literature, 167.
Simonians, 160, 423.
"Sinned, He has not," 275.
Sinopē, 241.
Sins on souls, stamping of, 499.
Siriadic land, 58.
Sirius, 58.
Sithians, 198.
Sixty, fatherhoods, 544; treasures, 540.
Skemmut, 505.
Skin, coats of, 190.
Slime, abysmal, 208.
Smith and Wace, 144.
Solomon, 557; odes of, 470; seal of, 317; *Wisdom of*, 298.
Solon, 39, 40.
Son, alone-begotten, 390; of God, 269, 565; of man, 189, 191, 199, 202, 378, 581; of father, 60; of living, 404;
Sons, of Adam, 599; God, 5, 266, 268, 303, 353, 354; light, 371, 511; Satan, 174; the man, 372; the plērōma, 511.
Sonship, 259, 260, 264, 354, 555; saviour of the, 262; second, 261; third, 262, 263, 265, 272, 303.
Sophia, 188, 189, 298, 304, 339, 561; fall of, 305; grief of, 346; mythus, 306, 333, 335, 469; ode to, 419; redemption of, 334.
Soria y Mata, 314, 322.
Soteriology, 355; of Basilides, 265.
Sothis, 58.
Soul, 277, 387, 496; clothed with a proper, 272; descent of, 334, 471; great, 467; hymn of the, 403; of Elias,

461; *On an Appended*, 277; *On the*, 251; plantal nature of, 277; mineral nature of, 277.
Souls, breathed out, 219; classes of, 139; coming and going of, 26; frenzied, 495; in incarnation, 488; return of, 23; saviours of, 492.
Space, blessed, 261; crucified in, 330; first, 492; limit, 267; middle, 173, 334, 348; of first mystery, inner, 478, 479; of ineffable, 477, 479; of twelve æons, 465; sun, 263.
Spaces, of light, three supernal, 478; three, 529; three-faced and two-faced, 551; twin, 463, 477; sublunary, 264, 268.
Spermatozoon, 331, 536.
Sphere, fate, 209; first, 464; second, 465.
Spheres, conversion of, 465, 466, 467; purgatorial, 381; seven, 379, 396.
Spider, 259.
Spiral, 331.
Spirit, 434, 475; baptism, 515, 522; counterfeit, 276, 496, 498, 499, 500, 504, 505; excellent, 305; fruits of, 338; gifts of the, 441; holy, 260, 261, 262, 278, 327, 353, 377, 378, 397, 422, 526; like a dove, 354; limitary, 266, 267, 269, 272, 343; living, 420; "shall come upon thee," 269; virginal, 203, 531, 583, 584.
Spirits, 276; mind-born, 563; mundane, 236.
Splendour, lord of, 562.
Srotāpanna, 370.
Standing one, 163.
Statute, 440, 564, 565; first, 463, 465.

Sublunary regions, 263; spaces, 264, 268.
Sun, 473; disk of, 510; in its true form, 476; light of, 498, 510; space, 263; worship of the, 55.
Superfluity of naughtiness, 524.
Supersubstantial, 566.
Supplementary development, 259.
Suppliant, 65.
Supplication, 346.
Supporters, 525; five, 529; great, 479.
Synesis, 588.
Syrian gnosis, 177.
Syzygy, 305, 423, 468, 472; law of, 321.
Sweat of bodies, 467.

T

Tabor, 597.
"Take courage," 460.
Tantra, 367.
Tau, 438.
Tears of their eyes, 467.
Ṭeḥuti (Thoth), 57.
Ten, 323; æons, 337; tribes, 89.
Tertullian, 149, 293, 590; pseudo, 149.
Tetrad, 323, 375, 377.
Tetrads, 357, 378.
Tetragrammaton, 132, 534.
Tetrahedron, 222, 317.
Tetraktys, 350, 373, 390.
Thalatth (Tiāmat), 209.
Thales, 37.
That-which-is, 553.
Thebaid, 101.
Thebes, 103.
Thelesis, 588.
Theocritus, 109.
Theodas, 294.
Theodoret, 150.
Theodotus, 288, 292, 294, 357;

Extracts from, 287, 292, 332, 356.
Theophrastus, 104, 223.
Theos, 329.
Therapeut, name, 66; order, 62.
Therapeutæ, 62, 66, 101.
Therapeutrides, 66.
Therapeuts, 60, 63, 64; books of the, 71; lay-pupils of the, 84; Philo's connection with, 84; prayers, of 70; rule, 72.
Theudas, 294.
Thiasi, 50.
Thieves and robbers, 353.
Third, of their light, 465; ventricle, 211.
Thirteenth æon, 325, 466, 468, 476, 511, 515, 520, 522, 528, 531, 532, 539.
Thirty hours, 460; two, 419; æons, 421.
Thirtyfold, 328.
Thomas, 602; *Acts of*, 419, 422, 424; palace of, 424; *Gospel according to*, 198, 201; Judas, 419, 424.
Thoth, 57.
Thousand, one in a, 506; years of light, 486.
Thrace, 42.
Thracian mysteries, 202.
Three times accomplished, 474.
Thrice-spiritual, 524, 529.
Thrones, 484.
Thyrsus, 185; bearers, 10.
Timæus, 39, 299.
Titus, 92.
Tobe (*see* Tybi), 278.
Tone, 547.
Tongue, of flesh, 438, 552, 578; of the ineffable, 482; wisdom's, 421.
Torments, 504.
"Torn myself asunder," 488, 505.
Transcendentalists, 186, 209.

Transfiguration, 459; story, 370.
Transmigration, 169, 276, 488, 499, 498, 503.
Treasure, 267; gates of, 474; house, 172; light of the, 512; of light, 477, 478, 509, 511, 514, 520, 522, 525; veil of, 468, 469; purgations of, 488; second light, 530.
Treasurers, 412.
Treasures, 172; of light, 527; of incorruptible, 192; sixty, 540; type of, 535.
Treasury, 406.
Tree, 221; fig, 218; fire, 172; hanging on, 342; life-giving, 446; of knowledge, 487, 505; of life, 487, 505.
Trees, 172, 194, 196; five, 523, 529, 544.
Triangle, 207; perfect, 74, 82.
Trismegistic literature, 57, 58, 223, 441.
Trismegistus, Hermes, 58, 440.
Trojan war, 43, 44, 168.
True God, 530, 533, 534, 535, 537, 542, 559, 587; gods, 543.
True Word, 150, 183.
Truth, 419, 549; body of, 366; diagram of, 367; father of, 377; gate of, 204; god of, 304, 367, 485, 486, 508; name of, 380; plain of, 230; saviour of, 381.
Twelve, 323, 420, 422, 461, 500; æons, 337, 465, 511, 531; depths, 548; incarnation of the, 460; mysteries, 485; saviours, 461; the, 538, 542; tribes, 202; years, 523.
Twin, of Jesus, 424; saviours, 529; spaces, 463, 477.
Twins, 423.
Tybi, 278, 459.

Typhon, 59.
Tyrants, 474, 465, 468.
Tübingen school, 166.
Turmoil, 276.

U

Unapproachable, 543, 544; god, 521, 528; god, hymn to the, 543; one and only, 531.
Uncontainables, 521, 529, 530, 545, 555, 566.
Under-meaning, 71, 79.
Unguent, 261, 262.
Unknowable, invisible, 565.
Unknown, great, 309.
Universality beyond being, 257.
Unstainables, 529, 564.
Untitled Apocalypse, 547.
Unutterable depth, 188.
Upanishads, 204, 301, 302, 307, 320, 439.

V

Valentinianism, 285, 286; schools of, 287.
Valentinus, 284, 289, 290, 294, 570, 578; gospel of, 298; myth of, 306; "they of," 285, 571; *Wisdom of*, 298; writings of, 297.
Vasus, 327.
Veil, 322; first, 509.
Veils, 538; of thirteenth æon, 468; of treasure, 468, 469.
Ventricle, third, 211.
Vesture, 547, 566; ineffable, 557; of light, 460, 483, 499; of shame, 598; of power, 558.
Vestures, 562; of glory, 472; of light, 463; of ineffable, 501.
Vine, true, 446.
Vineyard, 475.
Virgin, 191, 377, 558; John the, 484; made body, 221; mother, 58; of life, 526; of light, 476, 491, 497, 517, (the judge), 498, 499; matter, 564; one, 218; with child, 203; womb, 215, 225.
Virginal spirit, 203, 531, 583, 584.
Virginity, 75, 520.
Virgins, 251; of light, seven, 525.
Vision, 328; of Ezekiel, 94; of Jacob, 202; *of Paul*, 227; of baptism mysteries, 514.
Voice, 435, 448; and name, 171.
Voices, seven, 516, 523, 524, 526, 529; three, 536, 541.
Volkmar, 234.
Vortex, 329, 331.

W

"Wake thou that sleepest," 201.
"Wanderer, I am a," 220.
Water, 210; above, living, 200; baptism of, 515, 522; "Except a man be born of," 221; image of, 424; life-giving, 197, 216, 515; of life, 201, 565, (baptism of), 524; of pure light, 584; whirl, 323.
Waters of Jordan, 185, 204.
Way, 433, 448; of error, 448; of the first man, 448; of midst, 498, 510, 511, 513, 514, 546; to god, 3, 32, 223.
Wedding, feast, great, 397; garment, 405.
"When two shall be one," 595.
"Where is he?" 475.
"Where, then, O Egypt," 466.
"Which things I hate," 239.
Whirlpool, vast, 331.
Whirlwind, mighty, 185.
"Why callest thou me Good," 201.
Wiedemann, 301.

Wine, jars of, 524.
"Wing or thought," 260.
Winged globe, 473.
Wings, 260.
Wisdom, 27, 37, 169, 226, 331, 333; above, 375, 396; below, 376, 396; Chaldæan, 89, 94; cup of, 516; declared in a mystery, 268; god of, 57; goddess of, 41; harmony of, 436; hymn to, 419; lovers, 60; of deity, 9; of Egypt, 38, 57; *of Jesus Christ*, 152, 580, 582, 589; *of Solomon*, 298; *of Valentinus*, 298;
Within, looking, 473, 474, 486.
Womb, impure, 215; virgin, 215, 225; world, 225.
Women disciples, 75, 251, 582.
Word (*see* Logos), 363, 368, 434, 435, 438, 448, 587; and life, 323, 336, 374; Christ is the, 448; made flesh, 390; one and only, 482.
Words, 354, 442, 507, 508; of the Lord, 138; of Saviour, 385; of truth, 485; or angels, 352; or minds, 351; unspeakable, 269.
Workman (*see* Demiurge), 349, 350, 351, 353.
Worm, 180, 189.
Wrath, 436; of their iniquity, 512; receivers of, 491, 497; workmen of, 497.

Wreath, 442, 555, 557.
Wreaths, 556.

X

Xerxes, 38.

Y

Yahoo, 534.
Yahweh, 92, 138, 179, 534; friends of God, enemies of, 225.
Yantras, 367.
Yhvh, 534.
Yoga, 302.
Yogins, 429.
Yod, 222.

Z

Zahn, 417.
Zama, zama, 462.
Zealot, 94.
Zealotism, 91, 92, 97.
Zeus, 511, 512; all-father, 41.
Zodiac, signs of, 209, 325, 379, 448.
Zoroaster, 7.
Zoroasters, last of the, 37.
Zoroastrian logia, 172; tradition, 87.
Zoroastrianism, 91, 177, 278.
Zorokothora (Melchizedec), 512, 525, 526.

INTRODUCTION.

> The whole creation groaneth and travaileth together waiting for the manifestation of the Sons of God.
> PAUL (according to Gnostic tradition.)

PROLEGOMENA.

MYSTERIOUS Time is once more big with child and labouring to bring forth her twentieth babe, as the Western world counts her progeny; for, according to the books, just nineteen children of her centenarian brood have lived and died since He appeared to whom all Christians look as Teacher of the Way to God. The common conscience of the General Church flows not only from the fact that all believe He is the Teacher of the Way, but from the faith, He is that Way itself. This is the common bond of Christians the world over, and this has been the symbol of their union throughout the centuries. Some nineteen hundred years ago the Illuminator appeared and light streamed forth into the world—such is the common creed of the adherents of the great religion of the Western world.

The Creed of Christendom.

As the honorific inscriptions said of the birthday of the Roman Emperor Augustus, so said after them all Christians of the natal day of Jesus:

4 FRAGMENTS OF A FAITH FORGOTTEN.

The New Era Two Thousand Years Ago.

"This day has given the earth an entirely new aspect. The world would have gone to destruction had there not streamed forth from him who is now born a common blessing.

"Rightly does he judge who recognises in this birth-day the beginning of life and of all the powers of life; now is that time ended when men pitied themselves for being born.

"From no other day does the individual or the community receive such benefit as from this natal day, full of blessing to all.

"The Providence which rules over all has filled this man with such gifts for the salvation of the world as designate him as Saviour for us and for the coming generations; of wars he will make an end, and establish all things worthily.

"By his appearing are the hopes of our forefathers fulfilled; not only has he surpassed the good deeds of earlier time, but it is impossible that one greater than he can ever appear.

"The birth-day of God has brought to the world glad tidings that are bound up in him.

"From his birth-day a new era begins."

So runs the most perfect of a number of inscriptions lately found in Asia Minor and set up to commemorate the introduction of the Julian Calendar by the Emperor Augustus. It bears a date corresponding to our B.C. 9 (See Harnack's article in *Die christliche Welt*, Dec. 1899).

The hope of the adherents of the Emperor-cult was speedily shattered; the expectation of

Christendom remains in great part unfulfilled, for the nineteen centuries which have passed away have severally grown old in years of bitter strife, of internecine and most bloody wars, of persecution and intolerance in things religious which no other period in the world's known history can parallel. Will the twentieth century witness the fulfilment of this so great expectation; can it be said of the present time that "the whole nature travaileth together waiting for the manifestation of the Sons of God"? *The New Hope of To-day.*

Can any who keenly survey the signs of the times, doubt but that now, at the dawn of the twentieth century, among Christian nations, the general nature of thought and feeling in things religious is being quickened and expanded, and as it were is labouring in the pains of some new birth? And if this be so, why should not the twentieth century witness some general realization of the long deferred hope by the souls that are to be born into it? Never in the Western world has the general mind been more ripe for the birth of understanding in things religious than it is to-day; never have conditions been more favourable for the wide holding of a wise view of the real nature of the Christ and the task He is working to achieve in the evolution of His world-faith.

Our present task will be to attempt, however imperfectly, to point to certain considerations which may tend to restore the grand figure of the Great Teacher to its natural environment in history and tradition, and disclose the intimate points of *Our Present Task.*

contact which the true ideal of the Christian religion has with the one world-faith of the most advanced souls of our common humanity—in brief, to restore the teaching of the Christ to its true spirit of universality. Not for one instant would we try to lessen the reverence and the love of any single soul for that Great Soul who watches over Christendom; our task will rather be to point to a soil in which that love can flourish ever more abundantly, and ever more confidently open its heart to the rational rays of the Spiritual Sun. That soil is rich enough for the full growth of the man-plant; it is part of the original soil, and gives nourishment to every branch of man's nature, emotional and moral, rational and spiritual.

The One Religion.

With many others we hold there is but One Religion for humanity; the many faiths and creeds are all streams or streamlets of this great river. This may perhaps seem a hard saying to some, but let us briefly consider its meaning. The Sun of Truth is one. His rays stream forth into the minds and hearts of men; surely if we believe anything at all, we hold this faith in the Fatherhood of God! Must we not then believe that our common Father is no respecter of persons and that at all times, in all lands, He has loved and loves and will love His children? We should be dull scholars indeed if nineteen hundred years of the teaching of the Christ had not taught us this. And yet how few *really* believe it? The whole history of the Churches of Christendom is a record of disbelief in this fundamental dogma of universal religion, and no greater foe has dogged the footsteps of Christainity than the evil genius of Jewish particularism, which has ever instigated it to every outbreak of intolerance and persecution. This same spirit also infused itself into Mohammedanism, and we can trace the results in the bloody pages of its history.

It may possibly be that this crude particularism and exclusiveness in religion is a necessary factor in the development of certain classes of souls, and that it is used for ultimate good purpose by the Wisdom that guides the world; but is not a greater portion of our Father's blessing possible to us now? Can we not see that it matters not whether a man have learned of the Path from the teaching of Kṛiṣhṇa or of the Buddha, of Mohammed or Zoroaster, or of the Christ,—provided he but set his foot upon that Path, it is all one to our common Father? He it was who sent Them all forth and illumined Them, that all might through Them have the spiritual food suited to their needs. Words fail even to hint at the sublimity of this conception, at the glorious glimpse into the stupendous reality of God's providence which this illuminating doctrine opens up. And to *realise* this—not to believe it in some half-hearted way and practically deny it by our other beliefs—how great the growth of the heart! It is in the sunshine of this most blessed doctrine of all the world-saviours that we would ask our readers to approach the consideration of the many forms of faith of earliest Christendom with which we shall have to deal in these pages. In this sunshine

The Sunshine of its Doctrine.

"heresy" and "false religion" frequently wear so changed an aspect that they seem quite beautiful alongside of the "orthodoxy" and "true religion" of their unsympathetic opponents.

The Comparative Science of Religion.

But let us be on our guard against all exaggeration and strive to get things in their true proportions, for it is only thus that we can realise the eternal providence of God, who by His Messengers in His own good time ever adjusts the balance. It has been said by Professor Max Müller that we should not speak of the comparative science of religion, but should rather employ the phrase, comparative science of theology. This is quite true of the work that has so far been done, and done well, by official scholarship; the main effort has been to discover differences, and exaggerate the analysis of details. So far there has been, outside of a small circle of writers, little attempt at synthesis.

We are not, however, prepared to abandon the term comparative science of religion; we believe there is such a science—the noblest perchance to which any man can set his hand. But it is one of the most difficult. It requires not only an intimate experience of human nature as well as a wide knowledge of history, but also a deep sympathy with the hopes and fears of the religious conscience, and above all things an unshakable faith in the unwinking providence of God in all human affairs.

Supposing it possible that a man could love and revere all the great Teachers known to history as deeply and earnestly as each exclusive religionist reveres and loves his own particular Master;

supposing that he could really believe in the truth of each of the great religions in as full measure, though without exclusiveness, as the orthodox of each great faith believes in the truth of his own revelation; supposing finally he could sense the Wisdom of Deity in active operation in all these manifestations,—what a glorious Religion would then be his! How vast and strong his Faith when supported by the evidences of all the world-bibles and the exhortations of all the world-teachers! Persuaded of the fact of re-birth, he would feel himself a true citizen of the world and heir presumptive to all the treasures of the sacred books. Little would he care for the gibes of "eclectic" or "syncretist" flung at him by the analysers of externals and seekers after difference, for he would be bathing in the life-stream of Religion, and would gladly leave them to survey its bed and channels, and scrutinize the mud of its bottom and the soil of its banks; least of all would he notice the cry of "heretic" hurled after him by some paddlers in a pool on the shore. Not, however, that he would think little of analysis or less of orthodoxy, but his analysis would be from within as well as from without, and he would find his orthodoxy in the life of the stream and not in the shape of the banks. The True Scholar of Religion.

The One Religion flows in the hearts of men and the Light-stream pours its rays into the soil of human nature. The analysis of a religion is therefore an analysis of human-kind. Every great religion has expressions as manifold as The Just Method of Comparison.

the minds and hearts of its adherents. The manifestation of its truth in the life and words of a great sage must differ widely from the feeble reflection of its light which is all the dull intellect and unclean life of the ignorant and immoral can express. It is true that its light and life are free for all; but as there are grades of souls, all at different stages of evolution, how can it be that all can equally reflect that light? How unwise is it then to compare the most enlightened views of one set of religionists with the most ignorant beliefs and most superstitious practices of another set! And yet this is a very favourite pastime with those who seek to gratify themselves with the persuasion that their own faith is superior to that of every other creature. This method will never lead us to a comprehension of true Religion or an understanding of our brother man.

The Analysis of Religion.

Analyse any of the great religions, and you find the same factors at work, the same problems of human imperfection to be studied, the many who are "called" and the few who are "chosen,"—there are in each religion, as there ever have been, "many Thyrsus-bearers but few Bacchi." To compare the Bacchi of one religion with the Thyrus-bearers of another is mere foolishness. All Hindus, for instance, are not unintelligent worshipers of idols and all Christians fervent imitators of the Christ. If we compare the two at all, let us put the image-adoration of the Roman Church or eikon-worship of the Greek Church alongside of the worship of four-faced

Brahmā and the rest of the figures of the pantheon; but if we would find the proper parallel to the holy life and best theology of Christendom, then we must go to the best theology and holiest livers among the Brāhmans.

So then if we analyse a religion, we find that the lowest of the people know little of it and cling desperately to many misconceptions and superstitions, and that from this travesty of what it really is, rises grade after grade of higher intelligence and less erroneous expression of it, until we arrive at that class of souls who consciously seek to welcome the light in all its fulness and make this the one object of their lives. It is within this class of minds that we must seek for the true nature of a religion. Here then we expect to find the real points of contact between the religion and its sister-faiths, and here we sense the presence of the glorious Spiritual Sun, the parent of all the Rays of Light poured into the world.

Now of all the great religions none can be of greater interest to any student of the comparative science of religion in the West than the Christian Faith. It presses on him at every turn; it is a problem he cannot escape. He is amazed at the general ignorance of everything connected with its history and origins. How few are there who have ever really studied the subject, outside of the comparatively small body of scholars whose profession is to deal with such researches—and even among them how few have thrown any real light on the subject, in spite of their admirable industry.

The Beginnings of Christianity.

The First Two Centuries.

Indeed it is difficult for any one possessed of the ideas we have endeavoured to express above, filled with enthusiasm for the unity of religion and with a living faith in the truly universal nature of the Christ's teaching, to gain much real help from the studies of either rationalists or apologists. For long he is confronted with libraries of books filled with mutually contradictory opinions, and only valuable as a means of sifting out material for future use. He finds as he prosecutes his studies, that every one of his preconceptions as to early times has to be considerably modified, and most of them indeed to be entirely rejected. He gradually works his way to a point whence he can obtain an unimpeded view of the remains of the first two centuries, and gazes round on a world that he has never heard of at school, and of which no word is breathed from the pulpit.

Is this the world of the Primitive Church of which he has read in the accepted manuals and been told of by pastors and masters? Is this the picture of the single and simple community of the followers of Jesus; this the one doctrine which he had been led to believe has been handed down in unbroken succession and in one form since the beginnings? He gazes round on a religious world of immense activity, a vast upheaval of thought and a strenuousness of religious endeavour to which the history of the Western world gives no parellel. Thousands of schools and communities on every hand, striving and contending, a vast freedom of thought, a mighty effort to live the religious life. Here he finds innumerable points of contact with other religions; he moves in an atmosphere of freedom of which he has previously had no experience in Christian tradition. Who are all these people—not fishermen and slaves and the poor and destitute, though those are striving too— but these men of learning and ascetic life, saints and sages as much as many others to whom the name has been given with far less reason? They are all heretics, say later Church writers, very pestilent folk and enemies of the True Faith which we have now established by our decrees and councils.

But the student prefers to look to the first two centuries themselves instead of listening to the opinions and decisions of those who come after, who, as farther away from the origins, can hardly be expected to know more of them than those they anathematised after their death.

Now it is remarkable that, though such abundantly minute and laborious research has been expended on the problem of the origins of Christianity by the analysis of canonical documents, so little critical attention has been bestowed on the writings of these "heretics," although by their means great light may be thrown on many of the obscure problems connected with the history of the beginnings; it is only of comparatively late years that the utility of their evidence has been recognised and that attempts have been made to bring them into court. The "general voice" of the Catholic Church since its ascendancy has stigmatised these "heretics" as the "first-born sons of Satan," and the faithful have believed unquestioningly that that voice was "*Sancto Spiritu suggerente.*" But for Protestantism at least such crude opinions can no longer satisfy the liberal mind in things religious at the beginning of the twentieth century.

The "Higher Criticism."

For upwards of one hundred years liberal Christendom has witnessed the most strenuous and courageous efforts to rescue the Bible from the hands of an ignorant obscurantism which had in many ways degraded it to the level of a literary fetish and deprived it of the light of reason. This policy of obscurantism is really one of despair, of want of confidence in the living and persisting presence of inspiration in the Church, a tacit confession that inspiration had ceased in the infancy of the Faith.

As is well known, the dogma of the verbal and literal inspiration by the Holy Ghost, in the fullest sense of the terms, of every canonical document was but lately universally held, and is still held by the majority of Christians to-day. The famous encyclical of Leo XIII. ("Providentissimus Deus"— 1893) formulates the orthodoxy of Roman Catholic Christendom in the following counsel of despair:

"Providentissimus Deus."

"It is absolutely wrong and forbidden, either to narrow inspiration to certain parts only of Holy Scripture, or to admit that the sacred writer has erred. For the system of those who, in order to rid themselves of these difficulties, do not hesitate to concede that Divine inspiration regards the things of faith and morals, and nothing beyond, because (as they wrongly think) in the question of the truth or falsehood of a passage, we should consider not so much what God has said as the reason and purpose which He had in mind in saying it—this system cannot be tolerated, for all the books which the Church receives as sacred and canonical are written wholly and entirely, with all their parts, at the dictation of the Holy Ghost; and so far is it from being possible that any error can co-exist with inspiration, that inspiration not only is essentially incompatible with error, but excludes and rejects it as absolutely and necessarily as it is impossible that God Himself, the supreme truth, can utter that which is not true. This is the ancient and unchanging faith of the Church, solemnly defined in the Councils of Florence and Trent, and finally confirmed and more expressly formulated by the Council of the Vatican. . . . Hence because the Holy Ghost employed men as His instruments, we cannot therefore say that it was these inspired instruments who, perchance, have fallen into error, and not the primary author. For, by supernatural power, He so moved and impelled them to write—He was so present to them—that the things which He ordered, and those only, they, first rightly understood, then willed faithfully to write down, and finally expressed in apt words and with infallible truth. Otherwise it could not be said that He was the author of the entire Scripture. Such has always been the persuasion of the Fathers. . . . It follows that those who maintain that an error is possible in any genuine passage of the sacred writings, either pervert the Catholic notion of inspiration, or make God the author of such error."

This encyclical is not a curious literary relic of mediævalism; it is the most solemn and authoritative voice of the Head of by far the largest and most powerful Church of Christendom, binding on all the faithful, and circulated broadcast at the end of the nineteenth century, in which we boasted ourselves to be so much better than our fathers.

Its Immediate Result.

It is, of course, perfectly patent that such a pronouncement is unavoidable by the Head of a Church which has given in its adhesion to the dogma of infallibility, and whose life depends on the maintenance of its unquestioned authority. The consequence, however, is that in order to reconcile this dogma with reason, its scholars have to resort to a casuistical method which is exceedingly distasteful to those who are nurtured in the free air of scientific research, and which unfortunately renders the writings of Roman Catholic critics open to the charge of insincerity. We need not, however, necessarily, doubt their sincerity, for in the domain of religion the commonest phenomenon is faith doing violence to reason; as students of life, therefore, we watch with keenest interest this tragedy of the human reason struggling in the bonds of a self-imposed authority, and as believers in Providence have confidence that the force thus generated will eventually be used for good, though at present it seems to many of us an unmixed evil.

This is one side of the picture, and indeed a

most interesting one for the student of human nature. Indubitably many millions still believe most firmly as they are bidden to believe by the Holy Father, and with a slight difference of contents and edition many millions of Protestants, who spurn the Pope's authority far from them, believe as blindly in this view of inspiration and are even more fervent bibliolaters than their Roman Catholic brethren. This conservative and reactionary force is apparently still necessary; it is the pressure which insists on ever greater and greater thoroughness from those who are clearing a way for the acceptance of a living doctrine of inspiration, to replace what for an ever-growing number appears to be the fossil of a lifeless dogma. This conservatism, we believe, will not prove an evil for Christendom in the long run, for it is largely dictated by a faith—though a blind one—in the reality of inspiration, in the sublimity of the "things not seen," which refuses to have its positive place in the human heart filled by what seems to it at present a negation of its most cherished convictions. But could such believers open the eyes of their understanding, they would see that the busy souls who are clearing away the obscurations of centuries of misunderstanding, are filled with as lively a faith as their own—and by their devotion to truth are doing God's work in preparing the way for a fuller realization of His eternal Wisdom and a deeper understanding of human nature. True, in order to achieve this task these energetic souls are filled with an enthusiasm for criticism which is perhaps exaggerated, but which nevertheless is the necessary

The Force of Reaction.

yoke-fellow of blind conservatism. It is the child of these twain that will bring light.

The Force of Progress.
For if we turn to the other side of the picture, we find the keen and trained mind of the scientific intellect scrutinizing every word and letter of Scripture to test the assertions of blind faith. Textual or the Lower Criticism has for ever shattered the pretension of the Council of Trent, to settle the question of a "Textus Receptus." The Received Text is proved to have suffered in its tradition so many misfortunes at the hands of ignorant scribes and dogmatic editors that the human reason stands amazed at the spectacle. Can it be possible, it asks, that any soul possessed of God's good gift of reason can believe the literal inspiration of such a collection of protean changes of words?

The Nature of Criticism.
It is perhaps a mistake to have given the name of Criticism to such research, because the ordinary person looks on the term as implying something hostile and inimical; the original meaning of the word, however, did not convey such an idea, but simply the sense of examining and judging well. But the wise man will not be dismayed by a term; he will look at the thing itself, and so far from finding anything impious in so admirable an art as that of textual criticism, will regard it as a most potent means for removing human error.

But Criticism does not end with the investigation of the text; it proceeds to a higher branch and busies itself with research into the date and history of the sacred books, the analysis and comparison of their several contents, and their relations with other writings; in brief, it surveys the whole field of Biblical literature as to contents in all its parts. The results of this investigation are so stupendous, that we seem to enter a new religious land. But before we enter the sun-lit waters of the harbour of this new country, we must have battled through many storms which no bark of blind faith will ever survive; the only vessel that can live through them is the ship of a rational faith.

In brief, the method of criticism is rational, it is that of private judgment; though indeed I doubt if there be any class of men who have sought more earnestly for help and guidance in their task than the great Critics of Christendom. It is this fact, the high moral worth of our Critics and their deep religious sense, which makes their work so valuable. It is the best in Christendom criticising itself—not a band of enemies without, trying to compass its discomfiture. A religion whose adherents can do this, is alive, and so long as this spirit exists cannot die. This spirit is as much the inspiration of the Holy Ghost as is the conviction of blind faith in the "*credo quia absurdum*" of the Roman tradition of verbal inspiration.

But we must not suppose that Criticism is an end in itself; it is but a means towards a new definition of the eternal problems of religion—a most potent means indeed, because these problems can now be defined with an intelligence and a knowledge of human nature which infinitely adds to their interest, and demands more pressingly than ever their solution; but Criticism cannot solve

The Resultant.

them, their solution depends on a still higher faculty, a faculty that will pass beyond the science of things seen to the gnosis of things unseen. This is the child that will come to birth from the congress of the two great forces of progress and reaction of which we have been speaking.

For, granting that the Bible is a library of books for the most part composed of scraps of other documents, of very various dates edited and re-edited; that the older deposits of the Jewish portion draw largely from the mythology of other nations and falsify history to an incredible extent; are in their oldest deposits profuse in unmoral doctrine and patent absurdities, and paint the picture of a God that revolts all thinking minds; that the more recent deposits of the Hebrew Scriptures, though breathing a far loftier spirit, are still open to many objections; and that the books of the Christian portion are equally called in question on numerous points;—still there is so much of beauty and lofty conception in the teachings of the Bible, and it has for so many centuries been regarded as the vehicle of God's revelation to man, that the problem of inspiration, instead of being lessened by these facts, becomes all the more pressing for solution.

What is the nature of this higher faculty which transcends the reason; and why are the records of its activity marred with imperfection and absurdities which the reason can so clearly detect?

This the scientist as scientist, the scholar as scholar, can never fully explain. Equally so the mystic as mystic cannot throw full light on the problem

What is required is the nature born of the union of the two—a nature so hard to find that it may almost be said to be non-existent. The mystic will not submit himself to the discipline and training of science; the scholar refuses to attach any validity to the methods of the mystic. And yet without the union of the two the child of understanding cannot be born.

For some three hundred years the Western world has been evolving a wonderful instrument of natural research, a subtle grade of mind trained in what we call the scientific method; it has been developing in this instrument numerous new senses, and chief among them the sense of history. Its conquests are so brilliant that men are disposed to believe that never have such things been before; we are scornful of the past, impatient of its methods, unsympathetic to its ideas, and little inclined to profit by the lessons it can teach. As has ever been the case with nations in their prime, we think that "we are the people, and wisdom will die with us." All this is perfectly natural and even necessary for the proper development of this keen intellectual instrument, this grade of mind of which we are all so proud. But the student of human nature and the scholar of the science of life keeps looking to the past in order that he may the better forecast the future; his sense of history extends beyond the domain of the "Higher Criticism" and strives to become clairvoyant.

Nineteen Centuries Ago and Now.

We have had three hundred years or so of

cataloguing and criticism, analysis and scepticism, of most brilliant physical research in all departments; the pious have feared for the overthrow of religion, and positivists have longed for the downfall of superstition. What has it all meant; for what good purpose is this sifting; how does the strife exemplify the wise providence of God?

Perhaps it may not be so difficult as it appears at first sight, to point to the direction in which the answers to these questions may be to some extent anticipated. That similar phenomena recur in the natural world is the unvarying experience of mankind; that time is the ever-moving image of eternity, and that the wheel of genesis is ever turning, is testified to by the wiser minds of humanity. Whither, then, should we look in the history of human affairs for phenomena similar to the happenings of these last three hundred years? Whither else more certainly than to the history of the times which witnessed the birth of the religion of the Christ? The many striking parallels between the social and religious aspects of the civilization of that critical epoch and of our own times have been already sketched by a few writers, but no general notice has been taken of their endeavours, least of all has any practical lesson been learned from the review of this experience of the past. For the experience of humanity is our own experience, if we have but wit enough to understand.

The soul of man returns again and again to learn the lessons of life in this great world-school, according to one of the great doctrines of general religion. If this be so, it follows that when similar conditions recur a similar class of souls returns to continue its lessons of experience. It may well be even that many of the identical souls who were embodied in the early centuries of Christianity are continuing their experience among ourselves to-day. For why otherwise do the same ideas recur, why do the same problems arise, the same ways of looking at things? They cannot fall into our midst from the "*Ewigkeit*"; must it not be that they have been brought back by minds to whom they have already been familiar? *The Return of Souls.*

It would of course be exceedingly unwise to stretch even a single one of our parallels into an identity; we must bear in mind that though many of the conditions are strikingly resemblant, some factors in great prominence in the civilization of the Græco-Roman world are only very faintly outlined in our present civilization, while some strongly marked features of our own times are but imperfectly traceable in that age. *The Conditions of the Comparison.*

We must further remember that the records of that time are frequently very imperfect, while the history of our own is inscribed in painful detail; and that though we can review the main outlines of the whole of that phase of civilization, we can only survey a portion of our own, for its cycle is not ended and the records of the future are not yet open to our understanding.

Finally, we must remember that the general quality of the life and mind-texture of our own age is generally far more subtle than it was nineteen hundred years ago—for humanity evolves.

All these considerations must be kept in mind if we would anticipate the future from a survey of the history of the past. But indeed it requires no great effort of the imagination for even the most superficial student of history to see a marked similarity between the general unrest and searching after a new ideal that marked the period of brilliant intellectual development which preceded the birth of Christianity, and the uncertainty and eager curiosity of the public mind in the closing years of the nineteenth century.

The Intensified Present.

The tendency is the same in kind though not in degree; the achievements of the scientists and scholars of Alexandria (to take the most conspicuous example) during the three hundred years which preceded the Christian era, have been vastly transcended by the conquests of their successors in our own time. To-day life is more intense, thought more active, experience more extended, the need of the solution of the problem more pressing. The modern mind took birth in Greece some two thousand five hundred years ago, and developed itself by intimate contact with the ancient East, a contact made physically possible by the "world-conquest" of Alexander, and subsequently by the organising genius of Rome.

But to-day it is not the conquests of an Alexander or the power of Rome which have built the ways of communication between the nations; it is the conquests of physical science which have in truth united the ends of the earth, and built up an arterial and nervous system for our common mother which she has never previously possessed. It is no longer the speculative mind of Greece and the practical genius of Rome that meet together, it is not even the mind of the then confined Occident meeting with the enthusiasm and mysticism of the then Orient; it is the meeting of the great waters, the developed thought and industrious observation of the whole Western world of to-day meeting with the old slow stream of the ancient and modern East. *Occident and Orient.*

The great impetus which the study of oriental languages and tongues long since dead has received during the last hundred years, has led to the initiation of a comparative science of ancient literature—of the world-bibles—and of religion which is slowly but surely modifying all our preconceptions. To-day it is not a Porphyry who disproves the authenticity of the Book of Daniel or a Marcion who makes havoc of what afterwards became the New Testament canon, but it is the "Higher Criticism" which has struck the death blow to unreasoning bibliolatry. The conflict between religion (or, if you will, theology) and science has produced a generation that longs and searches for a reconciliation. That reconciliation will come; Heaven and Earth will once more kiss each other. It came in the past for those souls who were searching for it, and it will come for those who seek it to-day. If the human heart seek the Light the Light will pour into it. It was so nineteen hundred *The Reconciliation of Science and Theology.*

years ago; men sought for the Light and the Light came in answer to their prayers. And if this view may at first appear strange to those who have been taught to regard the state of affairs before the coming of the Christ as one of unmixed depravity, the reading of these pages may perhaps lead them to a more reasonable view of the conditions which called for the coming of so great a Soul for the helping of mankind.

The Coming and Going of Souls.

The Light was received by men in proportion to their capacity to understand it, and the Life was poured into them as their natures were capable of expansion. And if the subsequent history of the times, when the dark cloud of ignorance and intolerance settled down on Christendom for so many centuries, makes it appear as if that Life had been poured out in vain, and that Light radiated to no purpose, we should remember that they were lavished on souls and not on bodies; that the path of individual souls is not to be traced in the evolution of racial bodies. The souls incarnated into the civilisation of Greece and Rome who were capable of receiving the Light, were far different from the souls who were incarnated into the half barbarous hordes which destroyed that civilization, and out of which the new races were to be developed. The old races which supplied the conditions for the experience of the more advanced souls, were to disappear gradually, and new races were to be developed, which in their childhood could not supply the necessary conditions for the incarnation of such subtle intellects, but which in their manhood would attract to them still higher souls perchance. This of course did not take place with suddenness, it was all very gradual, there was much overlapping of races, as the old units and atoms were slowly replaced by new ones.

But how is it to be expected that Vandal and Goth could understand the great problems which delighted the minds of the philosophers and mystics of Greece and Rome? And further, must it not all have been foreseen and provided for by the Wisdom that watches over human affairs?

<small>The Birth and Death of Races.</small>

Races and nations are born, and die, as men are born and die; they may be long-lived or short-lived, they may be good, bad, or indifferent. But whatever their characters and characteristics as compared with other races, their early period is that of childhood, their middle period that of manhood, and their later period that of old age.

It follows then that as a general rule the class of souls which seeks experience in them in their childhood, is not the same as the grade of souls which incarnates in them in their middle age, or in their old age. Of course there are numerous individual exceptions, for the above is the merest outline of the elements of the problem; the details are so complicated, the permutations and combinations so innumerable, that no mind can fully grasp them.

Moreover races and nations so overlap and blend, their origins and disappearings so shade off into other nations and races, that the analogy of their lives with the lives of men must not be overstrained. The moment of birth and the moment of death is very hard to detect in the case of a race, and the embryonic period and stages of disintegration cannot be clearly defined. Nevertheless we can trace the main moments of their evolution and perceive the differences in their main periods of age.

<small>The Manhood of the Western World.</small>

Our Western world, the vehicle of the modern mind, has had its period of childhood; it was born from the womb of Greek and Roman civilisation, and its lusty childhood was a natural period of ignorance and passion. Such considerations will enable us better to understand the otherwise sad spectacle of the dark and middle ages in Europe; they were the natural concomitants of childhood, and were followed by the intellectual development of youth and early manhood. The Western world is apparently just coming of age, and in the future we may hope it will think and act as a man and put away childish things.

The problems which will in future occupy the attention of its developed intelligence were foreshadowed in the womb of its parent, and our more immediate task will be to deal with some of the outlines of that foreshadowing.

SOME ROUGH OUTLINES OF THE BACKGROUND OF THE GNOSIS.

PRELIMINARY CONSIDERATIONS.

THE familiar story of the origins of Christianity which we have all drunk in as it were with our mothers' milk, may be said to be almost a part of the consciousness of the Western world. It is interwoven with our earlist recollections; it has been stamped upon our infant consciousness with a solemnity which has repressed all questioning; it has become the "thing we have grown used to." It has upon its side that stupendous power of inertia, the force of custom, against which but few have the strength to struggle. But once let the ordinary man desire to know more about the greatest story in the world, as all its tellers assert, and he must begin the struggle. Previously he has been led to believe not only that the story is absolutely unique, but that it is entirely supernatural. In brief, if he analyses his own understanding of the story he finds it violently divorced from all historical environment, a thing of

The Greatest Story in the World.

itself, standing alone, in unnatural isolation. His picture has no background.

The Need of a Background.

Moreover he will find it very difficult to fill in that background, no matter how industriously he may labour. He may read many books on the "Life and Times of our Lord," only to find that for the most part the environment has been made to fit the story and its main features have been taken from it; in brief, he does not feel that he has been put in contact with the natural environment for which he is seeking.

There are of course a few works which are not of this nature, but the general reader seldom hears of them, for they are generally regarded as "dangerous" and "disturbing."

But even if we go deeper into the matter and make a special study of the history of the origins, with the largest of libraries at our disposal, we find that no writer has as yet given us a really sufficient sketch of the environment, and without this it is impossible to have a real comprehension of the nature of infant Christianity and the full scope of its illumination; without it we shall never understand its real naturalness and its vast power of adaptation to that environment.

The Main Means to a Recovery of the Outlines.

For if we look back to the evidence of the first two centuries of our era (and to our mind no evidence with regard to the origins subsequent to this period is of any validity) for an understanding of the actual state of affairs, instead of one Church and one form of faith, we find innumerable communities and innumerable modes of expression—communities united for the living of a Life and systems striving to express the radiance of a Light. In many of these communities and these expressions we find intimate points of contact with the life and faith of the best in universal religion, and a means that will help us to fill in the outlines of the background of the origins with a greater feeling of confidence than we had previously thought possible.

So far from finding the sharp divorcement between science (or philosophy) and religion (or theology) which has characterised all later periods of the Christian era up to our own day, it was just the boast of many of these communities that religion was a science; they boldly claimed that it was possible to know the things of the soul as definitely as the things of the body; so far from limiting the illumination which they had received to the comprehension of the poorest intellect, or confining it to the region of blind faith, they claimed that it had supplied them with the means of formulating a world-philosophy capable of satisfying the most exacting intellect. Never perhaps has the world witnessed more daring efforts to reach a solution of the world-problem than were attempted by some of these mystic philosophers and religio-scientists. That their attempts are for the most part incomprehensible to the modern mind is partly owing to the fact that our record of them is so imperfect, and partly due to the natural impossibility of expressing in human language the stupendous realities to which they aspired; nevertheless their "heaven-storming," when we can understand its nature, is a spectacle to move our admiration and (if we cast aside all prejudice) make us bow our heads before the Power which inspired their efforts.

The Gnostic Schools. They strove for the knowledge of God, the science of realities, the gnosis of the things-that-are; wisdom was their goal; the holy things of life their study. They were called by many names by those who subsequently haled them from their hidden retreats to ridicule their efforts and anathematise their doctrines, and one of the names which they used for themselves, custom has selected to be their present general title. They are now generally referred to in Church history as the Gnostics, those whose goal was the Gnosis,—if indeed that be the right meaning; for one of their earliest existing documents expressly declares that Gnosis is not the end—it is the beginning of the path, the end is God—and hence the Gnostics would be those who used the Gnosis as the means to set their feet upon the Way to God.

Where to Look for their Origins. The question which at once presses itself upon the attention of the student of history is: Whence did these men come? Did they arise suddenly in the midst of a world that cared not for these things; were they entirely out of touch with the past; had they no predecessors? By no means; those who so bitterly opposed them, who—boasting themselves to be the only legitimate inheritors of the illumination of the Christ—in their most angry mood, stigmatised the Gnostics as "the first-born of Satan," may help us to set our feet in the direction where we shall find some materials on which to base an answer. In less bitter mood, the Church Fathers tell us that the doctrines of the Gnosis are of Plato and Pythagoras, of Aristotle and of Heracleitus, of the Mysteries and Initiations of the nations, and not of Christ. Let us then try for a brief space to follow this lead and fill in some rough outlines of the background of the Gnosis; we shall then be better able to say whether or no we join our voices to the hue and cry of the heresy-hunters.

In what follows we shall only attempt the vaguest indications of the vast field of research in which the student of the Christian origins has to labour, before he can really appreciate the nature of the soil in which the seed was sown. The political history and social conditions of the time have to be carefully studied and continually borne in mind, but the most important field to be surveyed is the nature of the religious world, especially during the three centuries prior to our era. How is it possible, we ask ourselves, as we gaze upon the blendings of cult, the syncretism of theogonies and cosmogonies and the mixtures of faith which abounded in these centuries, to separate them into their original elements? The problem seems as hopeless as the endeavour to trace the mixtures of races and sub-races, of nations and families, which were the material means of these blendings of cult and religion. Where can we begin? For if we begin where known history fails (as is usually the case), and imagine that we have here

The Nature of the Field to be Surveyed.

reached a state of things primitive, we are forced to be ever revising our hypotheses by each new archæological and ethnological discovery. Tribes which we have regarded as primitive savages are found to be the decaying remnants of once great nations, their superstitions and barbarous practices are found blended with the remnants of high ideas which no savagery could evolve; where shall we seize a beginning in this material of protean change? Surely we cannot trace it on the lines of material evolution alone? May it not be that there is the "soul of a people" as well which has to be reckoned with?

The Soil of the Field.

Just as the bodies of men are born from other bodies, so are nations born from nations. But if the physical heredity of a man is difficult to trace (since the farther it is pushed back the more it ramifies), far more difficult is the heredity of a nation, for whereas a man has but two parents a nation may have many, and whereas the bodies of a man's parents at death are hidden away to decay in the earth, [the bodies of nations decay in the sight of all, and persist mingled with their children and grand-children, and all the family-tree which they share with other nations. Nations may have certain distinguishing characteristics, but they are not individualised in the same way as a man is individualised; and the problem of their inner heredity is more difficult to solve than even that of the nature of the animal soul, for it is on a vaster scale.

Such then being the nature of the physical vehicle of the general religious consciousness, it is not surprising to find that the history of the evolution of religious ideas is one of the most difficult of studies.

If we bear all these presuppositions in mind, it requires the greatest courage to venture on any attempt at generalization; we feel that every statement ought to be qualified by so many other considerations that we are almost disgusted with its crudity, and know that we are only tracing the bones of skeletons when we ought to be clothing them with flesh, and making them vibrant with life.

But to return to the antecedents of the special period and movement we have in view.

Three main streams mingle their waters together in the tumbling torrent that swirls through the land in these critical centuries.

Three main elements are combining their substance and transmuting their natures in the seething crucible of the first centuries of the Christian era.

Greece, Egypt, and Jewry receive the child in their arms, suckle the body of the new born babe, and watch round its cradle. The irrational soul of it is like to the animal souls of its nurses; its rational soul is of like heredity with their minds, but the spirit within it is illumined by the Christ. It is the heredity of its rational and spiritual soul, however, to which we shall pay the greatest attention; for in this is to be found the inner side of the religions of Jewry, Egypt, and Greece.

Three Mother Streams.

We have then to search most carefully in the direction in which this can be found; we shall not find it in the cult and practice of the people, but in the religion and discipline of the philosopher and sage, of the prophet and priest. For antiquity, there were as many degrees in religion as there were grades in human nature; the instruction in the inner degrees was reserved to those who were fit to comprehend; mystery-institutions and schools of initiation of every degree were to be found in all great nations, and to them we must look for the best in their religions—not infrequently, alas, for the worst as well, for the worst is the corruption of the best; but of this we will speak elsewhere.

Let us then first turn our attention to the religion of the intelligence of Greece.

GREECE.

The Greece of 600 B.C.
IF we turn to the Greece of the sixth century prior to our era, we can perceive the signs of the birth of a new spirit in the Western world, the beginning of a great intellectual activity; it is, so to speak, the age of puberty of the Greek genius, new powers of thought are coming into activity, and the old-time myths and ancient oracular wisdom are receiving new expression in the infant science of empirical physics and the birth of philosophy.

This activity is part and parcel of a great quickening, an outpouring of power, which may be traced in other lands as well; it is an intensification of the religious consciousness of the nations, and it intensified the religious instinct of Greece in a remarkable manner. Its most marked characteristic is the application of the intellect to things religious, owing to the accelerated development of this faculty in man.

The greatest pioneers of this activity were men whose names still live in the temple of fame. In the far East we have Confucius and Laotze, in India Gautama the Buddha, in Persia the last of the Zoroasters, in Greece Pythagoras; there were others doubtless elsewhere who acted as messengers of the Light, but our existing records are too imperfect to permit us to trace their paths.

Can any who believe in the providence of Wisdom in human affairs, doubt but that this was part of some great plan for man's advancement? If there be a Providence " that shapes our ends," where can we see its hand more clearly than in such great happenings?

But to confine ourselves to Greece; we must not suppose that Pythagoras was without predecessors; for though his later followers would have us think that all philosophy flowed from him, we cannot believe in this so sudden appearance of it, and we doubt not that Pythagoras regarded himself as the enunciator of old truths and but one of the teachers of a line of doctrine. He had Pherecydes and Anaximander and Thales before him in Asia Minor, and other teachers in Egypt and Chaldæa and elsewhere. Indeed in these early days it is almost impossible to separate philosophy from mythology and all the ancient ideas connected with it. If we look to the times of Thales, who is regarded as the herald of the first elements of philosophy in the Grecian world, and

The Precursors of Pythagoras.

who lived a century earlier than Pythagoras, we find a state of affairs somewhat as follows.

The educated and travelled of the Greeks of the time regarded Egypt as the centre of all learning and culture and their own forbears as of no account in such matters. The rhapsodists of the Homeric poems flattered their vanity by singing of the prowess of their ancient heroes, but could tell the intelligent nothing of religion; as for Hesiod and his theogany and the rest, they could make but little of them. He was doubtless more intelligible than the archaic fragments of the Orphic poems which enshrined the most ancient elements of the religious tradition of Hellas. But he fell far short of the wisdom of Egypt. As for the Orphic fragments, they were the relics of their barbarous ancestors, and no one believed in them but the superstitious and ignorant.

But a nation that is to be something of itself and not a mere copier of others must have confidence in its past traditions, and we find about this time that there arose a growing interest in these old fragments, which gradually led to their collection and translation into the Greek of the period. This took place at the end of the sixth century, and the name identified most closely with this activity to recover the fragments of the old tradition was that of Onomacritus.

It is interesting to notice how that this was done just prior to the period when Greece cast back the invading hosts of Xerxes from the shores of Europe. The effort seems to have been to revive in Greece the memory of its past by recovering the channel of its ancient inspiration, and at the same time to let her feel the strength of her peculiar genius in thinking out the old oracular wisdom in terms of her fresh intellect, that so she might feel courage to hurl back the invading forces of the East, and pave the way to her future conquests of that same East in the days of Alexander.

At this period, then, we notice the rise of philosophy and the revival of the Orphic tradition. But this is not all; the leaven is working within as well as without, and we find an enormously increased activity in those most sacred institutions of the religious life of Greece—the Mysteries. But before we proceed to consider briefly this perhaps the most important point of all, let us try to take a hasty retrospect along the line of the Orphic tradition; for those who studied such matters in later Greece more deeply than the rest, assert with one voice that the line of their descent was from Orpheus through Pythagoras and Plato.

The Orphic Tradition.

The Greeks known to history seem to have formed part of one of the waves of immigration into Europe of the great Aryan stock. Of the main wave there were doubtless many wavelets.

Primitive Hellas.

If we may venture to believe that some germ of history underlies the records of the priests of Saïs communicated to Solon and preserved to us by Plato in his *Critias* and *Timæus*; according to them, so long ago as ten thousand years before our era, Attica was occupied by the long-forgotten ancestors of the Hellenes. Then came the great flood when the Atlantic Island was destroyed, and the shores of the Mediterranean rendered uninhabitable by seismic disturbances of which the great cataclysm was but one of a number, the third it is said before the "Flood of Deucalion." It was the time of Egypt "before the flood" of which we have mention in the writings of Manetho.

If this be true, we can imagine how the wavelet of the conquering Aryan race which then occupied Hellas—the overlords of the "autochthones" of the period—was driven back, and how the country was left for long to the occupation of these same "autochthones" whom Herodotus calls "Pelasgi." They were to the Greeks, what the Dravidians were and are to the Indo-Aryans, "autochthones" if you will, but with a long history of their own if we could recover their records.

The polity of the ancient Greek inhabitants of Attica, according to the notes of Solon, bears a striking resemblance to the polity of the ancient Aryans in India, and doubtless their primitive religious traditions came from a common stock.

As for the "Pelasgi," who knows their traditions, or the blendings of races that had taken place before the remains of them could be classed as an indiscriminate mass? We are told, that they were ruled over by chiefs from the Atlantic Island who busily pushed its conquests to the most distant shores of the Great Sea (the Mediterranean), and that the ancient Hellenes disputed the lordship with this dominant race. What enormous possibilities of cult-mixtures myth-blending, and theocrasia have we here! It was these Atlanteans who introduced the cults of Poseidon and Hephæstus (Vulcan), the mighty powers of the sea and of subterranean fire, which had destroyed their fathers.

For the Aryan Hellenic stock there was All-father Zeus and the Goddess of Wisdom, Pallas Athene, who was also a warrior goddess, as befitted a warlike race. What the Greek religion was at this period, who shall say ? But it is not so wild a guess to suppose that it may have been of a bardic nature—hymn-bursts suited to warriors, of which we have relics in the legends of Druid and Bard and in all those ancient traditions of the Celt, in the mythology of the Teuton and Norseman, and even in the legend-lore preserved by the ancient Slavs.

We may imagine how in these early years, as the strong current of the Aryan flood swept them onward, wavelet overlapped wavelet, horde fought with horde, and that the smiling land of Hellas was a rich prize for the strongest. We may imagine how when the effects of the "floods" had subsided and in course of many many years seismic disturbances had lessened, the Hellenic stock reoccupied the ground again, not only in Greece itself but also on the shores of Asia Minor. But how many wavelets of immigration flowed in until Homeric times who shall say ? Perhaps some day it may be possible to sift out from the myths some deposit of history, and perceive how a Cecrops, an Erectheus, and an Ion did not follow each other in rapid succession, but were great leaders who established kingdoms separated by long periods of time. *The Wavelets of Aryan Immigration.*

May it not further be that with these conquering kings came bards to advise and encourage, and supply what of religion was thought good for them? May we not seek for the prototype of Orpheus here, and to one of the later wavelets trace the archaic fragments of the most ancient religious poems? We may almost see some religious pomp of the time passing down the Sacred Way to Eleusis, ever the most sacred spot in Greece, with some Orpheus of the time rousing the warriors to enthusiasm by his songs, harp in hand, with his grey locks streaming in the breeze, while the regular march of the warriors kept time to the strain, and emphasized it by the rhythmic clashing of their shields.

The Orphic Line. It would be vain to look for any intellectual presentation of religion along this line; whatever it was, it must have been inspirational, prophetical, and oracular; and indeed this is the peculiar characteristic of the Orphic tradition.

But even in these early days was the tradition a pure one? Scarcely; the various races must have fought their way through other races, and settled for a time among them before they reached Hellas, and the main line of their march seems to have been round the south shores of the Black Sea and through Thrace.

In Thrace they would meet with the cult of Dionysus and absorb some of its traditions; not that Thrace was the home of this cult, its origins appear to reach eastwards and back into time—a wide-spreading cultus with its roots in the soil of an archaic Semitism, the traces of which are hard to discover in the obscure and fragmentary records that we now possess. Moreover there is some mixture of the Chaldean tradition in the Orphic line, but whether it existed at this period or was superadded later is hard to say.

What the precise religion of the earlier of these successive wavelets was like, when they had settled in the rich lands of Greece, and became more civilized, we can no longer say, for we have no records, but doubtless they were watched over and sufficient inspiration given them for their needs.

If we now turn to the Greece of Homer, and try to find traces of Orpheus, we are doomed to disappointment; but this is not altogether inexplicable. Homer sings of a Greece that seems to have entirely forgotten its ancient bards, of heroes who had left their religion at home, as it were. The yellow-haired Greeks who won the supremacy subsequent to Ion's time, were a stock that paid little attention to religion; they give one the impression of being some sort of Viking warriors who cared little for the agricultural pursuits in which their predecessors were engaged, if we can judge from the tradition preserved by Hesiod. We see a number of independent chieftains occupying the many vales of Greece, whose idea of providing for an increasing population is by foray and conquest.

The Greece of Homer.

There may have been a fickle Helen and a too gallant Paris who violated the hospitality of his hosts, but the Trojan War was more probably a foray of these warriors to gain new lands,—a foray not against an alien race, but against those of their own general kin; for the Trojans were Greeks, somewhat orientalised in their customs perhaps, by settlement in contact with the nations of Asia, but for all that Greeks,—dark-haired Greeks, with a cult like the cult of the fair-haired ones, and with perchance for the most part as little understanding concerning it.

It is, however, just this absence of the priest, or the very subordinate position he holds, which is an indication of the germ of that independence of thought which is the marked characteristic of the Greek mind that was subsequently developed, and of which the Greece of history was the special and carefully watched depository, that it might evolve for the world-purpose for which it was destined. It was good for men to look the gods manfully in the face and battle with them if need be.

"Homer" was the bard of these Viking heroes; but the bard of their predecessors (who were equally Greeks) of the Hellenic stock which they had dominated, was "Orpheus." The descendants of the heroes of Troy naturally looked to "Homer" as the singer of the deeds of *their* forefathers, and as the recorder of their customs and cult; they were too proud to listen to "Orpheus" and the old "theologers" who had been the bards of the conquered; so the old songs and sagas of this bardic line, the lays and legends of this older Greece, were left to the people and to consequent neglect and lack of understanding.

"Orpheus" returns to Greece.

Such was the state of affairs when philosophy arose in the seventh century; it was then found by the few that Homer could not suffice for the religious needs of thinking men; there was nothing in Homer to compare with the religious traditions of Egypt and Chaldæa; the Greeks apparently had nothing of religion, their ancestors were barbarians. Then it occurred to some to collect and compare the ancient oracles and religious myths of the people—the fragments of the Orphic songs—and therein they found proofs of an ancient Greek tradition of things unseen that could be favourably compared with much that Egypt and Chaldæa could tell them. Greece had a religious tradition; their forebears were not barbarous.

Those who busied themselves with such matters at this critical period, we may believe, were not left without guidance; and poets and thinkers were helped as they could receive it. The fragments of this activity in Orphic poesy which have come down to us, show signs of this inspiration; we do not refer to the late "Orphic Hymns," some eighty in number, which may be read in English in Taylor's translation, but to the ancient fragments scattered in the works of classical and patristic writers.

Many of these were based on the archaic fragments of the pre-Homeric times, and looked back to this archaic tradition as their foundation. But the mystic and mythological setting of these poems, their enthusiastic and prophetic character, though all-sufficient for many, were not suited to the nascent intellectuality of Greece which was asserting itself with such vigour. Therefore the greatest leaders of that thought sought means to clothe the ideas which were enshrined in myth and poesy, in modes more suitable to the intellectuals of the time; and we have the philosophy of a Pythagoras and subsequently of a Plato.

The Mysteries.

But alongside of the public cults and popular traditions there existed an inner organism of religion and channels of secret traditions concealed within the Mystery-institutions. If it is difficult to form any precise notion of the evolution of popular religious ideas in Greece, much more difficult is it to trace the various lines of the Mystery-traditions, which were regarded with the greatest possible reverence and guarded with the greatest possible secrecy, the slightest violation of the oath being punishable by death.

The idea that underlay the Mystery-tradition in Greece was similar to that which underlay all similar institutions in antiquity, and it is difficult to find any cult of importance without this inner side. In these institutions, in the inner shrines of the temple, were to be found the means of a more intimate participation in the cult and instruction in the dogmas.

The institution of the Mysteries is the most interesting phenomenon in the study of religion. The idea of antiquity was that there was something to be *known* in religion, secrets or mysteries into which it was possible to be initiated; that there was a gradual process of unfolding in things religious; in fine, that there was a science of the soul, a knowledge of things unseen.

A persistent tradition in connection with all the great Mystery-institutions was that their several founders were the introducers of all the arts of civilization; they were either themselves gods or were instructed in them by the gods—

in brief, that they were men of far greater knowledge than any who had come after; they were the teachers of infant races. And not only did they teach them the arts, but they instructed them in the nature of the gods, of the human soul, and the unseen world, and set forth how the world came into existence and much else.

We find the ancient world honey-combed with these institutions. They were of all sorts and kinds, from the purest and most noble down to the most degraded; in them we find the best and worst of the religion and superstition of humanity. Nor should we be surprised at this, for when human nature is intensified, not only is the better in it stimulated but also the worse in it finds greater scope. *Their Corruption.*

When knowledge is given, power is acquired, and it depends on the recipients whether or no they use it for good or evil. The teachers of humanity have ever been opposed by the innate forces of selfishness, for evolution is slow, and mankind wayward; moreover, men cannot be forced, they must come of their own free-will, "for love is the fulfilling of the law"; and so again though "many are the 'called,' few are the 'chosen.'"

It is said that these earliest teachers of humanity who founded the Mystery-institutions as the most efficient means of giving infant humanity instruction in higher things, were souls belonging to a more highly developed humanity than our own. The men of our infant humanity were children with minds but little developed, and only capable of *The Reason of it.*

understanding what they distinctly saw and felt. In the earliest times, according to this view, the Mysteries were conducted by those who had a knowledge of nature-powers which was the acquisition of a prior perfected humanity not necessarily earth-born, and the wonders shown therein such that none of our humanity could of themselves produce. As time went on and our humanity more and more developed the faculty of reason, and were thought strong enough to stand on their own feet, the teachers gradually withdrew, and the Mysteries were committed to the care of the most advanced pupils of this humanity, who had finally to substitute symbols and devices, dramas and scenic representations, of what had previously been revealed by higher means.

Then it was that corruption crept in, and man was left to win his own divinty by self-conquest and persistent struggling against the lower elements in his nature. The teachers remained unseen, ever ready to help, but no longer moving visibly among men, to compel their reverence and worship. So runs the tradition.

The Various Traditions. If, as we have seen, the origin and evolution of the popular cults of Greece are difficult to trace, much more difficult are the beginnings and development of the Greek Mystery-cultus. The main characteristic of the Mysteries was the profound secrecy in which their traditions were kept; we therefore have no adequate materials upon which to work, and have to rely mainly on hints and veiled allusions. This much, however, is certain, that the Mystery-side of religion was the initiation into its higher cult and doctrine; the highest praise is bestowed upon the Mysteries by the greatest thinkers among the Greeks, who tell us that they purified the nature, and not only made men live better lives here on earth but enabled them to depart from life with brighter hopes of the future.

What the primitive Mystery-cultus traditions along the lines of Orphic, Dionysiac, and Eleusinian descent may have been, it is unnecessary to speculate in this rough outline sketch; but if we come down to the days of Plato we find existing Mystery-institutions which may be roughly characterised as political, private, and philosophic.

The political Mysteries—that is to say the State-Mysteries—were the famous Eleusinia, with their gorgeous external pageants and their splendid inner rites. At this period almost every respectable citizen of Athens was initiated, and we can easily see that the tests could not have been very stringent, when so many were admitted every year. In fact, these State-Mysteries, though providing for a grade or several grades of advancement along the path of right living and of right comprehension of life, had become somewhat perfunctory, as all departments of a State-religion are bound to become in time. *The Political Mysteries.*

Alongside of the Eleusinia there existed certain private Mysteries, not recognised by the State, the number of which subsequently increased enormously, so that almost every variety of Oriental Mystery-cultus found its adherents in Greece, as may be seen *The Private Mysteries.*

from a study of the religious associations among the Greeks known as Thiasi, Erani, and Orgeones; among private communities and societies of this kind there were to be found naturally many undesirable elements, but at the same time they satisfied the needs of many who could derive no spiritual nourishment from the State-religion.

<small>The Orphic Communities.</small>
Among these private foundations were communities of rigid ascetics, men and women, who gave themselves entirely to holy living; such people were said to live the "Orphic life" and were generally known as Orphics. Of course there were charlatans who parodied them and pretended to their purity and knowledge, but we are at present following the indications of those whose conduct squared with their profession.

These Orphic communities appear to have been the refuges of those who yearned after the religious life, and among them were the Pythagorean schools. Pythagoras did not establish something entirely new in Greece when he founded his famous school at Crotona; he developed something already existing, and when his original school was broken up and its members had to flee they sought refuge among the Orphics. The Pythagorean schools disappear into the Orphic communities.

It is in the Pythagorean tradition that we see the signs of what I have called the philosophic Mysteries; it is, therefore, in the best of the Orphic and Pythagorean traditions that we have to find the indications of the nature of the real Mysteries, and not in the political Eleusinia or in the disorderly elements of the Oriental cults.

In fact the Orphics did much to improve the Eleusinia and supported them as a most necessary means for educating the ordinary man towards a comprehension of the higher life. It stands to reason, however, that the Mysteries which satisfied the aspirations of Orphics and Pythagoreans were somewhat higher than the State-Mysteries of the ordinary citizen. These Pythagoreans were famous throughout antiquity for the purity of their lives and the loftiness of their aims, and the Mysteries they regarded with such profound reverence must have been something beyond the Eleusinia, something to which the Eleusinia were but one of the outer approaches. *The Philosophic Mysteries.*

We have then to seek for the innermost religious life of Greece in this direction, and to remember that the inner experiences of this life were kept a profound secret and not paraded on the house-tops. Pythagoras is said to have been initiated into the Egyptian, Chaldæan, Orphic, and Eleusinian Mysteries; at the same time he was one of the chief founders of Greek philosophy. His philosophy however, was not a thing of itself, but the application of his intellect — especially of his mathematical genius — to the best in these Mystery-traditions; he saw that it was necessary to attempt to lead the rapidly evolving intellectuality of Greece along its own lines to the contemplation of the inner nature of things; otherwise in the joy of its freedom it would get entirely out of hand and reject the truths of the ancient wisdom. *Pythagoras and Plato.*

Plato continued this task, though on somewhat different lines; he worked more in the world than Pythagoras, and his main effort was to clear the ground from misconceptions, so that the intellect might be purified and brought into a fit state to contemplate the things-that-are. He spent his life in this task, building up not so much a system of knowledge, as clearing the way so that the great truths of the Gnosis of things-that-are, as Pythagoras termed it, might become apparent of themselves.

It is a mistake to suppose that Plato formulated a distinctly new system of philosophy; his main conceptions are part and parcel of the old wisdom handed down by the seers of the Mysteries; but he does not formulate them so much as clear the ground by his dialetical method, so that the mind may be brought into a fit state to receive them.

Therefore are the conclusions of his dialogues nearly always negative, and only at the end of his long life, probably against his better judgment and in response to the importunity of his pupils, does he set forth a positive document in the *Timæus*, composed of scraps from the unpublished writings of Pythagoreans and others.

Unfortunately most of those who immediately followed him, imagined that his dialectical method was an end in itself, and so instead of living the life of philosophy and seeking the clear vision of true initiation, they degenerated into empty argument and ended in negation.

Aristotle followed with his admirable method

of analysis and exact observation of phenomena, and as he treated of the without rather than of the within he was from one point of view better understood than Plato, but from another more misunderstood, in that his method also was taken as an end in itself rather than as a means simply. And so we come to the three centuries prior to the present era, when the intellectual life of Greece was centred at Alexandria. *Aristotle and Scepticism.*

It was a far more extended Greece than the Hellas of Plato; it was a Greece whose physical prowess had conquered the Orient, and which boasted itself that its intellectual vigour would conquer the world. Everywhere it matched its vigorous intellect against the ancient East, and for a time imagined that victory was with it.

Its independence of thought had given rise to innumerable schools warring with each other, and the spectacle it offers us is very similar to the spectacle of modern Europe during the last three hundred years.

We see there at work, though on a smaller scale—in germ as it were—the same intellectual activity which has charcterized the rise of the modern scientific method, and with it the same breaking down of old views, the same unrest, the same spirit of scepticism.

If we look to the surface of things merely, we might almost say that Greece had entirely forgotten the Mystery-tradition and gloried solely in the unaided strength of her intellect. But if we look deeper we shall find that this is not the case. In the days of Plato the Orient and Egypt were brought to Greece so to speak, whereas later on Greece went to Egypt and the East.

East and West.

Now the ancient wisdom had its home in Egypt and Chaldæa and the Orient generally, so that though the Orphic and Pythagorean communities of Plato's time imported into Greece a modified Orientalism which they adapted to the Greek genius along the lines of their own ancient wisdom-tradition, when the Greeks in their thousands went forth into the East, those of them who were prepared by contact with these schools, came into closer intimacy with the ancient wisdom of the East, and drank it in readily.

As for the generality, just as the introduction of Orientalism into Greece among the people brought with it abuses and enthusiastic rites of an undesirable character, while at the same time it intensified the religious life and gave greater satisfaction to the religious emotions, so the Greek conquest of the Orient spread abroad a spirit of scepticism and unbelief, while sharpening the intellectual faculties.

But all this was a very gradual process, and the more scepticism increased, the intenser became the desire of numbers to withdraw from the warring clash of opinions, and seek refuge in the contemplative life that offered them knowledge. Oriental thinkers and mystics became Hellenized along the lines of Pythagorean and Platonic philosophy, and Greek philosophers became Orientalized by contact with members of the many communities that honeycombed not only Egypt and the rest of the "barbarian" nations subject to Greece, but also Asia Minor and even Hellas herself. How numerous were these communities in the first century may be seen from a study of the writings of Philo Judæus and the life of Apollonius of Tyana, and from the picture of mystic Greece which may be recovered from the ethical and theosophical essays of Plutarch, and also from the many recently discovered inscriptions relating to the innumerable Religious Associations in Greece.

When the Greek kingdoms of the Successors of Alexander were in their turn humbled beneath the conquering power of Rome, the organizing Italic genius policed the world, somewhat in a similar way to the fashion of the present British occupation of India. The legal mind and practical genius of Rome was never really at home in the metaphysical subtleties of Greek philosophy, or the mysticism of the East. In literature and art she could only copy Greece; in philosophy she sought for a rule of conduct rather than a system of knowledge, and so we find her, in the persons of her best men, the follower of Stoic naturalism, which summed up its code of ethics in the ideal of "*honestas*." *Rome.*

Nevertheless Rome could no more than Greece avoid religious contact with the East, and we find her passing through the same experiences as Greece, though in much more modified form. The chief point of contact among the many religions of the Roman Empire was in the common worship of the Sun, and the inner core of this most popular cult was, from about B.C. 70 *The Mysteries of Mithras.*

onwards, to be found in the Mysteries of Mithras.

"The worship of Mithras, or of the sun-god, was the most popular of heathen cults, and the principal antagonist of the truth during the first four centuries of our period." Such is the statement of one who looks at it from the point of view of a Christian ecclesiastic, and indeed the Church Fathers from the time of Justin Martyr onward have declared that the Devil, in the Mysteries of Mithras, had plagiarized their most sacred rites by anticipation.

The Mithriac Mysteries represented the esoteric side of a great international religious movement, which the uniting together of many peoples into the Græco-Roman world had made possible, and which resulted from the contact of Greece and Rome with the thought of the East.

National and local cults were gradually influenced by the form of symbolism employed by the modified Chaldæo-Persian tradition; the worship of the Spiritual Sun, the Logos, with the natural symbol of the glorious orb of day, which was common in one form or other to all great cults, and the rest of the solar symbolism, gradually permeated the popular indigenous forms of religion. In course of time, Mithra, the visible sun for the ignorant, the Spiritual Sun, the Mediator between the Light and Darkness, as Plutarch tells us, for the instructed, caused his rays to shine to the uttermost limits of the Roman Empire. And just as his outer cult dominated the restricted forms of national worship, so did the tradition of his Mysteries modify the Mystery-cultus of the ancient Western world.

EGYPT.

LET us now turn to Egypt and cast a glance on the vista which has to be surveyed, before the outlines of this part of the background of the Gnosis can be filled in.

In spite of her reserve and immeasurable contempt for the upstart Greek genius, Egypt had, even in the times of the earliest Ptolemies, given of her wisdom to Greece. There had been an enormous activity of translation of records and documents, the origin of which is associated with the name of Manetho. It is very probable that Plutarch in his treatise on the Mysteries of Isis drew the bulk of his information from Manetho, and it is very evident that the doctrines therein set forward as the traditional wisdom of Egypt have innumerable points of contact with the Greek Trismegistic literature, those mystic and theosophic treatises which formed the manuals of instruction in the inner Hermetic schools, mystic communities which handed on the wisdom-tradition of Thoth, or Ṭehuti, the God of Wisdom, whose name, as Jamblichus tells us, was "common to all priests," that is to say, was the source of inspiration of the wisdom-tradition in all its branches.

The Wisdom of Egypt.

The Greeks, finding in their own Hermes some points of similarity with the charactistics of Ṭehuti, called him by that name, with the added title

Trismegistus, or Thrice-greatest, because of his great wisdom. That the contents, though not the form, of the oldest treatises of this Trismegistic literature were largely Egyptian is further evidenced by Jamblichus in his treatise on the Mysteries of the Egyptians and Chaldæans.

Along these lines of contact between Egypt and Greece we can proceed to inspect the Egyptian wisdom on its own soil, and find in it many doctrines fully developed which without this investigation we should have considered as entirely indigenous to purely Christian soil. Indeed, in the Trismegistic literature we find a number of the distinctive doctrines of Gnostic Christianity but without the historic Christ; and all of these doctrines are seen to have existed for thousands of years previously in direct Egyptian tradition—especially the doctrines of the Logos, of the Saviour and Virgin Mother, of the second birth and final union with God.

The Blendings of Tradition.

But as in the case of Greece, so in the case of Egypt, within the Egyptian tradition itself there are all manners of conflation of doctrines, of syncretism and blendings, not only in the external popular cults but also in the inner traditions.

To take a single instance, there was a strong Semitic blend dating from the line of the Hyksōs (2000-1500 B.C.). At that time Seth, perchance identical with the title of the Supreme in the tongue of the Semitic conquerors, was a name of great honour. It was identified with Sothis, Sirius, the guardian star of Egypt, the Siriadic Land; and the Mysteries of Seth were doubtless blended in some fashion with those of Osiris. After the hated Hyksōs were expelled it is true that Seth or Set was gradually identified with Typhon, the opponent of Osiris, the Logos; but this no more affects the real doctrines of the Mysteries of Seth, than the fact that the Iranian Aryans used the name Daevos to designate evil entities, destroyed the beneficent nature of the Devas of the Indo-Aryans; it simply registers a rivalry of cult and race and points to a previous epoch when there was intimate contact between the races and their religions. Equally so the Christian use of the term Demon does not dispose of the fact that the Daimones of the Greeks were beneficent beings; witness the Daimon of Socrates "who prevented him if he were about to do anything not rightly."

The ancient close political relations between Chaldæa and Egypt disclosed by archæological research, and the later Persian conquest of Egypt, must also have discovered points of contact in the domain of religion, especially in the Mystery-traditions, and future researches in the many hitherto unworked fields of Egyptology will doubtless throw fresh light on the mixed heredity of religion in Egypt, which is perhaps even more complicated than that of the cults of Greece.

In any case we cannot but feel the sublimity of many of the conceptions of the inner religion of Egypt, in spite of our present inability to classify them in a satisfactory manner. The vast and mysterious background of the cults of Egypt, the sonorous phrases and grandiose titles which we sift out from the present unintelligibility of myth and symbol, persuade us that there was something great working within, and we find the innermost strivings of the mystics devoted to the "Birth of Horus," a shadowing forth of that greatest of all mysteries, the spiritual birth of man, whence man becomes a god and a son of the Father.

The Mystic Communities.

The Egyptians themselves, according to Greek writers, looked back to a time when their initiated priesthood was in possession of greater wisdom than was theirs in later times; they confess that they had fallen away from this high standard and had lost the key to much of their knowledge. Nevertheless the desire for wisdom was still strong in many of the nation, and Egypt was ever one of the most religious countries of the world. Thus we find the Jew Philo, in writing of the wisdom-lovers about A.D. 25, declaring that "this natural class of men is to be found in many parts of the inhabited world, both the Grecian and non-Grecian world, sharing in the perfect good. In Egypt there are crowds of them in every province, or nome as they call it, and especially round Alexandria."

The Therapeuts.

These wisdom-lovers Philo calls by the common name of Therapeuts, either because they professed an art of *healing* superior to that in ordinary use, for they healed souls as well as bodies, or because they were *servants* of God. He describes one of their communities, which evidently belonged to the circle of mystic Judaism; but the many other communities he mentions were also devoted to the same ends, their members were strenuous searchers after wisdom and devoted practisers of the holy life. These secret brotherhoods left no records; they kept themselves apart from the world, and the world knew them not. But it is just these communities which were the immediate links in the chain of heredity of the Gnosis.

We must, therefore, make the most we can of what Philo has to tell us of these Healers; in order to do this thoroughly, it would of course be necessary to search through the whole of his voluminous works and submit the material thus collected to a critical examination—a task outside the scope of these short sketches. But as the matter is of vital importance, we cannot refrain from presenting the reader with a translation of the main source in Philo's writings from which we derive our information. But before giving this translation it is necessary to prefix a few words by way of introduction.

The appearance in 1895 of Conybeare's admirable edition of the text of Philo's famous treatise *On the Contemplative Life* has at length set one of the ingeniously inverted pyramids of the origins squarely on its base again.

The Earliest Christians of Eusebius.

The full title of this important work is: *Philo about the Contemplative Life,* or *the Fourth Book of the Treatise concerning the Virtues,*—critically edited with a defence of its genuineness by Fred C. Conybeare, M.A. (Oxford, 1895). This book contains a most excellent bibliography of works relating to the subject.

The survival of the voluminous works of Philo through the neglect and vandalism of the Dark and

Middle Ages is owing to the fact that Eusebius, in his efforts to construct history without materials, eagerly seized upon Philo's description of the externals of the Therapeut order, and boldly declared it to be the earliest Christian Church of Alexandria.

This view remained unchallenged until the rise of Protestantism, and was only then called in question because the Papal party rested their defence of the antiquity of Christian monkdom on this famous treatise.

For three centuries the whole of the batteries of Protestant scholarship have been turned on this main position of the Roman and Greek Churches. For if the treatise were genuine, then the earliest Church was a community of rigid ascetics, men and women; monkdom, the *bête noire* of Protestantism, was coëval with the origins.

The Pseudo-Philo Theory. These three centuries of attack have finally evolved a theory, which, on its perfection by Grätz, Nicolas, and Lucius, has been accepted by nearly all our leading Protestant scholars, and is claimed to have demolished the objectionable document for ever. According to this theory, "the Therapeutæ are still Christians, as they were for Eusebius; but no longer of a primitive cast. For the ascription of the work to Philo is declared to be false, and the ascetics described therein to be in reality monks of about the year 300 A.D.; within a few years of which date the treatise is assumed to have been forged" (*op. cit.*, p. vi.).

The consequence is that every recent Protestant Church history, dictionary, and encyclopædia, when treating of the Therapeuts, is plentifully besprinkled with references to the ingenious invention, called the " Pseudo-Philo."

This pyramid of the origins was kept propped upon its apex until 1895, when Conybeare's work was published, and all the props knocked from under it. Strange to say, it was then and only then that a critical text of this so violently attacked treatise was placed in our hands. At last all the MSS. and versions have been collated. With relentless persistence Conybeare has marshalled his Testimonia, and with admirable patience paralleled every distinctive phrase and technical expression with voluminous citations from the rest of Philo's works, of which there is so " prevalent and regrettable an ignorance." To this he has added an extensive Excursus on the Philonean authorship of the tract. If Philo did not write the *De Vita Contemplativa* then every canon of literary criticism is a delusion; the evidence adduced by the sometime Fellow of University College for the authenticity of the treatise is irresistible. We have thus a new departure in Philonean research. [margin: Its Death-blow.]

The danger to certain orthodox presumptions which a thorough study of the rest of Philo's works would threaten, is evidenced by the concluding paragraph of Conybeare's preface, where he writes:

" It is barely credible, and somewhat of a reproach to Oxford as a place of learning, that not a single line of Philo, nor any work bearing specially on him, is recommended to be read by students in our Honour School of Theology; and that, although this most spiritual of authors is by the admission, tacit or express, of a long line of Catholic teachers, from Eusebius and Ambrose in the fourth century down to Bull and Döllinger in modern times, the father not only of Christian exegesis, but also, to a great extent, of Christian dogmatics" (*op. cit.*, p. x.).

An Interesting Question of Date.It is thus established that the *De Vita Contemplativa* is a genuine Philonean tract. As to its date, we are confronted with some difficulties; but the expert opinion of Conybeare assures us that "every reperusal of the works of Philo confirms my feeling that the D.U.C. is one of his earliest works" (*op. cit.*, p. 276). Now as Philo was born about the year 30 B.C., the date of the treatise may be roughly ascribed to the first quarter of the first century. ("About the year 22 or 23"—*op. cit.*, p. 290). The question naturally arises: At such a date, can the Therapeuts of Philo be identified with the earliest Christian Church of Alexandria? If the accepted dates of the origins are correct, the answer must be emphatically, No. If, on the contrary, the accepted dates are incorrect, then a vast problem is opened up, of the first importance for the origins of the Christian faith. Be this as it may, the contents of the *D.V.C.* are of immense importance and interest as affording us a glimpse into those mysterious communities in which Christians for so many centuries recognized their forerunners. The Therapeuts were not Christians; Philo knows absolutely nothing of Christianity in any possible sense in which the word is used to-day. Who, then, were they? The answer to this question demands an entire reformulation of the accepted history of the origins.

The Title and Context.

The treatise bears in some MSS. the superscription, "The Suppliants, or Concerning the Virtues, Book IV., or Concerning the Virtue of the Suppliants, Book IV." By "Suppliant" Philo tells us he means "one who has fled to God and taken refuge with Him." (*De Sac. Ab. et C.*, i. 186, 33). It is highly probable that our tract formed part of the fourth book of Philo's voluminous work *De Legatione*, fragments only of which have survived.

"Time and Christian editors have truncated the *De Legatione* in a threefold way. Firstly, a good part of the second book has been removed, perhaps because it ran counter to Christian tradition concerning Pontius Pilate. Secondly, the entire fourth book was removed, as forming a whole by itself; and the first part of it has been lost, all except the scrap on the Essenes which Eusebius has preserved to us in the *Præparatio Evangelica*; while the account of the Therapeutæ was put by itself and preserved as a separate book. . . Thirdly, the palinode which formed the fifth book has been lost" (*op. cit.*, p. 284).

But to the tractate itself.

PHILO ON THE CONTEMPLATIVE LIFE.

The Essæans.
"As I have already treated of Essæans who assiduously practise the [religious] life of action, carrying it out in all, or, not to speak too presumptuously, in most of its degrees, I will at once, following the sequence of my subject, proceed to say as much as is proper concerning those who embrace [the life of] contemplation; and that too without adding anything of my own to better the matter—as all the poets and history-writers are accustomed to do in the scarcity of good material—but artlessly holding to the truth itself, for even the most skilful [writer], I know, will fail to speak in accordance with her.

"Nevertheless the endeavour must be made and we must struggle through with it; for the greatness of the virtue of these men ought not to be a cause of silence for those who deem it right that no good thing should be kept silent.

The Name Therapeut.
"Now the purpose of our wisdom-lovers is immediately apparent from their name. They are called Therapeutæ and Therapeutrides [men and women] in the original sense of the word; either because they profess an art of healing superior to that in use in cities (for that only heals (θεραπεύει) bodies, whereas this [heals our] souls as well when laid hold of by difficult and scarce curable diseases, which pleasure and desire, and grief and fear, selfishness and folly, and injustice, and

the endless multitude of passions and vices, inflict upon them), or else because they have been schooled by nature and the sacred laws to serve ($\theta\epsilon\rho\alpha\pi\epsilon\acute{\upsilon}\epsilon\iota\nu$) That which is better than the Good and purer than the One and more ancient than the Monad."

Philo here indulges in a digression, contrasting the unintelligent worship of externals by the misinstructed in all religions with the worship of true Deity by those who follow the contemplative life. Those who are content to worship externals are blind; let them then remain deprived of sight. And he adds significantly, that he is not speaking of the sight of the body, but of that of the soul, by which alone truth and falsehood are distinguished from each other.

"But as for the race of devotees [the Therapeuts], who are ever taught more and more to see, let them strive for the intuition of That which is; let them transcend the sun which men perceive [and gaze upon the Light beyond], nor ever leave this rank [order, space, or plane], which leads to perfect blessedness. Now they who betake themselves to [the divine] service [do so], not because of any custom, or on some one's advice or appeal, but carried away with heavenly love, like those initiated into the Bacchic and Corybantic Mysteries; they are afire with God until they behold the object of their love.

"Then it is that, through their yearning for that deathless and blessed Life, thinking that their mortal life is already ended, they leave their possessions to their sons and daughters, or, may

Their Abandonment of the World.

be, other relatives, with willing resolution making them their heirs before the time; while those who have no relatives [give their property] to their companions and friends."

In a digression Philo points out the difference between the sober orderly abandonment of property to follow the philosophic life, which he praises, and the wild exaggerations of the popular legends, which told how Anaxagoras and Democritus, when seized with the love of wisdom, allowed all their estates to be devoured by cattle.

"Whenever then [our wisdom-lovers] take the step of renouncing their goods, they are no longer enticed away by any one, but hurry on without once turning back, leaving behind them brethren, children, wives, parents, the multitudinous ties of relationship, and bonds of friendship, their native lands in which they have been born and reared; for the habitual is a drag and most powerful allurement.

Their Retreats.

"Nor do they emigrate to some other city (like illused or worthless slaves who, in claiming purchase from their owners, only procure for themselves a change of masters and not freedom), for every city, even the best governed one, is full of innumerable tumults, forms of destruction, and disorders which would be insupportable to a man who has once taken wisdom as a guide.

"But they make their abode outside the walls in [shut in] woods or enclosed lands in pursuit of solitude, [and this] not to indulge any feeling of churlish dislike to their fellow-men, but from a knowledge that continual contact with those of dispositions dissimilar to their own is unprofitable and harmful.

"Now this natural class of men [*lit.* race] is to be found in many parts of the inhabited world, both the Grecian and non-Grecian world sharing in the perfect good.

"In Egypt there are crowds of them in every province, or nome as they call it, and especially round Alexandria. For they who are in every way [or in every nome] the most highly advanced come as colonists, as it were, to the Therapeutic fatherland, to a spot exceedingly well adapted for the purpose, perched on a fairly high terrace [small plateau or group of small hills] overlooking Lake Marea or Lake Mareōtis immediately south of Alexandria, in a most favourable situation both for security and mildness of temperature. Security [*sci.* from robbers] is ensured by the belt of homesteads and villages [which surrounds the terrace], and the mildness of temperature is due to the continual breezes sent up by the lake, which opens into the sea, and from the proximity of the open sea itself. The breezes from the sea are light, while those from the lake are heavy, and their combination produces a most healthy condition [of the atmosphere].

The Mareōtic Colony.

"The dwellings of the community are very simple, merely providing shelter against the two greatest necessities,—the extreme heat of the sun and the extreme cold of the air. The dwellings are not close together as those in towns, for neighbourhood is irksome and unpleasing to those

Their Dwellings.

who are seeking for solitude; nor are they far apart, because of the intercourse which is so dear to them, and also for mutual help in case of attack by robbers.

<small>The Original Meaning of the Term Monastery.</small>

"In each dwelling is a sacred place, called a shrine or monastery [a small chamber, closet, or cell], in which in solitude they perform the mysteries of the holy life, taking into it neither drink, nor food, nor anything else requisite for the needs of the body, but only the laws and inspired sayings of prophets, and hymns, and the rest, whereby knowledge and devotion grow together and are perfected.

"Thus they preserve an unbroken memory of God, so that even in their dream-consciousness nothing is presented to their minds but the glories of the divine virtues and powers. Hence many of them give out the rhythmic doctrines of the sacred wisdom, which they have obtained in the visions of dream-life.

<small>Their Prayers and Exercises.</small>

"Twice a day, at dawn and even, they are accustomed to offer up prayers; as the sun rises praying for the sunshine, the real sunshine, that their minds may be filled with heavenly Light, and as it sets praying that their soul, completely lightened of the lust of senses and sensations, may withdraw to its own congregation and council-chamber, there to track out truth.

"The whole interval from dawn to sunset they devote to their exercises. Taking the sacred writings they spend their time in study [*lit.* philosophise], interpreting their ancestral code allegorically, for they think that the words of the literal meaning are symbols of a hidden nature which is made plain [only] by the under-meaning.

"They have also works of ancient authors who were once heads of their school, and left behind them many monuments of the method used in their allegorical works; taking these as patterns, as it were, they imitate the practice of their predecessors. They do not then spend their time in contemplation and nothing else, but they compose songs and hymns to God in all sorts of metres and melodies, outlined necessarily upon [a background of] the more solemn numbers [*lit.* rhythms]. *The Nature of their Books.*

"For six days on end every one remains apart in solitude with himself in his 'monastery,' as it is called, engaged in study, never setting foot out of door, or even looking out of window. But every seventh day they come together as it were to a general assembly, and take their seats in order according to their 'age' [that is, the length of their membership in the order], in the prescribed attitude, with their hands palms downwards, the right between the breast and chin, the left by the side. Then he who is the senior most skilled in the doctrines comes foward and discourses, with steadfast eyes and steadfast voice, with reason and thoughtfulness, not making a display of word-cleverness, as the rhetoricians and sophists of to-day, but examining closely and explaining the precise meaning in the thoughts, a meaning which does not merely light on the tips of the ears, but pierces the ear and reaches the soul and steadfastly *Their Mode of Meeting.*

abides there. The rest all listen in silence, signifying their approval merely by a look in the eye or a nod of the head.

<small>The Sanctuary.</small>

"Now this general sanctuary in which they assemble every seventh day consists of two enclosures: one separated off for men, and the other for women. For women too habitually form part of the audience, possessing the same eager desire and having made the same deliberate choice [as the men].

"The division, however, between the two halls is only partly built up, some three or four cubits from the floor, like a breast-work, the rest of it, to the roof, being left open, and this for two reasons: in the first place for the preservation of that modesty which so becomes woman's nature, and in the second that sitting within earshot they may hear easily, since there is nothing in the way of the speaker's voice.

<small>Their Rule.</small>

"Now [our Therapeuts] first of all lay down continence as a foundation, as it were for the soul, and then proceed to build up the rest of the virtues upon it. Accordingly none of them would think of taking food or drink before sundown, for they consider that the practice of philosophy deserves the light, while the necessities of the body [may content themselves with] darkness; hence they assign the day to the former, and a brief portion of the night to the latter.

"A number of them, in whom the thirst for wisdom is implanted to a greater degree, remind themselves of their food but once in three days,

while a few are so cheered and fare so sumptuously *Fasting.*
at wisdom's banquet of teachings which she so
richly and unstintingly sets before them, that they
can last for twice the time, and even after six days
barely take a mouthful of the most necessary food,
being trained to live on air, as they say the
grasshoppers do [Plato, *Phaedr.*], their needs made
light by their singing methinks.

"Since then they regard the seventh day as all- *The*
hallowed and high festival, they consider it worthy *Seventh Day Common*
of special honour, and on it, after paying due *Meal.*
attention to the soul, they anoint the body, giving
it, as also indeed they do their cattle, respite from
continual labour. Still they partake of no dainty
fare, but plain bread with salt for seasoning, which
the gourmands supplement with an extra relish of
hyssop; while for drink they have water from the
spring. Thus in mollifying those tyrants which
nature has set over the mortal race—hunger and
thirst, they offer them nothing to tickle their
vanity, but only such bare necessities as make life
possible. Accordingly they eat only to escape
hunger, and drink only to escape thirst, avoiding
satiety as an enemy of and a plotter against both
soul and body.

"Now there are two kinds of covering—clothes
and house. As to their dwelling I have already *Housing*
stated above that it is anything but beautiful to *and Clothing.*
look at, and put together anyhow, being made to
answer only its most absolutely necessary purpose;
and as to their clothing, it is equally of the
plainest description, just to protect them from cold

and heat; in winter a thick mantle instead of a woolly hide, and in summer a sleeveless robe of fine linen.

"For in everything they practise simplicity, knowing that vanity has falsehood for its origin, but simplicity truth, each of them containing the innate power of its source; for from falsehood stream forth the manifold kinds of evils, while from truth come the abundant blessings of good both human and divine.

_{Their Sacred Feasts.} "I would also touch upon the general meetings in which they pass the time in greater festivity than usual banqueting together, contrasting them with the banquets of others."

Philo here indulges in a long digression in which he paints in the strongest colours the debauchery and extravagance of the banquets of voluptuaries, in order to contrast them as much as possible with the sacred feasts of the Therapeuts.

"In the first place they all come together at the end of every seventh week, for they reverence not only the simple period of seven days, but also the period of the power [or square] of seven, since they know that the 'seven' is pure and ever-virgin. Their seventh day festival then is only a prelude to their greatest feast, which is assigned to the fiftieth, the most holy and natural of numbers, [the sum] of the powers of the [perfect] right-angled triangle, which has been appointed as the origin of the generation of the cosmic elements.

"When then they have assembled together, clad in white robes, with joyous looks and with the greatest solemnity, at sign from one of the Ephemereuts for the day (for this is the usual name for those who are engaged in such duties), and before sitting down, standing one beside the other in rows in a certain order, and raising their eyes and hands to heaven—their eyes, since they are trained to gaze on things worthy of contemplation; and their hands, since they are pure of gain, unstained by any pretence of money-making affairs—they offer prayer unto God that their banquet may be pleasing and acceptable. *The Banquet on the Fiftieth Day.*

"After prayers the seniors sit down to table, following the order of their election. For they do not regard as seniors merely those who are advanced in years and have reached old age (nay, they regard such as quite young children if they have only lately fallen in love with the higher life), but such as have grown up and arrived at maturity in the contemplative part of philosophy, which is unqestionably its fairest and most divine portion. *Seniority.*

"And women also share in the banquet, most of whom have grown old in virginity, preserving their purity not from necessity (as some of the priestesses among the Greeks), but rather of their own free-will, through their zealous love of wisdom, with whom they are so keenly desirous of spending their lives that they pay no attention to the pleasures of the body. Their longing is not for mortal children, but for a deathless progeny which the soul that is in love with God can alone bring forth, when the Father has implanted in it those spiritual light-beams, with which it shall *The Women Disciples.*

contemplate the laws of wisdom. There is, however, a division made between them in their places at table, the men being apart on the right, and the women apart on the left."

(It should be remembered that it was the custom in the Greco-Roman world to recline at table, leaning on the left elbow with a cushion under the arm. The person reclining to the right of another was said to lie on the latter's breast (ἀνακεῖσθαι ἐν τῷ κόλπῳ). *Cf.* the canonical phrase, "the disciple who lay on His breast at meat.")

The Plain Couches.

"Perhaps you suspect that cushions, if not luxurious at any rate of tolerable softness, are provided for people well-born and well-bred and students of philosophy, whereas they have nothing but mattresses of the more easily procurable material (the papyrus of the country), over which [they throw] the plainest possible rugs, slightly raised at the elbow for them to lean upon. For on the one hand they somewhat relax their [usual] Spartan rigour of life [on such occasions], while on the other [even at the banquets] they always study the most liberal frugality in everything, rejecting the allurements of pleasure with all their might.

The Servers.

"Nor are they waited upon by slaves, since they consider the possession of servants in general to be contrary to nature. For nature has created all men free; but the injustice and selfishness of those who strive after inequality (the root of all evil), have set the yoke of power on the necks of the weaker and harnessed them to [the chariots of] the stronger.

"So in this holy banquet there is no slave, as I have said, but it is served by free men who perform the necessary service, not by compulsion, or waiting for orders, but of their own free-will anticipating the requests [of the guests] with promptitude and eagerness. For they are not chance free men who are appointed for such service, but juniors of the order who have been selected in order of merit with every possible care, who (as those noble and well-born and anxious to reach the summit of virtue should) with affectionate rivalry, as though they were their legitimate children, wait upon these fathers and mothers of theirs, regarding them as their common parents, bound to them with closer ties than their parents by blood: since, for those who think, there is no closer tie than virtue and goodness. And they come in to serve ungirdled, with their robes let down, so that no resemblance to a slave's dress may be introduced.

"I know that some of my readers will laugh at such a banquet as this: but such laughter will bring them weeping and sorrow.

"Nor is wine brought in on these occasions, but the clearest water, cold for the majority, and warmed for those of the older men whose tastes are delicate. The table moreover contains nothing that has blood in it, for the food is bread with salt for seasoning, to which hyssop is added as an extra relish for the gourmands. For just as right reason bids priests make offerings free from wine and blood, so does it bid these sages live. For wine is a drug that brings on madness, and costly

The Frugal Fare.

seasonings rouse up desire, the most insatiable of beasts. So much, then, for the preliminaries of the banquet.

The President.

"Now, after the guests have taken their places in the ranks I have described, and the waiters have taken their stand in order, ready to serve, when complete silence is gained—(and when is there not? you may say; but then there is deeper silence than before, so that no one ventures to make a sound or even breathe at all hard)—the president searches out some passage in the sacred scriptures or solves some difficulty propounded by one of the members, without any thought of display, for he does not aim at a reputation for cleverness in words, but is simply desirous of getting a clearer view of some points [of doctrine]; and when he has done so, he unselfishly shares it with those who, though they have not such keen vision as himself, nevertheless have as great a longing to learn.

The Instruction.

"The president for his part employs a somewhat leisurely method of imparting instruction, pausing at intervals and stopping for frequent recapitulations, impressing the ideas on their souls. (For when, in giving an interpretation, one continues to speak rapidly without pausing for breath, the mind of the hearers is left behind unable to keep up the pace, and fails to comprehend what is said.) While they, on their side, fixing all their attention upon him, remain in one and the same attitude listing attentively, showing their understanding and comprehension [of his words] by nod and look; praise of the speaker by a pleased expression and the thoughtful turning to him of their faces, and hesitation by a mild shake of the head and a motion of the forefinger of the right hand. And the juniors who stand at service are just as attentive as the seniors at table.

"Now the interpretation of the sacred scriptures is based upon the under-meanings in the allegorical narratives; for these men look upon the whole of their law-code as being like to a living thing, having for body the spoken commands, and for soul the unseen thought stored up in the words (in which thought the rational soul [of the student] begins to contemplate things native to its own nature more than in anything else)—the interpretation, as it were, in the mirror of the names, catching sight of the extraordinary beauties of the ideas contained in them, unwrapping and unrobing the symbols from them, and bringing to light the naked inner meanings, for those who are able with a little suggestion to arrive at the intuition of the hidden sense from the apparent meaning. *The Interpretation of Scripture.*

"When then the president seems to have discoursed long enough, and the discourse, according to its range, to have in his case made good practice at the points aimed at, and in theirs [to have met with due] attention, there is a burst of applause from the company, as though they would offer their congratulations, but this is restricted to three claps of the hands.

"Then the president, rising, chants a hymn which has been made in God's honour, either a new one which he has himself composed, or an old one of *The Singing of Hymns.*

the ancient poets. For they have left behind them many metres and tunes in trimetric epics, processional hymns, libation odes, altar-chants, stationary choruses, and dance-songs, [all] admirably measured off in diversified strains.

"And after him the others also in bands, in proper order, [take up the chanting], while the rest listen in deep silence, except when they have to join in the burden and refrains; for they all, both men and women, join in.

Bread and Salt.

Then when hymns are over, the juniors bring in the table, which was mentioned shortly before, with the all-pure food upon it, leavened bread, with flavouring of salt mingled with hyssop, out of respect to the holy table set up in the holy place of the temple. For on this table are loaves and salt without seasoning; the loaves are unleavened and the salt unmixed with anything else; for it was fitting that the simplest and purest things should be allotted to the most excellent division of the priests, the reward of their ministry, while the rest should strive after things of similar purity, but abstain from the same food [as the priests], in order that the more excellent should have this privilege.

The Sacred Dancing.

"After the banquet they keep the holy all-night festival. And this is how it is kept. They all stand up in a body, and about the middle of the entertainment they first of all separate into two bands, men in one and women in the other, And a leader is chosen for each, the conductor whose reputation is greatest and the one most suitable for the post.

They then chant hymns made in God's honour in many metres and melodies, sometimes singing in chorus, sometimes one band beating time to the answering chant of the other, [now] dancing to its music, [now] inspiring it, at one time in processional hymns, at another in standing songs, turning and returning in the dance.

"Then when each band has feasted [that is, has sung and danced] apart by itself, drinking of God-pleasing [nectar], just as in the Bacchic rites men drink the wine unmixed, then they join together, and one chorus is formed of the two bands, in imitation of the joined chorus on the banks of the Red Sea because of the wonderful works that had been there wrought. For the sea at God's command became for one party a cause of safety and for the other a cause of ruin."

(Philo here refers to the fabled dance of triumph of the Israelites at the destruction of Pharaoh and his host, when Moses led the men and Miriam the women in a common dance; but the Therapeuts all over the world could not have traced the custom to this myth.)

"So the chorus of men and women Therapeuts, being formed as closely as possible on this model, by means of melodies in parts and harmony—the high notes of the women answering to the deep tones of the men—produces a harmonious and most musical symphony. The ideas are of the most beautiful, the expressions of the most beautiful, and the dancers reverent; while the goal of the ideas, expressions, and dancers is piety.

The Morning Prayer.

"Thus drunken unto morning's light with this fair drunkenness, with no head-heaviness or drowsiness, but with eyes and body fresher even than when they came to the banquet, they take their stand at dawn, when, catching sight of the rising sun, they raise their hands to heaven, praying for sunlight and truth and keenness of spiritual vision. After this prayer each returns to his own sanctuary, to his accustomed traffic in philosophy and labour in its fields.

"So far then about the Therapeuts, who are devoted to the contemplation of nature and live in it and in the soul alone, citizens of heaven and the world, legitimately recommended to the Father and Creator of the Universe by their virtue, which procures them His love, virtue that sets before it for its prize the most suitable reward of nobility and goodness, outstripping every gift of fortune, and the first comer in the race to the very goal of blessedness."

A Note on the Sacred Numbers.

With regard to the mystic numbers 7 and 50 mentioned in the text above, it may be of interest to remark that Philo elsewhere (*Leg. Alleg.*, i. 46) tells us that the Pythagoreans called the number 7 the ever-virgin, because "it neither produces any of the numbers within the decad [*i.e.*, from 1 to 10] nor is produced by any of them." The power or square of 7 is 49, and the great feast therefore took place every fiftieth day. The number 50 is based on the proportioned of the sides of the "perfect" right-angled triangle, the famous Pythagorean triangle, so often referred to by Plato. (*Cf. The Nuptial Number of Plato*, by James Adam, M.A., Cambridge, 1891; the best work on the subject.) The sides of this triangle bear the proportions of 3, 4, and 5, and $3^2 + 4^2 = 5^2$, or $9 + 16 = 25$; and $9 + 16 + 25 = 50$.

In another treatise (*Qu. in Gen.*, iii. 39) we get some further interesting information concerning the 50. Philo speaks of two series, which he calls triangles and squares, namely 1, 3, 6, 10, and 1, 4, 9, 16. At first sight it is difficult to discover why Philo should call the first series of numbers triangles, but it has occurred to me that he had in mind some such arrangement as the following.

Many interesting correspondences may be made out from the study of the apparently simple ordering of these points, monads, or atoms, but we are at present only engaged on the consideration of the number 50.

With regard to the triangular series, 1, 3, 6, 10, it is to be noticed that $1 = 1$; $3 = 1 + 2$; $6 = 1 + 2 + 3$; and $10 = 1 + 2 + 3 + 4$.

With regard to the square series, 1, 4, 9, 16, we see at once that $1 = 1^2$; $4 = 2^2$; $9 = 3^2$; and $16 = 4^2$. Moreover $1 + 3 + 6 + 10 = 20$; and $1 + 4 + 9 + 16 = 30$; and finally $20 + 30 = 50$.

Much more could be said; but our space is limited, and those who are interested in the matter can easily work out details for themselves.

In reading this treatise and the rest of the references to the Therapeuts scattered through Philo's writings, the chief questions that naturally arise are: What was Philo's connection with them; and how far can we rely on his account? There is an important passage in his writings which gives us the critical point of departure in seeking an answer. Philo (*Leg. Alleg.*, i. 81) writes:

Philo's Connection with the Therapeuts.

"I too have ofttimes left my kindred and my friends and country, and have gone into the wilderness [or into solitude] in order to comprehend the things worthy to be seen, yet have profited nothing; but my soul was scattered or stung with passion, and lapsed into the very opposite current."

We learn from this interesting item of autobiography that Philo had himself enjoyed no success in the contemplative life. This accounts for his great reverence and high respect for those who had succeeded in comprehending the things "worthy to be seen." Now as Philo never abandoned his property, he could therefore not have been a full accepted member of one of these brotherhoods. In all probability he belonged to one of their outer circles. As was the case with the Pythagoreans and Essenes, the Therapeuts had lay-pupils who lived in the world and who perhaps resorted to the community now and again for a period of "retreat," and then returned again to the world.

That these lay-disciples were men of great ability

and insight is amply shown by the works of Philo himself, but that there was a large literature of a still loftier and more inspired character is also evident from what Philo has to say of his teachers. What has become of all these works, commentaries, interpretations, hymns, sermons, expositions, apocalypses—works which aroused the admiration of so distinguished a writer as Philo? It seems to me that though we may have some scraps of them embedded in the Jewish Pseudepigrapha which have come down to us, many of them belonged to the now lost precursors of the fragments of the Gnostic literature which have survived.

The Lay Disciples.

But were the Therapeuts Jews, as Philo would lead us to believe in his apology for that nation? It is evident from his own statements that the community which he describes, and with which he was probably connected as lay-pupil, was but one of a vast number scattered all over the world. Philo would have us believe that his particular community was the chief of all, doubtless because it was mainly Jewish, though not orthodoxly so, for they were "sun-worshippers."

It is therefore reasonable to conclude that there were at this time numerous communities of mystics and ascetics devoted to the holy life and sacred science scattered throughout the world, and that Philo's Mareotic community was *one* of these. Others may have been tinged as strongly with Eygptian, or Chaldæan, or Zoroastrian, or Orphic elements, as the one south of Alexandria was tinged with Judaism. It is further not incredible

The Variety of Communities.

that there were also truly eclectic communities among them who combined and synthesized the various traditions and initiations handed down by the doctrinally more exclusive communities, and it is in this direction therefore that we must look for light on the origins of Gnosticism and for the occult background of Christianity. These communities did not at this time propagandize, though they may have indirectly been at the back of some of the greatest propagandist efforts, as in the case of Philo. I also think that the later Gnostic communities did not propagandize directly, and that whatever works they may have put foward for lay-pupils or by lay-pupils were only a small part of their literature. For the people there were the Law and the Prophets and the Gospel; for the lay-pupils, the intermediate literature; and for those within, those most highly mystical and abstruse treatises that none but the trained mystics could possibly understand or were expected to understand.

JEWRY.

<small>The Influence of Babylon.</small>

THE third stream which poured into the matrix of the Christian origins, was that of Jewry. Even before the Exile the undisciplined tribes composing this peculiar nation had had their "Schools of the Prophets," small communities holding themselves apart and recruited by seers and visionaries. Up to this time the traditions of the Jews and their conceptions of religion had been mostly of a very crude nature compared to those of the more highly civilized nations which surrounded them, although of course they were distinguished by the particularism of a nascent exclusive monotheism and a growing detestation of idolatry.

In Babylon, however, they came into intimate contact with a great and very ancient civilization, and the impression it made upon them can be clearly traced in the history of their subsequent religious development.

Most of the nation remained contentedly in Babylon, while the leaders of those who returned set to work to rewrite their old traditions and reformulate their religious conceptions, by the light of the wider views they had absorbed—all of which is to be clearly traced in the various stages of evolution of their national scripture, the various deposits of which are revealed to us by the patient researches of scientific Biblical scholars and the ever new discoveries of archæology.

The Jewish writers appropriated to themselves the traditions of the great Semitic race and of the nations of Chaldæa and of Babylon, and used them for the glorification of their own origins and history, in the strange conviction that they all applied to them as the "chosen people" of God. The elaborate doctrine of purity on which the Persian Zoroastrian tradition laid such stress was eagerly adopted by their priesthood, and we perceive in their library of religious books the gradual elimination of the cruder ideas of Deity and the gradual development of far higher conceptions in (at times) most wonderful poetic outbursts.

The Writing of Scripture History.

It must not be supposed, however, that the re-writers and editors of the old traditions were forgers and falsifiers in any ordinary sense of the word. Antiquity in general had no conception of literary morality in its modern meaning, and all writing of a religious character was the outcome of an inner impulse. The wealth of technical terms bestowed on these ancient writers and their methods by modern Biblical critics forces the student almost unconsciously to read into those times ideas and standards that had then no existence. Again, a common fault is to endow these ancient worthies of the Jews with motives of action and refinements of belief which only belong to the best in Christendom; and so we not only do grave injustice to their memories, but we read into their history an atmosphere of too great refinement for the actual Jew of the period to have lived in. It should also be remembered that the mythologizing of history and the historicizing of mythology were not peculiar to the Jews, but common to the times; what was peculiar to them was their fanatical belief in Divine favouritism and their egregious claim to the monopoly of God's providence.

The Mythology of History.

Now the Jews, as all children of the desert, had ingrained in them an invincible longing for freedom, and at the same time they had the innate poetic imagination of all those who live in close contact with nature.

The two "kingdoms" that were always fighting

among themselves and with their neighbours, "Israel" and "Judah," were successively deported by the Assyrian authorities, to remove a centre of perpetual disturbance.

The "ten tribes" who were the first to be deported, consisting as they did of elements more adaptable to their surroundings than the Judæans, settled down in Babylonia and gradually adapted themselves to their new environment; it would be interesting to know what development occurred in the schools of *their* prophets in contact with the ancient Chaldæan wisdom, and the subsequent history of that "Israel" which not only thus settled in Babylon, but remained there.

When the more turbulent Judæan tribes were subsequently in their turn deported, some of them followed the example of their kinsfolk; but most of the Judæans refused to adapt themselves to the new conditions, they pined for their freedom, and in spite of their being surrounded by the monuments of a great civilisation, looked back to their poor settlement of Jerusalem as though it had been in the land of Paradise, and its meagre homes the palaces of kings. The fathers wove for the children stories of the beauty and richness of their native land, of the glories of its palaces, and the great deeds of their ancient sheiks; above all things they insisted on their peculiar destiny as men who had made a compact with a God who had promised them victory over all foes. The fathers, who had gradually grown to believe their own stories, died before the conqueror Cyrus, in gratitude for their help against the Assyrian power, granted the return of the Judæan folk. Those who returned were of the next generation, and they reoccupied the ruins of Jerusalem with ideas of a former greatness which existed in the poetic imagination and love of freedom of their sires rather than in actual history.

Filled with an enthusiasm for the past, they wrote what their fathers had told them, expanding the old records into a splendid "history," and bringing into it all that they had developed of religion by controversy with the Babylonians and Persians—a controversy which consisted in persistently maintaining that their religion was better than their opponents', claiming the best in their opponents' position or tradition as their own, and ever asserting that they had something still higher as well.

<small>Honest Self-delusion.</small>

Now the Jew had such a firm conviction that he was the Chosen of God that he probably really believed all his assertions; in any case the sense of history did not exist in those days, and there was no one to check the enthusiasm of these early scribes.

They probably argued: We are the chosen people of God: our religion is better than any other religion, in fact all other religions are false, all other Gods false; the palmy days of our religion were before the Captivity; those times must have been greater than the best times in other nations, our temple must have been grander, our sacrifices greater than any other in the world; our fathers have said it and we feel it is true. In such a frame of mind and with the innate poetic fervour of their nature they felt impelled to write, and by their writing transformed the old records out of all historic recognition, and from such beginnings gradually evolved a literature which future generations received without question, not only as a precise record of fact but as a divinely written scripture verbally inspired.

The development of this literature was a natural growth, though the distinct factors which played a part in it are somewhat difficult to disentangle; but there are distinct signs of repeated modifications of cruder conceptions, and of the leavening of the nation by a steadily developing spiritual force. Whence came this persistent spiritualizing of the old conceptions?

In seeking for an answer to this question, the point of departure may be found in the fact that the majority of the nation did not return; and not only this, but that the majority of the Jews in course of time preferred to live among the Gentiles. In fact the members of the nation gradually became the great traders of the ancient world, so that we find colonies of them scattered abroad in all the great centres; for instance, shortly after the founding of Alexandria we hear of a colony of no fewer than 40,000 Jews planted there. These Jews of the Diaspora or Dispersion were in constant contact with their Palestinian co-religionists on the one side, and on the other in intimate contact with the great civilizations in which they found a home. *The Spiritualizing of Judaism.*

The expectation of the salvation of the race and of a Saviour of the race, which the Jews absorbed from Zoroastrianism, they adapted to *Zealotism.*

their own needs and to the conviction that Israel was the Chosen of God. This expectation was for long entirely of a material nature; they looked for a king who should restore them to freedom and tread under foot the nations of the world, when he would reign for one thousand years in Jerusalem. All this was to be effected by the direct interposition of Yahweh, their God. For some four hundred years, up to the final destruction of Jerusalem by Titus, we are presented with the spectacle of a most determined struggle for freedom; for the Jews were ever disappointed of their hopes, and had to submit to the successive overlordship of Greece and Rome. But hope ever sprang up again and again after every new disappointment, and we find in their literature the record of a determined opposition to the conqueror, fanned into fever heat by the fiery exhortations and denunciations of a pseudoprophetical character which has no parallel in the history of the world. If in the Greek genius was centred the struggle for the freedom of the intellect, in the Jewish nation was centred the struggle for personal freedom; and in the Roman Empire, after the destruction of Jerusalem, Jewry finally became the centre of all disaffection and revolutionary ideas.

Pharisaism. At the back of all of this was the peculiarly exclusive faith which the Jew had evolved, and which from a Roman point of view constituted him "the hater of mankind." But this fanatical Zealotism, although it was directly nourished by the more unbalanced pronouncements of the religious writers and prophets, became more and more distasteful to the better elements in the nation. These better elements we find represented by the more spiritual views that by degrees worked into the sacred literature, and the nation was gradually leavened by Pharisaism, which, though running to the extreme of minute ceremonial and the most elaborate rules of external purity, was nevertheless a most potent factor in the widening of the religious horizon. The external side of Pharisaism is fairly well known to us; but the inner side of this great movement, to which all the most learned of the Jews belonged, is but little understood.

Pharisaism was in course of time divided into numerous schools, the strictest of which led the life of rigid internal purity. Leading such a life, it could not but be that their ideas became of a more spiritual nature; indeed Pharisaism had its origin in Babylon, and it represented the main stream of Chaldæan and Persian influence on Jewry.

Along this line of tradition we find gradually evolved a far more spiritual view of the Messiah-doctrine; Israel was not the physical nation of the Jews, but the Elect of God chosen out of all nations; the servants of God were those who served Him with their hearts and not with their lips; the God of this Israel abhorred their blood sacrifices.

The Chassidim and Essenes.

But such views as these, although they indirectly influenced the public scripture of the nation, could not be boldly declared among a people that had ever stoned its prophets and delighted in blood-sacrifice. Such views could only be safely discussed in private, and we find numerous records of the existence of schools of Chassidim and those whom Josephus calls Essenes, among whom were the most pure and learned of the Jews, the "Rabbis of the South," living apart and in retirement.

These schools and communities seem to have looked back to the stern physical discipline of the Schools of the Prophets on the one hand, and to have been in contact with the spiritual ideas of the Babylonian wisdom-discipline on the other.

The Inner Schools.

In Babylon we see how one of the nation's seers contacted part of the Chaldæan wisdom-tradition, and the famous "Vision of Ezekiel" was subsequently invoked as canonical authority for all that range of ideas which we find revived so many hundreds of years later in Mediæval Kabalism. But in order to understand the nature of the studies and inner experiences of the members of these mystic schools of Chassidim and their imitators, it is necessary to have a critical acquaintance with non-canonical Jewish writings, especially the wisdom-literature and those numerous apocrypha, and apocalypses, and apologies for unfulfilled prophecy — a mass of pseudepigraphs which were so busily produced in the last centuries preceding our era and in its earliest centuries. It is true we possess only the fragmentary remains of this once enormous literature, most probably only the works that were written for general circulation, and principally by those members of these communities who were still obsessed by the Zealot conception of Israel; but enough remains to fill in some very necessary outlines of the background of the Gnosis, and to enable us to realise how earnestly men were striving for a purer life and greater knowledge of God in those early days.

These mystic schools of Jewish theosophy had an enormous influence on nascent Christianity; the innermost schools influenced the inner schools of Christendom, and the general literature of the intermediate circles left a deep mark on general Christianity.

Most of these mystic schools and communities, whether of Greek or Egyptian or Jewish descent, when they came in contact with each other, gave and received. True that some of them refused to mix in person or doctrine, and there were rigidly conservative mystic schools of all three lines of descent; others, however, if not in their corporate capacity, at any rate in the persons of their individual members, gave and received, and so modified their preconceptions and enlarged their horizon. Indeed, in the last two centuries prior to and first two centuries of our era there was an enormous enthusiasm for syncretism and syntheticism among the members of such schools, the effects of which are plainly traceable in the fragments of the Gnosis preserved to us by the polemical citations of the heresiologists of later orthodoxy.

ALEXANDRIA.

The rough outlines of the background of the Gnosis which we have endeavoured to sketch, are of necessity of the vaguest, for each of the many subjects touched upon is deserving of a volume or several volumes. Our intention has only been to give some general idea of the manifold lines along which its complicated heredity has to be traced. But our sketch is so vague that perhaps it may be as well, before proceeding further, to give the reader some notion of the more immediate *outer* conditions in which the Christian Gnosis lived and —we will not say died, but—disappeared. Insistence upon some of the points already touched upon and a few more details may serve to make the matter clearer; and the best spot from which to make our observation is Alexandria, and the best time for a retrospect is the epoch when General Christianity had definitely won its victory and driven the Gnosis from the field.

It should be remembered that in the following sketch we shall attempt to depict only the outer appearances of things; within, as we have already suggested and as we shall show in the sequel, there was a hidden life of great activity. If there was an enormous public library at Alexandria, there were also many private libraries of the inner schools dealing with the sacred science of unseen things. It was precisely from these private circles that all mystic writings proceeded, and we can see from the nature of the Gnostic and other works of this kind which have reached us, that their authors and compilers had access to large libraries of mystic lore.

A Bird's-eye View of the City. Let us then carry our minds foward to the last quarter of the fourth century of the present era, when Hypatia was a girl, after the hopes of the School that traced its descent through Plato and Pythagoras from Orpheus, had received so rude a shock from the early death of Julian, the emperor-philosopher; just in time to see the Serapeum still standing, unviolated by the iconoclastic hands of a fanaticism that was the immediate progeny of Jewish Zealotism and entirely foreign to the teaching of the Christ. Let us ascend the great lighthouse, 400 feet high, on the island off the mainland, the world-famous Pharos, and take a bird's-eye view of the intellectual centre of the ancient Western world.

The city lies out before us on a long ribbon of land or isthmus, between the sea front and the great lake towards the south, Lake Mareotis. Far away to the left is the most westerly mouth of the Nile, called the Canopic, and a great canal winds out that way to Canopus, where is the sacred shrine of Serapis. Along it, if it were festival-time, you would see crowds of pilgrims, hastening, on gaily decorated barges, to pay their homage to certain wise priests, one of whom about this time was a distinguished member of the later Platonic School.

The great city with its teeming populace stretches out before us with a sea-frontage of some four or five miles; in shape it is oblong, for when Alexander the Great, hundreds of years ago, in 331 B.C., marked out its original walls with the flour his Macedonian veterans carried (perhaps according to some national rite), he traced it in the form of a chlamys, a scarf twice as long as it was broad. Two great streets or main arteries, in the form of a cross, divide it into four quarters. These thoroughfares are far wider than any of our modern streets, and the longer one, parallel to the shore, and extending through the outlying suburbs, has a length of three leagues, so that the Alexandrians consider it quite a journey to traverse their city.

Where these streets cross is a great square surrounded with handsome buildings, and adorned with fountains, statues and trees. There are many other squares and forums also, but none so vast as the great square. Many pillars and obelisks adorn the city; the most conspicuous of them being a flat-topped pillar of red stone, on a hill near the shore, and two obelisks on the shore itself, one of which is the present Cleopatra's Needle.

The island on which we are standing is joined to the main-land by a huge mole almost a mile long, with two water-ways cutting it, spanned with bridges, and defended with towers. This mole helps to form the great harbour on our right, and the smaller and less safe harbour on our left. There is also a third huge dock, or basin, in the north-west quarter of the city, closed also by a bridge.

The two main thoroughfares divide Alexandria into four quarters, which together with the first suburb of the city were originally called by the first five letters of the alphabet. The great quarter on our left is, however, more generally known as the Bruchion, perhaps from the palace Ptolemy Soter set aside to form the nucleus of the great library. It is the Greek quarter, the most fashionable, and architecturally very magnificent. There you see the vast mausoleum of Alexander the Great, containing the golden coffin in which the body of the world-conquering hero has been preserved for hundreds of years. There, too, are the splendid tombs of the Ptolemies, who ruled Egypt from the time of the division of Alexander's empire till the latter part of the first century B.C. when the Romans wrested the kingdom from Cleopatra. Observe next the great temple of Poseidon, god of the sea, a favourite deity of the sailor populace. There, too, is the Museum, the centre of the university, with all its lecture rooms and halls, not the original Museum of the Ptolemies, but a later building. Baths, too, you see everywhere, thousands of them, magnificent buildings where the luxurious Alexandrians spend so much of their time.

On the right is the Egyptian quarter, the north-western, called Rhacotis, a very old name dating back to a time when Alexandria did not exist, and an old Egyptian burg, called Ragadouah, occupied its site. The difference in the style of achitecture at once strikes you, for it is for the most part in the more sombre Egyptian style; and that great building you see in the eastern part of the quarter is the far-famed Serapeum; it is not so much a single building as a group of buildings, the temple of course being the chief of them. It is a fort-like place, with plain heavy walls, older than the Greek buildings, gloomy and severe and suited to the Egyptian character; it is the centre of the "Heathen" schools, that is to say, the Barbarian or non-Greek lecture halls. You will always remember the Serapeum by its vast flights of steps bordered with innumerable sphinxes, both inside and outside the great gate.

If you could see underneath the buildings, you would be struck with the network of vaults and crypts on which the whole city seems to have been built; these vaults are used mostly as underground cisterns for the storage of water—a most necessary provision in so poorly rain-fed a country as Egypt.

The south-eastern quarter, behind the Bruchion, is the centre of the Jewish colony, which dates back to the days of Alexander himself, and has never numbered less than 40,000 Hebrews.

The great open space to the left of the Bruchion is the Hippodrome or race-course, and further east still along the shore is the fashionable suburb of Nicopolis, where perchance Hypatia lives. On the other side of the city, beyond Rhacotis, is a huge cemetery adorned with innumerable statues and columns, and known as Necropolis.

The Populace. But the various styles of architecture and distinct characteristics of the various quarters can give but little idea of the mixed and heterogeneous populace assembled on the spot where Europe, Asia, and Africa meet together. First you have the better class Egyptians and Greeks, mostly extremely refined, haughty and effeminate; of Romans but a few—the magistrates and military, the legionaries of the guard who patrolled the city and quelled the frequent riots of religious disputants; for all of whom, Jew or Christian, Gnostic or Heathen, they had a bluff and impartial contempt.

In the more menial offices you see the lower-class

mixed Egyptians, the descendants of the aboriginal populace, perchance, crowds of them. Thousands of Ethiopians and negroes also, in the brightest possible colours.

There, too, you see bands of monks from the Thebaid, many from the Nitrian Valley, two or three days' journey south into the desert, beyond the great lake; they are easily distinguishable, with their tangled unkempt locks, and skins for sole clothing—for the most part at this time a violent, ignorant, and ungovernable set of fanatics. Mixed with them are people in black, ecclesiastics, deacons and officers of the Christian churches.

Down by the harbours, however, we shall come across many other types, difficult to distinguish for the most part because of the interblending and mixture. Thousands of them come and go on the small ships which crowd the harbours in fleets. Many are akin to the once great nation of the so-called "Hittites"; Phœnician and Carthaginian sailor-folk in numbers, and traders from far more distant ports.

Jews everywhere and those akin to Jews, in all the trading parts; some resembling Afghans; ascetics, too, from Syria, descended from the Essenes, perchance, or Therapeutæ, paying great attention to cleanliness. Also a few tall golden-haired people, Goths and Teutons perchance, extremely contemptuous of the rest, whom they regard as an effeminate crowd—big, tall, strong, rough fellows. A few Persians also, and more distant Orientals.

Perhaps, however, you are more interested in the

Christian populace, a most mixed crowd without and within. The city ecclesiastics are busied more with politics than with religion; the rest of the faithful can be divided into two classes, offering widely different presentments of Christianity.

On the one hand, the lowest classes and many of the monks, bigoted and ignorant, contemptuous of all education, devoted to the cult of the martyrs, thirsting for the blood of the Jews, and wild to overthrow every statue and raze every temple to the ground. On the other hand, a set of refined disputants, philosophical theologians, arguing always, eager to enter the lists with the Pagan philosophers, spending their lives in public discussions, while the crowds who come to hear them are mostly indifferent to the right or wrong of the matter, and applaud every debating point with contemptuous impartiality, enjoying the wrangle from the point of view of a refined scepticism.

The Library. But we must hasten on with our task, and complete our sketch of the city with a brief reference to two of its most famous institutions, the Library and Museum. Even if most of us have had no previous acquaintance with the topography of Alexandria, and are perfectly ignorant of the history of its schools, we have at any rate all heard of its world-famed Library.

When the kingdom of Alexander was divided among his generals, the rich kingdom of Egypt fell to the lot of Ptolemy I., called Soter, the Saviour. Believing that Greek culture was the most civilising factor in the known world, and Greek methods the most enlightened, Soter determined not only to make a small Greece in Egypt, but also to make his court at Alexandria the asylum of all the learning of the Grecian world. Fired with this noble ambition he founded a Museum or University, dedicated to the arts and sciences, and a Library. Had not Aristotle the philosopher taught his great leader, Alexander, the art of government; and should not the chief of his generals therefore gather together all the works that dealt with so useful a science? Fortunately, however, the original plan of a purely political library was speedily abandoned and more universal views prevailed. It is, however, not unlikely that Ptolemy, as an Egyptian ruler, did but found a new library for his capital in emulation of the many libraries already existing in that ancient land. We have only to recall the vast collection of Osymandyas at Thebes, the "Remedy of the Soul," to be persuaded of the fact. Therefore, though the Alexandrian Library was the first great public Grecian library, it was by no means the first in Egypt. Nor was it even the first library in Greece; for Polycrates of Samos, Pisistratus and Eucleides of Athens, Nicocrates of Cyprus, Euripides the poet, and Aristotle himself, had all large collections of books.

To be brief; the first collection was placed in the part of the royal palaces near the Canopic Gate, the chief of these palaces being called the Bruchion, close to the Museum. A librarian and a staff were appointed—an army of copyists and calligraphists. There were also scholars to revise and correct the texts, and chōrizontes (χωρίζοντες) to select the authentic and best editions; also makers of catalogues, categories and analytics.

Under the first Ptolemies the collecting of books became quite a mania. Ptolemy Soter had letters sent to all the reigning sovereigns begging for copies of every work their country possessed, whether of poets, logographers, or writers of sacred aphorisms, orators, sophists, doctors, medical philosophers, historians, etc. Ptolemy II. (Philadelphus) commissioned every captain of a vessel to bring him MSS., for which he paid so royally that many forgeries were speedily put on the market. Attalus and Eumenes, kings of Pergamus, in north-west Asia Minor, established a rival library in their capital, and prosecuted the search for books with such ardour that the library of Aristotle, bequeathed to Theophrastus and handed on to Neleus of Scepsis, had to be buried to escape the hands of their rapacious collectors, only to find its way, however, to Alexandria at last. Philadelphus accordingly issued an order against the exportation of papyrus from Egypt, and thus the rival collectors of Pergamus had to be content with vellum; hence, some say, pergamene, parchemin, parchment. The commerce of MSS. was carried on throughout all Greece, Rhodes and Athens being the chief marts.

Thus Alexandria became possessed of the most ancient MSS. of Homer and Hesiod and the Cyclic poets; of Plato and Aristotle, of Æschylus, Sophocles and Euripides, and many other treasures.

Moreover, large numbers of translators were

employed to turn the books of other nations into Greek. The sacred books of the nations were translated, and the Septuagint version of the Hebrew Bible was added to the number, not without miracle, if we are to believe the legend recounted by Josephus.

Even by the time of Ptolemy III. (Euergetes) the Bruchion could not contain all the books, and a fresh nucleus was established in the buildings of the Serapeum, on the other side of the city, but not in the temple itself with its four hundred pillars, of all of which Pompey's Pillar alone remains to us.

What a wealth of books in so short a time! Even in the times of the first three Ptolemies, we read of 400,000 rolls or volumes. What then must have been the number in later years? Some say they exceeded a million rolls and papyri. Let us, however, remember that a "book" or "roll" was generally not a volume as with us, but rather the chapter of a work. We read of men writing "six thousand books"! The rolls had to be comparatively small, for the sake of convenience, and a work often had as many rolls as it contained books. We must, therefore, bearing this in mind, be on our guard against exaggerating the size of the great Library.

The Serapeum, however, soon contained as many books as the Bruchion, and all went well till 47 B.C., when the great fire which destroyed Cæsar's fleet, burnt the Bruchion to the ground. An imaginative versifier, Lucian, asserts that the glow of the conflagration could be seen as far as Rome!

So they had to rebuild the Bruchion, and put into the new building the famous library of Pergamus, which the city had bequeathed to the Senate, and which the infatuated Mark Antony handed over to Cleopatra, last of the Ptolemies.

When the glory of Alexandria began to depart, its library began to share its fate. Julian, the emperor (360-363), took many volumes to enrich his own library; when the "Christian" fanatics in 387 stormed the Serapeum, they razed the temple to its foundation, and nothing of the library was left but the empty shelves. Finally in 641 Amru, general of Omar, second in sucession to the Prophet, fed the furnaces of the 4000 baths of Alexandria for full six months with the Bruchion's priceless treasures. If what the rolls contained were in the Korān, they were useless, if what they taught were not in the Korān, they were pernicious; in either case, burn them! Some Mohammedan apologists have lately tried to whitewash Omar and deny the whole story; but perhaps he is as little to be excused as the "Christian" barbarians who devastated the shelves of the Serapeum.

The Museum.

Such was the written material on which the scholars, scientists and philosophers of Alexandria had to work. And not only was there a library, but also a kind of university, called the Museum, dedicated to the arts and sciences, and embracing among other things an observatory, an amphitheatre of anatomy, a vast botanical garden, an immense menagerie, and many other collections of things useful for physical research.

It was an institution conceived on a most liberal plan, an assembly of savants lodged in a palace, richly endowed with the liberality of princes, exempt from public charges. Without distinction of race or creed, with no imposed regulations, no set plan of study or lecture lists, the members of this distinguished assembly were left free to prosecute their researches and studies untrammelled and unhampered. In their ranks were innumerable poets, historians, geometricians, mathematicians, astronomers, translators, critics, commentators, physicians, professors of natural science, philologists, grammarians, archæologists; in brief, savants of all sorts laying the first foundations of those researches which have once more in our own time, after the lapse of centuries, claimed the attention of the world. True, the Museum of Alexandria made but faltering steps where we to-day stride on with such assurance; but the spirit and method were the same, feeble compared to our strength, but the same spirit now made strong by palingenesis.

Very like was the temper then, in the last three centuries before the Christian era, to the temper that has marked the last three centuries of our own time. Religion had lost its hold on the educated; scepticism and "science" and misunderstood Aristotelian philosophy were alone worthy of a man of genius. There were "emancipated women" too, "dialectical daughters," common enough in those latter days of Greece.

Had not, thought these schoolmen, their great founder, Alexander, conquered the political world by following the advice of his master Aristotle? They also, would follow the teaching of the famous Stagirite, who had mapped out heaven and earth and all things therein, and soon they too would conquer what else of the world there was to be conquered, both natural and intellectual. It seemed so probable then, so simple and logical. It seems to be probable even now—to some minds!

So they set to work with their commenting, and criticizing, their philologizing, their grammar, and accentuation, their categorizing and cataloguing. They set to work to measure things; being pupils of Euclid, they attempted to measure the distance of the sun from the earth; and Eratosthenes, by copper armillæ, or circles for determining the equinox, calculated the obliquity of the ecliptic, and by further researches calculated the circumference of the earth; he also mapped out the world from all the books of travel and earth-knowledge in the great Library. In mechanics, Archimedes solved the mysteries of the lever and hydrostatic pressue which are the basis of our modern statics and hydrostatics. Hipparchus too thought out a theory of the heavens, upside down in fact, but correct enough to calculate eclipses and the rest; and this, three hundred years later, under the Antonines, was revamped by a certain Ptolemy, a commentator merely and not an inventor, the patent now standing in his name. Hipparchus was also the father of plane and spherical trigonometry.

But enough has already been said to give us an idea of the temper of the times, and it would be too long to dwell on the long list of famous names in

ALEXANDRIA. 109

other departments—encyclopædists and grammarians like Callimachus and Aristophanes; poets such as Theocritus.

Thus with the destruction of the building in the fire of Cæsar's fleet and with the Roman conquest the first Museum came to an end. It is true that a new Museum was established in the reign of Claudius (41-50 A.D.), but it was a mere shadow of its former self, no true home of the Muses, but the official auditorium of the wearisome writings of an emperor-scribbler. Claudius had written in Greek, *magis inepte quam ineleganter*, as Suetonius remarks, eight books of a history of Carthage, and twenty books of a history of Etruria. He would, therefore, establish a Museum and have his precious writings read to sycophant professordom once a year at least. Thus passed away the glory of that incarnation of scholarship and science; it was a soulless thing at best, marking a period of unbelief and scepticism, and destined to pass away when once man woke again to the fact that he was a soul.

And what of the outer schools of so-called philosophy during that period? They, too, were barren enough. The old sages of Greece were no more. Pythagoras, Socrates, Plato, and Aristotle had passed from the sight of mortals. The men who followed them were for the most part word-splitters and phrase-weavers. Dialectic arguers of the Megaran school, Eristics or wranglers, Pyrrhonists or doubters, Cyrenaics who believed in the senses alone as the only avenues of knowledge, pessimists and annihilationists, a host of later

The Schools of the Sophists.

Sceptics, Cynics, Epicureans, Academics, Peripatetics and Stoics—Epicureans who sought to live comfortably; Stoics who, in opposition to Plato's doctrine of social virtues, asserted the solitary dignity of human individualism.

After the three great reigns of the first Ptolemies, Alexandria fell morally, together with its rulers; for one hundred and eighty years "sophists wrangled, pedants fought over accents and readings with the true *odium grammaticum*," till Cleopatra, like Helen, betrayed her country to the Romans, and Egypt became a tributary province. So far there had been no philosophy in the proper sense of the word; that did not enter into the curriculum of the Museum.

The Dawn-Land.

Hitherto Alexandria had had no philosophy of her own, but now she is destined to be the crucible in which philosophic thought of every kind will be fused together;—and not only philosophy, but more important still, religio-philosophy and theosophy of every kind will be poured into the melting pot, and many strange systems and some things admirably good and true will be moulded out of the matter cast into this seething crucible. So far the Grecian genius has only thought of airing its own methods and views before the East. Into Egypt, Syria, Persia, into India even, it has flitted and sunned itself. It has taken many a year to convince Greek complacency that the period of world-genius is not bounded on one hand by Homer and on the other by Aristotle. Slowly but remorselessly it is borne in upon Hellenic ingenuity that there is an antiquity in the world beside which it is a mere *parvenu*. The Greek may despise the Orientals and call them mere "barber" or Barbarians, because they are strangers to the Attic tongue; but the Barbarian is to laugh last and laugh best after all, for he has a carefully guarded heirloom of wisdom, which he has not yet quite forgotten. The Greeks have had the tradition, too, and have even revived it, but have now forgotten again; the sceptics have replaced Orpheus by Homer, and Pythagoras and the real Plato by Aristotle. Their Mysteries are now masonic and no longer real—except for the very very few.

And if the Greek despised the Barbarian, the Barbarian, in his turn, thought but little of the Greek. " You Greeks are but children, O Solon," said the wise priest of Saïs to the Attic law-giver. You Greeks misunderstand and change the sacred myths you have adopted, fickle and careless, and superficial in things religious. Such was the criticism of the ancient Barbarian on the young and innovating Greek.

Slowly but surely the wisdom of the Egyptians, of the Babylonians and Chaldæans, and its reflection in some of the Jewish doctors, of Persia, too, and perhaps even of India, begins to react on the centre of Grecian thought, and religion and all the great problems of the human soil begin to oust mere scholasticism, *beaux arts* and *belles lettres*, from the schools; Alexandria is no longer to be a mere literary city, but a city of philosophy in the old sense of the term: it is to be wisdom-loving; not that it will eventually succeed even in this, but it will try to succeed.

There is to be a new method too. The concealed and hidden for so many centuries will be discussed and analyzed; there will be eclecticism, or a choosing out and synthesizing; there will be syncretism and a mingling of the most heterogeneous elements into some sort of patchwork; there will be analogeticism or comparison and correspondencing; efforts to discover a world-religion; to reconcile the irreconcilable; to synthesize as well science, philosophy and religion; to create a theosophy. It will apparently fail, for the race is nearing its end; it is the searching for truth at the end of a long life with an old brain, with too many old tendencies and prejudices to eradicate. The race will die and the souls that ensouled it will go out of incarnation, to reappear in due time when the wheel has turned. The old race is to be replaced with new blood and new physical vigour; but the mind of the new race is incapable of grasping the problems of its predecessors: Goths, Teutons, Vandals, Huns, Celts, Britons, and Arabs are bodies for a far less developed batch of souls. True the new race will also grow and develop and in its turn reach to manhood and old age, and far transcend its predecessor in every way; but when a child it will think as a child, when a man as a man, and when aged as the aged. What could the barbarian Huns and Goths and Arabs make of the great problems that confronted the highly civilised Alexandrians?

For the new race a new religion therefore, suited to its needs, suited perchance to its genius, suited to its age. What its actual historic origins were are so far shrouded in impenetrable obscurity; what the real history of its Founder was is impossible to discover.

This much, however, is certain, that a new keynote was struck for the tuning up of the new instrument. It is always a dangerous thing to generalize too freely, and paint the past in too staring splashes of colour, for in human affairs we find nothing unmixed; good was mixed with evil in the old method, and evil with good in the new. The new method was to force out into the open for all men a portion of the sacred Mysteries and secret teachings of the few. The adherents of the new religion itself professed to throw open "everything"; and many believed that it had revealed all that was revealable. That was because they were as yet children. So bright was the light to them that they perforce believed it came directly from the God of all gods—or rather from God alone, for they would have no more of gods; the gods were straightway transmuted into devils. The "many" had begun to play with psychic and spiritual forces, let loose from the Mysteries, and the "many" went mad for a time, and have not yet regained their sanity. Let us dwell on this intensely interesting phenomenon for a few moments.

<small>The New Religion.</small>

It is true that in the Roman Empire, which had now reduced the "world" to its sway, and thus politically united so many streams of ancient civilisation and barbarism into one ocean, things were in a very parlous state, morally and socially. The ancient order was beginning to draw to an end. Political freedom and independence were of the past, but intellectual and religious tolerance were still guaranteed, for so far the ancient world knew not the meaning of intolerance.

States were politically subordinated to the control of the Cæsars, but the religious institutions of such states, on which their social life and national existence depended, were left in absolute freedom. Nevertheless the spirit of reality had long left the ancient institutions; they were still maintained as part and parcel of statecraft, and as necessary for the people, who must have a cult, and festivals, and religious shows, then as now; but few took the matter really seriously. For the educated there was philosophy, and the shadow of the ancient Mysteries.

But these things were not for the people, not for the uneducated; the priestly orders had forgotten their duties, and, using their knowledge for self-aggrandisement, had now almost entirely forgotten what they once had known. It is an old, old story. The ancient church was corrupt, the ancient state enslaved. There must be a protest, partly right, partly wrong, as usual good and evil protesting against evil and good.

It is true that the Mysteries are free and open to all—who are worthy.

It is true that morals and virtues are absolutely essential pre-requisites—but not these alone.

It is true that there is One God—but Yahweh is not that Deity.

It is true that there are grades of being and intelligence between the Supreme and man—but the gods are not the work of men's hands or devils, while the angels are creatures of light.

It is true that philosophy alone cannot solve the problem—but it must not be neglected.

It is true that all men will be "saved"—but not rather the poor than the rich, the ignorant than the learned.

In protestantism in things religious there is no middle ground among the uninstructed. They fly to the opposite pole. Therefore, when the new impulse seizes on the people, we are to have a breaking down of old barriers and a striving after a new order of things, but at the same time a wild intolerance, a glorification of ignorance, a wholesale condemnation; a social upheaval, followed by a political triumph. One thing, however, is acquired definitely, a new lease of life for faith.

It was good for the people to believe with all their heart after so much disbelief; it was good for them to make virtue paramount as the first all-necessary step to a knowledge of God. It was good to set aside the things of the body and love the things of the soul; it was good to bring reality of life once more into the hearts of men.

What might have been if more temperate counsels had prevailed, who can say?

The main fact was that one race was dying and another being born. The memories of the past crowded into the old brain, but the new brain was unable to register them except in their cruder forms. The memory which succeeded in eventually impressing itself with most distinctness on the new brain, was perchance the most suited to the vigorous and warlike races that were to replace the old races of the Roman Empire; this memory was the tradition of the Jew.

We are of course in this only looking at the popular and outer side of the great movement which transformed the general religious consciousness of the ancient world. Within was much of great excellence, only a portion of which could be understood by the young brain of the new race. But now that the race is growing into manhood it will remember more of it; it has already recovered its memory of science and philosophy, and its memory of religion will doubtless ere long be brought through.

Jewish and Christian Schools.

We are still, however, looking at the outer conditions among which the Gnosis was working. At Alexandria, ever since its foundation, the Jews had been an important element in the life of the city. Though the translation of the Hebrew scriptures by the so-called "Seventy" had been begun in the reign of Ptolemy Philadelphus, it does not seem to have attracted the attention of the Greek official savants. Jewish ideas at Alexandria were at that time confined to Jews,—and naturally so, for in the beginning these most exclusive and intolerant religionists kept their ideas to themselves and guarded them jealously from the Gentiles. Later on the Jewish schools at Alexandria were so esteemed by their nation throughout the East, that the Alexandrian Rabbis were known as the "Light of Israel," and continued to be the centre of

Jewish thought and learning for several centuries. Within these it was that the Jews perfected their theories of religion and worked out what they had gleaned of "kabalistic" lore from the Chaldæans and Babylonians, and also from the wisdom-traditions of Egypt.

Many of the Hebrew doctors, moreover, were students of Grecian thought and literature, and are therefore known as Hellenists. Some of these wrote in Greek, and it was chiefly through their works that the Grecian world derived its information on things Jewish.

Aristobulus, whose date is unknown, but is conjecturally about B.C. 150, had endeavoured to maintain that the Peripatetic philosophy was derived from Moses—a wild theory that was subsequently developed and expanded to a ludicrous extent, and (Plato being substituted for Aristotle) was in the greatest favour even among such enlightened Church Fathers as Clement of Alexandria and Origen. This theory of Aristobulus was the forerunner of the still more fantastic theory, invented by Justin Martyr, that the wisdom of antiquity, wherever found, was a "plagiarism by anticipation" of the Devil, in order to spite the new religion; and this pitiful hypothesis has been faithfully reproduced by Christian apologists almost down to our own time.

Philo (circa B.C. 25—A.D. 45), however, is the most renowned of the Hellenists. He was a great admirer of Plato, and his work brings out many similarities between Rabbinical religious thought and Greek philosophy. It is true that Philo's method of allegorical exegesis, whereby he reads high philosophical conceptions into the crude narratives of the myths of Israel, is no longer regarded as legitimate; but his writings are nevertheless of great value. Philo believed not only that the Old Covenant documents were inspired in every part, but also that every name therein contained a hidden meaning of highest import. In this way he strove to explain away the crudities of the literal narrative.

But though Philo's method—whereby he could invoke the authority of "Moses" for the ideas of his school—is scientifically inadmissible, when the Bible documents are submitted to the searching of historic and philological criticism, nevertheless his numerous tractates are of great importance as supplying us with a record of the ideas which were current in the circles or schools with which Philo was in contact. They are a precious indication of the existence of communities who thought as Philo thought, and a valuable means of becoming acquainted with the scope of the Jewish Gnosis in a propagandist form.

Josephus (A.D. 37—100), the famous historian, also wrote in Greek, and so made known his nation far and wide throughout the Græco-Roman world.

Here, therefore, we have indications of the direct points of contact between Greek and propagandist Jewish thought. Now Christianity in its popular origins had entirely entangled itself with the popular Jewish tradition of religion, a tradition that was innocent of all philosophy or kabalistic mysticism. The Gentiles who were admitted into the new faith, however, soon grew restive at the imposition of the rite of circumcision, which the earliest propagandists insisted upon; and so the first "heresy" arose, and the "Church of Jerusalem," which remained essentially Jewish in all things, speedily resolved itself into a narrow sect, even for those who regarded Judaism as the only forerunner of the new faith. As time went on, however, and either men of greater education joined their ranks, or in their propaganda they were forced to study themselves to meet the objections of educated opponents, wider and more liberal views obtained among a number of the Christians, and the other great religious traditions and philosophies contacted the popular stream. All such views, however, were looked upon with great suspicion by the "orthodox," or rather that view which finally became orthodox. And so as time went on, even the very moderate liberalism of Clemens and Origen was regarded as a grave danger; and with the triumph of narrow orthodoxy, and the condemnation of learning, Origen himself was at last anathematized.

It was the Alexandrian school of Christian philosophy, of which the most famous doctors were the same Clemens and Origen, which laid the first foundations of General Christian theology; and that school owed its evolution to its contact with Grecian thought. There is a pleasant story of its first beginnings to which we may briefly refer. Towards the end of the first century the Christians established a school in Alexandria, the city of schools. It was a Sunday-school for children, called the Didascaleion. With courageous faith it was established hard by the door of the world-famous Museum, from whose chairs the general Christians, owing to their ignorance of art and science and philosophy, were excluded. From that same Sunday-school, however, arose the vast fabric of Catholic theology; for the teachers of the Didascaleion were forced to look to their laurels, and they soon numbered in their ranks men who had already received education in the Grecian schools of thought and training.

Such is a brief sketch of Alexandria and her schools, and it was in outer contact with such a seething world of thought and endeavour, that some of the greatest of the Gnostic doctors lived. They were found of course elsewhere in the world—in Syria, Asia Minor, and Italy, in Gaul and Spain; but the best picture of the ancient world with which they were in outer contact, is to be sketched in the city where Egypt and Africa, Rome and Greece, Syria and Arabia met together.

GENERAL AND GNOSTIC CHRISTIANITY.

THE EVOLUTION OF CATHOLIC CHRISTIANITY.

THE historical origins of Christianity are hidden in impenetrable obscurity. Of the actual history of the first half of the first century we have no knowledge. Of the history of the next hundred years also we have for the most part to rely on conjecture. The now universally received canonical account was a selection from a mass of tradition and legend; it is only in the second half of the second century that the idea of a Canon of the New Testament makes its appearance, and is gradually developed by the Church of Rome and the Western Fathers. The early Alexandrian theologians, such as Clement, are still ignorant of a precise Canon. Following on the lines of the earliest apologists of a special view of Christianity, such as Justin, and using this evolving Canon as the sole test of orthodoxy, Irenæus, Tertullian and Hippolytus, supported by the Roman Church, lay the foundations of "catholicity,"

The Canon.

and begin to raise the first courses of that enormous edifice of dogma which is to-day regarded as the *only* authentic view of the Church of Christ.

The first two centuries, however, instead of confirming the boast of the later orthodox, "one church, one faith, always and everywhere," on the contrary present us with the picture of many lines of evolution of belief, practice, and organisation. The struggle for life was being fiercely waged, and though the "survival of the fittest" resulted as usual, there were frequent crises in which the final "fittest" is hardly discernible and at times disappears from view.

The Gospels.

The view of the Christian origins which eventually became the orthodox tradition based itself mainly upon Gospel-documents composed, in all probability, some time in the reign of Hadrian (A.D. 117-138). The skeleton of three of these Gospels was presumably a collection of Sayings and a narrative of Doings in the form of an ideal life, a sketch composed by one of the "Apostles" of the inner communities and designed for public circulation. Round this nucleus the compilers of the three documents wove other matter selected from a vast mass of myth, legend, and tradition; they were evidently men of great piety, and their selection of material produced narratives of great dignity, and cast aside much in circulation that was foolish and fantastic, the remains of which we have still preserved in some of the apocryphal Gospels. The writer of the fourth document was a natural mystic who adorned his account with a beauty of conception

EVOLUTION OF CATHOLIC CHRISTIANITY. 123

and a charm of feeling that reflect the highest inspiration.

At the same time the canonical selection most fortunately preserved for us documents of far greater historic value.

In the Letters of Paul, the majority of which are in the main, I believe, authentic, we have the earliest historic records of Christianity which we possess. The Pauline Letters date back to the middle of the first century, and are the true point of departure for any really historic research into the origins. On reading these Letters it is almost impossible to persuade ourselves that Paul was acquainted with the statements of the later historicized account of the four canonical Gospels; all his conceptions breathe a totally different atmosphere. Instead of preaching the Jesus of the historicized Gospels, he preaches the doctrine of the mystic Christ. He not only seems to be ignorant of the Doings but even of the Sayings in any form known to us; nevertheless it is almost certain that some collection of Sayings must have existed and been used by the followers of the public teaching in his time. Though innumerable opportunities occur in his writings for reference to the canonical Sayings and Doings, whereby the power of his exhortations would have been enormously increased, he abstains from making any. On the other hand, we find his Letters replete with conceptions and technical terms which receive no explanation in the traditions of General Christianity, but are fundamental with the handers-on of the Gnosis.

The Letters of Paul.

124   FRAGMENTS OF A FAITH FORGOTTEN.

The picture which the letters of Paul give us of the actual state of affairs in the middle of the first century is that of an independent propagandist, with his own illumination, in contact with the ideas of an inner school on the one hand, and with outer communities of various kinds on the other. Whatever the inner schools may have been, the outer communities among which Paul laboured were Jewish, synagogues of the orthodox Jews, synagogues of the outer communities of the Essenes, communities which had received some tradition of the public teaching of Jesus as well, and understood or misunderstood it as the case may have been.

<small>The Gentilisation of Christianity.</small> Paul's mission was to break down Jewish exclusiveness and pioneer the way for the gentilization of Christianity. The century which followed this propaganda of Paul (50-150) is, according to Harnack, characterised by the following features:

(i) The rapid disappearance of Jewish (that is to say, primitive and original) [popular] Christianity.

(ii) Every member of the community was supposed to have received the "Spirit of God"; the teaching was "charismatic," that is to say, of the nature of "spiritual gifts."

(iii) The expectation of the approaching end of the age, and the reign of Christ on earth for a thousand years — "chiliasm" — was in universal favour.

(iv) Christianity was a mode of life, not a dogma.

(v) There were no fixed doctrinal forms, and accordingly the greatest freedom in Christian preaching.

(vi) The Sayings of the Lord and the Old Testament were not as yet absolute authorities; the "Spirit" could set them aside.

(vii) There was no fixed political union of the Churches; each community was independent.

(viii) This period gave rise to "a quite unique literature, in which were manufactured facts for the past and for the future, and which did not submit to the usual literary rules and forms, but came forward with the loftiest pretensions."

(ix) Particular sayings and arguments of assumed "Apostolic Teachers" were brought forward as being of great authority.

At the same time, besides this gentilizing tendency, which was always really subordinated to the Jewish original impulse, though flattering itself that it had entirely shaken off the fetters of the "circumcision," there was a truly universalizing tendency at work in the background; and it is this endeavour to universalize Christianity which is the grand inspiration underlying the best of the Gnostic efforts we have to review. But this universalizing does not belong to the line of the origins along which General Christiaity subsequently traced its descent.

THE EBIONITES.

The Nazoræans.

Epiphanius would have it that the Christians were first called Iessæi, and says they are mentioned under this name in the writings of Philo. The followers of the earliest converts of Jesus are also said to have been called Nazoræi. Even towards the end of the fourth century the Nazoræans were still found scattered throughout Cœle-Syria, Decapolis, Pella (whither they fled at the destruction of Jerusalem), the region beyond Jordan, and far away to Mesopotamia. Their collection of the *logoi* was called *The Gospel according to the Hebrews*, and differed greatly from the synoptic accounts of the Canon. Even to this day a remnant of the Nazoræans is said by some to survive in the Mandaïtes, a strange sect dwelling in the marshes of Southern Babylonia, but their curious scripture, *The Book of Adam,* as preserved in the *Codex Nasaræus*, bears no resemblance whatever to the known fragments of *The Gospel according to the Hebrews*, though some of their rites are very similar to the rites of some communities of the "Righteous" referred to in that strange Jewish pseudepigraph *The Sibylline Oracles.*

Who the original Iessæans or Nazoræans were, is wrapped in the greatest obscurity; under another of their designations, however, the Ebionites or "Poor Men," we can obtain some further information. These early outer followers of Jesus were finally ostracized from the orthodox fold, and so completely were their origin and history obscured by the subsequent industry of heresy-hunters, that we finally find them fathered on a certain Ebion, who is as non-existent as several other heretics, such as Epiphanes, Kolarbasus and Elkesai, who were invented by the zeal and ignorance of fourth-century hæresiologists and "historians." Epiphanes is the later personification of an unnamed "distinguished" *(epiphanes)* teacher; Kolarbasus is the personification of the "sacred four" *(kol-arba)*, and Elkesai the personification of the "hidden power" *(elkesai)*. So eager were the later refutators to add to their list of heretics, that they invented the names of persons from epithets and doctrines. So with Ebion.

The Ebionites were originally so called because they were "poor"; the later orthodox subsequently added "in intelligence" or "in their ideas about Christ." And this may very well have been the case, and doubtless many grossly misunderstood the public teaching of Jesus, for it should not be forgotten that one of the main factors to be taken into account in reviewing the subsequent rapid progress of the new religion was the social revolution. In the minds of the most ignorant of the earliest followers of the public teaching, the greatest hope aroused may well have been the near approach of the day when the "poor" should be elevated above the "rich." But this was the view of the most ignorant only; though doubtless they were numerous enough.

<small>The Poor Men.</small>

Nevertheless it was Ebionism which preserved the tradition of the earliest converts of the public teaching, and the Ebionite communities doubtless possessed a collection of the public Sayings and based their lives upon them.

It was against these original followers of the public teaching of Jesus that Paul contended in his efforts to gentilize Christianity. For many a long year this Petro-Pauline controversy was waged with great bitterness, and the Canon of the New Testament is thought by some to have been the means adopted to form the basis of a future reconciliation; the Petrine and Pauline documents were carefully edited, and between the Gospel portion and the Pauline letters was inserted the new-forged link of the *Acts of the Apostles*, a carefully edited selection from a huge mass of legendary *Acts*, welded together into a narrative and embellished with speeches after the manner of Thucydides.

The Ebionite Tradition of Jesus.

How then did the original Ebionites view the person and teaching of Jesus? They regarded their leader as a wise man, a prophet, a Jonas, nay even a Solomon. Moreover, he was a manifestation of the Messiah, the Anointed, who was to come, but he had not yet appeared as the Messiah; that would only be at his second coming. In his birth as Jesus, he was a prophet simply. The New Dispensation was but the continuation of the Old Law; all was essentially Jewish. They therefore expected the coming of the Messiah as literally prophesied by their men of old. He was to come as king, and then all the nations would be subjected to the power of the Chosen People, and for a thousand years there would be peace and prosperity and plenty on earth.

Jesus was a man, born as all men, the human son of Joseph and Mary. It was only at his baptism, at thirty years of age, that the Spirit descended upon him and he became a prophet. They, therefore, guarded his Sayings as a precious deposit, handing them down by word of mouth. The Ebionites knew nothing of the pre-existence or divinity of their revered prophet. It is true that Jesus was "christ," but so also would all be who fulfilled the Law. Thus they naturally repudiated Paul and his new doctrine entirely; for them Paul was a deceiver and an apostate from the Law, they even denied that he was a Jew.

It was only later that they used *The Gospel according to the Hebrews*, which Jerome says was the same as *The Gospel of the Twelve Apostles* and *The Gospel of the Nazarenes*, that is to say, of the Nazoræans. It should be remembered that these Nazoræans knew nothing of the Nazareth legend, which was subsequently developed by the "in order that it might be fulfilled" school of historicizers.

The Ebionites did not return to Jerusalem when the emperor permitted the new colony of Ælia Capitolina to be established in 138, for no Jew was allowed to return. The new town was Gentile. Therefore, when we read of "the re-constitution of the mother church" at Ælia Colonia, in Church historians, little reliance can be placed upon such assertions. The "mother church," based on the public teaching, was Ebionite and remained Ebionite, the community at Ælia Colonia was Gentile and therefore Pauline.

K

Christianity, as understood by the Ebionites, being an essentially national doctrine, Paulinism was a necessity if any public attempt at universality was to be made; therefore it was that the true historical side of popular Christianity (the orginal Ebionite tradition) became more and more obscured, until finally it had so completely disappeared from the area of such tradition, that a new "history" could with safety be developed to suit the dogmatic evolution inaugurated by Paul.

The later forms of Ebionism, however, which survived for several centuries, were of a Gnostic nature, and reveal the contact of these outer communities of primitive Christendom based on the public teaching with an inner Jewish tradition, which evidently existed contemporaneously with Paul, and may have existed far earlier.

THE ESSENES.

BASING themselves on the Sayings preserved in the canonical Gospels and on the description of the communities given in the *Acts*, many have supposed that Jesus was a member of or intimately acquainted with the doctrines and discipline of the Essene communities. Who then were these Essenes or Healers?

For centuries before the Christian era Essene communities had dwelt on the shores of the Dead Sea. These Essenes or Essæans, in the days of Philo and Josephus, were imbued with the utmost reverence for Moses and the Law. They believed in God, the creator, in the immortality of the soul, and in a future state of retribution. Finding it impossible to carry out in ordinary life the minute regulations of the laws of purity, they had adopted the life of ascetic communism. Their chief characteristic was the doctrine of love—love to God, love of virtue, and love of mankind—and the practical way in which they carried out their precepts aroused the admiration of all.

Their strict observance of the purificatory discipline enacted by the Levitical institutions thus compelled them to become a self-supporting community; all worked at a trade, they cultivated their own fields, manufactured all the articles of food and dress which they used, and thus in every way avoided contact with those who did not observe the same rules. They also appear in their inner circles to have been strict celibates.

Their Manner of Life.

Their manner of life was as follows: they rose before the sun, and no word was uttered until they had assembled together and, with faces turned towards the dawn, offered up prayers for the renewal of the light. Each then went to his appointed task under the supervision of the stewards or overseers ("bishops") elected by universal suffrage. At eleven o'clock they again assembled and, putting off their working clothes, performed the daily rite of baptism in cold water; then clothing themselves in white linen robes, they proceeded to the common meal, which they regarded as a sacrament; the refectory was a "holy temple." They ate in silence, and the food was of the plainest—bread and vegetables. Before the meal a blessing was invoked, and at the end thanks were rendered. The members took their seats according to seniority. They then went forth to work again until the evening, when they again assembled for the common meal. Certain hours of the day, however, were devoted to the study of the mysteries of nature and of revelation, as well as of the powers of the celestial hierarchies, the names of the angels, etc.; for they had an inner instruction, which was guarded with the utmost secrecy.

This was the rule for the week-days, while the Sabbath was kept with extreme rigour. They had, however, no priests, and any one who was "moved" to do so, took up the reading of the Law, and the exposition of the mysteries connected with the Tetragrammaton, or four-lettered mystery-name of the Creative Power, and the angelic worlds. The

Essenes, therefore, were evidently in contact with Chaldæan "kabalism" and the Zoroastrian tradition of the discipline of purity; logic and metaphysics, however, were eschewed as injurious to a devotional life.

There were four degrees in the community: (i.) novices; (ii.) approachers; (iii.) new full members, or associates; (iv.) old members, or elders.

(i.) After the first year the novice gave all his possessions to the common treasury, and received a copy of the regulations, a spade (for the purpose described in Moses' camp-regulations), and a white robe, the symbol of purity; but the novice was still excluded from the lustral rites and common meal.

(ii.) After two years more, the novice shared in the lustral rites, but was still excluded from the common meal.

(iii.) The associates were bound by the most solemn assurances, and in case of any delinquency could only be judged by the "assembly," consisting of one hundred members.

Essenism is said by some to have been an exaggerated form of Pharisaism; and it may be a matter of surprise to those whose only knowledge of the Pharisees is derived from canonical documents, to learn that the highest aim of this enlightened school of Judaism was to attain to such a state of holiness as to be able to perform miraculous cures and to prophesy. The "degrees of holiness" practised by the Pharisees are said to have been: (i.) the study of the Law and circumspection; (ii.) the noviciate, in which the apron was the symbol of purity; (iii.) external

The Degrees of Holiness.

purity, by means of lustrations or baptisms; (iv.) celibacy; (v.) inward purity, purity of thought; (vi.) a higher stage still, which is not further defined; (vii.) meekness and holiness; (viii.) dread of every sin; (ix.) the highest stage of holiness; (x.) the stage which enabled the adept to heal the sick and raise the dead.

We should, however, remember that the Healers absolutely refused to have anything to do with the blood-sacrifices of the Temple-worship, and refused to believe in the resurrection of the physical body, which the rest of the Pharisees held as a cardinal doctrine.

In this brief sketch it is of course impossible to point out the striking similarities between the discipline of the Essenes and that of the Therapeutæ of Egypt and of the Orphic and Pythagorean schools. Every subject referred to in these essays requires a volume or several volumes for its proper treatment; we can only set up a few finger-posts, and leave the reader to make his own investigations.

But before leaving this most interesting theme, it will be necessary to point to the identity between many of the Essene regulations and the Gospel teachings and traditions.

Points of Contact with Christianity.

Converts were required to sell their possessions and give to the poor, for the laying up of treasure was regarded as injurious to a spiritual life. Not only did the Essenes despise riches, but they lived a life of self-imposed poverty. Love of the brotherhood and of one's neighbour was the soul of Essene life, and the basis of all action; and this characteristic of their discipline called forth universal admiration. The members lived together as in a family, had all things in common, and appointed a steward to manage the common bag. When travelling they would lodge with brethren whom they had never seen before, as though with the oldest and most intimate friends; and thus they took nothing with them when they went on a journey. All members were set on the same level, and the authority of one over another was forbidden; nevertheless mutual service was strictly enjoined. They were also great lovers of peace, and so refused to take arms or manufacture warlike weapons; moreover they proscribed slavery. Finally, the end of the Essenes was to be meek and lowly in spirit, to mortify all sinful lusts, to be pure in heart, to hate evil but reclaim the evildoer, and to be merciful to all men. Moreover, their yea was to be yea, and their nay, nay. They were devoted to the curing of the sick, the healing of both body and soul, and regarded the power to perform miraculous cures and cast out evil spirits as the highest stage of discipline. In brief, they strove to be so pure as to become temples of the Holy Spirit, and thus seers and prophets.

To these inner communities were attached outer circles of pupils living in the world, and found in all the main centres of the Diaspora.

Philo distinguishes the Essenes from the Therapeuts by saying that the former were devoted to the "practical" life, while the latter proceeded to the higher stage of the "contemplative" life, and devoted themselves to still higher problems of religion and philosophy, and it is in this direction that we must look for the best in Gnosticism.

THE TENDENCIES OF GNOSTICISM.

The "Secularizing" of Christianity.

BUT here again accurate historical data are out of the question, and we have for the most part to deal with what the Germans call "*Tendenz.*" Harnack speaks of the tendency, which by long convention is generally called Gnostic, as the "acute secularizing of Christianity." What then is the meaning of this phrase? Catholic dogma is said to be the outcome of the *gradual* hellenizing of general Christianity, that is to say, the modification of popular tradition by the philosophical and theological method. All evolution of popular beliefs takes time, and the results arrived at by the general mind only after centuries, are invariably anticipated by minds of greater instruction generations before. The Galileos of the world are invariably condemned by their contemporaries. The Gnostic mind rapidly arrived on the one hand at many conclusions which the Catholics gradually adopted only after generations of hesitation, and on the other at a number of conclusions which even to our present generation seem too premature. All theosophic students are, in matters of religion, centuries before their time, for the simple reason that they are endeavouring by every means in their power to shorten the time of normal evolution and reach the mystic goal, which at every moment of time is near at hand *within*, but for the majority is far distant along the normal path of external evolution.

The phrase "acute secularizing of Christianity," then, represents the rapid theologizing and systematizing of Christianity; but I doubt whether this altogether accounts for the facts. The Gnosis was pre-Christian; the Christ illumined its tradition, and by His public teaching practically threw open to all what had previously been kept "secret from the creation of the world"—to speak more accurately, the intermediate grades of the Mysteries. The leaven worked, and in course of time much that had been previously kept for the "worthy" alone, was forced into publicity and made common property. It was forced out by the stress of circumstances, inaugurated by the propaganda of Paul, and intensified by subsequent hæresiological controversy. The Gnostics claimed that there were two lines of tradition—the public sayings, and the inner teachings which dealt with things that the people in the world could not understand. This side of their teaching they kept at first entirely to themselves, and only gradually put forth a small portion of it; the rest they kept in closest secrecy, as they knew it could not possibly be understood.

The Gnostics were, then, the first Christian theologists, and if it is a cause for reprehension that the real historical side of the new movement was obscured in order to suit the necessities of a religion which aspired to universality, then the Gnostics are the chief culprits.

Catholicism finally, by accepting the Old Testament Canon in its literal interpretation, adopted the beliefs of popular Judaism and the Yahweh-cult, but in the earlier years it had been inclined to seek for an allegorical interpretation. Gnosticism, on the contrary, whenever it did not entirely reject the Old Covenant documents, invariably adopted not only the allegorical method, but also a canon of criticism which minutely classified the "inspiration" and so sifted out most of the objectionable passages from the Jewish Canon.

Yahweh not "the Father" of Jesus.

Thus, in persuit of a universal ideal, the tribal God—or rather, the crude views of the uninstructed Jewish populace as to Yahweh—was, when not entirely rejected, placed in a very subordinate position. In brief, the Yahweh of the Elohīm was not the Father of Jesus; the Demiurgos, or creative power of the world, was not the Mystery God over all.

The Inner Teaching.

And just as this idea of the true God transcended the popular notions of deity, so did the true teaching of the Gnosis illumine the enigmatical sayings or parables. The ethical teachings, or "Words of the Lord," and the parables, required interpretation; the literal meaning was sufficient for the people, but for the truly spiritual minded there was an infinite vista of inner meaning which could be revealed to the eye of the true Gnostic. Thus the plain ethical teaching and the unintelligible dark sayings were for the uninstructed; but there was a further instruction, an esoteric or inner doctrine, which was imparted to the worthy alone. Many gospels and apocalypses were thus compiled under the inspiration of the "Spirit," as it was claimed—all purporting to be the instruction vouchsafed by Jesus to His disciples after the "resurrection from the dead," which mystical phrase they mostly represented as meaning the new birth or Gnostic illumination, the coming to life of the soul from its previous dead state. But even these Gnostic treatises did not reveal the whole matter; true, they explained many things in terms of internal states and spiritual processes; but they still left much unexplained, and the final revelation was only communicated by word of mouth in the body, and by vision out of the body.

Thus it was a custom with them to divide mankind into three classes: (a) the lowest, or "hylics," were those who were so entirely dead to spiritual things that they were as the *hylē*, or unperceptive matter of the world; (b) the intermediate class were called "phychics," for though believers in things spiritual, they were believers simply, and required miracles and signs to strengthen their faith; (c) whereas the "pneu matics," or spiritual, the highest class, were those capable of knowledge of spiritual matters, those who could receive the Gnosis. Various Classes of Souls.

It is somewhat the custom in our days in extreme circles to claim that all men are "equal." The modern theologian wisely qualifies this claim by the adverb "morally." Thus stated the idea is by no means a peculiarly Christian view—for the doctrine is common to all the great religions, seeing that it simply asserts the great principle of justice as one of the manifestations of Diety. The Gnostic view, however, is far clearer, and more in accord with the facts of evolution; it admits the "morally equal," but it further asserts difference of degree, not only in body and soul, but also in spirit, in order to make the morality proportional, and so to carry out the inner meaning of the parable of the talents.

This classification obtained not only among men, but also among powers; and the prophets of the Old Testament as instruments of such powers were, as stated above, thus sorted out into an order of dignity.

<small>The Person of Jesus.</small>

The personality of Jesus, the prophet of the new tidings proved, however, a very difficult problem for the Gnostic doctors, and we can find examples of every shade of opinion among them—from the original Ebionite view that he was simply a good and holy man, to the very antipodes of belief; that he was not only a descent of the Logos of God—a familiar idea to Oriental antiquity —but in deed and in his person very God of very God, a necessity forced upon faith by the boastful spirit of an enthusiasm which sought to transcend the claims of every existing religion.

The person of Jesus was thus made to bear the burden of every possibility of the occult world and every hidden power of human nature. In their endeavours to reconcile the ideas of a suffering man and of a triumphant initiator and king of the universe (both sensible and intellectual), they had recourse to the expedient of Docetism, a theory which could cover every phase of contradiction in the sharp juxtaposition of the divine and human natures of their ideal. The docetic theory is the theory of "appearance." A sharp distinction was made between Christ, the divine æon or perfected "man," and Jesus the personality. The God, or rather God, in Christ, did not suffer, but appeared to suffer; the lower man, Jesus, alone suffered. Or again, Christ was not really incarnated in a man Jesus, but took to himself a phantasmal body called Jesus. But these were subsequent doctrinal developments on the ground of certain inner facts: (*a*) that a phantasmal body can be used by the "perfect," be made to appear and disappear at will, and become dense or materialised, so as to be felt physically; and (*b*) that the physical body of another, usually a pupil, can be used by a master of wisdom as a medium for instruction. Such underlying ideas occur in Gnostic treatises and form an important part of their christology, especially with regard to the period of instruction after the "resurrection."

In fact no problem appeared too lofty for the intuition of the Gnostic philosopher; the whence, whither, why, and how of things, were searched into with amazing daring. Not only was their cosmogony of the most sublime and complex character, but the limits of the sensible world were too narrow to contain it, so that they sought for its origins in the intellectual and spiritual regions of the immanent mind of deity, wherein they postulated a transcendent æonology which pourtrayed the energizings of the divine ideation. Equally complex was their anthropogony, and equally sublime the potentialities which they postulated of the human soul and spirit.

<small>The Main Doctrines.</small>

As to their soteriology, or theory of the salvation or regeneration of mankind, they did not confine the idea to the crude and limited notion of a physical passion by a single individual, but expanded it into a stupendous cosmical process, wrought by the volition of the Logos in His own nature.

Their eschatology, or doctrine of the "last things," again painted for mankind at the end of the world-cycle a future which gave "*nirvāṇa*" to the "spiritual" and æonian bliss to the "psychic," while the "hylic" remained in the obscuration of matter until the end of the "Great Peace"—a picture somewhat different from the crude expectation of the good feasting time on earth of the "Poor Men," which Harnack technically refers to as a "sensuous eudæmonistic eschatology."

Finally, the whole of their doctrine revolved round the conception of cyclic law for both the universal and the individual soul. Thus we find the Gnostics invariably teaching the doctrine not only of the preëxistence but also of the rebirth of human souls; and though a chief feature of their dogmas was the main doctrine of forgiveness of sins, they nevertheless held rigidly to the infallible working out of the great law of cause and effect. It is somewhat curious that these two main doctrines, which explain so much in Gnosticism and throw light on so many dark places, have been either entirely overlooked or, when not unintelligently slurred over, despatched with a few hurried remarks in which the critic is more at pains to apologize for touching on such ridiculous superstitions as "metempsychosis" and "fate," than to elucidate tenets which are a key to the whole position.

THE LITERATURE AND SOURCES OF GNOSTICISM.

The study of Gnosticism has so far been almost entirely confined to specialists, whose works cannot be understanded of the people; the ordinary reader is deterred by the wealth of detail, by the difficulty of the technical terms, by the obscurity of theological phraseology, and by the feeling that he is expected to know many things of which he has never even heard. It is to be hoped that ere long some competent English scholar, endowed with the genius of lucid generalization, may be induced to write a popular sketch of the subject, in order that thinking men and women who have not enjoyed the advantages of a technical training in Church history and dogmatics, may understand its importance and absorbing interest.

Meantime our present essay may, perhaps, to some extent serve as a "guide to the perplexed," yet not conceived on the plan or carried out with the ability of a Maimonides, but rather the mere jotting down of a few notes and indications which may spare the general reader the years of labour the writer has spent in searching through many books.

First, then, as to books; what are the best works on Gnosticism? The best books without exception are by German scholars. Here, then, we are confronted with our first difficulty, for the general reader as a rule is a man of one language only. For the ordinary English reader, therefore, such works are closed books, and he must have recourse to

Literature.

translations, if such exist. Unfortunately only two of such works are procurable in English dress.

The second volume of the translation (Bohn, new ed., 1890) of Neander's *Church History* (1825, etc.), deals with the Gnostics, but the great German theologian's work is now out of date.

The best general review of Gnosticism by the light of the most recent researches, is to be found in Harnack's admirable *History of Dogma*, in the first volume, translated in 1894.

For a more detailed account, Smith and Wace's *Dictionary of Christian Biography* (1877-1887) is absolutely indispensable. The scheme of this useful work contains a general article, with lengthy articles on every Gnostic teacher, and shorter articles on a number of the technical terms of the Gnosis. Lipsius, Salmon, and Hort are responsible for the work, and their names are a sufficient guarantee of thoroughness.

The last two works are all that are necessary for a preliminary grasp of the subject, and are the outcome of profound scholarship and admirable critical acumen. It is a pleasure to subscribe one's tribute of praise to such work, although the point of view assumed by these distinguished scholars is not sufficiently liberal for one who is deeply convinced that the inspiration of every honest effort to formulate the inner truth of things is *really* from above.

Of other English works we may mention King's *Gnostics and their Remains* (2nd ed., 1887), a work intended for the general reader. King strongly insists on a distinct Indian influence in Gnosticism, and deals with a number of interesting points; but his work lacks the thoroughness of the specialist. He is, however, far removed from "orthodoxy," and has an exceeding great sympathy for the Gnostics. The weakest point of King's work is the side he has brought into chief prominence; the so-called "remains" of the Gnostics, amulets, talismans, etc., in which King as a numismatologist took special interest, are now stated by the best authorities to have had most probably no connection with our philosophers. Nevertheless King's book is well worth reading.

Mansel's posthumous work, *The Gnostic Heresies of the First and Second Centuries* (1875), is not only unsympathetic, but for the most part does grave injustice to the Gnostics, by insisting on treating their leading ideas as a metaphysic to be judged by the standard of modern German philosophical methods, the Dean having himself once held a chair of philosophy.

Norton, in his *Evidences of the Genuineness of the Gospels* (1847), devotes his second volume to the Gnostics, but the value of his work is small.

Burton's *Inquiry into the Heresies of the Apostolic Age* (1829) might have been written by an early Church Father. The Bampton lecturer's effort and Norton's are now both out of date; moreover their books and that of Mansel are only procurable in the second-hand market.

So much for works in English dealing directly with Gnosticism.

The student will find in Harnack brief but discriminating bibliographies after each chapter, in which all the best works are given, especially those of German scholars; in Smith and Wace's Dictionary each article is also followed by a fair bibliography. A short general bibliography, and also a list of nearly all the latest work done on the only direct documents of Gnosticism which we possess, is to be found in the Introduction to my translation of the Gnostic treatise *Pistis Sophia* (1896); and a classified bibliography of all the most important works is appended to this essay. The student will be surprised to see how unfavourably the paucity of information in English compares with the mass of encyclopædic work in German, and how France also in this department of Church history and theological research runs England very close. But the consideration of these works does not fall into the plan of this short essay.

Indirect Sources. So much, then, for the general literature of the subject in English; we have now to consider briefly the indirect and direct documents of Gnosticism. By "indirect" documents I mean the polemical writings of the Fathers of what subsequently established itself as the orthodox Catholic Church. These indirect documents were practically the only sources of information until 1853, when Schwartze's translation of the *Pistis Sophia* was published. By "direct" documents I mean the few Gnostic treatises which have reached our hands through the medium of Coptic translation.

Our indirect sources of information, therefore,

come through the hands of the most violent opponents of the Gnosis; and we have only to remember the intense bitterness of religious controversy at all times, and especially in the early centuries of the Church, to make us profoundly sceptical of the reliability of such sources of information. Moreover, the earlier and more contemporaneous, and therefore comparatively more reliable, sources are to be found mostly in the writings of the Fathers of the Western Church, who were less capable of understanding the philosophical and mystical problems which agitated the Eastern communities. The Roman and occidental mind could never really grasp Greek and oriental thought, and the Western Fathers were always the main champions of " orthodoxy."

We should further remember that we have extant no contemporary "refutation" of the first century (if any ever existed), or of the first three quarters of the second. The great "store-house of Gnosticism" is the Refutation of Irenæus, who wrote at Lyons in Gaul, far away from the real scene of action, in about the penultimate decade of the second century. All subsequent refutators base themselves more or less on the treatise of Irenæus, and frequently copy the work of the Gallic bishop. If, then, Irenæus can be shown to be unreliable, the whole edifice of refutation is endangered by the insecurity of its foundation. This important point will be considered later on.

Prior to Irenæus a certain Agrippa Castor, who flourished late in the reign of Hadrian, about 135 A.D., is said by Eusebius to have been the first to write against heresies. His work is unfortunately lost.

Justin Martyr, the apologist, also composed a work against heresies; this Syntagma or Compendium is also unfortunately lost. Judging from Justin's account of the Gospel-story in his extant works, it would appear that the "Memoirs of the Apostles" to which he repeatedly refers, were not identical with our four canonical Gospels, though it may well be that these Gospels were assuming their present shape at this period. It may therefore be supposed that his work upon heresies threw too strong a light on pre-canonical controversy to make its continued use desirable. This may also be the reason of the disappearance of the work of Agrippa Castor. Justin flourished about 140-160 A.D.

Clement of Alexandria, whose greatest literary activity was from about 190-203 A.D., lived in the greatest centre of Gnostic activity, and was personally acquainted with some of the great doctors of the Gnosis. His works are for the most part free from those wholesale accusations of immorality with which the general run of Church Fathers in after years loved to bespatter the character of the Gnostics of the first two centuries. All the critics are now agreed that these accusations were unfounded calumnies as far as the great schools and their teachers were concerned, seeing that the majority were rigid ascetics. But this point will come out more clearly later on.

Clement is supposed to have dealt with the higher problems of Gnosticism in his lost work, *The Outlines*, in which he endeavoured to construct a complete system of Christian teaching, the first three books of which bore a strong resemblance to the three stages of the Platonists : (i.) Purification, (ii.) Initiation, (iii.) Direct Vision. This work is also unfortunately lost. It was the continuation of his famous *Miscellanies*, in which the Christian philosopher laboured to show that he was a true Gnostic himself.

Tertullian of Carthage (fl. 200-220 A.D.), whose intolerance, "fiery zeal," and violently abusive language are notorious, wrote against heresies, mostly copying Irenæus. For the Marcionites, however, he is an independent authority. Part of the treatise against heresies ascribed to Tertullian is written by some unknown refutator, and so we have a Pseudo-Tertullian to take into consideration.

Hippolytus, Bishop of Portus at the mouth of the Tiber, was the disciple of Irenæus. He wrote a Compendium against all heresies, based almost entirely on Irenæus, which is lost; but a much larger work of the same Father was in 1842 discovered at Mount Athos. This purported to be a *Refutation of All Heresies*, and adds considerably to our information from indirect sources; for the work is not a mere copy of Irenæus, but adds a large mass of new matter, with quotations from some Gnostic MSS. which had fallen into Hippolytus' hands. The composition of this work may be dated somewhere about 222 A.D.

About this time also (225-250) Origen, the great Alexandrian Father, wrote a refutation against a certain Celsus, who is supposed to have been the first opponent of Christianity among the philosophers, and who lived some seventy-five years before Origen's time. In this there are passages referring to some of the Gnostics. If then we include Origen's work against *The True Word* of Celsus, we have mentioned all the Fathers who are of any real value for the indirect sources of Gnosticism in the first two centuries

Philaster, bishop of Brescia in Italy, Epiphanius, bishop of Salamis in Cyprus, and Jerome, fall about the last quarter of the fourth century, and are therefore (unless, of course, they quote from earlier writers) too late for accuracy with regard to the things of the first two centuries. Philaster, moreover, is generally put out of court owing to his overweening credulity; and the reliability of Epiphanius is often open to grave suspicion, owing to his great faculty of inventing or retailing scandals and all kinds of foulness.

Eusebius is fifty years earlier, but there is little to be gleaned from him on the subject, and his reputation for accuracy has been called into question by many independent historical critics.

Theodoret's Compendium, based on his predecessors and dating about the middle of the fifth century, is far too late to add to our knowledge of the first two centuries.

The study of these indirect documents has exercised the ingenuity of the critics and resulted in a marvellously clever feat of scholarship. Lipsius has demonstrated that Epiphanius, Philaster, and

Pseudo-Tertullian all draw from a common source, which was the lost Syntagma or Compendium of Hippolytus, consisting mainly of notes of the lectures of Irenæus; that is to say, in all probability, of the polemical tractates which the bishop read to his community, and on which he based his larger work. Thus reconstructing the lost document, he compares it with Irenæus, and infers for both a common authority, probably the lost Syntagma of Justin.

We thus see that our main source is Irenæus. The *Refutation* of Irenæus is the "store-house of Gnosticism"—according to the Fathers—for the first two centuries. Irenæus lived far away in the wilds of Gaul; is his evidence reliable? Setting aside the general presumption that no ecclesiastical writer at such a time could, in the nature of things, have been fair to the views of his opponents, which he perforce regarded as the direct product of the prince of all iniquity, we shall shortly see that fate has at length—only a few years ago—placed the final proof of this presumption in our hands.

But meantime let us turn our attention to our direct sources of imformation. We have now no less than three Codices containing Coptic translations of original Greek Gnostic works.

Direct Sources.

(i.) The Askew Codex, vellum, British Museum, London: containing the *Pistis Sophia* treatise and extracts from *The Books of the Saviour*.

(ii.) The Bruce Codex (consisting of two distinct MSS.), papyrus, Bodleian Library, Oxford: containing a series of lengthy fragments under the general title *The Book of the Great Logos according to the Mystery;* another treatise of great sublimity but without a title; and a fragment or fragments of yet another treatise.

(iii.) The Akhmīm Codex, papyrus, Egyptian Museum, Berlin: containing *The Gospel of Mary* (or *Apocryphon of John*), *The Wisdom of Jesus Christ*, and *The Acts of Peter*.

The Akhmīm Codex was only discovered in 1896. Prior to 1853, when the Askew Codex was translated into Latin, nothing of a practical nature was known of its contents, while the contents of the Bruce Codex were not known till 1891-1892, when translations appeared in French and German. We have to reflect on the indifference which allowed these important documents to remain, in the one case (Cod. Ask.) for eighty years without translation, and in the other (Cod. Bruc.) one hundred and twenty years! The first attempt at translation in English appeared only in 1896 in my version of *Pistis Sophia*.

It will thus be seen that the study of Gnosticism from direct sources is quite recent, and that all but the most recent research is out of date. This new view is all the more forced upon us by the latest discovery which in the Akhmīm MS. places in our hands the means of testing the accuracy of Irenæus, the sheet-anchor of hæresiologists. *The Gospel of Mary* is one of the original sources that Irenæus used. We are now enabled in one case to control the Church Father point by point—and find that he has so condensed and paraphrased his original that the consistent system of the school of Gnosticism which he is endeavouring to refute, appears as an incomprehensible jumble.

This recent activity among specialists in Gnostic research, at a time when a widespread interest in a revival of theosophic studies has prepared the way for a reconsideration of Gnosticism from a totally different standpoint to that of pure criticism or refutation, is a curious coincidence.

From the above considerations it is evident that so far are the Gnostics and their ideas from being buried in that oblivion which their opponents have so fervently desired and so busily striven to ensure, that now at the opening of the twentieth century, at a time when Biblical criticism is working with the reincarnated energy and independence of a Marcion, the memory of these universalizers of Christianity is coming once more to the front and occupying the attention of earnest students of religion.

In addition to these indirect and direct sources there is also another source that may yield us some valuable information, when submitted to the searching of an enlightened criticism. The legends and traditions preserved in the Gnostic *Acts* deserve closer attention than they have hitherto received, as we shall hope to show in the sequel by quotations from several of them.

THE GNOSIS ACCORDING TO
ITS FOES.

Oh that mine adversary had written a book!

Job (according to the Authorised Version).

SOME GNOSTIC FRAGMENTS RECOVERED FROM THE POLEMICAL WRITINGS OF THE CHURCH FATHERS.

WE shall now proceed to introduce the reader to the chief teachers and schools of Gnosticism, as far as they are known to us from the polemical writings of the Church Fathers. Unfortunately we are not in a position to present the student with a satisfactory classification of the Gnostic schools; every classification previously attempted has completely broken down, and in the present state of our knowledge we must be content to sift the different phases of development out of the heap as best we can. Clement of Alexandria, at the end of the second century, tried the rough expedient of dividing these schools of Christendom into ascetic and licentious sects; Neander at the beginning of the present century endeavoured to classify them by their friendly or unfriendly relations to Judaism; Baur followed with an attempt which took into consideration not

No Classification Possible.

only how they regarded Judaism, but also their attitude to Heathenism; Matter adopted a geographical distribution into the schools of Syria, Asia Minor, and Egypt; and Lipsius followed with a more general division into the Gnosticism of Syria and of Alexandria.

All these classifications break down on many important points; and we are thus compelled to follow the imperfect indications of the earliest Patristic hæresiologists, who vaguely and uncritically ascribed the origin of Gnosticism to "Simon Magus." It is, however, certain that the origin of Gnostic ideas, so far from being simple and traceable to an individual, was of a most complex nature; some have thought that it has to be sought for along the line of so-called "Ophitism," which is a general term among the hæresiologists for almost everything they cannot ascribe to a particular teacher. But the medley of schools and tendencies which the Fathers indiscriminately jumble together as Ophite, contains the most heterogeneous elements, good and bad. The name Ophite, or "serpent-worshipper," is simply a term of abuse used solely by the refutators, while the adherents of these schools called themselves generally "Gnostics," and were apparently the first to use the term.

We shall, therefore, first of all follow the so-called "Simonian" line of descent until the first quarter of the second century; then plunge into the indefinite chaos of the "Gnostics"; next retrace our steps along a Gnostic phase of the Ebionite tradition; and finally treat of the most brilliant epoch of Gnosticism known to us—when Basilides, Valentinus, and Bardesanes lived and worked and thought, and Marcion amazed infant orthodoxy with a "higher criticism" which for boldness has perhaps not yet been equalled even in our own day. It was an epoch which gave birth to works of such excellence that, in the words of Dr. Carl Schmidt (in the Introduction to his edition of the Codex Brucianus), "we stand amazed, marvelling at the boldness of the speculations, dazzled by the richness of thought, touched by the depth of soul of the author"—"a period when Gnostic genius like a mighty eagle left the world behind it, and soared in wide and ever wider circles towards pure light, towards pure knowledge, in which it lost itself in ecstasy."

We should, however, in studying the lives and teachings of these Gnostics always bear in mind that our only sources of information have hitherto been the caricatures of the hæresiologists, and remember that only the points which seemed fantastic to the refutators were selected, and then exaggerated by every art of hostile criticism; the ethical and general teachings which provided no such points, were almost invariably passed over. It is, therefore, impossible to obtain anything but a most distorted portrait of men whose greatest sin was that they were centuries before their time. It should further be remembered, that the term "heresy" in the first two centuries, did not generally connote the narrow meaning assigned to it later on. It was simply the usual term for a school of philosophy; thus we read of the heresy of Plato, of Zeno, of Aristotle. The Gnostics, and the rest of Christendom also, were thus divided into a number of schools or "heresies," which in those early times were more or less of equal dignity and authenticity.

THE "SIMONIANS."

The Origin of the Name.

THERE is no reason to suppose that the Gnostics whom the Church Fathers call "Simonians" would have themselves answered to the name, or have recognized the line of descent imagined for them by their opponents as founded on any basis in fact. As early as Justin Martyr (c. 150 A.D.), "Simon" assumed a prominence out of all proportion to his place in history. Evidently Justin regarded him with great detestation, and accused the Romans of worshipping him as a god, on the strength of an inscription on a statue at Rome. Justin gives the inscription as "*Simoni Deo Sancto*"—"To Simon, the holy God." But (alas! for the reputation of Justin's accuracy when engaged in controversy) archæology has discovered the statue—and finds it dedicated to a Sabine deity, "Semo Sancus"! Justin's assertion, however, was received without question by subsequent hæresiologists, as all such assertions were in that uncritical age.

Now it is very probable that Justin, in his innumerable controversies in defence of his particular view of Christianity, was met with some argument in which Simon was quoted as an example. It may have been that Justin argued that the miracles of Jesus proved all that Justin claimed on His behalf, and was met by the counter-argument that Simon also was a great wonder-worker, and made great claims, so that miracles did not prove Justin's contentions. Thus it may have been that Justin grew to detest the memory of Simon, and saw him and his supporters everywhere, even at Rome in a statue to a Sabine godling.

It may well have been that some wonder-worker called Simon may have astonished people in Samaria with his psychological tricks, and that stories were still in Justin's time told of him among the people. But what did most to stereotype the legend that Simon was the first heretic, was the insertion of his name in one of the stories included in the subsequently canonical *Acts of the Apostles*. This took place later than Justin, and so we have the first moments in the evolution of the legend of the origin of heresy (and therefore, according to the Fathers, of Gnosticism). What then is told us about "Simon" and the "Simonians," is only of interest for a recovery of some of the ideas which the subsequently Catholic party was striving to controvert; it has no value as history.

DOSITHEUS.

A Follower of John the Baptist.

The legendary background of the Pseudo-Clementine polemic informs us that the precursor of "Simon Magus" was a certain Dositheus. He is mentioned in the lists of the earliest hæresiologists, in a Samaritan Chronicle, and in the Chronicle of Aboulfatah (fourteenth century); the notices, however, are all legendary, and nothing of a really reliable character can be asserted of the man. That however he was not an unimportant personage is evidenced by the persistence of the sect of the Dositheans to the sixth century; Aboulfatah says even to the fourteenth. Both Dositheus and "Simon Magus" were, according to tradition, followers of John the Baptist; they were, however, said to be inimical to Jesus. Dositheus is said to have claimed to be the promised prophet, "like unto Moses," and "Simon" to have made a still higher claim. In fact, like so many others in those days, both were claimants to the Messiahship. The Dositheans followed a mode of life closely resembling that of the Essenes; they had also their own secret volumes, and apparently a not inconsiderable literature.

Dositheus (Dousis, Dusis, or Dosthai) was apparently an Arab, and in Arabia, we have every reason to believe, there were many mystic communities allied to those of the Essenes and Therapeuts. One of the Gospels used by Justin, under the general title "Memoirs of the Apostles," states that the "wise men" came from Arabia. One legend even claims Dositheus as the founder of the sect of the Sadducees! Later tradition assigned to him a group of thirty disciples, or to be more precise twenty-nine and a-half (the number of days in a month), one of them being a woman. That is to say, the system of Dositheus turned on a lunar basis, just as subsequent systems ascribed to Jesus turned on a solar basis, the twelve disciples typifying the solar months or zodiacal signs, or rather certain facts of the wisdom-tradition which underlie that symbolism. Dositheus is said to have claimed to be a manifestation of the "Standing One" or unchanging principle, the name also ascribed to the supreme principle of the "Simonians." The one female disciple was Helena (the name of the moon or month, Selēnē, in Greek), who appears also in the legend of Simon.

On the dim screen of Dosithean tradition we can thus see shadows passing of the sources of a pre-Christian Gnosis — Arab, Phœnician, Syrian, Babylonian shadows. More interesting still, we can thus, perhaps, point to a source to which may be traced, along another line of descent, the subsequent thirty æons of the Valentinian plērōma or ideal world, with the divided thirtieth, Sophia (within and without, above and below), the lower aspect of which constituted the World-soul or the primordial substance of a world-system.

The Pre-Christian Gnosis.

It is also to be observed that Aboulfatah places Dositheus 100 years B.C. Of course only very qualified credence can be given to this late chronicler, but still it is possible that he may have drawn from sources no longer accessible to us. The statement is interesting as showing that the chronicler recognized the fact of a pre-Christian Gnosis; though how he reconciles this John the Baptist date with the orthodox chronology is a puzzle. Can he have been influenced by the Talmudic tradition of the date of Jesus, which places him a century prior to our era? Together with Dositheus and "Simon," Hegesippus (according to Eusebius) also mentions Cleobius, Gorthæus, and Masbotheus as prominent leaders of primitive Christian schools.

"SIMON MAGUS."

"SIMON MAGUS," as we have already said, is mentioned in the *Acts of the Apostles*, a document of the New Testament collection, said not to be quoted prior to 177 A.D. Irenæus and his successors repeat the *Acts* legend. Justin Martyr (*c.* 150) speaks of a certain Simon of Gitta whom nearly all the Samaritans regarded with the greatest reverence; this Simon, he said, claimed to be an incarnation of the "Great Power," and had many followers. Justin, however, makes no reference to the *Acts* story, and so some have assumed two Simons, but this does not seem to be necessary. The Justin account is the nucleus of the huge Simonian legend which was mainly developed by the cycle of Pseudo-Clementine literature of the third century, based on the second century *Circuits of Peter*.

Hippolytus alone, at the beginning of the third

century, has preserved a few scraps from the extensive literature of the "Simonians"; the bishop of Portus quotes from a work entitled *The Great Announcement*, and so we are able to form some idea of one of the systems of these Gnostics. The scheme of the Gnosis contained in this document, so far from presenting a crude form, or mere germ, of Gnostic doctrine, hands on to us a highly developed phase of Gnostic tradition, which, though not so elaborated as the Valentinian system, nevertheless is almost as mature as the Barbēlō scheme, referred to so cursorily by Irenæus, and now partly recovered in the newly-discovered *Gospel of Mary*.

In the earliest times to which Catholic Christians subsequently traced the origin of their traditions, there were, as we know from various sources, numerous movements in and about Palestine of a prophetical and reformatory nature, many prophets and teachers of ethical, mystical, religio-philosophical, and Gnostic doctrines. The Ebionite communities found themselves in conflict with the followers of these teachers on many points, and Ebionite tradition handed on a garbled account of these doctrinal conflicts. Above all things, the Ebionites were in bitterest strife with the Pauline churches. Later on General Christianity set itself to work to reconcile the Petrine and Pauline differences, principally by the *Acts* document; and in course of time Ebionite tradition was also edited by the light of the new view, and the name of Simon substituted for the great "heretic" with whom the Ebionites had striven.

The Ebionite "Simon."

And so the modified Ebionite tradition, which was

presumably first committed to writing in the *Circuits of Peter*, gradually evolved a romance, in which the conflicts between Simon Peter the Ebionite, and Simon the Magician, are graphically pourtrayed, the magical arts of the Samaritan are foiled, and his false theology is exposed, by the doughty champion of the "Poor Men." The latest recension of this cycle of romance gave the whole a Roman setting, and so we find Simon finally routed by Peter at Rome (to suit the legend of the Roman Church that Peter had come to Rome), but in earlier recensions Peter does not travel beyond the East, and Simon is finally routed at Antioch.

A close inspection of the Pseudo-Clementine literature reveals a number of literary deposits or strata of legend, one of which is of a very remarkable nature. Baur was the first to point this out, and his followers in the Tübingen school elaborated his views into the theory that Simon Magus is simply the legendary symbol for Paul. The remarkable similarity of the doctrinal points at issue in both the Petro-Simonian and Petro-Pauline controversies cannot be denied, and the scholarly reputation of the Tübingen school puts out of court mere *à priori* impossibility. Although, of course, it would not be prudent to take the extreme view that wherever Simon Magus is mentioned, Paul is meant, nevertheless we may not unclearly distinguish this identity in at least one of the strata of the legend.

The "Simonian" systems, as described by the Fathers, reveal the main features of the Gnosis: the Father over all, the Logos-idea, the æon-world, or ideal universe, its emanation, and its positive and negative aspects represented as pairs or syzygies; the world-soul represented as the thought or female aspect of the Logos; the descent of the soul; the creation of the sensible world by the builders; the doctrines of reincarnation, redemption, etc.

The Simonian Literature.

The main characteristic of the "Simonians" is said to have been the practice of "magic," which "Simon" is reported to have learned in Egypt, and which gave rise to most of the fantastic stories invented by their opponents. But it is very probable that the title Magus covers much more than the story of the Samaritan wonder-worker, and puts us in touch with a Gnostic link with Persia and the Magi; and indeed the fire-symbolism used in the MS. quoted from by Hippolytus amply confirms this hypothesis.

In other respects the "Simonian" Gnosis was on similar lines to the Barbēlō-Gnostic and Basilido-Valentinian developments; this is to be clearly seen in the fragments of *The Great Announcement* preserved by Hippolytus.

The rest of the "Simonian" literature has perished; one of their chief documents, however, was a book called *The Four Quarters of the World*, and another famous treatise contained a number of controversial points *(Refutatorii Sermones)* ascribed to "Simon," which submitted the idea of the God of the Old Testament to a searching criticism, especially dealing with the serpent-legend in Genesis.

The main symbolism, which the evolvers of the

Simon-legend parodied into the myth of Simon and Helen, appears to have been sidereal; thus the Logos and his Thought, the World-soul, were symbolized as the Sun (Simon) and Moon (Selēnē, Helen); so with the microcosm, Helen was the human soul fallen into matter and Simon the mind which brings about her redemption. Moreover one of the systems appears to have attempted to interpret the Trojan legend and myth of Helen in a spiritual and psychological fashion.

This is interesting as showing an attempt to invoke the authority of the popular Greek "Bible," the cycle of Homeric legend, in support of Gnostic ideas. It was the extension of the method of the Jewish allegorizers into the domain of Greek mythology.

The detractors of the "Simonians," among the Church Fathers, however, evolved the legend, that Helen was a prostitute whom Simon had picked up at Tyre. The name of this city presumably led Baur to suggest that the Simon (שמש, Sun) and Helen (Σελήνη, Moon) terminology is connected with the Phœnician cult of the sun and moon deities which was still practised in that ancient city. Doubtless the old Phœnician and Syrian ideas of cosmogony were familiar to many students of religion at that period, but we need not be too precise in matters so obscure.

The "Simonian" System of Irenæus.

Irenæus gives the following outline of the system he ascribes to the "Simonians." It is the dramatic myth of the Logos and the World-soul, the Sophia, or Wisdom. Irenæus, however, would have it that it was the personal claim of Simon concerning

Helen; he evidently bases himself on a MS. in which the Christ, as the Logos, is represented as speaking in the first person, and we shall therefore endeavour to restore it partially to its original form.

"'Wisdom was the first Conception (or Thought) of My Mind, the Mother of All, by whom in the beginning I conceived in My Mind the making of the Angels and Archangels. This Thought leaping forth from Me, and knowing what was the will of her Father, descended to the lower regions and generated the Angels and Powers, by whom also the world was made. And after she had generated them, she was detained by them through envy, for they did not wish to be thought the progeny of any other. As for Myself, I am entirely unknown to them.'

"And Thought," continues Irenæus, summarising from the MS., "was made prisoner by the Powers and Angels that had been emanated by her. And she suffered every kind of indignity at their hands, to prevent her reascending to her Father, even to being imprisoned in the human body and transmigrating into other female [?] bodies, as from one vessel into another. . . . So she, transmigrating from body to body, and thereby also continually undergoing indignity, last of all even stood for hire in a brothel; and she was the 'lost sheep.'

"'Wherefore, also, am I come to take her away for the first time, and free her from her bonds; to make sure salvation to men by My Gnosis.'

"For as the Angels," writes the Church Father,

"were mismanaging the world, since each of them desired the sovereignty, He had come to set matters right; and He had descended, tranforming Himself and being made like to the Powers and Principalities and Angels; so that He appeared to men as a man, although He was not a man; and was thought to have suffered in Judæa, although He did not really suffer. The prophets, moreover, had spoken their prophecies under the inspiration of the Angels who made the world."

All of these doctrines proceeded from circles who believed in the mystical Christ, and are common to many other systems; if Irenæus had only told us the history of the document which he was summarizing and glossing, if he had but copied it verbally, how much labour would he have saved posterity! True, he may have been copying from Justin's controversial writings, and Justin had already done some of the summarizing and commenting; but in any case a single paragraph of the original would have given us a better ground on which to form a judgment than all the paraphrazing and rhetoric of these two ancient worthies who so cordially detested the Gnostics.

The Great Announcement. Fortunately Hippolytus, who came later, is more correct in his quotations, and occasionally copies verbally portions of the MSS. which had come into his hands. One of these he erroneously attributes to "Simon" himself, presumably because he considered it the oldest Gnostic MS. in his possession; most critics, however, consider it a later form of the Gnosis than the system summarized by Irenæus, but there is nothing to warrant this assumption. By this time the legend that "Simon" was the first heretic had become "history" for the hæresiologists, and no doubt Hippolytus felt himself fully justified in ascribing the contents of the MS. to one whom he supposed to be the oldest leader of the Gnosis.

The title of the MS. was *The Great Announcement*, probably a synonym for The Gospel, in the Basilidian sense of the term; and it opened with the following words: "This is the Writing of the Revelation of Voice-and-Name from Thought, the Great Power, the Boundless. Wherefore shall it be sealed, hidden, concealed, laid in the Dwelling of which the Universal Root is the Foundation."

The Dwelling is said to be man, the temple of the Holy Spirit. The symbol of the Boundless Power and Universal Root was Fire. Fire was conceived as being of a twofold nature—the concealed and the manifested; the concealed parts of the Fire are hidden in the manifested, and the manifested produced by the concealed. The manifested side of the Fire has all things in itself which a man can perceive of things visible, or which he unconsciously fails to perceive; whereas the concealed side is everything which one can conceive as intelligible, even though it escape sensation, or which a man fails to conceive.

The Hidden Fire.

Before we come to the direct quotation, however, Hippolytus treats us to a lengthy summary of the Gnostic exposition before him, from which we may take the following as representing the thought of the writer of the MS. less erroneously than the rest.

"Of all things that are concealed and manifested,

The Fire Tree. the Fire which is above the heavens is the treasure-house, as it were a great Tree from which all flesh is nourished. The manifested side of the Fire is the trunk, branches, leaves, and the outside bark. All these parts of the great Tree are set on fire from the all-devouring flame of the Fire and destroyed. But the fruit of the Tree, if its imaging has been perfected and it takes shape of itself, is placed in the store-house (or treasure), and not cast into the Fire. For the fruit is produced to be placed in the store-house, but the husk to be committed to the Fire; that is to say, the trunk, which is generated not for its own sake but for that of the fruit."

This symbolism is of great interest as revealing points of contact with the " Trees " and " Treasures " of the elaborate systems recoverable from the Coptic Gnostic works, and also with the line of tradition of the Chaldæan and Zoroastrian Logia, which were the favourite study of so many of the later Platonic school. The fruit of the Fire-tree and the " Flower of Fire " are the symbols of (among other things) the man immortal, the garnered spiritual consciousness of the man-plant; but the full interpretation of this graphic symbolism would include both the genesis of the cosmos and the divinizing of man.

Man (teaches the Gnosis we are endeavouring to recover from Hippolytus) is subject to generation and suffering so long as he remains in potentiality; but, once that his " imaging forth " is accomplished, he becomes like unto God, and, freed from the bonds of suffering and birth, he attains perfection. But to our quotation from *The Great Announcement*, taken apparently from the very beginning of the treatise, immediately following the superscription:

"To you, therefore, I say what I say, and write what I write. And the writing is this:

"Of the universal Æons there are two growths, without beginning or end, springing from one Root, which is the Power Silence invisible, inapprehensible. Of these one appears from above, which is the Great Power, the Universal Mind, ordering all things, male; and the other from below, the Great Thought (or Conception), female, producing all things.

The Æons.

"Hence matching each other, they unite and manifest the Middle Space, incomprehensible Air [Spirit], without beginning or end. In this [Air] is the [second] Father who sustains and nourishes all things which have beginning and end.

"This [Father] is He who has stood, stands and will stand, a male-female power, like the pre-existing Boundless Power, which has neither beginning nor end, existing in oneness. It was from this Boundless Power that Thought, which had previously been hidden in oneness, first proceeded and became twain.

"He [the Boundless] was one; having her in Himself, He was alone. Yet was He not 'first,' though 'pre-existing,' for it was only when He was manifested to Himself from Himself that there was a 'second.' Nor was He called Father before [Thought] called Him Father.

"As, therefore, producing Himself by Himself, He manifested to Himself His own Thought, so also His manifested Thought did not make the [manifested—the second] Father, but contemplating Him hid him—that is, His power—in herself and is male-female, Power and Thought.

"Hence they match each other, being one; for there is no difference between Power and Thought. From the things above is discovered Power, and from those below Thought.

"Thus it comes to pass that that which is manifested from them, though one, is found to be two, male-female, having the female in itself. Equally so is Mind in Thought; they really are one, but when separated from each other they appear as two."

So much for *The Great Announcement* of "Simon." That some document may yet be discovered which will throw fresh light on the subject is not an impossibility; in the meantime we can reserve our judgment, and regard all positive statements that "Simon" was the "first-born son of Satan" as foreign to the question.

MENANDER.

ONE of the teachers of the "Simonian" Gnosis who was singled out by Justin for special mention, because of his having led "many" away, even as Marcion was gaining an enormous following in Justin's own time, is Menander, a native, we are told, of the Samaritan town Capparatea. The notice in Justin shows us that Menander was a man of a past generation, and that he was specially famous because of his numerous following. We know that the dates of this period are exceedingly obscure even for Justin, our earliest authority. For instance, writing about 150 A.D., he says that Jesus lived 150 years before his time. His "Simon" and Menander dates are equally vague; Menander may have lived a generation or four generations before Justin's time, or still earlier.

His Date.

The centre of activity of Menander is said to have been at Antioch, one of the most important commercial and literary cities of the Græco-Roman world, on the highway of communication between East and West. He seems to have handed on the general outlines of the Gnosis; especially insisting on the distinction between the God over all and the creative power or powers, the "forces of nature." Wisdom, he taught, was to be attained by the practical discipline of transcendental "magic"; that is to say, the Gnosis was not to be attained by faith alone, but by definite endeavour and conscious striving along the path of cosmological and psychological science. Menander professed to teach a knowledge of the powers of

His Doctrines.

nature, and the way whereby they could be subjected to the purified human will; he is also said to have claimed to be the Saviour sent down by the higher Powers of the spiritual world, to teach men the sacred knowledge whereby they could free themselves from the dominion of the lower Angels.

It is, however, almost certain that Menander made no more claim to be the Saviour (in the Catholic meaning of the term) than did "Simon." The Saviour was the Logos, as we have seen above. The claim of the Gnostics was that a man might so perfect himself that he became a conscious worker with the Logos; all those who did so, became "Christs," and as such were Saviours, but not in the sense of being the Logos Himself.

The neophyte on receiving "baptism," that is to say, on reaching a certain state of interior purification or enlightenment, was said to "rise from the dead"; thereafter, he "never grew old and became immortal," that is to say, he obtained possession of the unbroken consciousness of his spiritual ego. Menander was especially opposed to the materialistic doctrine of the resurrection of the body, and this was made a special ground of complaint against him by the Patristic writers of the subsequent centuries.

The followers of Menander were called Menandrists, and we can only regret that no record has been left of them and their writings. As they seem to have been centralized at Antioch—seeing that tradition assigns the founding of the Church of Antioch to Paul, and assigns to it Peter as its first bishop; seeing again that the "withstanding to the face" incident is placed by the *Acts* tradition in the same city—it may be that their writings would have thrown some light on these obscure traditions.

I would, however, suggest that Mainandros should be placed far earlier than "Simon," and that we should see in him one of the earliest links between Gnosticism and the Magian tradition. It may be even that the Gnostics traced the tradition of their æon-lore to this disciple of the Magi, for the root of their æonology is to be found in the Zoroastrian Amshaspends, the personal emanations of Ahuramazda, as Mills and others have shown; though I myself would seek the origin of the æon-doctrine in Egypt.

A Link with Zoroastrianism.

SATURNINUS.

SATURNINUS, or more correctly Satornilus, is generally regarded as the founder of the Syrian Gnosis, but there is every reason to suppose that Gnosticism was widespread in Syria prior to his time. Justin Martyr (*Trypho*, xxxv.), writing between 150 and 160, speaks of the Satornilians as a very important body, for he brackets them with the Marcians (? Marcionites), Basilidians and Valentinians, the most important schools of the Gnosis in his time. Saturninus, Basilides and Valentinus were separated from each other respectively by at least a generation, and Saturninus may thus be placed somewhere about the end of the first and the beginning of the second century; but this assignment of date rests entirely upon the Patristic statements that Menander was the

The Chain of Teachers.

teacher of Saturninus, Saturninus of Basilides, and Basilides of Valentinus. It is, however, not improbable that, with regard to the first two, a general similarity of doctrine alone was sufficient reason for the hæresiologists to father the origin of Saturninus' system upon Menander himself, whereas in reality a generation or two may have elapsed between them, and they may have never as a matter of fact met face to face.

Asceticism. Saturninus is said to have taught at Antioch, but (as is almost the invariable case with the Gnostic doctors) we have no information as to his nationality or the incidents of his life. He was especially distinguished for his rigid asceticism, or encratism. His followers abstained from marriage and from animal food of all kinds, and the rigidity of their mode of life attracted many zealous adherents. Salmon says that Saturninus seems to have been the first to have introduced encratism "among those who called themselves Christians." Protestant theologians especially regard encratism as a heretical practice; but there seems no sufficient reason for assuming that so common a feature of the religious life can be traced to any particular teacher.

Summary of Doctrines. Our information as to the Saturninian system is unfortunately exceedingly defective; the short summary of Irenæus is presumably based on, or a copy of, the lost Compendium of Justin. This is all the more regrettable as fuller information would have probably enabled us to trace its connection with the "Ophite" and "Barbēlō" developments, and to define the relations of all three to the Gnosticism of Basilides and Valentinus. The main features are of the same nature as those of the "Simonian" and Menandrian Gnosis; we should, however, always bear in mind that these early systems, instead of being germinal, or simple expressions, may have been elaborate enough. The mere fact that Irenæus gives a summary which presents comparatively simple features, is no guarantee that the systems themselves may not have been full and carefully worked out expositions. We may with safety regard the summary of the bishop of Lyons as a rough indication of heads of docrine, as a catalogue of subjects deprived of their content. Thus we learn that Saturninus taught the Unknown Father; the great intermediate hierarchies, archangels, angels, and powers; the seven creative spheres and their rulers; the builders of the universe and the fashioners of man. There were numerous inimical hierarchies and their rulers, and a scheme of regeneration whereby a World-saviour in the apparent form of man, though not really a man, brings about not only the defeat of the evil powers, but also rescues all who have the light-spark within them, from the powers of the creative hierarchies, among whom was placed the Yahweh of the Jews. The Jewish scriptures were imperfect and erroneous; some prophecies being inspired by the creative angels, but others by the evil powers.

The most interesting feature of the system which Irenæus has preserved for us, is the myth of the creation of man by the angels, or rather the fabrication of man's external envelope by the hierarchies of the builders.

The Making of Man.
The making of man was on this wise. A shining image or type was shown by the Logos to the demiurgic angels; but when they were unable to seize hold upon it, for it was withdrawn immediately, they said to one another: "Let us make man according to [this] image and likeness." They accordingly endeavoured to do so, but the nature-powers could only evolve an envelope or plasm, which could not stand upright, but lay on the ground helpless and crawling like a worm. Then the Power Above, in compassion, sent forth the life-spark, and the plasm rose upright, and limbs developed and were knit together, that is to say, it hardened or became denser as race succeeded race; and so the body of man was evolved, and the light-spark, or real man, tabernacled in it. This light-spark hastens back after death to those of its own nature, and the rest of the elements of the body are dissolved.

Here we have in rough suggestion the same theory of the evolution of the bodies of the early races as we find advanced, from totally different sources and an entirely different standpoint, by a number of modern writers on theosophic doctrines—and, therefore, we all the more regret that the orthodox prejudices of Irenæus or his informant have treated Saturninus and his "heresy" with so scant notice.

THE "OPHITES."

THE task we have now to attempt is by far the most difficult which can be undertaken by the student of Patristic Gnosticism. When we have the name of an individual teacher to guide us, there is at least a point round which certain ideas and statements may be grouped; but when we have no such indications, but only scraps of information, or summaries of "some say" and "others maintain," as in Irenæus; or vague designations of widespread schools of various periods, as in Hippolytus; when further we reflect that among such surroundings we are face to face with one of the main streams of evolving Gnosticism, and realize the complete absence of any definite landmarks, where all should have been carefully surveyed—a feeling almost of despair comes over even the most enthusiastic student.

The Obscurity of the Subject.

It has been supposed that up to the time of Irenæus Gnostic documents were freely circulated; but that by the time of Hippolytus (that is to say, after the lapse of a generation or more) orthodoxy had made such headway that the Gnostic documents were withdrawn from circulation and hidden, and that this accounts for the glee of Hippolytus, who taunts the Gnostics with his possession of some of their secret MSS. I am, however, convinced that the most recondite and technical treatises of the Gnostics were never circulated; the adherents of the Gnosis were too much imbued with the idea of a "secret doctrine" and grades of initiation to blazon their inner tenets forth on the house-tops.

Also I doubt exceedingly whether these intertwined schools and phases of doctrine were separated from one another in any very precise fashion, or that the Basilidians, Valentinians, and the rest, distinguished themselves by such designations. Gnosticism was a living thing, no crystallized system or dead orthodoxy; each competent student thought out the main features of the Gnosis in his own fashion, and generally phrased it in his own terms.

In treating this part of our essay also another difficulty presents itself; we are writing for those who are presumably but slightly acquainted with the subject, and who would only be confused by a mass of details. It is, however, precisely these details which are of interest and importance, and therefore a summary must at best be exceedingly imperfect and liable to misconstruction. We have thus to set up our finger-posts as best we may.

The Term "Ophite." As stated above, the term "Ophite" is exceedingly erroneous; it does not generally describe the schools of which we are treating; it was not used by the adherents of the schools themselves, who mostly preferred the term Gnostic; even where the symbolism of the serpent enters into the exposition of their systems, it is by no means the characteristic feature. In brief, this term, which originated in the fallacy of taking a very small part for the whole—a favourite trick of the hæresiologist, whose main weapon was to exaggerate a minor detail into a main characteristic—has been used as a vague designation for all exposition of Gnostic doctrine which could not be ascribed to a definite teacher. It is in this foundling asylum, so to say, that we must look for the general outlines which form the basis of the teachings of even Basilides and Valentinus, each of whom, like the rest of the Gnostics, modified the general tradition in his own peculiar fashion.

This "Ophite" Gnosticism is said by Philaster to be pre-Christian; Irenæus, after detailing a system, which Theodoret when copying from him calls "Ophite," says that it was from the Valentinian school. Celsus, the Pagan philosopher, in his *True Word*, writing about the third quarter of the second century, makes no distinction between the rest of the Christian world and those whom Origen, almost a century afterwards, in his refutation of Celsus, calls "Ophiani."

The latest criticism is of opinion that Philaster has blundered, but the statement is sufficient evidence that there was *a* body of pre-Christian Gnosis, that the stream flowed unbrokenly and in ever-increasing volume during the first two centuries, and that the erroneous designation "Ophite" still marks out one of its main channels.

The serpent-symbol played a great part in the Mysteries of the ancients, especially in Greece, Egypt, and Phœnicia; thence we can trace it back to Syria, Babylonia, and farther East to India, where it still survives and receives due explanation. It figured forth the most intimate processes of the generation of the universe and of man, and also of the mystic birth. It was the glyph of the creative power, and in its

[The Serpent Symbol.]

lowest form was debased into a phallic emblem. Physical procreation and the processes of conception are lower manifestations of the energizing of the great creative will and the evolutionary world-process. But the one is as far removed from the other, as man's body is from the body of the universe, as man's animal desire from the divine will of deity.

The mysteries of sex were explained in the adyta of the ancient temples; and naturally enough the attempt to get behind the great passion of mankind was fraught with the greatest peril. A knowledge of the mystery led many to asceticism; a mere curious prying into the matter led to abuse. Illumination, seership, and spiritual knowledge, were the reward of the pure in body and mind; sexual excess and depravity punished the prying of the unfit. This explains one of the most curious phenomena in religious history; the bright and dark sides are almost invariably found together; whenever an attempt is made to shed some light on the mystery of the world and of man, the whole nature is quickened, and if the animal is the stronger, it becomes all the more uncontrolled owing to the quickening. Thus we find that some obscure groups of dabblers in the mystery-tradition fell into grave errors, not only of theory but of practice, and that Patristic writers of the subsequent centuries tried by every means to exaggerate this particular into a general charge against "error"; whereas, as a matter of fact, it is in the writings of the Gnostics themselves that we find the severest condemnation of such abuses.

As man was generated in the womb from a "serpent" and an "egg," so was the universe; but the serpent of the universe was the Great Power, the Mighty Whirlwind, the Vast Vortex, and the egg was the All-Envelope of the world system, the primordial "fire-mist." The serpent was thus the glyph of the Divine Will, the Divine Reason, the Mind of Deity, the Logos. The egg was the Thought, the Conception, the Mother of All. The germinal universe was figured as a circle with a serpent lying diagonally along its field, or twined a certain number of times round it. This serpentine force fashioned the universe, and fashioned man. It created him; and yet he in his turn could use it for creation, if he would only cease from generation. The Caduceus, or Rod of Mercury, and the Thyrsus in the Greek Mysteries, which conducted the soul from life to death, and from death to life, figured forth the serpentine power in man, and the path whereby it would carry the "man" aloft to the height, if he would but cause the "Waters of the Jordan" to "flow upwards."

The serpent of *Genesis*, the serpent-rod of Moses, and the uplifting of the brazen serpent in the wilderness, were promptly seized upon by Jewish Gnostics as mythological ideas similar to the myths of the Mysteries. To give the reader an insight into their methods of mystical exegesis, which looked to an inner psychological science, we may here append their interpretation of what may be called "The Myth of the Going-forth."

The Myth was common to a number of schools, but Hippolytus ascribes it to an otherwise unknown

The Myth of the Going-forth.

school called the Peratæ, supposed to mean Transcendentalists, or those who by means of the Gnosis had "passed beyond" or "crossed over." Thus then they explained the Exodus-myth. Egypt is the body; all those who identify themselves with the body are the ignorant, the Egyptians. To "come forth" out of Egypt is to leave the body; and to pass through the Red Sea is to cross over the ocean of generation, the animal and sensual nature, which is hidden within the blood. Yet even then they are not safe; crossing the Red Sea they enter the Desert, the intermediate state of the doubting lower mind. There they are attacked by the "gods of destruction," which Moses called the "serpents of the desert," and which plague those who seek to escape from the "gods of generation." To them Moses, the teacher, shows the true serpent crucified on the cross of matter, and by its means they escape from the Desert and enter the Promised Land, the realm of the spiritual mind, where there is the Heavenly Jordan, the World-soul. When the Waters of the Jordan flow downwards, then is the generation of men; but when they flow upward, then is the creation of the gods. Jesus (Joshua) was one who had caused the Waters of the Jordan to flow upwards.

Many of the ancient myths had a historico-legendary background, but their use as myths, or religious and mystic romances, had gradually effaced the traces of history. Those instructed in the Mysteries were practised in the science of mythology, and thus the learned Gnostics at once perceived the mythological nature of the Exodus and its adaptability to a mystical interpretation. The above instance is a very good example of this method of exegesis; a great deal of such interpretation, however, was exceedingly strained, when not decidedly silly. The religious mind of the times loved to exercise its ingenuity on such interpretations, and the difference between Gnostic exegesis and that of the subsequent Orthodox, is that the former tried to discover soul-processes in the myths and parables of scripture, whereas the Orthodox regarded a theological and dogmatic interpretation as alone legitimate.

Judged by our present knowledge of language, the "silliest" element which entered into such pious pastimes was the method of word-play, or pseudo-philology, which is found everywhere in the writings of the Babylonians, Egyptians, Indians, Jews, and Greeks. Among the Gnostic and Patristic writers, therefore, we find the most fantastic derivations of names, which were put forward in support of theological doctrines, but which were destitute of the most rudimentary philological accuracy. Men, such as Plato, who in many other respects were giants of intellect, were content to resort to such methods. It is, however, pleasant to notice that the nature of the soul and the truths of the spiritual life were the chief interest for such ancient "philologists," and not the grubbing up of "roots"; nevertheless, we should be careful when detecting the limitation of such minds in certain directions, to guard against the error of closing our eyes to the limitations of

Pseudo-philology.

our own modern methods in directions where the ancients have done much good work.

We will now proceed to give a brief sketch of the main outlines of one of the presentations of general Gnostic ideas preserved by Irenæus.

AN ANONYMOUS SYSTEM FROM IRENÆUS.

The Spiritual Creation.

IN the Unutterable Depth were two Great Lights, the First Man, or Father, and his Son, the Second Man; and also the Holy Spirit, the First Woman, or Mother of all living. Below this triad was a sluggish mass composed of the four great "elements," called Water, Darkness, Abyss, and Chaos. The *Universal* Mother brooded over the Waters; enamoured of her beauty, the First and Second Man produced from her the third Great Light, the Christ; and He, ascending above, formed with the First and Second Man the Holy Church. This was the right-hand birth of the Great Mother. But a Drop of Light fell downwards to the left hand into chaotic matter; this was called Sophia, or Wisdom, the *World*-Mother. The Waters of the Æther were thus set in motion, and formed a body for Sophia (the Light-Æon), *viz.*, the Heaven-sphere. And she, freeing herself, left her body behind, and ascended to the Middle Region below her Mother (the *Universal* Mother), who formed the boundary of the Ideal Universe.

By her mere contact with the Space-Waters she had aleady generated a son, the chief Creative Power of the Sensible World, who retained some of the

ANONYMOUS SYSTEM FROM IRENÆUS. 189

Light-fluid; this son was Ialdabaōth (said by some to mean the Child of Chaos), who in his turn produced a son, and he another, until there were seven in all, the great Formative Powers of the Sensible Universe. And they were "fighters," and quarrelled much with their fathers. And by means of this interplay of forces on matter came forth the "mind," which was "serpent-formed," and "spirit," and "soul," and all things in the world.

And Ialdabaōth was boastful and arrogant, and exclaimed: "I am Father and God, and beyond me is none other." But Sophia hearing this cried out to her son: "Lie not, Ialdabaōth, for above thee is the Father of All, the First Man, and Man the Son of Man." And all the Powers were astonished at the word; but Ialdabaōth, to call off their attention, cried out: "Let us make 'man' after our image." So they made "man," and he lay like a worm on the ground, until they brought him to Ialdabaōth, who breathed into him the "breath of life," that is to say the Light-fluid he had received from Sophia, and so emptied himself of his Light. And "man" receiving it, immediately gave thanks to the First Man and disregarded his fabricators (the Elohīm). Yahweh Ialdabaōth.

Whereupon Ialdabaōth (Yahweh) was jealous and planned to deprive Adam of the Light-spark by forming "woman." And the six creative powers were enamoured of Eve, and by her generated sons, namely, the angels. And so Adam again fell under the power of Ialdabaōth and the Elohīm; then Sophia or Wisdom sent the "serpent" ("mind") into the Paradise of Ialdabaōth, and Adam and Eve O. T. Exegesis.

listened to its wise councils, and so once more "man" was freed from the dominion of the Creative Power, and transgressed the ordinance of ignorance of any power higher than himself imposed by Ialdabaōth. Whereupon Ialdabaōth drove them out of his Paradise, and together with them the "serpent" or "mind"; but Sophia would not permit the Light-spark to descend, and so withdrew it to avoid profanation. And "mind" (the lower mind) the serpent-formed, the first product of Ialdabaōth, brought forth six sons, and these are the "dæmonial" powers, which plague men because their father was cast down for their sake.

Now Adam and Eve before the fall had spiritual bodies, like the "angels" born of this Eve; but after their fall, down from the Paradise of Ialdabaōth, their bodies grew more and more dense, and more and more languid, and became "coats of skin," till finally Sophia in compassion restored to them the sweet odour of the Light, and they knew that they carried death about with them. And so a recollection of their former state came back to them, and they were patient, knowing that the body was put on only for a time.

The system then goes on to grapple with the legends of *Genesis* touching Cain and Noah, etc., and the Old Testament record generally, with moderate success; the main idea being that the prophets were inspired by one or other of the seven Elohīm, but occasionally Sophia had succeeded in impressing them with fragmentary revelations about the First Man and the Christ above.

ANONYMOUS SYSTEM FROM IRENÆUS.   191

The rest of the system is devoted to the question of the scheme of regeneration and the interpretation of the Mystery-myths. Sophia, or Wisdom, finding no rest in heaven or earth, implored the help of the Great Mother, and she in compassion begged of the First Man that the Christ should be sent to help her. And then Wisdom, knowing that her brother and spouse was coming to her aid, announced his coming by John, and by means of the "baptism of repentance" Jesus was made ready to receive him, as in a clean vessel. And so the Christ descended through the seven spheres, likening himself unto the Rulers, and draining them of their power, the Light they had retained all flowing back to him. And first of all the Christ clothed his sister Sophia with the Light-vesture, and they rejoiced together, and this is the mystical "marriage" of the "bridegroom and the bride." Now Jesus, having been born of a "virgin" by the working of God (in other words, after the spiritual "second birth" had been attained by the ascetic Jesus), Christ and Sophia, the one enfolding the other, descended upon him and he became Jesus Christ.

Christology.

Then it was that he began to do mighty works, to heal, and to proclaim the Unknown Father, and profess himself openly the Son of the First Man. Whereupon the Powers and especially Ialdabaôth took measures to slay him, and so Jesus, the man, was "crucified" by them, but Christ and Sophia mounted aloft to the Incorruptible Æon. But Christ did not forget the one in whom He had tabernacled, and so sent a power which raised up his body, not

Jesus.

indeed his gross physical envelope, but a psychic and spiritual body. And those of his disciples who saw this body, thought he was risen in his physical frame, but to certain of them who were capable of receiving it, he explained the mystery, and taught them many other mysteries of the spiritual life. And Jesus now sits at the right hand of his father, Ialdabaōth, and receives the souls who have received these mysteries. And in proportion as he enriches himself with souls, in such measure is Ialdabaōth deprived of power; so that he is no longer able to send back holy souls into the world of reincarnation, but only those of his own substance; and the consummation of all things will be when all the Light shall once more be gathered up and stored in the treasures of the Incorruptible Æon.

Such is the account of this by no means absurd scheme of the Gnosis preserved to us in the barbarous Latin translation of Irenæus' summary. That the original system was far more elaborate we may assume from the now known method of Irenæus to make a very brief summary of the tenets he criticized. The main features of the christological and soteriological part of the system is identical with the main outlines of the system of the *Pistis Sophia*, and of one of the treatises of the Codex Brucianus. This is a very important point, and indicates that the dates of these treatises need not necessarily be later than the time of the bishop of Lyons, but the consideration of this important subject must be reserved for the sequel. Interesting again is it to remark the influence of the Orphic,

Pythagoræan, Platonic, and Hermetic tradition in the cosmological part, and to observe how both the Hellenic and Jewish myths find a common element in the Chaldæan tradition.

AN EARLY "OPHITE" SYSTEM.

HIPPOLYTUS devotes the fifth book of his Refutation to the "Ophites," who, however, all call themselves followers of the Gnosis, and not "Ophites," as explained above; he seems to regard them as the most ancient stream of the Gnosis. After treating of three great schools, to which we shall subsequently refer, he specially singles out for notice a certain Justinus, who is mentioned by no other hæresiologist. This account of Hippolytus is all the more important, seeing that the system with which the name of Justinus is associated, represents apparently one of the oldest forms of the Gnosis of which we have record. This has been disputed by Salmon, but to my mind his arguments are unconvincing; the fact that the Justinian school, in its mystical exegesis, makes no reference to the texts of the New Testament collection, although freely quoting from the Old, should decide the point. One short saying is referred to Jesus, but it is nowhere found in the canonical texts.

Justinus.

This circle had a large literature, from which Hippolytus selects a single volume, *The Book of Baruch*, as giving the most complete form of the system. The members were bound by an oath of secrecy not to reveal the tenets of the school, and the form of the oath is given. The cosmogony is based on a Syrian creation-myth, a variant of which is preserved by Herodotus (iv. 8-10), in which Hercules (the Sun-god) plays the principal part, and a stratum of which is also found in Genesis. The myth has intimate points of contact with Chaldæan and ancient Semitic traditions. The following is the outline of the system.

The Book of Baruch.
There are three principles of the Universe: (i.) The Good, or all-wise Deity; (ii.) the Father, or Spirit, the creative power, called Elohīm; and (iii.) the World-Soul, symbolized as a woman above the middle and a serpent below, called Eden. From Elohīm (a plural used as a collective) and Eden twenty-four cosmic powers or angels come forth, twelve follow the will of the Father-Spirit, and twelve the nature of the Mother-Soul. The lower twelve are the World-Trees of the Garden of Eden. The Trees are divided into four groups, of three each, representing the four Rivers of Eden. The Trees are evidently of the same nature as the cosmic forces which are represented by the Hindus as having their roots or sources above and their branches or streams below. The name Eden means Pleasure or Desire.

Thus the whole creation comes into existence, and finally from the animal part of the Mother-Soul are generated animals, and from the human part men. The upper part of the Garden is called the "most beautiful Earth"; that is to say, Cosmic Earth, and the body of man is formed of the finest. Man having thus been formed, Eden and Elohīm depute their powers unto him; the World-Soul bestows on him the soul, and the World-Spirit infuses into him the spirit. Thus were men and women constituted.

And all creation was subjected to the four groups of the twelve powers of the World-Soul, according to their cycles, as they move round as in a circular dance

But when the man-stage was reached, the turning-point of the world—process, Elohīm, the Spirit, ascended into the celestial spaces, taking with him his own twelve powers. And in the highest part of the heaven he beheld the Great Light shining through the Gate (? the physical sun), which led to the Light-world of The Good. And he who had hitherto thought himself Lord of Creation, perceived that there was one above him, and cried aloud: "Open me the gates that I may acknowledge the [true] Lord; for I considered myself to be the Lord." And a voice came forth, saying: "This is the Gate of the Lord; through this the righteous enter in." And leaving his angels in the highest part of the heavens, the World-Father entered in and sat down at the right hand of the Good One.

And Elohīm desired to recover by force his spirit which was bound to men, from further degradation; but the Good Deity restrained him, for now that he had ascended to the Light-realm he could work no destruction.

And the Soul (Eden) perceiving herself abandoned by Elohīm, tricked herself out so as to entice him back; but the Spirit would not return to the arms of

Mother Nature (now that the middle point of evolution was passed). Thereupon, the spirit that was left behind in man, was plagued by the soul; for the spirit or mind desired to follow its Father into the height, but the soul, incited by the powers of the Mother—Soul, and especially by the first group who rule over sexual passion and excess, gave way to adulteries and even greater vice; and the spirit in man was thereby tormented.

Baruch.

Now the angel, or power, of the World-Soul, which especially incited the human soul to such misdeeds, was the third of the first group, called Naas (Heb. *Nachash*), the serpent, the symbol of animal passion. And Elohīm, seeing this, sent forth the third of his own angels, called Baruch, to succour the spirit in man. And Baruch came and stood in the midst of the Trees (the powers of the World-Soul), and declared unto man that of all the Trees of the Garden of Eden he might eat the fruit, but of the Tree Naas, he might not, for Naas had transgressed the law, and had given rise to adultery and unnatural intercourse.

And Baruch had also appeared to Moses and the prophets through the spirit in man, that the people might be converted to the Good One; but Naas had invariably obscured his precepts through the soul in man. And not only had Baruch taught the prophets of the Hebrews, but also the prophets of the uncircumcised. Thus, for instance, Hercules among the Syrians had been instructed, and his twelve labours were his conflicts with the twelve powers of the World-Soul. Yet Hercules also had finally failed, for after seeming to accomplish his labours, he is vanquished by Omphalē, or Venus, who divests him of his power by clothing him with her own robe, the power of Eden below.

Last of all Baruch appeared unto Jesus, a shepherd boy, son of Joseph and Mary, a child of twelve years. And Jesus remained faithful to the teachings of Baruch, in spite of the enticements of Naas. And Naas in wrath caused him to be "crucified," but he, leaving on the "tree" the body of Eden—that is to say, the psychic body or soul, and the gross physical body—and committing his spirit or mind to the hands of his Father (Elohīm), ascended to the Good One. And there he beholds " whatever things eye hath not seen and ear hath not heard, and which have not entered into the heart of man"; and bathes in the ocean of life-giving water, no longer in the water below the firmament, the ocean of generation in which the physical and psychic bodies are bathed. This ocean of generation is, of course, the same as the Brāhmanical and Buddhistic *saṁsāra*, the ocean of rebirth.

Christology.

Hippolytus tries to make out that Justinus was a very vile person, because he fearlessly pointed out one of the main obstacles to the spiritual life, and the horrors of animal sensuality; but Justinus evidently preached a doctrine of rigid asceticism, and ascribed the success of Jesus to his triumphant purity.

THE NAASSENI.

PRIOR to the section on Justinus, Hippolytus treats of three schools under the names Naasseni, Peratæ, and Sethians or Sithians. All three schools apparently belong to the same cycle, and the first two present features so identical as to make it highly probable that the Naassene work and the two Peratic treatises from which Hippolytus quotes, pertain to the same Gnostic circle.

Although the name Naassene is derived from the Hebrew *Nachash*, a serpent, Hippolytus does not call the Naassenes Ophites, but Gnostics; in fact, he reserves the name Ophite for a small body to which he also gives (viii. 20) the names Cainites and Nochaïtæ (? Nachaïtæ from *Nachash*), and considers them of not sufficient importance for further mention.

Their Literature.

The Naassenes possessed many books, and also regarded as authoritative the following scriptures: *The Gospel of Perfection, The Gospel of Eve, The Questions of Mary, Concerning the Offspring of Mary, The Gospel of Philip, The Gospel according to Thomas,* and *The Gospel according to the Egyptians.* One of their MSS. had fallen into the hands of Hippolytus. It was a treatise of a mystical, psychological, devotional, and exegetical character, rather than a cosmological exposition, and therefore the system is somewhat difficult to make out from Hippolytus' quotations. Indeed, the Naassene Document, when analysed into its sources, is found to be the Christian overworking

THE NAASSENI.

of the Jewish overworking of a Pagan commentary on a Hymn of the Mysteries. The date of the Christian overwriter may be placed about the middle of the second century, and the document is especially valuable as pointing out the identity of the inner teachings of Gnostic Christianity with the tenets of the Mysteries—Phrygian, Eleusinian, Dionysian, Samothracian, Egyptian, Assyrian, etc.

The Christian writer claimed that his tradition was handed down from James to a certain Mariamne. This Miriam, or Mary, is somewhat of a puzzle to scholarship; it seems, however, probable that the treatise belonged to the same cycle of tradition as *The Greater* and *Lesser Questions of Mary, The Gospel of Mary*, etc., in the frame of which the *Pistis Sophia* treatise is also set.

The main features of the system are that the cosmos is symbolized as the (Heavenly) Man, male-female, of three natures, spiritual (or intelligible), psychic and material; that these three natures found themselves in perfection in Jesus, who was therefore truly the Son of Man. Mankind is divided into three classes, assemblies, or churches: the elect, the called, and the bound (or in other words, the spiritual or angelic, the psychic, and the choïc or material), according as one or other of these natures predominates.

After this brief outline, Hippolytus proceeds to plunge into the mystical exegesis of the writer and overwriters (whom he of course regards as one person) and their interpretation of the Mysteries, which is mixed up here and there with specimens of

<small>Their Mystical Exegesis.</small>

the pseudo-philological word-play so dear to the heart of Plato's *Cratylus*, as remarked above. The system is supposed to underlie all mythologies, Pagan, Jewish and Christian. It is the old teaching of macrocosm and microcosm, and the Self hidden in the heart of all.

The technical character of this exegesis and the nature of our essay compel us to give only a brief summary of the main ideas; but the subject is important enough to demand a special study in itself.

The spirit or mind of man is imprisoned in the soul, his animal nature, and the soul in the body. The nature and evolution of this soul were set forth in *The Gospel according to the Egyptians*, a work which is unfortunately lost.

The Assyrian Mysteries.

Now the Assyrians (following the Chaldæans, who, together with the Egyptians, were regarded by antiquity as the sacred nation *par excellence*) first taught that man was threefold and yet a unity. The soul is the desire-principle, and all things have souls, even stones, for they increase and decrease.

The real "man" is male-female, devoid of sex; therefore he strives to abandon the animal nature and return to the eternal essence above, where there is neither male nor female but a new creature.

Baptism was not the mere symbolical washing with physical water, but the bathing of the spirit or mind in the "living water above," the eternal world, beyond the ocean of generation and destruction; and the anointing with oil was the introduction of the candidate into unfading bliss, thus becoming a Christ.

The kingdom of heaven is to be sought for within a man; it is the "blessed nature of all things which were, and are, and are still to be," spoken of in the Phrygian Mysteries. It is of the nature of the spirit or mind, for, as it is written in *The Gospel according to Thomas*: "He who seeks me shall find me in children from the age of seven years"; and this is the representative of the Logos in man.

Among the Egyptians, Osiris is the Water of Life, the Spirit or Mind, while Isis is "seven-robed nature, surrounded by and robed in seven æthereal mantles," the spheres of ever-changing generation, which metamorphose the ineffable, unimaginable, incomprehensible mother-substance; while the Mind, the Self, makes all things but remains unchanged, according to the saying: "I become what I will, and I am what I am; wherefore, say I, immovable is the mover of all. For He remains what He is, making all things, and is naught of the things which are." This also is called The Good, hence the saying: "Why callest thou Me Good? One only is Good, My Father in the heavens." _{The Egyptian.}

Among the Greeks, Hermes is the Logos. He is the conductor and reconductor (the psychagogue and psychopomp), and originator of souls. They are brought down from the Heavenly Man above into the plasm of clay, the body, and thus made slaves to the demiurge of the world, the fiery or passionate god of creation. Therefore Hermes "holds a rod in his hands, beautiful, golden, wherewith he spell-binds the eyes of men whomsoever he would, and wakes them again from sleep." Therefore the saying: "Wake thou that sleepest, and rise, and Christ shall _{The Greek.}

give thee light." This is the Christ, the Son of the Man, in all who are born; and this was set forth in the Eleusinian rites. This is also Ocean, "the generation of gods and the generation of men," the Great Jordan, as explained in the Myth of the Going-forth, given above.

The Samothracian.

The Samothracians also taught the same truth; and in the temple of their Mysteries were two statues, representing the Heavenly Man, and the regenerate or spiritual man, in all things co-essential with that Man. Such a one was the Christ, but His disciples had not yet reached to perfection. Hence the saying: "If ye drink not My blood and eat not My flesh, ye shall by no means enter into the Kingdom of the Heavens; but even if ye drink of the cup which I drink of, whither I go ye cannot come." And the Gnostic writer adds: "For He knew of what nature each of His disciples was, and that it needs must be that each of them should go to his own nature. For from the twelve 'tribes' He chose twelve disciples, and through them He spake to every 'tribe.' Wherefore (also) neither have all men hearkened to the preaching of the twelve disciples, nor if they hearken can they receive it."

The Phrygian.

The mysteries of the Thracians and Phrygians are then referred to, and the same ideas further explained from the Old Testament documents. The vision of Jacob is explained as referring to the descent of spirit into matter, down the ladder of evolution, the Stream of the Logos flowing downward, and then again upward, through the Gate of the Lord. Wherefore the saying: "I am the true gate." The Phrygians also called the spirit in man the "dead," because it was buried in the tomb and sepulchre of the body. Wherefore the saying; "Ye are whitened sepulchres, filled within with the bones of the dead,"—"for the living man is not in you." And again: "The dead shall leap forth from the tombs"; that is to say, "from their material bodies, regenerated spiritual men, not carnal." For "this is the resurrection which takes place through the gate of the heavens, and they who pass not through it, all remain dead."

Many other interpretations of a similar nature are given, and it is shown that the Lesser Mysteries pertained to "fleshly generation," whereas the Greater dealt with the new birth. "For this is the Gate of Heaven, and this is the House of God, where the Good God dwells alone, into which no impure man shall come, no psychic, no fleshly man; but it is kept under watch for the spiritual alone, where they must come, and, casting away their garments, all become bridegrooms made virgin by the Virginal Spirit. For such a man is the virgin with child, who conceives and brings forth a son, which is neither psychic, animal, nor fleshly, but a blessed æon of æons."

This is the Kingdom of the Heavens, the "grain of mustard seed, the indivisible point, which is the primeval spark in the body, and which no man knoweth save only the spiritual."

The school of the Naasseni, it is said, were all initiated into the Mysteries of the Great Mother, because they found that the whole mystery of rebirth was taught in these rites; they

<small>The Mysteries of the Great Mother.</small>

were also rigid ascetics. The name Naasseni was given them because they represented the "Moist Essence" of the universe—without which nothing that exists, "whether immortal or mortal, whether animate or inanimate, could hold together"—by the symbol of a serpent. This is the cosmic Ākāsha of the Upaniṣhads, and the Kuṇḍalinī, or serpentine force in man, which when following animal impulse is the force of generation, but when applied to spiritual things makes of a man a god. It is the Waters of Great Jordan flowing downwards (the generation of men) and upwards (the generation of gods); the Ākāsha-gangā or Heavenly Ganges of the Purāṇas, the Heavenly Nile of mystic Egypt.

"He distributes beauty and bloom to all who are, just as the [river] 'proceeding forth out of Eden and dividing itself into four streams.'" In man, they said, Eden is the brain "compressed in surrounding vestures like heavens," and Paradise the man as far as the head only. These four streams are sight, hearing, smell, and taste. The river is the "water above the firmament [of the body]."

Thus, to use another set of symbolic terms, "the spiritual choose for themselves from the living waters of the Euphrates [the subtle world], which flows through the midst of Babylon [the gross world or body], what is fit, passing through the gate of truth, which is Jesus, the blessed," *i.e.*, the "gate of the heavens," or the sun, cosmically; and microcosmically the passing out of the body consciously through the highest centre in the head, which Hindu mystics cal-

the Brahmarandhra. Thus these Gnostics claimed to be the true Christians because they were anointed with the "ineffable chrism," poured out by the serpentine "horn of plenty," another symbol for the spiritual power of enlightenment.

We will conclude this brief sketch of these most interesting mystics by quoting one of their hymns. The text is unfortunately so corrupt that parts of it are hopeless, nevertheless sufficient remains to "sense" the thought. It tells of the World-Mind, the Father, of Chaos, the Cosmic Mother, and of the third member of the primordial trinity, the World-Soul. Thence the individual soul, the pilgrim, and its sorrows and rebirth. Finally the descent of the Saviour, the firstborn of the Great Mind, and the regeneration of all. Behind all is the Ineffable, then comes first the First-born, the Logos:

The Fragment of a Hymn.

"Mind was the first, the generative law of all;
Second was Chaos diffused, [spouse] of the first-born;
Thirdly, the toiling Soul received the law;
Wherefore surrounded with a watery form
It weary grows, subdued by death. . . .
Now holding sway, it sees the light;
Anon, cast into piteous plight, it weeps.
Whiles it weeps, it rejoices;
Now wails and is judged;
And now is judged and dies.
And now it cannot pass . . . .
Into the labyrinth [of rebirth] it has wandered.
[Jesus] said: Father!
A searching after evil on the earth

Makes [man] to wander from thy Spirit.
He seeks to shun the bitter Chaos,
But knows not how to flee.
Wherefore, send me, O Father!
Seals in my hands, I will descend;
Through every æon I will tread my way;
All mysteries will I reveal,
And show the shapes of gods;
The hidden secrets of the Holy Path
Shall take the name of Gnosis,
And I will hand them on."

THE PERATÆ.

The Source of their Tradition

HIPPOLYTUS says that the mysteries symbolized by the serpent are at the root of all Gnosticism; and though the Church Father himself has not any idea what these mysteries really are, as is amply proved by all his remarks, we agree with him, as we have endeavoured to show above. He then proceeds to treat of the system of the Peratæ, to whom we have already referred, and whose Mysteries (Hippolytus calls them their "blasphemy against Christ") had been kept secret "for many years." We know from other sources that the school was prior to Clement of Alexandria. The system of the Peratæ was based on an analogy with sidereal considerations, and depended on the tradition of the ancient Chaldæan star-cult. In Book iv., Hippolytus has already endeavoured to refute the Chaldæan system of the star-spheres; but though he makes some good points against the vulgar astrology of the time, he does not affect the mysterious doctrine of the septenary spheres, of which the empirical horoscopists had long lost the secret, and for which they had substituted the physical planets. Hippolytus had the Peratic school especially in mind in his attempted refutation of the art of the astrologers and mathematicians, of which, however, he admits he had no practical knowledge, but space compels us simply to refer the student to the fourth book of his *Philosophumena* for the outline of astrology which the Church Father presents.

According to the Peratic school, the universe was symbolized by a circle enclosing a triangle. The triangle denoted the primal trichotomy into the three worlds, ingenerable, self-generable, and generable. Thus there were for them three aspects of the Logos, or, from another point of view, three Gods, or three Logoi, or three Minds, or three Men. When the world-process had reached the completion of its devolution, the Saviour descended from the ingenerable world or æon; the type of the Saviour is that of a man perfected, "with a threefold nature, and threefold body, and threefold power, having in himself all [species of] concretions and potentialities from the three divisions of the universe." According to the Pauline phrase: "It pleased Him that in him should dwell all fulness (plērōma) bodily."

The Three Worlds.

It is from the two higher worlds, the ingenerable and self-generable, that the seeds of all kinds of potentialities are sent down into this generable or formal world.

Hippolytus here breaks off, and, after informing

us that the founders of the school were a certain Euphrates (whom Origen calls the founder of those Ophites to whom Celsus referred about 175 A.D.) and Celbes, whom he elsewhere calls Acembes and Ademes, proceeds to tell us something more of the Chaldæan art. He then says that he will quote from a number of Peratic treatises to show that their ideas were similar to those of the Chaldæans.

The Saviour has not only a human but a cosmic task to perform; the cosmic task is to separate the good from the bad among the sidereal powers and influences; the same peculiarity of soteriology is brought into prominence in the *Pistis Sophia* treatise, to which we shall refer later on. The "wars in heaven" precede the conflict of good and evil on earth.

A Direct Quotation.

The treatise from which Hippolytus proceeds to quote is evidently a Gnostic commentary on an old Babylonian or Syrian cosmogonic scripture, which the commentator endeavours to explain in Greek mythological terms. The beginning of this mysterious treatise runs as follows:

"I am the voice of awakening from slumber in the æon (world) of night. Henceforth I begin to strip naked the power that proceedeth from Chaos. It is the power of the abysmal slime, which raiseth up the clay of the imperishable vast moist [principle], the whole might of convulsion of the colour of water, ever moving, supporting the steady, checking the tottering, . . . the faithful steward of the track of the æthers, rejoicing in that which streameth forth from the twelve founts of the Law, the power which taketh its type from the impress of the power of the invisible waters above."

This power is called Thalassa, evidently the Thalatth (Tiāmat), or World-Mother, of the Babylonians. The twelve sources are also called twelve mouths, or pipes, through which the world-powers pour hissing. It is the power which is surrounded by a dodecagonal pyramid or dodecahedron—a hint which should persuade astrologers to reconsider their "signs of the zodiac."

Hippolytus' quotations and summary here become very obscure and require a critical treatment which has not yet been accorded them; we are finally told that the matter is taken from a treatise dealing with the formal or generable world, for it is denominated *The Proasteioi up to the Æther;* that is to say, the hierarchies of powers as far as the æther, which were probably represented diagramatically by a series of concentric circles, a "*proasteion*" being the space round a city's walls.

Hippolytus here again points out the correspondence between astrological symbolism and the teaching of this school of Gnosticism; it is, he says, simply astrology allegorized, or rather we should say cosmogony theologized. These Peratics, or Transcendentalists, derive their name from the following considerations.

They believed that nothing which exists by generation can survive destruction, and thus the sphere of generation is also the fate-sphere. He then who knows nothing beyond this, is bound to the wheel of fate; but "he who is conversant with the

The Meaning of the Name.

P

compulsion of generation [*saṁsāra*], and the paths through which man has entered into the [generable] world," can proceed through and pass beyond (transcend) destruction. This destruction is the "Water" which is the "generation of men," and which is the element in which the hierarchies of generation hold their sway, and have their being. It is called water because it is of that colour, namely, the lower ether.

The treatise from which Hippolytus quotes, again dives into the depths of mythology, and among other things adduces the Myth of the Going-forth, and its mystical interpretation; finally, the Gnostic commentator explains the opening verses of the proem to the fourth canonical Gospel. Hippolytus, however, is beginning to be baffled by the amazing intricacy of the system, as he tells us, and thus breaks off, and apparently takes up another treatise from which to quote. The new treatise is of an exceedingly mystical character, and seemingly deals with the psychological physiology of the school.

Psychological Physiology. The universe is figured forth as triple: Father, Son, and Matter (Hylē), each of endless potentialities. The Son, the fashioning Logos, stands midway between the immovable Father and moving Matter. At one time He is turned to the Father and receives the powers in His disk (face, or "person"), and then turning casts them into Matter, which is devoid of form; and thus the Matter is moulded and the formal world is produced.

We here see an attempt to graft a higher teaching, of the same nature as the Platonic doctrine of types and ideas, on to the primitive symbolism of imperfectly observed natural phenomena. The sun is the Father, the moon is the Son, and the earth is Matter. The moon is figured as a serpent, owing to its serpentine path, and its phases are imagined as the turning of its face towards the sun, and again towards the earth. If this is correct, however, the immobility of the sun and the motion of the earth give us reason to believe that the Chaldæans were better acquainted with astronomy than the followers of the far later Hipparcho-Ptolemæic geocentricism. The Gnostic writer has also a correct theory of magnetic and other influences, which he quaintly sets forth. We can, moreover, distinguish three strata of interpretation: (i.) metaphysical and spiritual—the ideal world, the intermediate, and the visible universe; (ii.) the world of generation—with its sun, moon and earth-forces; and (iii.) the analogical psycho-physiological process in man.

The last is thus explained. The brain is the Father, the cerebellum the Son, and the medulla Matter or Hylē. "The cerebellum, by an ineffable and inscrutable process, attracts through the pineal gland the spiritual and life-giving essence from the vaulted chamber [? third ventricle]. And on receiving this, the cerebellum [also] in an ineffable manner imparts the 'ideas,' just as the Son does, to Matter; or, in other words, the seeds and the genera of things produced according to the flesh flow along into the spinal marrow." And, adds Hippolytus, the main secrets of the school depend on a knowledge of these correspondences, but it would be impious for him to say anything more on the matter—a scruple which is surprising to find in a Church Father, and especially in Hippolytus, who devoted the second and third books of his Refutation to an exposition of the Mysteries.

The Lost Books of Hippolytus.
Now it is a curious fact that these two books have been bodily removed from the MS. Did Hippolytus, then, reveal too much of the "plagiarism by anticipation" of the rites and doctrines of the Church, and did those who came after him consider it unwise to keep such evidence on record? For one would have thought that above all things the orthodox Fathers would have delighted in parading the possession of such information before the heathen and heretics, and would have specially preserved these two books from destruction. But indeed it is altogether strange that this, the most important Refutation of all the hæresiological documents which we possess, was made no use of by the successors of Hippolytus. The only MS. known to the western world was brought from Mount Athos in 1842, and its contents (because of the number of direct quotations) have revolutionized our ideas on Gnosticism on many points. Had the two books on the Mysteries been preserved, we might perchance have had our ideas even further revolutionized.

THE SETHIANS.

CLOSELY connected with the Gnostics above described are the Sethians, to whom Hippolytus next devotes his attention. He speaks of their "innumerable commentaries," and refers his readers especially to a certain treatise, called *The Paraphrase of Seth*, for a digest of their doctrines. But whether or not Hippolytus quotes from this document himself, or from some other treatise or treatises, is not apparent. The title, *Paraphrase of Seth*, is exceedingly puzzling; it is difficult to say what is the exact meaning of the term "*paraphrasis*," and the doctrines set forth by Hippolytus have no connection with the Seth-legend.

Seth.

The term Sethians, as used by Hippolytus, is not only puzzling on this account, but also because his summary differs entirely from the scraps of information on the system of the Sethites supposed to have been mentioned in his lost Syntagma, and allied to the doctrine of the Nicolaïtans by the epitomizers. In the latter fragments the hero Seth was chosen as the type of the good man, the perfect, the prototype of Christ.

Can it possibly be that there is a connection between the name "Seth" and the mysterious "Setheus" of the Codex Brucianus? And further, are we to look for the origin of the Sethians along the Egyptian line of tradition of the Hyksōs-cult, the Semitic background of which made Seth the Mystery-God?

An Outline of their System.

The Sethians of whom we are treating begin with a trinity; Light, Spirit and Darkness. The Spirit is not, however, to be thought of as a breath or wind, but as it were a subtle odour spreading everywhere. All three principles then are intermingled one with another. And the Darkness strives to retain the Light and the Spirit, and imprison the light-sparks in matter; while the Light and the Spirit, on their side, strive to raise their powers aloft and rescue them from the Darkness.

All genera and species and individuals, nay the heaven and earth itself, are images of "seals"; they are produced according to certain pre-existent types. It was from the first concourse of the three original principles or powers that the first great form was produced, the impression of the great seal, namely, heaven and earth. This is symbolized by the world-egg in the womb of the universe, and the rest of creation is worked out on the same analogy. The egg is in the waters, which are thrown into waves by the creative power, and it depends on the nature of the waves as to what the various creatures will be. Here we have the whole theory of vibrations and the germ-cell idea in full activity.

Into the bodies thus brought into existence by the waves of the waters (the vehicles of subtle matter) the light-spark and the fragrance of the Spirit descend, and thus "mind or man" is "moulded into various species."

"And this [light-spark] is a perfect god, who from the ingenerable Light from above, and from the Spirit, is borne down into the natural man, as into a

shrine, by the tide of nature and the motion of the wind [the creative power which causes the waves].
. . . Thus a minute spark, a divided splinter from above, like the ray of a star, has been mingled in the much compounded waters [bodies of various kinds of subtle matter] of many (existences).
. . . Every thought, then, and solicitude actuating the Light from above is as to how and in what manner mind may be set free from death—the evil and dark body—from the 'father' below, the [generative impulse] wind, which with agitation and tumult raised up the waves, and [finally] produced a perfect mind, his own son, and yet not his own in essence. For he [the mind] was a ray from above, from that perfect Light, overpowered in the dark and fearsome, and bitter, and blood-stained water; he also is a light-spirit floating on the water."

The generative power is called not only "wind," but also "beast," and "serpent," the latter because of the hissing sound it produces, just like the whirling wind. Now the impure womb, or sphere of generation, can only produce mortal men, but the virgin or pure womb, the Sphere of Light, can produce men immortal or gods. It is the descent of the Perfect Man or Logos into the pure man that alone can still the birth-pangs of the carnal man.

This natural and spiritual process is shown forth in the Mysteries; after passing through the Lesser Mysteries, which pertain to the cycle of generation, the candidate is washed or baptised, and stripping off the dress of a servant, puts on a heavenly garment, and drinks of the cup

The Mysteries.

of life-giving water. That is to say, he leaves his servile form, the body which is subjected to the necessity of generation and is thus a slave, and ascends in his spiritual body to the state where is the ocean of immortality.

The Sethian school supported their theosophic tenets by analogies drawn from natural philosophy, and by the allegorical interpretation of the Old Testament; but, says Hippolytus, their system is nothing else than the tenets of the Orphic Mysteries, which were celebrated in Achæa at Phlium, long before the Eleusinian. No doubt the Sethians based their theories on one or more of the traditions of the Mystery-cult, but we need not follow Hippolytus in his selection of only one tradition, and that too in its grossest and most ignorant phase of vulgar phallicism.

The school seems also to have had affinities with the Hermetic tradition, and used the analogy of natural and "alchemical" processes for the explanation of spiritual matters. For instance, after citing the example of the magnet, one of their books continues: "Thus the light-ray [human soul], mingled with the water [animal soul], having obtained through discipline and instruction its own proper region, hastens towards the Logos [divine soul] that comes down from above in servile form [body]; and along with the Logos becomes Logos there where the Logos has His being, more speedily than iron [hastens] to the magnet."

THE DOCETÆ.

As previously remarked, the remains of the ancient bed of the stream of the Gnosis which we are endeavouring to survey, are so fragmentary, that nothing can be attempted, but a most imperfect outline, or rather a series of rough sketches of certain sections that some day further discovery may enable us to throw into the form of a map. Chronological indications are almost entirely wanting, and we can as yet form no idea of the correct sequence of these general Gnostic schools. We must therefore proceed at haphazard somewhat, and will next turn our attention to a school which Hippolytus (Bk. viii.) calls the Docetæ, seeing that their tenets are very similar to those of the three schools of which we have just treated. There is nothing, however, to show why this name is especially selected, except the obscure reason that it is derived from the attempt of these Gnostics to theorise on "inaccessible and incomprehensible matter." It may, therefore, be possible that they believed in the doctrine of the non-reality of matter; and that the name Docetæ ("Illusionists") is of similar derivation to the Māyā-vādins of the Hindus. The system of this Gnostic circle bears a strong family likeness to the doctrines of the Basilidian and Valentinian schools; but the doctrine of the non-physical nature of the body of the Christ, which is the general characteristic of ordinary Docetism, is not more prominent with them than with many other schools. The outline of their tenets given by Hippolytus is as follows.

God.

The Primal Being is symbolized as the seed of a fig-tree, the mathematical point, which is everywhere, smaller than small, yet greater than great, containing in itself infinite potentialities. He is the "refuge of the terror-striken, the covering of the naked," and much else as allegorically set forth in the Scriptures. The manner of the infinite generation of things is also figured by the fig-tree, for from the seed comes the stem, then branches, and then leaves, and then fruit, the fruit in its turn containing seeds, and thence other stems, and so on in infinite manner; so all things come forth.

The Æons.

In this way, even before the sensible world was formed, there was an emanation of a divine or ideal world of three root-æons, each consisting of so many sub-æons, male-female; that is to say, worlds, or beings, or planes, of self-generating powers. And this æon-world of Light came forth from the one ideal seed or root of the universe, the ingenerable. Then the host of self-generable æons uniting together produce from the One Virgin (ideal cosmic substance), the Alone-begotten (-generated) one, the Saviour of the universe, the perfect æon; containing in Himself all the powers of the ideal world of the æons, equal in power in all things to the orignal seed of the universe, the ingenerable. Thus was the Saviour of the ideal universe produced, the perfect æon. And thus all in that spiritual world was perfected, all being of the nature of That which transcends intellect, free from all deficiency. Thus was accomplished the eternal and ideal world-process in the spaces of the æons.

Next with regard to the emanation of the ideal world into the sensible universe. The third root-æon, in its turn, made itself threefold, containing in itself all the supernal potentialities. Thus, then, its Light shone down upon the primordial chaotic substance, and the souls of all genera and species of living beings were infused into it. And when the third æon, or Logos, perceived that His ideas and impressions and types or seals ($\chi\alpha\rho\alpha\tau\hat{\eta}\rho\epsilon\varsigma$)—the souls—were seized upon by the darkness, He separated the light from the darkness, and placed a firmament between; but this was only done after all the infinite species of the third æon had been intercepted in the darkness. And last of all the resemblance of the third æon himself was impressed upon the lower universe, and this resemblance is a "life-giving fire, generated from the light." Now this fire is the creative god which fashions the world, as in the Mosaic account. This fabricating deity, having no substance of his own, uses the darkness (gross matter) as his substance, out of which he makes bodies, and thus perpetually treats despitefully the eternal attributes of light which are imprisoned in the darkness. Thus until the coming of the Saviour, there was a vast delusion of souls, for these "ideas" are called souls ($\psi\upsilon\chi\alpha\iota$) because they have been breathed out ($\dot{\alpha}\pi o\psi\upsilon\gamma\epsilon\hat{\iota}\sigma\alpha\iota$) from the (æons) above. These souls spend their lives in darkness, passing from one to another of the bodies which are under the ward of the creative power or world-fabricator.

Cosmos and Man.

In support of this the Gnostic author refers to the saying: "And if ye will receive it, this is Elias that was for to come; he that hath ears to hear, let him hear"; and also to Job ii. 9: "And I am a wanderer, changing place after place and house after house." The latter passage is found in the version of the Seventy, but is omitted in the English translation.

<small>The Saviour.</small> It is by means of the Saviour that souls are set free from the circle of rebirth (*metensomatosis*), and faith is aroused in men that their sins should be remitted. Thus, then, the Alone-begotten Son gazing upon the soul-tragedy—the "images" of the supernal æons changing perpetually from one body to another of the darkness—willed to descend for their deliverance.

Now the individual æons above were not able to endure the whole fullness of the divine world, *i.e.*, the Son; and had they beheld it they would have been thrown into confusion at its greatness and the glory of its power, and would have feared for their existence. So the Saviour indrew His glory into Himself, as it were the vastest of lightning-flashes into the minutest of bodies, or as the sudden cessation of light when the eyelids close, and so descended to the heavenly dome; and reaching the star-belt there, again indrew His glory, for even the apparently most minute light-giver of the star-sphere is a sun illuminating all space; and so the Saviour withdrew His glory again and entered into the domain of the third sphere of the third æon. And so He entered even into the darkness; that is to say, was incarnated in a body.

And His baptism was in this wise: He washed himself in the Jordan (the stream of the Logos), and after this purification in the water He became possessed of a spiritual body, a copy or impression of his virgin-made physical body; so that when the world-ruler (the god of generation) condemned his own plasm (the physical body) to death, *i.e.*, the cross, the spiritual body, nourished in the virgin physical body, might strip off the physical body, and nail it to the "tree," and thus the Christ would triumph over the powers and authorities of the world-ruler, and not be found naked; for He would put on His new spiritual body of perfection instead of another body of flesh. Thus the saying: "Except a man be born of water and of the spirit he cannot enter into the kingdom of the heavens; that which is born of the flesh is flesh."

As to Jesus Christ, the Gnostic writer wisely remarks that this ideal can be seen from many sides; that each school has its own view, some a low, some a high view; and that this is in the nature of things. Finally none but the real Gnostics, that is those who have passed through initiations similar to those of Jesus, can understand the mystery face to face.

It would seem hardly necessary to point out to the student of Gnosticism the striking similarity between the general outlines of this system and the leading ideas of the contents of the Bruce and Askew Codices; and yet no one has previously remarked them.

MONOÏMUS.

HIPPOLYTUS devotes his next section to a certain Monoïmus, who is only mentioned by one other hæresiologist, namely Theodoret, in a brief paragraph. Monoïmus was an Arabian and lived somewhere in the latter half of the second century. His system is based on the idea of the Heavenly Man, the universe, and the Son of this Man, the perfect man, all other men being but imperfect reflections of the one ideal type.

Number-theories. His general ideas attach themselves to the cycle of Gnostic literature of which we are treating, and are elaborated by many mathematical and geometrical considerations from the Pythagoræan and Platonic traditions. The theory of numbers and the geometrical composition of the universe from elements which are symbolized by the five Platonic solids—namely, the tetrahedron, cube, octahedron, dodecahedron and icosahedron—are developed. All these geometrical symbols are produced by the monad, which he calls the iōta, the yod, and the "one horn." It is our old friend the serpentine force, the horn of plenty, the rod of Moses and of Hermes; in other words, it is the atom which is said by seers to be a "conical" swirl of forces. This monad is in numbers the decad, the perfect number and completion of the first series of numbers, after which the whole process begins again.

Now it was Moses' rod which brought to pass the plagues of Egypt according to the myth. These "plagues" are nothing else but transmutations of the matter of the physical body, *e.g.*, water into blood, etc., all of which is quaintly worked out by the writer.

The whole of this system, indeed, opens up a number of important considerations which would lead us far beyond the scope of the present essay. Monoïmus was undoubtedly a contemporary of the Valentinian school, if not a pupil of Valentinus, and the garbled version of his system as preserved by Hippolytus can be made to yield many important points which will throw light on the "theological arithmetic" of the Gnostic doctors. This may be proved some day still to preserve a seed which may grow into a tree of real mathematical knowledge.

We will conclude our sketch of the tenets of Monoïmus by quoting his opinion on the way to seek for God. In a letter to a certain Theophrastus, he writes: "Cease to seek after God (as without thee), and the universe, and things similar to these; seek Him from out of thyself, and learn who it is, who once and for all appropriateth all in thee unto Himself, and sayeth: 'My god, my mind, my reason, my soul, my body.' And learn whence is sorrow and joy, and love and hate, and waking though one would not, and sleeping though one would not, and getting angry though one would not, and falling in love though one would not. And if thou shouldst closely investigate these things, thou wilt find Him in thyself, one and many, just as the atom; thus finding from thyself a way out of thyself."

How to Seek after God.

All of this re-echoes very distinctly the teaching of the earlier Trismegistic literature.

THE SO-CALLED CAINITES.

The Obscurity of the Subject.

BEFORE returning again towards the time of the origins along another line of tradition, of which one or two obscure indications still remain — the Carpocrates-Cerinthus trace—we will briefly refer to the obscure chaos of tendencies classed together under the term "Cainite" and its variants. Our sources of information are scanty, and (if we exclude the mere mention of the name) are confined to Irenæus and Epiphanius; the latter, moreover, copies from Irenæus, and with the exception of his own reflections and lucubrations, has only a scrap or two of fresh information to add.

This line of tradition is again generally classed as "Ophite," and as usual we find that its adherents called themselves simply Gnostics. They were distinguished by the honour they paid to Cain and Judas; which fact, taken by itself, was sufficient to overwhelm them with the execrations of the orthodox, who ascribed the perpetration of every iniquity to them. Thus we find that Epiphanius, who wrote two hundred years after Irenæus, embroiders considerably on the account of the Bishop of Lyons, even where he is in other respects simply copying from his predecessor. We will now proceed to see the reason why these Gnostics entertained an apparently so strange belief.

If the reader will bear in mind the systems of Justinus and of the Sethians, he will be in a better position to comprehend what follows. The main features of the system of these Gnostics, then, is as follows.

The creator of the world was not the God over all; the absolute power from above was stronger than the weaker (ὑστέρα—hystera) power of generation, which was symbolized as the power of the impure world-womb, containing heaven and earth within it —the sensible world. But this sensible world was, as it were, an after-birth (ὕστερα—hystera), compared with the true birth from the virgin spiritual womb, the ideal world of the æons above. Epiphanius has made a great muddle of this part of the system; it is evidently consanguineous with the Valentinian "deficiency" (ὑστέρημα—hysterēma), or "abortion," the sensible world, without or external to the ideal fullness or perfection (πλήρωμα—plērōma), or world of the æons.

The inferior power, therefore, was the God of generation, the superior the God of enlightenment and wisdom. The Old Testament idea of God went no further than obedience to the commands of the inferior power. Those who had obeyed its behests were regarded as the worthies of old by the followers of the External Law, who, seeing no further, had in their traditions vilified all who refused to follow this law, the commands of the inferior power of generation. Thus Abel and Jacob and Lot and Moses were praised by the followers of the law of generation; whereas in reality it was the opponents of these who ought to be praised, as followers of the Higher Law who despised the laws of the powers of generation, and were thus

The Enemies of Yahweh the Friends of God.

protected by Wisdom and taken to herself, to the æon above. They therefore claimed that Cain and Esau, and the inhabitants of the Cities of the Plain, and Coran, Dathan and Abiram, were types of those individuals or nations who had followed a higher law, and who, apparently, were calumniated by the followers of Yahweh.

We can here see very plainly the traces of the same antitheses as those worked out by Justinus; the influence of the psychic powers or angels being traceable along the Abel line of descent, and that of the spiritual powers along the Cain line. Abel was the offerer of blood-sacrifices, while Cain offered the fruits of the field. This antithetical device, in one form or other, was common enough—as for instance, the later Ebionite antitheses of superior and inferior men (Isaac-Ishmael, Jacob-Esau, Moses-Aaron), or the Marcionite antitheses of the God of freedom and the God of the law, the God of the Christ and the Yahweh of the Old Testament—but the school whose tenets we are describing, seem, in their contempt for Yahweh, to have pushed their theories to the most extravagant conclusion of any. This is especially brought out in their ideas of New Testament history, which, in spite of their strangeness, may nevertheless contain a small trace of the true tradition of the cause of Jesus' death.

Judas. This Gnostic circle had a number of writings, chief amongst which were two small summaries of instruction, one called *The Gospel of Judas*, and the other *The Ascent of Paul*. To take the latter first; *The Ascent of Paul* purported to contain the record of the ineffable things which Paul is reported to have seen when he ascended into the third heaven. Whether this was the same as *The Apocalypse of Paul* referred to by Augustine is uncertain; in any case it is lost. A more orthodox version of one of the documents of the same cycle has come down to us in *The Vision of Paul*, a translation of which may be read in the last volume of the Ante-Nicene Christian Library (1897). If we can rely on this title, for which Epiphanius alone is responsible, the school of the Cainites is consequently post-Pauline.

But the strangest and, from one point of view, the most interesting development of their theory, was the view they took of Judas. The "Poor Men's" (Ebionite) tradition had consistently handed over Judas to universal execration; there was, however, apparently another tradition, presumably Essene in the first place, which took a different view of the matter. Obscure traces of this seem to be preserved in the unintelligent Irenæus-Epiphanius account of the Cainite doctrines.

This circle of students looked upon Judas as a man far advanced in the discipline of the Gnosis, and one who had a very clear idea of the true God as distinguished from the God of generation; he consequently taught a complete divorcement from the things of the world and thus from the inferior power, which had made the heaven, the world and the flesh. Man was to ascend to the highest region through the crucifixion of the Christ. The Christ was the spirit which came down from above, in order that the stronger power of the spiritual world might be perfected in man; and so Jesus triumphed over the weaker power of generation at the expense of his body, which he handed over to death, one of the manifestations of the God of generation. This was the christological doctrine of the school, and it was apparently, judging from the "he says" of Epiphanius, taken from *The Gospel of Judas*.

A Scrap of History.

But besides this general mystical teaching, there was also a historical tradition: that Jesus, after becoming the Christ and teaching the higher doctrine, fell away, in their opinion, and endeavoured to overset the law and corrupt the holy doctrine, and therefore Judas had him handed over to the authorities. That is to say, those to whom Jesus originally taught the higher doctrine considered that his too open preaching to the people was a divulging of the Mysteries, and so finally brought about his condemnation for blasphemy by the orthodox Jewish authorities.

Yet another more mystical tradition, preserved in one of their books, declared that, on the contrary, the Christ had not made a mistake, but that all had been done according to the heavenly wisdom. For the world-rulers knew that if the Christ were betrayed to the cross, that is to say, were incarnated, the inferior power would be drained out of them and they would ascend to the spiritual æon. Now Judas knew this, and, in his great faith, used every means to bring about His betrayal, and in this way the salvation of the world. These Gnostics consequently praised Judas as being one of the main factors in the scheme of salvation; without him the mystic "salvation of the cross" would not have been consummated, nor the consequent revelation of the realms above.

The Cainite circle, therefore, from their doctrines appear to have been rigid ascetics. But, says Epiphanius, embroidering on Irenæus, they were very dreadful people, and, like Carpocrates, taught that a man could not be saved without going through every kind of experience. We will therefore now take a brief glance at the views of the Carpocratians.

THE CARPOCRATIANS.

OUR main source of information is Irenæus; Tertullian, Hippolytus and Epiphanius simply copy their predecessor. Carpocrates, or Carpocras, was (according to Eusebius) a Platonic philosopher who taught at Alexandria in the reign of Hadrian (A.D. 117-138); he was also the head of a Gnostic circle, whom the Church fathers call Carpocratians, but who called themselves simply Gnostics. With regard to the charge which Epiphanius brings against them two hundred and fifty years afterwards, it is evidently founded on a complete misunderstanding of the jumbled account of Irenæus, if not of malice prepense; for the Bishop of Lyons distinctly says, that he by no means believes that they did the things which he thinks they ought to have done, if they had consistently carried out their teachings! As a matter of fact, the whole confusion arises through the incapacity of the latter Church Father to understand the elements of the doctrine of rebirth. The main tenets of the school were as follows.

Their Idea of Jesus.

The sensible world was made by the fabricating powers, or builders, far inferior to the ineffable power of the unknown ingenerable Father. Jesus was the son of Joseph and Mary, and was born like all other men; he differed from the rest in that his soul, being strong and pure, *remembered* what it saw in its orbit round (or conversation with) the ineffable Father. This is also the idea (lying behind the Pythagorean, Platonic and Hermetic traditions) of the orderly course of the soul in harmonious circuit round the Spiritual Sun, in the Plain of Truth, when it is in its own nature. In consequence of this reminiscence (which is the source of all wisdom and virtue) the Father clothed him with powers, whereby he might escape from the dominion of the rulers of the world, and passing through all their spheres, and being freed from each, finally ascend to the Father. In like manner all souls of a like nature who put forth similar efforts, shall ascend to the Father. Though the soul of Jesus was brought up in the ordinary Jewish views, he soared above them, and thus by the powers he received from above, he triumphed over human passions.

Believing, then, that all souls which rise above the constraints of the world-building rulers, will receive similar powers and perform like wonders, these Gnostics still further claimed that some of their number had actually attained to the same degree of perfection as Jesus, if not to a higher degree, and were stronger than Peter and Paul, and the other Apostles who had attained similar powers.

In fact they boldly taught that men could reach higher degrees of illumination than Jesus; it is not, however, clear whether they made the usual distinction between Jesus and the Christ. These powers were of a "magical" nature, and the next paragraph of Irenæus puts us strongly in mind of the tenets of the "Simonian" school. Such ideas seem to have been very prevalent, so much so that Irenæus complains that outsiders were induced to think that such views were the common belief of Christianity.

The next paragraph deals with the doctrine that there is no essential evil in the universe, but that things are bad and good in man's opinion only. Let us, therefore, see how Irenæus, from his summary of their doctrine of rebirth, arrives at this generalisation. *[Reincarnation.]*

The soul has to pass through every kind of existence and activity in its cycle of rebirth. Irenæus is apparently drawing his information from a MS. which asserted that this could be done in one life; that is to say, apparently, that some souls then existing in the world could pay their kārmic debt in one life. For the MS. quotes the saying, "Agree with thine adversary quickly whiles thou art in the way with him, lest at any time thine adversary deliver thee to the judge, and the judge deliver thee to his officer, and thou be cast into prison. Amen, I say unto thee, thou shalt not come forth thence till thou has paid the uttermost farthing." Now, the adversary is the accuser (diabolus), that is to say the kārmic record in the man's own nature; the judge is the chief of the world-building powers; the officer is the builder of the new body; the prison is the body. Thus the MS. explains the text—precisely the same exegesis as is given to it in the *Pistis Sophia* treatise, which explains all in the fullest manner on the lines of reincarnation and what Indian philosophers call karma.

But not so will Irenæus have it. He asserts that the doctrine means that the soul must pass through all experience good and bad, and until every experience has been learned, no one can be set free. That some souls can do all this in one life! That the Carpocratians, therefore, must have indulged in the most unmentionable crimes because they wished to fill full the tale of all experience good and bad, and so come to an end of the necessity of experience.

Irenæus, however, immediately afterwards adds that he does not believe the Carpocratians actually do such things, although he is forced to deduce such a logical consequence from their books. It is, however, evident that the whole absurd conclusion is entirely due to the stupidity of the Bishop of Lyons, who, owing to his inability to understand the most elementary facts of the doctrine of reincarnation, has started with entirely erroneous premises, although the matter was as clear as daylight to a beginner in Gnosticism.

The circle of the Carpocratians is said to have established a branch at Rome, about 150, under a certain Marcellina. They had pictures and statues of many great teachers who were held in honour by their school, such as Pythagoras, Plato, and Aristotle, and also a portrait of Jesus.

It is curious to remark that Celsus, as quoted by Origen (c. 62), in referring to these Marcellians, also mentions the Harpocratians who derived their tenets from Salōmē. Is it possible that this is the correct form of the name, and not Carpocratians? Harpocrates was the Græcised form of Horus, the Mystery-God of the Egyptians; and Salōmē, we know, was a prominent figure in the lost *Gospel according to the Egyptians*.

"EPIPHANES."

WE next pass on to the contradictory and manifestly absurd legends, which Patristic writers have woven round the second best-known name of the Carpocratian circle. We have already referred to the extraordinary blunder of Epiphanius, who has ascribed a whole system of the Gnosis, which he found in Irenæus assigned simply to a "distinguished teacher" (probably the Valentinian Marcus), to this Epiphanes; the Greek for "distinguished" being also "*epiphanes.*"

This is excusable in a certain measure, seeing that Epiphanius wrote at the end of the fourth century (at least 250 years after the time of the actual Epiphanes) when any means of discrediting a heretic were considered justifiable; but what shall we say of Clement of Alexandria, who is generally fair, and who lived in the same century as Epiphanes? His blunder is even more extraordinary. This is his legend. Epiphanes was the son of Carpocrates and Alexandria, a lady of Cephallenia. He died at the early age of seventeen, and was worshipped as a god with the most elaborate and lascivious rites by the Cephallenians, in the great temple of Samē, on the day of the new moon.

Such an extraordinary legend could not long escape the penetrating criticism of modern scholarship, and as early as Mosheim the key was found to the mystery. Volkmar has worked this out in detail, showing that the festival at Samē was in honour of the moon-god, and accompanied with licentious rites. It was called the Epiphany ($\tau \grave{a}$ Ἐπιφάνια) in honour of Epiphanes ($\acute{o}$ Ἐπιφανής), the "newly-appearing one," the new moon. This moon lasted some seventeen days. Thus Clement of Alexandria, deceived by the similarity of the names and also by the story of licentious rites, bequeathed to posterity a scandalous libel. It is almost to be doubted whether any Epiphanes existed. Clement further asserts that among the Carpocratians one of their most circulated books was a treatise *On Justice*, of which he had seen a copy. He ascribes this to Epiphanes, but it is scarcely possible to believe that a boy of seventeen or less could have composed an abstract dissertation on justice.

Communism.
We thus come to the conclusion that the Carpocratians, or Harpocratians, were a Gnostic circle in Alexandria at the beginning of the second century, and that some of their ideas were

set forth in a book concerning justice, a copy of which had come into the hands of Clement. This Gnostic community was much exercised with the idea of communism as practised by the early Christian circles; being also students of Plato, they wished to reduce the idea to the form of a philosophical principle and carry it out to its logical conclusion. The false ideas of *meum* and *tuum* were no longer to exist; private property was the origin of all human miseries and the departure from the happy days of early freedom. There was, therefore, to be community of everything, wives and husbands included—thus carrying out in some fashion that most curious idea, of Plato's as set forth in *The Republic*. We have, however, no reliable evidence that our Gnostics carried these ideas into practice; it is also highly improbable that men of education and refinement, as the Gnostics usually were, who came to such views through the Pythagorean and Platonic discipline, and through the teachings of Jesus—the *sine quâ non* condition of such ideal communities being that they should consist of "gnostics" and be ruled by "philosophers"—should have turned their meetings into orgies of lasciviousness. Such, however, is the accusation brought against them by Clement. This has already been in part refuted by what has been said above; but it is not improbable that there were communities at Alexandria and elsewhere, calling themselves Christian, who did confuse the Agapæ or Love-feasts of the early times with the orgies and feasts of the ignorant populace. The Pagans brought such accusations against the Christians indiscriminately, and the Christian sects against one another; and it is quite credible that such abuses did creep in among the ignorant and vicious.

The Monadic Gnosis. The Carpocratian school has been sometimes claimed, though I think improperly, as the originator of the so-called Monadic Gnosis. This idea has been worked out in much detail by Neander. The following summary by Salmon will, however, be sufficient for the general reader to form an idea of the theory.

"From one eternal Monad all existence has flowed, and to this it strives to return. But the finite spirits who rule over several portions of the world counteract this universal striving after unity. From them the different popular religions, and in particular the Jewish, have proceeded. Perfection is attained by those souls who, led on by reminiscences of their former conditions, soar above all limitation and diversity to the contemplation of the higher unity. They despise the restriction imposed by the mundane spirits; they regard externals as of no importance, and faith and love as the only essentials; meaning by faith, mystical brooding of the mind absorbed in the original unity. In this way they escape the dominion of the finite mundane spirits; their souls are freed from imprisonment in matter, and they obtain a state of perfect repose (corresponding to the Buddhist Nirvāna) when they have completely ascended above the world of appearance."

CERINTHUS.

CONTINUING to pick our way back along this trace towards the times of the origins, we next come upon the circle of the Cerinthians (or the Merinthians, according to the variant of Epiphanius). They are said to derive their name from a certain Cerinthus, who is placed in "apostolic times," that is to say the latter half of the first century.

Epiphanius has busied himself exceedingly over Cerinthus, and cleverly made him a scapegoat for the "pillar-apostles'" antagonism to Paul. Most writers have followed his lead, and explained away a number of compromising statements in the Acts and Pauline Letters by this device. Impartial criticism, however, has to reject the lucubrations of the late Epiphanius, and go back to the short account of Irenæus, from whom all later writers have copied. Irenæus, who was himself a full century after Cerinthus, has only a brief paragraph on the subject.

The Scapegoat for the "Pillar-apostles."

Cerinthus is the strongest trace between Ebionism, or the original external non-Pauline tradition, and the beginning of the second century. He is supposed to have come into personal contact with John, the reputed writer of the fourth Gospel; but the same story is told of the mythic Ebion, and it must therefore be dismissed as destitute of all historical value.

Cerinthus is said to have been trained in the "Egyptian discipline," and to have taught in Asia Minor. The Egyptian discipline is supposed to mean the Philonic school, but this is a mere assumption. In any case the importance of Cerinthus, whom some Gnostics claimed to have been the writer of the Apocalypse orthodoxly ascribed to John, is that his name has preserved one of the earliest forms of Christian tradition. Its cosmogony declared the stupendous excellence of the God over all, beyond the subordinate power, the World-fashioner. Its christology declared that Jesus was son of Joseph and Mary; that at his "baptism" the Christ, the "Father in the form of a dove," descended upon him, and only then did he begin to prophesy and do mighty works, and preach the hitherto unknown Father (unknown to the Jews), the God over all. That the Christ then left him; and then Jesus suffered, and rose again (that is, appeared to his followers after death).

Such is the account of Irenæus, which seems to be straightforward and reliable enough as far as it goes. The scripture of the Cerinthians was not the recension of the Sayings ascribed to "Matthew," but a still earlier collection in Hebrew. All other collections and recensions were rejected as utterly apocryphal. The Greek writer of the fourth canonical Gospel is said to have composed his account in opposition to the school of Cerinthus, but this hypothesis is not borne out by any evidence.

The Overwriter of the Apocalypse.

NICOLAUS.

WE have now got back to such early times that even the faintest glimmer of historical light fails us; we are deep down in the sombre region of legend and speculation. We will, therefore, plunge no farther into the dark depths of the cave of the origins, but once more retrace our steps to the mouth of the cavern, where at least some fitful gleams of daylight struggle through. But before doing so, we must call the reader's attention to a just discernible shadow of early Gnosticism, the circle of the Nicolaïtans. These Gnostics are of special interest to the orthodox, because the over-writer of the *Apocalypse* has twice gone out of his way to tell us that he hates their doings. Encouraged by this phrase, Irenæus includes the Nicolaïtans in the writer's condemnation of some of the members of the church of Pergamus, who apparently "ate things sacrificed to idols and committed fornication." Subsequent hæresiologists, in their turn encouraged by Irenæus, added further embellishments, until finally Epiphanius makes Nicolaus the father of every enormity he had collected or invented against the Gnostics. And then, with all this "evidence" of his iniquity before him, Epiphanius proceeds rhetorically to address the shade of the unfortunate Gnostic: "What, then, am I to say to thee, O Nicolaus?" For ourselves we are surprised that so inventive a genius as the Bishop of Salamis should have drawn breath even to put so rhetorical a question.

"Which things I hate."

Tradition claims Nicolaus as an ascetic, and relates an exaggerated instance of his freedom from passion. Even granted that he taught that the eating of sacrificial viands was not a deadly sin, there seems no reason why we to-day should follow these Church Fathers in their condemnation of everything but their own particular view of the Christ's doctrine.

CERDO.

<small>The Master of Marcion.</small>

LET us now return to the historical twilight of the second century, and turn our attention to the great Basilidian and Valentinian developments. But before doing so, it will be convenient to give a brief sketch of the great and contemporaneous Marcionite movement, which at one time threatened to absorb the whole of Christendom. The method of this school was the direct prototype of the method of modern criticism. Its conclusions, however, were far more sweeping; for it not only rejected the Old Testament entirely, but also the whole of the documents of the " in order that it might be fulfilled " school of Gospel-compilation.

The predecessor of Marcion is said to have been a certain Cerdo, of Syrian extraction, who flourished at Rome about 135 A.D. But the fame of Marcion so eclipsed the name of his preceptor, that Patristic writers frequently confuse not only their teachings but even the men themselves. It is interesting to note that, though Cerdo's relationship with the Church of Rome was unsettled, no distinct sentence of excommunication is recorded against him; it would, therefore, appear that the idea of a rigid canon of orthodoxy was not yet developed even in the exclusive mind of the Roman presbytery. It was no doubt the success of Marcion that precipitated the formulation of the idea of the canon in the mind of the Roman church, the pioneer of subsequent orthodoxy.

MARCION.

MARCION was a rich shipowner of Sinopē, the chief port of Pontus, on the southern shore of the Black Sea; he was also a bishop and the son of a bishop. His chief activity at Rome may be placed somewhere between the years 150 and 160. At first he was in communion with the church at Rome, and contributed handsomely to its funds; as, however, the presbyters could not explain his difficulties and refused to face the important questions he set before them, he is said to have threatened to make a schism in the church; and apparently was finally excommunicated. But as a matter of fact the origin of Marcionism is entirely wrapped in obscurity, and we know nothing of a reliable nature of the lives of either Cerdo or Marcion.

The Church writers at the end of the second century, who are our best authorities, cannot tell the story of the beginning of the movement with any certainty. For all we know, Marcion may have developed his theories long before he

The Spread of Marcionism.

came to Rome, and may have based them on information he gleaned and opinions he heard on his long voyages. This much we know, that the views of Marcion spread rapidly over the "whole world," to use the usual Patristic phrase for the Græco-Roman dominions; and as late as the fifth century we hear of Theodoret converting more than a thousand Marcionites. In Italy, Egypt, Palestine, Arabia, Syria, Asia Minor and Persia, Marcionite churches sprang up, splendidly organised, with their own bishops and the rest of the ecclesiastical discipline, with a cult and service of the same nature as those of what subsequently became the Catholic Church. Orthodoxy had not declared for any party as yet, and the Marcionite view had then as good a chance as any other of becoming the universal one. What then was the secret of Marcion's success? As already pointed out, it was the same as that of the success of modern criticism as applied to the problem of the Old Testament.

The "Higher Criticism."

Marcion's view was in some respects even more moderate than the judgment of some of our modern thinkers; he was willing to admit that the Yahweh of the Old Testament was just. With great acumen he arranged the sayings and doings ascribed to Yahweh by the writers, and compilers, and editors of the heterogeneous books of the Old Testament collection, in parallel columns, so to say, with the sayings and teachings of the Christ—in a series of antitheses which brought out in startling fashion the fact, that though the best of the former might be ascribed to the idea of a

Just God, they were foreign to the ideal of the Good God preached by the Christ. We know how in these latter days the best minds in the Church have rejected the horrible sayings and doings ascribed to God in some of the Old Testament documents, and we thus see how Marcion formulated a protest which must have already declared itself in the hearts of thousands of the more enlightened of the Christian name.

As for the New Testament, in Marcion's time, the idea of a canon was not yet or was only just being thought of. Marcion, too, had an idea of a canon, but it was the antipodes of the views which afterwards became the basis of the orthodox canon.

The Christ had preached a universal doctrine, a new revelation of the Good God, the Father over all. They who tried to graft this on to Judaism, the imperfect creed of one small nation, were in grievous error, and had totally misunderstood the teaching of the Christ. The Christ was not the Messiah promised to the Jews. That Messiah was to be an earthly king, was intended for the Jews alone, and had not yet come. Therefore the pseudo-historical "in order that it might be fulfilled" school had adulterated and garbled the original Sayings of the Lord, the universal glad tidings, by the unintelligent and erroneous glosses they had woven into their collections of the teachings. It was the most terrific indictment of the cycle of New Testament "history" that has ever been formulated. Men were tired of all the contradictions and obscurities of the innumerable and mutually destructive variants of the traditions concerning the person of Jesus. No man could say what was the truth, now that "history" had been so altered to suit the new Messiah-theory of the Jewish converts.

The Gospel of Paul.
As to actual history, then, Marcion started with Paul; he was the first who had really understood the mission of the Christ, and had rescued the teaching from the obscurantism of Jewish sectarianism. Of the manifold versions of the Gospel, he would have the Pauline alone. He rejected every other recension, including those now ascribed to Matthew, Mark, and John. The Gospel according to Luke, the "follower of Paul," he also rejected, regarding it as a recension to suit the views of the Judaising party. His Gospel was presumably the collection of Sayings in use among the Pauline churches of his day. Of course the Patristic writers say that Marcion mutilated Luke's version; but it is almost impossible to believe that, if he did this, so keen a critic as Marcion should have retained certain verses which made against his strong anti-Judaistic views. The Marcionites, on the contrary, contended that their Gospel was written by Paul from the direct tradition, and that Luke had nothing to do with it. But this is also a difficulty, for it is highly improbable that Paul wrote any Gospel.

So many orthodox apologists wrote against Marcion after his death, that it is possible to reconstruct almost the whole of his Gospel. It begins with the public preaching of the Christ at Capernaum; it is shorter than the present Luke document, and some writers of great ability have held that it was the original of Luke's version, but this is not very credible. As for the rest of the documents included in the present collection of the New Testament, Marcion would have nothing to do with any of them, except ten of the Letters of Paul, parts of which he also rejected as interpolations by the reconciliators of the Petro-Pauline controversy. These ten Letters were called *The Apostle*.

The longest criticism of Marcion's views is to be found in Tertullian's invective *Against Marcion*, written in 207 and the following years. This has always been regarded by the orthodox as a most brilliant piece of work; but by the light of the conclusions arrived at by the industry of modern criticism, and also to ordinary common sense, it appears but a sorry piece of angry rhetoric. Tertullian tries to show that Marcion taught two Gods, the Just and the Good. Marcion, however, taught that the *idea* of the Jews about God, as set forth in the Old Testament, was inferior and antagonistic to the ideal of the Good God revealed by the Christ. This he set forth in the usual Gnostic fashion. But we can hardly expect a dispassionate treatment of a grave problem, which has only in the last few years reached a satisfactory solution in Christendom, from the violent Tertullian, whose temper may be gleaned from his angry address to the Marcionites: "Now then, ye dogs, whom the apostle puts outside, and who yelp at the God of truth, let us come to your various questions! These are the bones of contention, which ye are perpetually gnawing!"

Eznik.

Enough has now been said to give the reader a general idea of the Marcionite position—a very strong one it must be admitted, both because of its simplicity and also because it formulated the protest of long slumbering discontent among the outer communities. It is, however, difficult to deduce anything like a clear system of cosmogony or christology from the onslaughts of the best known hæresiologists on Marcionite doctrines. It has even been doubted whether Marcion should be classed as a Gnostic, but this point is set at rest by the work of Eznik (Eznig or Esnig), an Armenian bishop, who flourished about 450 A.D. In his treatise *The Destruction of False Doctrines*, he devotes the fourth and last book to the Marcionites, who seem to have been even at that late date a most flourishing body. Although it is doubted whether the ideas there described are precisely the same as the original system of Marcion, it is evident that the Marcionite tradition was of a distinctly Gnostic tendency, and that Marcion owed more to his predecessors in Gnosticism than was usully supposed prior to the first translation of Eznik's treatise (into French) in 1833.

It will be sufficient here to shorten Salmon's summary of this curious Marcionite myth, calling the reader's attention to the similarity of parts of its structure to the system of Justinus.

There were three Heavens; in the highest was the Good God; in the intermediate the God of the Law; in the lowest, his Angels. Beneath lay Hylē or root-matter. The world was the joint product of the God of the Law and Hylē. The Creative Power perceiving that the world was very good, desired to make man to inhabit it. So Hylē gave him his body and the Creative Power the breath of life, his spirit. And Adam and Eve lived in innocence in Paradise, and did not beget children. And the God of the Law desired to take Adam from Hylē and make him serve him alone. So taking him aside, he said: "Adam, I am God and beside me there is no other; if thou worshippest any other God thou shalt die the death." And Adam on hearing of death was afraid, and withdrew himself from Hylē. Now Hylē had been wont to serve Adam; but when she found that he withdrew from her, in revenge she filled the world with idolatry, so that men ceased to adore the Lord of Creation. Then was the Creator wrath, and as men died he cast them into Hell (Hades—the Unseen World), from Adam onwards.

A Marcionite System.

But at length the Good God looked down from Heaven, and saw the miseries which man suffered through Hylē and the Creator. And He took compassion on them, and sent them down His Son to deliver them, saying: "Go down, take on Thee the form of a servant [? a body], and make Thyself like the sons of the Law. Heal their wounds, give sight to their blind, bring their dead to life, perform without reward the greatest miracles of healing; then will the God of the Law be jealous and instigate his servants to crucify thee. Then go down to Hell, which will open her mouth to receive Thee, supposing

Thee to be one of the dead. Then liberate the captives Thou shalt find there, and bring them up to Me."

And thus the souls were freed from Hell and carried up to the Father. Whereupon the God of the Law was enraged, and rent his clothes and tore the curtain of his palace, and darkened the sun and veiled the world in darkness. Then the Christ descended a second time, but now in the glory of His divinity, to plead with the God of the Law. And the God of the Law was compelled to acknowledge that he had done wrong in thinking that there was no higher power than himself. And the Christ said unto him: "I have a controversy with thee, but I will take no other judge between us but thy own law. Is it not written in thy law that whoso killeth another shall himself be killed; that whoso sheddeth innocent blood shall have his own blood shed? Let me, then, kill thee and shed thy blood, for I am innocent and thou hast shed My blood."

And then He went on to recount the benefits He had bestowed on the children of the Creator, and how He had in return been crucified; and the God of the Law could find no defence, and confessed and said: "I was ignorant; I thought Thee but a man, and did not know Thee to be a god; take the revenge that is Thy due."

And the Christ thereupon left him, and betook himself to Paul, and revealed the path of truth.

The Marcionites were the most rigid of ascetics, abstaining from marriage, flesh and wine, the latter being excluded from their Eucharist. They also rejoiced beyond all other sects in the number of their martyrs. The Marcionites have also given us the most ancient dated Christian inscription. It was discovered over the doorway of a house in a Syrian village, and formerly marked the site of a Marcionite meeting-house or church, which curiously enough was called a synagogue. The date is October 1, A.D. 318, and the most remarkable point about it is that the church was dedicated to "The Lord and Saviour Jesus, the Good"—Chrēstos not Christos. In early times there seems to have been much confusion between the two titles. Christos is the Greek for the Hebrew Messiah, Anointed, and was the title used by those who believed that Jesus was the Jewish Messiah. This was denied, not only by the Marcionites, but also by many of their Gnostic predecessors and successors. The title Chrēstos was used of one perfected, the holy one, the saint; no doubt in later days the orthodox, who subsequently had the sole editing of the texts, in pure ignorance changed Chrēstos into Christos wherever it occurred; so that instead of finding the promise of perfection in the religious history of all the nations, they limited it to the Jewish tradition alone, and struck a fatal blow at the universality of history and doctrine.

There was naturally a number of sub-schools of the Marcion school, and in its ranks were a number of distinguished teachers, of whom, however, we have only space to refer to Apelles.

APELLES.

His Wide Tolerance.

WE owe our most reliable information on this Gnostic to a certain Rhodon, who opposed his views some time in the reign of Commodus (180-193 A.D); an excerpt from this lost "refutation" has fortunately been preserved for us by Eusebius. At this time Apelles was a very old man and refused the controversy, saying that all sincere believers would ultimately be saved, whatever their theology might be—a most enlightened doctrine and worthy of the best in Gnosticism. As Hort says: "The picture which Rhodon unwittingly furnishes of his [Apelles'] old age is pleasant to look upon. We see a man unwearied in the pursuit of truth, diffident and tolerant, resting in beliefs which he could not reconcile, but studious to maintain the moral character of theology."

Apelles seems to have taken up a less exclusive position than Marcion, though his book of *Reasonings*, directed against the Mosaic theology, seems to have been drastic enough; and he is further said by Eusebius to have written a "multitude of books" of the same nature.

Philumēnē.

He was, however, specially taken to task for his belief in the clairvoyant faculty of a certain Philumēnē, whom he came across in his old age. Her visions were recorded in a book called *The Manifestations*, by which Apelles set great store. Strangely enough, the man who pours on his head the greatest abuse for this, accompanied with the usual charges of immorality, is Tertullian, who, in his own treatise *On the Soul*, following out his own Montanist convictions, confesses his full belief in the prophetical power of a certain voyante of his own congregation, in a most entertaining and naïve fashion! Rhodon, on the contrary, who knew Apelles personally at Alexandria, says that the old gentleman thought himself protected from such slanderous insinuations, by his age and well-known character.

Philumēnē seems to have enjoyed certain psychic faculties, and also to have been a "medium" for physical phenomena, as a modern spiritist would say. She belonged to the class of holy women or "virgins," who were numerous enough in the early Church, though it is exceedingly doubtful whether any of them were trained secresses, except in the most advanced Gnostic circles.

There is an entertaining account of Philumēnē in a curious fragment of an anonymous author, which was printed in the early editions of Augustine's work *On Heresies*, in the section devoted to the Severians. The following is Hort's rendering of the passage:

"He [Apelles] moreover used to say that a certain girl named Philumēnē was divinely inspired to predict future events. He used to refer to her his dreams, and the perturbations of his mind, and to forewarn himself secretly by her divinations or presages." [Here some words appear to be missing.] "The same phantom, he said, showed itself to the same Philumēnē in the form of a boy. This seeming boy sometimes declared himself to be Christ, some-

Her Visions.

times Paul. By questioning this phantom she used to supply the answers which she pronounced to her hearers. He added that she was accustomed to perform some wonders, of which the following was the chief: she used to make a large loaf enter a glass vase with a very small mouth, and to take it out uninjured with the tips of her fingers; and was content with that food alone, as if it had been given her from above."

All of which is very monkish and very spiritistic, and quite in keeping with the records of phenomenalism.

We should, however, remember that this account is not from the side of the Gnostics, but from an unfriendly source. We shall perhaps never know whether Apelles had a knowledge of the sources of the phenomena he witnessed; or, like the vast majority of that time, as indeed of all times, ignorantly assumed that the fact of psychic powers proved the truth of theological doctrines.

THE BASILIDIAN GNOSIS.

LET us now return to the early years of the second century, and devote our attention to Basilides and his followers ("them of Basilides"), who elaborated one of the most abstruse and consistent systems of the Gnosis, the outlines of which are plainly recoverable from the garbled fragments that Patristic polemics have left us.

<small>Basilides and his Writings.</small>

Of the life of this great doctor of the Gnosis we know nothing beyond the fact that he taught at Alexandria. His date is entirely conjectural; he is, however, generally supposed to have been immediately prior to Valentinus. If, therefore, we say that he flourished somewhere about A.D. 120-130, it should be understood that a margin of ten years or so either way has to be allowed for. Of his nationality again we know nothing. But whether he was Greek, or Egyptian, or Syrian, he was steeped in Hellenic culture, and learned in the wisdom of the Egyptians. He was also well versed in the Hebrew scriptures as set forth in the Greek version of the Seventy. The Gospel teaching was his delight, and he wrote no fewer than twenty-four books of commentaries thereon, although he does not appear to have used the subsequently canonical versions. He also quotes from several of the Pauline Letters.

Of the writings of Basilides the most important were the commentaries already referred to; they were the first commentaries on the Gospel-teachings written by a Christian philosopher; and in this, as in all other departments of theology, the Gnostics led the way. Basilides is further said to have written a Gospel himself, and to have claimed to be the disciple of a certain Glaucias, who was an "interpreter of Peter." There is also mention of certain Traditions of Matthias, as held in great honour by the school. These purported to be teachings given to Matthias in secret by Jesus after the "resurrection." It may, therefore, be supposed that the Gospel of Basilides was not a new historical setting of the Sayings of the Lord, but an exposition of that "knowledge of supermundane things," which was the definition he gave to the Gospel. Basilides presumably wrote a commentary on the Sayings and Doings of the Lord, which were in general circulation in many traditions, with or without the various historical settings; and also his own elaboration of certain inner instructions that had been handed down by a secret tradition. Whether or not this inner Gospel formed part of the twenty-four books of his *Exegetica* is doubtful; most critics, however, are in favour of this view. In any case, it is to be supposed that his commentaries aimed at explaining the public Sayings and Parables by the light of this secret Gospel. But there is another hypothesis, which, if true, would be of intense interest. It is suggested that it was Matthias, one of the heads of the inner schools, who wrote the original sketch of Sayings and Doings underlying our Synoptic accounts, and that these accounts were expansions by various presbyters of the outer churches in Egypt. The original draft was presumably a Life intended for public circulation, and designed to be capable of an interpretation according to the inner tenets of the Gnosis.

Basilides is also said to have written certain Odes, but of these no fragment has reached us.

Our main sources of information for recovering an outline of the Basilidian Gnosis are three in number, and consist of the very fragmentary quotations: (i.) of Hippolytus in his later work, *The Philosophumena*; (ii.) of Clement of Alexandria in his *Miscellanies*; and (iii.) presumably in the first place (either of the lost Syntagma of Justin or) of the lost work of Agrippa Castor, who is said by Eusebius to have written a refutation of the views of Basilides in the reign of Hadrian (c. 133 A.D.), and whose very unsatisfactory and inaccurate data were copied by Irenæus, and the epitomators of the earlier, smaller, and now lost work of Hippolytus.

Our Sources of Information.

Turning to the great work of Hippolytus, we come upon the most valuable information extant for the reconstruction of this most highly metaphysical system. The Church Father had evidently before him a treatise of Basilides, but whether it was the *Exegetica* or not, is by no means clear; what is certain, however, is that it set forth the Gospel, or "knowledge of supermundane things," as Basilides understood it; and we can only regret that we have not the original text of the Gnostic doctor himself before us, instead of a most faulty copy of the text of the Church Father's *Refutation*, whose method is of the most provoking. Hippolytus muddles up his own glosses and criticisms with mutilated quotations, imperfectly summarizes important passages, which treat of conceptions requiring the greatest subtlety and nicety of language; and in other respects does scant justice to a thinker whose faith in Christianity was so great, that, far from confining it to the narrow limits of a dogmatic theology, he would have it that the Gospel was also a universal philosophy explanatory of the whole world-drama.

Let us then raise our thoughts to those sublime heights to which the genius of Basilides soared so many centuries ago, when faith in the universal possibilities of the Glad Tidings was really living. And first we must rise to that stupendous intuition of Deity, which transcends even Being, and which to the narrow minds of earth seems pure nothingness, instead of being that which beggars all fullness. Beyond time, beyond space, beyond consciousness, beyond Being itself—

The Divinity Beyond Being.

"There was when naught was; nay, even that 'naught' was not aught of things that are [even in the world of reality]. But nakedly, conjecture and mental quibbling apart, there was absolutely not even the One [the Logos of the world of reality]. And when I use the term 'was,' I do not mean to say that it was [that is to say, in any state of being]; but merely to give some suggestion of what I wish to indicate, I use the expression 'there was absolutely naught.' For that 'naught' is not simply the so-called Ineffable; it is beyond that. For that which is *really* ineffable is not named Ineffable, but is superior to every name that is used.

"The names [we use] are not sufficient even for the [manifested] universe [which is outside the world of real being], so diversified is it; they fall short."

Much less, then, he continues to argue, can we find appropriate names for the beings of the world of reality and their operations; and far more impossible, therefore, is it to give names to That which transcends even reality. Thus we see that Basilides soared beyond even the ideal world of Plato, and ascended to the untranscendable intuition of the Orient—the That which cannot be named, to be worshipped in silence alone.

We next come to the inception of the Seed of Universality, in this state beyond being, a discrete stage, so to speak, beyond the unmanifested or noumenal world even.

Universality Beyond Being.

Hippolytus summarizes this condition of nonbeing, which transcends all being from the original treatise as follows.

"Naught was, neither matter, nor substance, nor voidness of substance, nor simplicity, nor impossibility-of-composition, nor inconceptibility, nor imperceptibility, neither man, nor angel, nor god; in fine, neither anything at all for which man has ever found a name, nor any operation which falls within the range either of his preception or conception. Such, or rather far more removed from the power of man's comprehension, was the state of non-being, when [if we can speak of 'when' in a state beyond time and space] the Deity beyond being, without thinking, or feeling, or determining, or choosing, or

s

being compelled, or desiring, willed to create universality.

"When I use the term 'will,'" writes Basilides, "I do so merely to suggest the idea of an operation transcending all volition, thought, or sensible action. And this universality also was not [our] dimensional and differentiable universe, which subsequently came into existence and was separated [from other universes], but the Seed of all universes."

This is evidently the same concept as the Mūlaprakṛiti of Indian philosophy, and the most admirable statement of the dogma of the "creation out of nothing" that has been put forward by any Christian philosopher.

"This universal Seed contained everything in itself, potentially, in some such fashion as the grain of mustard seed contains the whole simultaneously in the minutest point—roots, stem, branches, leaves, and the innumerable germs that come from the seeds of the plant, and which in their turn produce still other and other plants in manifold series.

"Thus the Divinity beyond being created universality beyond being from elements beyond being, positing and causing to subsist a single something"—which poverty of language compels us to call a Seed, but which was really the potentiality of potentialities, seeing that it was "containing in itself the entire all-seed-potency of the universe." From such a "Seed," which is everywhere and nowhere, and which treasures in its bosom everything that was or is or is to be, all things must come into manifestation in their "proper natures and cycles" and times, at the will of the Deity beyond all. How this is brought about is by no means clear. Basilides seems to have had some idea of a "supplementary development" (κατὰ προσθήκην αὐξανόμενα), which, however, is beyond definition; one thing is clear, that he entirely repudiated every idea of emanation, projection, or pullulation (προβολή).

"For of what sort of emanation is there need, or of what sort of matter must we make supposition, in order that God should make the universe, like as a spider weaves its web [from itself], or mortal man takes brass or timber or other matter out of which to make something? But 'He spake and it was,' and this is what is the meaning of the saying of Moses, 'Let there be light, and there was light.' Whence, then, was the light? From naught. For it is not written whence, but only from the voice of the Speaker of the word. And He who spake the word, was not; and that which was, was not. For the Seed of the universe, the word that was spoken, 'Let there be light,' was from the state beyond being. And this was what was spoken in the Gospel, 'It was the true light which lighteth every man that cometh into the world.' Man both deriveth his principles from that Seed and is also enlightened by it." This primordial Light and Life is the source of all things.

Ex Nihilo.

The next stage deals with the outcome, first-fruits, highest product, or sublimest consummation, of universal potentiality, which Basilides calls the Sonship.

"In the absolute Seed there was a triple Sonship in every way consubstantial with the God beyond being, coming into being from the state beyond being. Of this triply divided Sonship, one aspect was the subtlest of the subtle, one less subtle, and one still stood in need of purification. The subtlest nature of the Sonship instantly and immediately, together with the depositing of the Seed of universality by the God beyond being, burst forth, rose aloft, and hastened from below upward, 'like wing or thought,' as Homer sings, and was with Him beyond being [πρὸς τὸν οὐκ ὄντα—'with,' the very same word as the mysterious preposition in the Proem now prefixed to the fourth canonical Gospel]. For every nature striveth after Him because of His transcendency of all beauty and loveliness, but some in one way and others in another.

The Sonship.

"The less subtle nature of the Sonship, on the other hand, still remained within the universal Seed; for though it would imitate the higher and ascend, it could not, seeing that it fell short of the degree of subtlety of the first Sonship, which had ascended through it [the second], and so it remained behind. The less subtle Sonship, accordingly, had to find for itself as it were wings on which to soar, . . . and these wings are the Holy Spirit."

Just as a bird cannot fly without wings, and the wings cannot soar without the bird, so the second Sonship and the Holy Spirit are complementary the one to the other, and confer mutual benefits on one another.

THE BASILIDIAN GNOSIS. 261

We here see that Basilides is dealing with the second aspect of the Logos, the positive-negative state; we also perceive the anticipation of the ground of the great controversies which subsequently arose generations later, such as the Arian and the "Filioque." But if we enquire whence was the Holy Spirit, Basilides will tell us, from the universal Seed, from which all things came forth under the will of Deity.

"The second Sonship, then, borne aloft by the Spirit, as by a wing, bears aloft the wing, that is the Spirit; but on drawing nigh to the first Sonship and the God beyond being, who createth from the state beyond being, it could no longer keep the Spirit with it, for it [the Spirit] was not of the same substance with it, nor had it a nature like unto that of the Sonship. But just as a pure and dry atmosphere is unnatural and harmful to fish, so to the Holy Spirit was that state of the Sonship together with the God beyond being—that state more ineffable than every ineffable and transcending every name.

"The Sonship, therefore, left it [the Spirit] behind near that Blessed Space, which can neither be conceived of, nor characterized by any word, yet not entirely deserted nor yet divorced from the Sonship. But even as the sweetest smelling unguent poured into a vessel, though the vessel be emptied of it with the greatest possible care, nevertheless some scent of the unguent still remains and is left behind—the vessel retains the scent of the unguent, though it no longer holds the unguent itself—in such a way has

The Holy Spirit.

the Holy Spirit remained emptied and divorced from the Sonship, yet at the same time retaining in itself as it were the power of the unguent, the savour of the Sonship. And this is the saying, 'Like the unguent on the head which ran down unto Aaron's beard'— the savour of the Holy Spirit permeating from above and below even as far as the formlessness [crude matter] and our state of existence, whence the [remaining] Sonship received its first impulse to ascend, borne aloft as it were on the wings of an eagle. For all things hasten from below upward, from worse to better, nor is anything in the better condition so bereft of intelligence as to plunge downward. But as yet this third Sonship still remains in the great conglomeration of the seed-mixture, conferring and receiving benefits," in a manner that will receive subsequent explanation.

The Holy Spirit, which in reality permeates everything, but phenomenally separates the sensible universe from the noumenal, constitutes what Basilides terms the Limitary Spirit, midway between things cosmic and supercosmic. This Firmament is far beyond the visible firmament whose locus is the moon's track.

The Great Ruler.

"After this, from the universal Seed and conglomeration of seed-mixture there burst forth and came into existence the Great Ruler, the head of the sensible universe, a beauty and magnitude and potency that nought can destroy." This is the demiurge; but let no mortal think that he can comprehend so great a being, "for he is more ineffable than ineffables, more potent than potencies, wiser than the wise, superior to every excellence that one can name.

"Coming into existence he raised himself aloft, and soared upward, and was borne above in all his entirety as far as the Great Firmament. There he remained, because he thought there was none above him, and so he became the most potent power of the universe," save only the third Sonship which yet remained in the seed-mixture. His limit, therefore, was his own ignorance of the supercosmic spaces, although his wisdom was the greatest of all in the cosmic realms.

"Thus thinking himself lord, and ruler, and a wise master-builder, he betook himself to the creation of the creatures of the universe."

This is the supercelestial or ætherial creation, which has its physical correspondence in the spaces beyond the moon; below the moon was our world and its "atmosphere." This atmosphere (the sublunary regions) terminated at the visible heaven, or lower firmament, its periphery, marked by the moon's path. In the sun-space lay the ætherial realms, which apparently no mortal eye has seen, but only the reflection of their inhabitants, the stars, in the surface of the sublunary waters of space.

The ætherial creation of the Great Ruler proceeds on the theory of similarity and analogy.

"First of all the Great Ruler, thinking it not right that he should be alone, made for himself, and brought into existence from the universal Seed, a Son far better and wiser than himself. For all this

The Ætherial Creation.

had been predetermined by the God beyond being, when He deposited the universal Seed.

"And the Great Ruler, on beholding his Son, was struck with wonder and love and amazement at his marvellously great beauty, and he caused him to sit at his right hand." And this space where is the throne of the Great Ruler they called the Ogdoad. "And the Great Demiurgos, the wise one, fabricated the whole ætherial creation with his own hand; but it was his Son, who was wiser still, who infused energy into him and suggested to him ideas."

That is to say, that the Great Ruler made the creatures of the ætherial spaces, and these evolved souls, or rather were ensouled. And thus it is that the son is, as it were, greater than the father, and sits on his right hand, or above him; the right hand in Gnostic symbolism signifying a higher condition. They mutually confer benefits also, one giving the body and the other the mind or soul to ætherial beings. All ætherial spaces then, down to the moon, are provided for and managed by the Son of the Great Ruler, the consummation or perfection of his evolution or creation.

The Sublunary Spaces.

"Next, there arose a second Ruler from the universal Seed, far inferior to the first, but greater than all below him, except the Sonship which still remained in the Seed." This was the Ruler of the sublunary spaces, from the moon to the earth. This Ruler is called effable, because men can speak of him with understanding, and the space over which he rules is named the Hebdomad. And the second Ruler also "brought forth a Son far greater than himself from the universal Seed, in like manner to the first," and the lower creation was ordered in the same manner as the higher. This lower creation is apparently still one of subtle matter.

As to the earth, the conglomeration of the seed-mixture is still in our own stage or space, and the things that come to pass in this state of existence, "come to pass according to nature, as having been primarily uttered by Him who hath planned the fitting time and form and manner of utterance of the things that were to be uttered. Of things here on the earth, then, there is no special chief or manager or creator, for sufficient for them is that plan which the God beyond being laid down when He deposited the universal Seed."

That is to say, that the earth-stage is the moment between the past and future, the turning-point of all choice, the field of new karman; here all things verily are in the hand of God alone, in the highest sense. Thus does Basilides avoid the difficulties both of fate and free-will absolute.

We next come to the soteriology of Basilides, the redemption and restoration of all things.

"When, then, the supercosmic planes and the whole universe [ætherial, sublunary, and terrestrial] were completed, and there was no deficiency," that is to say, when the evolutionary stream of creative energy began to return on itself, "there still remained behind in the universal Seed the third Sonship, which bestows and receives benefits.

"But it needs must be that this Sonship also

Soteriology.

should be manifested, and restored to its place above, there beyond the highest Firmament, the Limitary Spirit of cosmos, with the most subtle Sonship, and the second which followed the example of its fellow, and the God beyond being, even as it was written, 'And the creation itself groaneth together and travaileth together, waiting for the manifestation of the Sons of God'"—the third Sonship.

The Sons of God are the divine sparks, the real spiritual men within, who have been left behind here in the seed-mixture, "to order and inform and correct and perfect our souls, which have a natural tendency downwards to remain in this state of existence."

Before the Gospel was preached, and the Gnosis came, the Great Ruler of the Ogdoad was considered even by the most spiritual among men to be the only God, nevertheless no name was given to him, because he was ineffable.

The inspiration of Moses, however, came from the Hebdomad only, as may be seen from the words, "I am the God of Abraham, Isaac and Jacob, but the name of God I did not make known unto them." This God to whom Moses and the Prophets gave names, was of the Hebdomad, which is effable, and their inspiration came from this source. But the Gospel was that Mystery which was ever unknown, not only to the nations, but also to them of the Hebdomad and the Ogdoad, and even to their Rulers.

"When, therefore, the time had come," says the

Gnostic doctor, "for the revelation of the children of God (who are ourselves), for whom the whole creation groaneth and travaileth in expectation, the Gospel [the Glad Tidings, the Gnosis] came into the universe, and passed through every principality, and authority, and lordship, and every title that man can use. It 'came' of very truth, not that anything 'came *down*' from above, or that the blessed Sonship 'departed from' that Blessed God beyond being, who transcends all thought. Nay, but just as the vapour of naphtha can catch fire from a flame a great way off from the naphtha, so do the powers of men's spirit pass from below from the formlessness of the conglomeration up to the Sonship.

The Mystic Gospel.

"The Son of the Great Ruler of the Ogdoad, catching fire as it were, lays hold of and seizes on the ideas from the blessed Sonship beyond the Limitary Spirit. For the power of the Sonship which is in the midst of the Holy Spirit, in the Limit Space, shares the flowing and rushing thoughts of the [supreme] Sonship with the Son of the Great Ruler.

"Thus the Gospel first came from the Sonship through the Son who sits by the Great Ruler, to that Ruler; and the Ruler learned that he was not the God over all, but a generable deity, and that above him was set the Treasure of the ineffable and unnameable That beyond being and of the Sonship. And he repented and feared on understanding in what ignorance he had been. This is the meaning of the words, 'The fear of the Lord is the beginning of wisdom.' For he began to grow wise through the instruction of the Christ sitting by him, learning what is That beyond being, what the Sonship, what the Holy Spirit, what the apparatus of the universe what the manner of its restoration. This is the 'wisdom, declared in a mystery,' concerning which Scripture uses the words, 'Not in words taught of human wisdom, but in those taught of the Spirit.'

"The great Ruler, then, being instructed and taught and made afraid, confessed the sin which he had done in boasting himself. This is the saying, 'I have recognized my sin, and I know my transgression, and I will confess it for the eternity.'

"After the instruction of the Great Ruler, the whole space of the Ogdoad was instructed and taught, and the Mystery became known to the powers above the heavens.

"Then was it that the Gospel should come to the Hebdomad, that its Ruler might be instructed and evangelized in like manner. Thereupon the Son of the Great Ruler lit up in the Son of the Ruler of the lower space, the Light which he himself had had kindled in him from above from the Sonship; and thus the Son of the Ruler of the Hebdomad was illumined, and preached the Gospel to the Ruler, who in his turn, like as the Great Ruler before him, feared and confessed [his sin]. And then all things in the sublunary spaces were enlightened and had the Gospel preached unto them.

The Sons of God.

"Therefore the time was ripe for the illumination of the formlessness of our own world, and for the Mystery to be revealed to the Sonship which had been left behind in the formlessness, as it were to one born out of due time (an abortion) —'the mystery which was not known unto former generations,' as it is written, 'By revelation was the mystery made known unto me,' and 'I heard unspeakable words, which it is not lawful for man to utter.'

"Thus, from the Hebdomad, the Light—which had already come down from above from the Ogdoad unto the Son of the Hebdomad—descended upon Jesus, son of Mary, and he was illumined, being caught on fire in harmony with the Light that streamed into him. This is the meaning of the saying, 'The Holy Spirit shall come upon thee'—that is to say, that which came from the Sonship through the Limitary Spirit to the Ogdoad and Hebdomad, down as far as Mary [the body]—and 'The Power of the Highest shall overshadow thee'—that is to say, the divine creative power which cometh from the [aetherial] heights above through the Demiurgos, which power belongeth to the Son."

The text of Hippolytus is here exceedingly involved, and he evidently did not seize the thought of Basilides. The "Son" apparently means the soul. The power belongs to the soul and not to Mary—the body; the divine creative power making of man a god, whereas the body can only exercise the power of physical procreation. Moreover, Jesus seems to stand for a type of every member of the Sonship, every Son of God.

"For the world shall hold together and not be dissolved until the whole Sonship—which has been left behind to benefit the souls in the state of formlessness, and to receive benefits, by evolving forms for them [the spirit requiring a psychic vehicle for conscious contact with this plane]—shall follow after and imitate Jesus, and hasten upward and come forth purified. [For by purification] it becometh most subtle, so that it is able to speed aloft through its own power, even as the first Sonship; for it hath all its power naturally consubsistent with the Light which shone down from above.

The Final Consummation.
"When, then, the whole Sonship shall have ascended, and passed beyond the Great Limit, the Spirit, then shall the whole creation become the object of the Great Mercy; for it groaneth until now and suffereth pain and awaiteth the manifestation of the Sons of God, namely that all the men of the Sonship may ascend beyond it [the creation]. And when this shall be effected, God will bring upon the whole universe the Great Ignorance [Mahā-pralaya], in order that all things may remain in their natural condition, and nothing long for anything which is contrary to its nature.

"Thus all the souls of this state of existence, whose nature is to remain immortal in this state of existence alone, remain without knowledge of anything different from or better than this state; nor shall there be any rumour or knowledge of things superior in higher states, in order that the lower souls may not suffer pain by striving after impossible objects, just as though it were fish longing to feed on the mountains with sheep, for such a desire would end in their destruction. All things are indestructible if they remain in their proper condition, but subject to destruction if they desire to overleap and transgress their natural limits.

"Thus the Ruler of the Hebdomad shall have no knowledge of the things above him, for the Great Ignorance shall take hold of him also, so that sorrow and pain and lamentation may go from him. He shall desire naught of things impossible for him to attain, and thus shall suffer no grief.

"And in like manner the Great Ignorance shall seize upon the Great Ruler of the Ogdoad, and also upon all the [ætherial] creations which are subject to him in similar fashion, so that nothing may long after anything contrary to nature and thus suffer pain.

"And thus shall be the restoration of all things, which have had their foundations laid down according to nature in the Seed of the universe in the beginning, and which will all be restored [to their original nature] in their appointed cycles.

"And that everything has its proper cycle and time, the Saviour is sufficient witness in the saying, 'My hour hath not yet come,' and also the Magi in their observation of His star. For He also was foreordained in the Seed to be subject to the nativity of the stars and the return of the time-periods to their starting places."

Now the Saviour, according to the Basilidian Gnosis, was the perfected spiritual "man," within the psychic and animal man or soul. And when a man reaches this stage of perfection, the Sonship in him leaves the soul behind here, "the soul being no longer mortal but remaining in its natural state [that is to say, having become immortal], just as the first Sonship [left behind] the Holy Spirit, the Great Limit, in its proper space or region"; for it is only then on reaching perfection, that the real "man" is "clothed with a proper [and really immortal] soul."

Jesus.

Every part of the creation goes up a stage, and the whole scheme of salvation is effected by the separating from their state of conglomeration the various principles into their proper states; and Jesus was the first-fruits, or great exemplar, of this process.

"Thus his physical part down here—which belongs to formless matter—alone suffered, and was restored to the formless state. His psychic vesture or vehicle—which belongs to the Hebdomad—arose and was restored to the Hebdomad. That vehicle in him which was of the nature of the height of the Great Ruler he raised aloft, and it remained with the Great Ruler. Moreover he raised still higher that which was of the nature of the Great Limit, and it remained in the Limitary Spirit. And it was thus through him that the third Sonship was purified, the Sonship left behind in the state of mixture [or impurity] for the purpose of helping and being helped, and it passed upwards through all of these purified principles unto the blessed Sonship above."

The main idea at the back of this system is the separating forth, classification or restoration of the various elements or principles confused in the original world-seed, or universal plasm, into their proper natures, by a process of purification which brought unto men the Gnosis or perfection of consciousness. Man was the crown of the world-process, and the perfected man, the Christ, the Saviour, was the crown of manhood, and therefore the manifestation of Deity, the Sonship.

So far Hippolytus, who in all probability gives us the outline of the true Basilidian system. It was only in 1851 that *The Philosophumena* were published to the world, after the discovery of the MS. in one of the libraries on Mount Athos in 1842; prior to this nothing but the short and garbled sketches of Irenæus and the Epitomators was known of this great Gnostic's sublime speculations. *The Philosophumena* account has revolutionized all prior views, and changed the whole enquiry, so that the misrepresentations of Irenæus, or those of his prior authority, are now referred to as "the spurious Basilidian system." To this we shall refer later on. Meantime let us turn to Clement of Alexandria, who deals purely with the ethical side of the Basilidian Gnosis, and therefore does not touch the "metaphysical" part—using the term "metaphysical" in the Aristotelian sense, namely, of things beyond the Hebdomad, the things of the Hebdomad or sublunary space being called "physics" or in the domain of physis or nature.

As to marriage, Basilides and his son Isidorus

T

taught that it was natural but not necessary, and seem to have taken a moderate ground between the compulsory asceticism of some schools and the glorification of procreation by the Jews, who taught that "he who is without a wife is no man."

As to the apparently undeserved sufferings of martyrs, Basilides, basing himself on the doctrines of reincarnation and karman, writes as follows in Book xxiii. of his *Exegetica*:

Karman and Reincarnation.

"I say that all those who fall into these so-called tribulations, are people who, only after transgressing in other matters without being discovered, are brought to this good end [martyrdom] by the kindness of Providence, so that, the offences they are charged with being quite different from those they have committed without discovery, they do not suffer as criminals for proved offences, reviled as adulterers or murderers, but suffer merely for being Christians; which fact is so consoling to them that they do not even appear to suffer. And even though it should happen that one comes to suffer without previously committing any outward transgression—a very rare case—he will not suffer at all through any plot of any [evil] power, but in exactly the same way as the babe who apparently has done no ill.

"For just as the babe, although it has done no wrong previously, or practically committed any sin, and yet has the capacity of sin in it [from its former lives], when it suffers, is advantaged and reaps many benefits which otherwise are difficult to gain; in just the selfsame way is it with the perfectly virtuous man also who has never sinned in deed, for he has still the tendency to sin in him; he has not committed actual sin [in this life], because he has not as yet been placed in the necessary circumstances. In the case even of such a man we should not be right in supposing entire freedom from sin. For just as it is the will to commit adultery which constitutes the adulterer, even though he does not find the opportunity of actually committing adultery, and the will to commit murder constitutes the murderer, although he may not be actually able to effect his purpose; for just this reason if I see such a 'sinless' man suffering [the pains of martyrdom], even if he has actually *done* no sin, I shall say that he is evil in so far as he has still the *will* to transgress. For I will say anything rather than that Providence is evil."

Moreover, even if the example of Jesus were to be flung in his face by those who preferred miracle to law, the sturdy defender of the Gnosis says that he should answer: "If you permit, I will say, He has not sinned; but was like a babe suffering." And if he were pressed even more closely, he would say: "The man you name is man, but God [alone] is righteous; for 'no one is pure from pollution,'" as Job said.

Men suffer, says Basilides, from their deeds in former lives; the "elect" soul suffers "honourably" through martyrdom, but souls of another nature by other appropriate punishments. The "elect" soul is evidently one that will suffer for an ideal; in other words it is possessed of faith, which is the "assent of the soul to any of the things which do not excite sensation"; such a soul, then, "discovers doctrines without demonstration by an intellective apprehension."

The vulgar superstition of transmigration, the passing of a human soul into the body of an animal—so often confused by the uninstructed with the doctrine of reincarnation, which denies such a possibility—received a rational explanation at the hand of the Basilidian school. It arose from a consideration of the animal nature in man, the animal soul, or body of desire, the ground in which the passions inhere; the doctrine being thus summarized by Clement:

The Theory of "Appendages."

"The Basilidians are accustomed to give the name of appendages [or accretions] to the passions. These essences, they say, have a certain substantial existence, and are attached to the rational soul, owing to a certain turmoil and primitive confusion."

The word translated essences is literally "spirits"; curiously enough the whole animal soul is called the "counterfeit spirit" in the *Pistis Sophia* treatise, and in *The Timæus* of Plato the same idea is called "turmoil," as may be seen from the commentary of Proclus. The primitive confusion is of course the chaotic conglomeration of the universal seed-mixture, and the differentiation of the "elemental essence" of some modern writers on theosophy.

"On to this nucleus other bastard and alien natures of the essence grow, such as those of the wolf, ape, lion, goat, etc. And when the peculiar qualities of such natures appear round the soul, they cause the desires of the soul to become like to the special natures of these animals, for they imitate the actions of those whose characteristics they bear. And not only do human souls thus intimately associate themselves with the impulses and impressions of irrational animals, but they even imitate the movements and beauties of plants, because they likewise bear the characteristics of plants appended to them. Nay, there are also certain characteristics [of minerals] shown by habits, such as the hardness of adamant."

But we are not to suppose that man is composed of several souls, and that it is proper for man to yield to his animal nature, and seek excuse for his misdeeds by saying that the foreign elements attached to him have compelled him to sin; far from it, the choice is his, the responsibility is his, the rational soul's. Thus in his book, *On an Appended Soul*, Isidorus, son of Basilides, writes:

"Were I to persuade anyone that the real soul is not a unit, but that the passions of the wicked are occasioned by the compulsion of the appended natures, no common excuse then would the worthless of mankind have for saying, 'I was compelled, I was carried away, I did it without wishing to do so, I acted unwillingly'; whereas it was the man himself who led his desire towards evil, and refused to battle with the constraints of the appendages. Our duty is to show ourselves rulers over the inferior creation within us, gaining the mastery by means of our rational principle."

Moral Responsibility.

In other words, the man is the same man, no

matter in what body or vesture he may be; the vestures are not the man.

One of the greatest festivals of the school was the celebration of the Baptism of Jesus on the fifteenth day of the Egyptian month Tobe or Tybi. "They of Basilides," says Clement, "celebrate His Baptism by a preliminary night-service of readings; and they say that 'the fifteenth year of Tiberius Cæsar' means the fifteenth day of the month Tybi." It was then that the Father "in the likeness of a dove"—which they explained as meaning the Minister or Holy Spirit—came upon Him.

In "the fifteenth [year] of Tib[erius]" we have, then, perhaps an interesting glimpse into the workshop of the "historicizers."

It is evident, therefore, that the Basilidians did not accept the accounts of the canonical gospels literally, as Hippolytus claims; on the contrary, they explained such incidents as historicized legends of initiation, the process of which is magnificently worked out in the *Pistis Sophia* treatise, to which I must refer the reader for further information.

A Trace of Zoroastrianism.

We learn from Agrippa Castor, as preserved by Eusebius, that Basilides imposed a silence of five years on his disciples, as was the custom in the Pythagorean school, and that he and his school set great store by the writings of a certain Barcabbas and Barcoph, and by other books of Orientals. Scholars are of opinion that Barcabbas and Barcoph, and their variants, point to the cycle of Zoroastrian literature which is now lost, but which was in great favour among many Gnostic communities. It must have been that among the learned Jews and Essenes, after the return from Babylonia, and also among the theosophically minded of the time, the traditions of the Magi and of the great Iranian faith were an important part of eclectic and syncretistic religion. The Avesta-literature that has come down to us is said to be a recovery from memory of a very small portion of the great library of Persepolis, destroyed by the "accursed Alexander," as Pārsī tradition has it. And it seems exceedingly probable, as Cumont has shown in his just-published monumental work on the subject, that the Mithriac mystery-tradition contains as authentic a tradition as the Pārsī line of descent, and throws a brilliant light on the Zoroastrianism with which Gnosticism was in contact.

Such, then, is all that can be deduced of the real Basilidian system from the writings of Hippolytus and Clemens Alexandrinus, who respectively selected only such points as they thought themselves capable of refuting; that is to say, such features of the system as they considered most erroneous. To the student of comparative religion it is evident that both Church Fathers misunderstood the tenets they quoted, seeing that even such hostilely selected passages easily fall into the general scheme of universal theosophy, once they are taken out of the setting of Patristic refutation, and allowed to stand on their own merits. It is therefore a matter of deep regret that the writings of the school have been lost or destroyed; they would doubtless have thrown much light not only on Christian theosophy but also on the obscure history of the origins.

The Spurious System.

It now remains for us to refer briefly to the "spurious" Basilidian system. The following points are taken from Irenæus and the epitomators, and are another proof of the unreliability of Irenæus, the sheet-anchor of orthodox hæresiology. The series of writers and copyists to which we refer, had evidently no first-hand information of the teaching of Basilides, and merely retailed whatever fantastic notions popular rumour and hearsay attributed to the school.

The main features of the confection thus brewed are as follows. The God of the Basilidians, they said, was a certain Abraxas or Abrasax, who was the ruler of their first heaven, of which heavens there were no less than 365. This power was so denominated because the sum of the numerical values of the Greek letters in the name Abrasax came to 365, the number of days in the year.

We learn, however, from Hippolytus (II.) that this part of the system had to do with a far lower stage of creation than the God beyond all. It is not, however, clear whether the Abrasax idea is to be identified with the Great Ruler of the Ogdoad, or the Ruler of the Hebdomad and the region of the "proasteioi up to the æther." In any case the 365 "heavens" pertained to the astrological and genetical considerations of Egyptian and Chaldæan occult science, and represented from one point of view the 365 "aspects" of the heavenly bodies (during the year), as reflected on the surface of the earth's "atmosphere" or envelope, which entended as far as the moon.

Now it is curious to notice that in the *Pistis Sophia* treatise the mysteries of embryology are consummated by a hierarchy of elemental powers, or builders, 365 in number, who follow the dictates of the kārmic law, and fashion the new body in accordance with past deeds. The whole is set forth in great detail, and also the astrological scheme of the one ruler of the four, which in their turn each rule over ninety, making in all 365 powers.

Not till Schwartze translated this treatise from the Coptic, in 1853, was any certain light thrown on the Abrasax idea, and this just two years after Miller in 1851 published his edition of *The Philosophumena*, and thus supplied the material for proving that the hitherto universal opinion that the "Abrasax" was the Basilidian name for the God over all, was a gross error based on ignorance or misrepresentation. It is also to be noticed that the ancient anonymous treatise which fills the superior MS. of the Codex Brucianus, makes great use of the number 365 among its endless hierarchies, but nowhere mentions the name Abrasax.

The elemental forces which fashion the body are the lowest servants of the kārmic law. It was presumably these lowest powers that made up the Abrasax of the populace. The God over all is the supreme ruler of an endless galaxy of rulers, gods, archangels, authorities, and powers, all of them superior to the 365.

In fact the mysteries of the unseen world were

so intricate in detail, that even those who devoted their lives to them with unwearied constancy could scarcely understand some of the lower processes, although the general idea was simple enough; and thus Basilides imposed a silence of five years on his disciples, and declared that "only one out of 1,000, and two out of 10,000," could really receive the Gnosis, which was the consummation of many lives of effort. Curiously enough this very phrase is also found in the *Pistis Sophia* treatise.

The term Abrasax is well known to students of Gnosticism, because of the number of gems on which it is found, and which are attributed to the followers of Basilides; in addition to the great Continental scholars who have treated the matter, in this country King has devoted much of his treatise to the subject. The best and latest authorities, however, are of opinion "that there is no tangible evidence for attributing any known gems to Basilidianism or any other form of Gnosticism."

Abrasax.

In fact, in the Abrasax matter, as in all other things, Gnosticism followed its natural tendency of going "one better," to use a colloquialism, on every form of belief, or even superstition. Doubtless the ignorant populace had long before believed in Abrasax as the great power which governed birth and everyday affairs, according to astrological notions; talismans, invocations, and the rest of the apparatus which the vulgar mind ever clamours for in some form or other, were all inscribed with this potent "name of power." Behind the superstition, however, there lay certain occult facts, of the real nature of which, of course, the vulgar astrologers and talisman-makers were naturally ignorant. There facts, however, seem to have been known to the doctors of the Gnosis, and they accordingly found the proper place for them in their universal systems. Thus Abrasax, the Great God of the ignorant, was placed among the lower hierarchies of the Gnosis, and the popular idea of him was assigned to the lowest building powers of the physical body.

As to the rest of the "spurious system" there is nothing of interest to record; we cannot, however, omit the silliest tale told against the Basilidians, which was as follows. They are said to have believed that at the crucifixion Jesus changed bodies with Simon of Cyrene, and then, when his substitute hung in agony, stood and mocked at those he had tricked! —with which cock-and-bull story we may come out of the Irenæic "store-house of Gnosticism" for a breathing space.

Of the history of the school we know nothing beyond the fact that Epiphanius, at the end of the fourth century, still met with students of the Basilidian Gnosis in the nomes west of the Delta, from Memphis to the sea. It seems more probable, however, that the school continued in the main stream of Gnosticism of the latter half of the second century, and was at the back of the great Valentinian movement of which we have next to treat. Indeed it is very probable that the followers of this, the main stream of the Gnosis, would have warmly resented being classed as "them of Basilides" or "them of

Valentinus"; they doubtless regarded these teachers as handers-on of a living tradition, each in his own way, and not as severally inspired revealers of new doctrines.

THE VALENTINIAN MOVEMENT.

The "Great Unknown" of Gnosticism.

BEHIND the whole Valentinian movement stands the commanding and mysterious figure of Valentinus himself, universally acknowledged to have been the greatest of the Gnostics. His learning and eloquence are admitted, even by his bitterest opponents, to have been of a most extraordinary nature, and no word has ever been breathed against his moral character. And yet, when we come to analyze the chaos of "information" which Patristic writers have left us on the subject of so-called Valentinianism, we find the mysterious character of the great master of the Gnosis ever receding before our respectful curiosity; he who has been made to give his name to the remodelling of the whole structure, still remains the "great unknown" of Gnosticism. We know nothing certain of him as a man, nothing definite of him as a writer, except the few mutilated scraps which hæresiological polemics have vouchsafed to us.

(I am of course leaving aside entirely the vexed question of, I will not say the authorship, but the compilation, of the treatises in the Askew and Bruce Codices. My own opinion is that we owe a great part of these elaborations to Valentinus; not that I think this can be proved in any satisfactory fashion with the present scanty sources of information open to us. On the contrary, however, I do not see how it is to be disproved. It is very strange that, in spite of the universally admitted transcendency of Valentinus, no one of his works has been preserved to us. They are said to have been exceedingly intricate and difficult; they are further said to have been syntheses and symphonies as it were of prior formulations of the Gnosis. Now distinctly this is not the case with the outline of the best known system ascribed to "them of Valentinus" by the Church Fathers. Whereas it is patently the case with the treatises in Coptic translations; they could have been elaborated by no one but the stoutest-headed among the Gnostics—and the best head-piece of them all is said to have been on the shoulders of Valentinus.)

In spite of this appalling ignorance of the man and his teachings, the so-called Valentinian Gnosis is the *pièce de résistance* of nearly every hæresiological treatise. We shall, therefore, have to trespass on the patience of the reader for a short space, while we set up a few finger-posts in the maze of Valentinianism, as seen through the eyes of its Patristic opponents. We should moreover always remember that "Valentinianism," so far from being a single separate formulation of the Gnosis, was the main stream of Gnosticism simply rechristened by the name of its greatest leader.

With the exception of the few fragments to which we have referred, all that has been written by the Fathers refers to the teachings of "them

"Them of Valentinus."

of Valentinus," and even then it is but very rarely that we have an unmutilated quotation from any written work of theirs; for the most part it all consists of fragments torn from their contexts, or mere hearsay. Now the followers of Valentinus were no slavish disciples who could do nothing else but repeat parrot-like the "words of the master"; the *ipse dixit* spirit was far from their independent genius. Each of them thought out the details of the scheme of universal philosophy in his own fashion. True that by this time the presentation of the Gnosis, from being of a most diverse nature, had become more settled in its main features, and perhaps Valentinus may have initiated this syntheticizing tendency, though it is far more probable that he developed and perfected it; neverthless it was still enormously free and independent in innumerable details of a very far-reaching character, and its adherents were imbued with that spirit of research, discovery, and adaptation which ever marks a period of spiritual and intellectual life.

Thus we understand the complaint of Irenæus, who laments that he never could find two Valentinians who agreed together. And if this be so, what good is there in any longer talking of the "Valentinian system"? We know next to nothing from the Church Fathers of the "system" of Valentinus himself; as to his followers, each introduced new modifications, which we can no longer follow in the confused representations of the Church Fathers, who make them flatly contradict not only one another, but also themselves.

From *The Philosophumena*, published in 1851, we first heard of an Eastern and Western (Anatolic and Italic) division of the school of Valentinus, thus explaining the title superscribed to the *Extracts from Theodotus* appended, in the only M.S. of them we possess, to *The Miscellanies* of Clement of Alexandria. A great deal has been made of this; the meagre differences of doctrine of the Anatolic and Italic schools of Valentinianism indicated by Hippolytus (II.) have been seized upon by criticism, and had their backs broken by the weight of argument which has been piled upon them. But when Lipsius demonstrates that the *Extracts from Theodotus*, which claim in their superscription to belong to the Eastern school, are, following the indications of Hippolytus, half Eastern and half Western, the ordinary student has to hold his head tightly on to his shoulders, and abandon all hope of light from the division of Valentinianism into Anatolic and Italic schools, in the present state of our ignorance;—unless indeed we simply assume that they were originally purely geographical designations, to which in later times a doctrinal signification was unsuccessfully attempted to be given.

The so-called Eastern and Western Schools.

Although we have no sure indication of the date of Valentinus himself, it may be conjectured to extend from about A.D. 100 to A.D. 180, as will be seen later on.

Of the other leaders of the movement, the earliest with whose names we are acquainted, are Secundus and Marcus. Now Marcus himself had a large

The Leaders of the Movement.

following as early as 150; his followers were not called Valentinians but Marcosians, or Marcians, and what we know of his system differs enormously from those of the rest of "them of Valentinus." Marcus is sometimes supposed to have been a contemporary of Irenæus, but this is only on the supposition that Irenæus, in using the second person in his hortatory and admonitory passages, is addressing a living person, and not employing the "thou" as a mere rhetorical effect, as Tertullian with Marcion.

Next, years later, we come to Ptolemæus, who again is supposed to have been a contemporary of Irenæus somewhere about A.D. 180.

Irenæus had certainly no personal knowledge of Ptolemæus, and dealt for the most part with his followers, who are said to have differed greatly from their teacher.

Later still is Heracleon, whom Clement (c. 193) calls the most distinguished of the disciples of Valentinus. Both Heracleon and Ptolemæus, however, are known not so much for the exposition of a system as for the exegetical treatment of scripture from the standpoint of the Gnosis of their time.

Still later, and as late as, say, about 220, Axionicus and Bardesanes flourished, the former of whom taught at Antioch, and the latter still farther east. They are therefore called, by some, heads of the Anatolic or Oriental school.

Theodotus, from whom the Excerpts appended to Clement's *Miscellanies* were taken, was of course far earlier in date, but of him we know nothing

We also hear of a certain Theotimus and Alexander, who are earlier than 220.

In brief, the influence of Valentinus spread far and wide, from Egypt eastwards to Syria, Asia Minor and Mesopotamia, and westwards to Rome, Gaul, and even Spain.

A short review of the teachings ascribed to these doctors of the Gnosis will bring our task to a close, as far as the indirect sources of Gnosticism for the first two centuries are concerned. But the fact we would again insist upon is, that we are face to face with a great movement and not a single system. On the one hand, such older forms of the Gnosis as had been exceedingly antagonistic to Judaism found a logical outcome in the great Marcionite movement, which cut Christianity entirely apart from Judaism; on the other, a basis of reconciliation was sought by the more moderate and mystical views of the movement now headed by Valentinus, which found room for every view in its all-embracing universality, and explained away contradictions by means of that inner secret teaching which was claimed to have come from the Saviour Himself.

The Synthetizing of the Gnosis.

The main outline of the movement of conciliation, which presumably had always been the attitude of the innermost circles, is perhaps to be most clearly seen to-day in the system of Basilides, but those infinite spaces, which either Basilides himself left unfilled, or Hippolytus (II.) has omitted to mention in his quotations, were also peopled with an infinitude of creations and creatures by the genius of the Gnostics, who could brook no deficiency in the exposition of their universal science. Into this general outline, or one closely resembling it, they fitted the various aspects of the ancient Gnosis and the postulates of the old religions and philosophies, adopting these world-old ideas, and adapting them by the light of the new revelation, retaining sometimes the old names, more frequently inventing new ones.

This syntheticizing of the Gnosis was mainly due to the initiative of the genius of Valentinus. His technical works, as we have observed above, are said to have been most abstruse and difficult of comprehension, as well they might be from the nature of the task he attempted. What has become of these writings? No Church Father seems to have been acquainted with a single one of his technical treatises; at best we have only a few ethical fragments from letters and homilies. But what of his own followers, whom Church Fathers and critics make responsible for a certain Valentinian system of a most chaotic nature? Were they in possession of MSS. of Valentinus; or did they depend on general notions derived from his lectures? Did Valentinus work out a consistent scheme of the Gnosis; or did he set forth several alternatives, owing to the difficulty of the matter, and the innumerable points of view from which it could be envisaged? If the *Pistis Sophia* document and the other two Codices can be made to throw any light on the matter, it will be a precious acquisition to our knowledge of this most important epoch; if not, we must be content to remain in the dark until some fresh document is discovered.

Meantime we must confine our attention to the certain traces of Valentinus and the general movement; but before doing so, we must briefly review our authorities among the Fathers. In this review I shall mostly follow Lipsius, who is not only one of the best authorities on the subject (Art. in S. and W.'s *Dict. of Christ. Biog.*, 1887), but who long ago inaugurated the admirable critical investigations into our Gnostic sources of information, by his analysis of *The Panarion* of Epiphanius. {*Sources of Information.*}

Tertullian informs us that prior to himself no fewer than four orthodox champions had undertaken the refutation of the Valentinians: namely, Justin Martyr, Miltiades, Irenæus and the Montanist Proculus. With the exception of the five books of Irenæus, the rest of these controversial writings are lost.

Irenæus wrote his treatise somewhere about A.D. 185-195. He devotes most of his first book to the Valentinians exclusively, and isolated notices are found in the remaining four books.

Irenæus claims to have come across certain Memoranda of the Valentinians and had conversations with some of their number. But these Notes belonged only to the followers of Ptolemæus, and only one short fragment is ascribed to a writing of Ptolemæus himself. The personal conversations were also held with followers of the same teacher, presumably in the Rhone district—not exactly a fertile soil in which to implant the abstruse tenets of the Gnosis, we should think, in spite of the "martyrs of Lyons."

In dealing with Marcus, Irenæus derived his information for the most part from the same unreliable oral communications, but he seems also to have been in possession of a Memoir of a Marcosian; Marcus himself living and working far away in Asia Minor years before.

In chapter xi. Irenæus professes to give the teaching of Valentinus himself; but here he is simply copying from the work of a prior refutator. Lipsius also points out that Irenæus drew some of his opening statements from the same source as Clement in *The Excerpts from Theodotus*.

From all of which it follows that we are face to face with a most provoking patch-work, and that the system of Valentinus himself is not to be found in *The Refutation* by the Bishop of Lyons.

Our next source of information is to be found in the *Excerpts* from the otherwise unknown Theodotus, which are supposed by Lipsius to have probably formed part of the first book of Clement's lost work, *The Outlines*. These excerpts "have been dislocated and their original coherence broken up" in so violent a manner, and so interspersed with "counter-observations and independent discussions" by Clement hinself, that it is exceedingly difficult to form a judgment upon them. When, moreover, Lipsius assigns part of these extracts to the Oriental and part to the Occidental school, he practically bids us erase the superscription which has always been associated with them—namely, *Extracts from the (Books) of Theodotus and the so-called Anatolic School.* In any case, we are again face to face with another patch-work.

Hippolytus (I.), in his lost Syntagma, recoverable from the epitomators Pseudo-Tertullian and Philaster, and Epiphanius, seems to have combined the first seven chapters of Irenæus with some other account, and the chaos is still further confused.

Hippolytus (II.), in that most precious of all hæresiological documents, *The Philosophumena*, gives an entirely independent account, in fact the most uniform and synoptical representation of any phase of the Gnosis of the Valentinian cycle that has reached us through the Fathers.

Tertullian simply copies from Irenæus, and so also for the most part does Epiphanius. The latter, however, has preserved the famous *Letter of Ptolemæus to Flora*, and also a list of " barbarous names" of the æons not found elsewhere. Theodoret of course simply copies Irenæus and Epiphanius.

So many, and of such a nature, then, are our indirect sources of information for an understanding of the Valentinian movement;—a sorry troop of blind guides, it must be confessed, where everything requires the greatest care and discrimination. Let us now return to Valentinus himself, and endeavour to patch together from the fragments that remain, some dim silhouette of a character that was universally acknowledged to have been the greatest among the Gnostics.

VALENTINUS.

Biography.
As to his biography, we know next to nothing. Valentinus was an Egyptian, educated at Alexandria in all that Egypt and Greece had to teach him. The mysterious lore of ancient Khem, the "mathēsis" of Pythagoras, the wisdom of Plato, all helped to fashion his character. But the greatest inspiration of all he found in the last outpouring from the same source from which the wisdom of every true philosopher comes—the stream of Christianity that was swirling along at full tide. But what kind of Christianity did Valentinus encounter at Alexandria? There was no Catechetical School when he was a boy. Pantænus and Clement were not as yet. There were the Logoi, the Sayings of the Lord, and many contradictory traditions; a Pauline community also, doubtless founded by some missionary from Asia Minor; and numerous legends of the mysterious Gnosis which Jesus had secretly taught to those who could comprehend. But, above all things, at the back were the inner schools and communities of the wisdom-traditions and the Gnosis. Valentinus must have been in closest intimacy with Basilides, though he is said to have stated that a certain Theodas, an "apostolic man," was his witness to the direct tradition of the Gnosis. Nothing is known of this Theodas or Theudas, and Ussher has even assumed that it was a contraction for Theodotus, a conjecture in which he has been followed by Zahn. This theory

would thus make the Theodotus of the Excerpts in Clement an older authority than Valentinus himself, which would still further complicate the Eastern and Western school question, and, in fact, change the whole problem of Valentinian origins. All we can say here is that the view is not entirely improbable, and would clear the ground on certain important points.

In addition there were at Alexandria, in the great library and in the private libraries of the mystics, all those various sources of information, and in the intellectual and religious atmosphere of the place all those synthetical and theosophical tendencies which make for the formulation of a universal system of religion. And this we know was the task that Valentinus set before him as his goal. He determined to syntheticize the Gnosis, every phase of which was already in some sort a synthesis. But in so doing, Valentinus did not propose to attack or abandon the general faith, or to estrange the popular evolution of Christianity which has since been called the Catholic Church. He most probably remained a Catholic Christian to the end of his life. It is true that we read of his excommunication in Tertullian, coupled with the favourite accusation brought against prominent heretics, that he apostatized from the Church because his candidature for the episcopal office was rejected. Tertullian imagined that this took place at Rome; but, even if so, did Rome speak in the name of the Catholic Church in those early days? Would Alexandria, the philosophic, recognize the ruling of disciplinarian Rome? Or did Rome excommunicate Valentinus after his death, a favourite way with her in after times of finishing a controversy? Or is not Tertullian romancing here as is not infrequently the case? Epiphanius distinctly states that Valentinus was regarded as orthodox so long as he was at Rome, and Tertullian himself also, in another place, adds fifteen years of orthodoxy on to the date of his leaving Rome.

Date. Valentinus seems to have passed the greater part of his life in Egypt; he was, however, if we can trust our authorities, for some considerable time at Rome, somewhere between 138 and 160. One authority also says that he was at Cyprus.

The date of his death is absolutely unknown; critics mostly reckon it about 161, but in order to arrive at this conclusion, they reject the distinct statement of Tertullian that Valentinus was still an orthodox member of the Church up to the time of Eleutherus (c. 175); and the equally distinct statement of Origen, that he was personally acquainted with Valentinus. This would set back Origen's own date of birth and advance the date of Valentinus' death; but as both are problematical, we have nothing to fear from the putting back of the one and the putting forward of the other ten years or so.

On the whole I am inclined to assign the date of Valentinus to the first eighty years of the second century. In further support of this length of days, I would invite the reader to reflect on the extraordinary fact that, though the name of Valentinus is in the mouth of everyone of the time, and though his fame entirely eclipses that of every other name of this most important Gnostic cycle, the words and deeds of the great coryphæus of Gnosticism are almost entirely without record, and, stranger than all, he is regarded, at any rate for the major part of his life, as orthodox. This strange fact requires explanation, and I would venture to suggest that the explanation is to be found to a great extent in the extraordinary reserve and secrecy of the man. He was an enigma not only to the generality, but even to those who regarded him as a teacher.

The Gnosis in his hands is trying to forestall "orthodoxy," to embrace everything, even the most dogmatic formulation of the traditions of the Master. The great popular movement and its incomprehensibilities were recognized by Valentinus as an integral part of the mighty out-pouring; he laboured to weave all together, external and internal, into one piece, devoted his life to the task, and doubtless only at his death perceived that for that age he was attempting the impossible. None but the very few could ever appreciate the ideal of the man, much less understand it.

None of his technical treatises were ever published; his letters and homilies alone were circulated.

After leaving Rome he is practically lost to the sight of the Western hæresiologists. Where he went, what he did, and how long he lived after that, is almost entirely conjectural. But if it be ever shown to be true that such documents as the *Pistis Sophia* are specimens of the workshop to which he belonged, we can at least conjecturally answer that he went back to Alexandria, where he

Writings.

finished his life in the retirement that such abstruse literary labours required.

Of his writings, besides the fact that they were numerous and his technical treatises exceedingly difficult and abstruse, we know very little. He composed numerous Letters and Homilies and Psalms. We are also told that he composed a Gospel, but this is supposed to be a false assumption—false, that is to say, if by Gospel is meant a Gospel containing the Sayings of the Lord. But may not Gospel here be used in the Basilidian sense of an exposition of the Gnosis, or knowledge of the things beyond the phenomenal world?

Tertullian also tells us that Valentinus composed a treatise entitled *Sophia*, or Wisdom. Some critics have asserted that the words of Tertullian do not refer to a book but to the Wisdom which Valentinus claimed to teach; but if this were so, the antithesis which Tertullian makes between the *Wisdom* of Valentinus and the *Wisdom* of Solomon would lose all its point. The *Wisdom* of Solomon is a book, the *Wisdom* of Valentinus should also be a book; if it were intended to mean simply the Gnosis which Valentinus taught, then its proper antithesis would have been the Wisdom of God and not of Solomon.

The Fragments that remain.

We have now to treat of the few fragments of the works of this prolific writer which have come down to us in the writings of the Church Fathers. The latest collection of them is by Hilgenfeld (1884), whose "emendations," however, we shall not always follow. The fragments consist of a few scraps of letters and homilies preserved by

Clement of Alexandria, and two pieces in *The Philosophumena*—the narrative of a vision and the scrap of a psalm.

i. From a Letter.

"And just as terror of that creature [*lit.*, plasm] seized hold of the angels [the fabricative powers], when it gave voice to things greater than had been used in its fashioning, owing to the presence in it of Him [the Logos] who, unseen to them [the powers], had bestowed on it the seed of the supernal essence [the ego], and who spake of realities face to face; in like manner also among the races of humanity, the works of men become a terror to them who make them—such as statues and images, and all things which [men's] hands fashion to bear the name of God. For Adam being fashioned to bear the name of the [Heavenly] Man [the Logos], spread abroad the terror of that pre-existing Man, for in very truth he had His being in him. And they [the powers] were struck with terror, and [in their terror] speedily marred the work [of their hands]."

Concerning the Creation of the First Race of Mankind.

Here we have the Gnostic myth of the genesis of man, which is already familiar to us in the general tradition of the Gnosis.

The plasm, or primitive form of man, which could neither stand nor walk—the embryonic sphere of Plato's *Timæus*—is evolved by the powers of nature, as the outcome of evolution; into it Deity breathes the mind, and man is immediately raised above the rest of the creation and its powers.

Nevertheless his body is still feeble, and the nature-powers, in fear of the mind within—the "name" of the Heavenly Man—war on him, and only by slow degrees does the mind of man learn to overcome them.

The Heavenly Man is the perfect type of all Humanities, and the "name" is no name, but that mysterious something which decides the nature and class and being of every creature. Man alone down here has the divine "name" or nature alive within him.

The "prehistoric" world, with which Egypt was in direct traditional contact, made much of this "name"; statues and talismans and amulets, if made in a certain manner, were supposed to be a nearer approach to the perfect type either of manhood or of nature-organism, and on these fabrications of men's hands the "name" of this or that supernal power was thought to be bestowed by "Him who speaks face to face." Here we have a hint of the explanation given of "idol-worship" by the initiated priests of antiquity, which idea was thus woven into the scheme of universal Gnosis by Valentinus.

ii. From a Letter.

On the Pure in Heart.

"One [alone] is Good, whose free utterance is His manifestation through his Son; it is by Him alone that the heart can become pure, [and that too only] when every evil essence has been expelled out of it. Now its purity is prevented by the many essences which take up their abode in it, for each of them accomplishes its own deeds, outraging it in divers fashions with unseemly lusts. As far as I can see, the heart seems to receive somewhat the same treatment as an inn [or caravanserai], which has holes and gaps made in its walls, and is frequently filled with dung, men living filthily in it and taking no care of the place as being someone else's property. Thus it is with the heart so long as it has no care taken of it, ever unclean and the abode of many dæmons [elemental essences]. But when the Alone Good Father hath regard unto it, it is sanctified and shineth with light; and he who possesseth such a heart, is so blessed that 'he shall see God.'"

Here we have the very same doctrine as that enunciated by Basilides and Isidorus with regard to the "appendages" of the soul, as indeed is pointed out by Clement. The doctrine was an exceedingly ancient one in Egypt. In the so-called *Book of the Dead* we read, that the "heart" is a distinct personality within the man (the "*purusha* [or man] in the æther of the heart" of the Upanishads); and not only this, but the formula referred to and its explanatory texts teach us that "it is not the heart that sins but only its fleshly envelope." (Cf. Wiedemann's *Relig. of the Ancient Egyptians*, p. 287; 1897.) Isidorus, as we have already seen, guarded against making the "appendages" the scapegoat, and fixed the responsibility on the "heart" proper, the "ancestral heart"—"guardian of my fleshes"—the reincarnating entity. It is, however, quite true that the passions are connected with the blood, and so with the "fleshly envelope," or physical heart, in which the real "heart" is said to be enshrined.

iii. From the Letter to Agathōpus.

Concerning One of the Powers of the Perfect Man.

The "free utterance," or perfect expression, of the Alone Good can only be manifested by the man made perfect. Such a man was Jesus. Thus we find Valentinus writing to Agathōpus as follows:

"It was by his unremitting self-denial in all things that Jesus attained to [*lit.*, gained by working] godship; he ate and drank in a peculiar manner, without any waste. The power of continence was so great in him, that his food did not decay in him, for he himself was without decay."

It is said that the physical body can be gradually accustomed to less and less nutriment, and innumerable cases are on record in the East of holy ascetics who have been able to support life on incredibly small quantities of food. The "power" described above by Valentinus is one of the *siddhis* mentioned in every treatise on *yoga* in India, and in the Upanishads we read that "very little waste" is one of the first signs of "success in *yoga*." We are also told that in the highest stages, after the particles of the body have been entirely refined and made to obey the higher will of the ascetic, a body of a still higher grade of matter can be gradually substituted; and apparently some such ideas as these (together with other notions) lay behind the doctrine of docetism which was an integral part of the Gnosis·

Clement himself also shared like views, and so did some other Fathers.

iv. From a Homily.

"From the very beginning have ye been immortal and children of life—such life as the æons enjoy; yet would ye have death shared up among you, to spend and lavish it, so that death might die in you and by your hands; for inasmuch as ye dissolve the world and are not dissolved yourselves, ye are lords of all creation and destruction." *Ye are the Sons of God.*

Here we have the burden of the teaching in one of the treatises of the Codex Brucianus—to crucify the world and not let the world crucify us—and of the *Pistis Sophia* treatise, "Know ye not that ye are all gods and lords?" The Self within the heart, the seed of the divine, the pneumatic light-spark, the dweller in light, the inner man, was the eternal pilgrim incarnated in matter; those who had this alive and conscious within them were the spiritual or pneumatic. To such Valentinus is speaking.

v. A few Sentences preserved in the Controversial Matter of Clement following the above Quotation, and probably taken from a Writing of Valentinus.

The "elect race," the third Sonship of Basilides, has incarnated here for the abolition of "death," the domain of the Ruler of the phenomenal world, the *saṁsāra* of the Buddhist and Indian philosophers, the realm of the "ever-becoming" of Plato. This Ruler is the God of the Old Testament. "No *The Face of God.*

man shall see the face of God and live." This is the face of death, but there is also a face of life, concerning which Valentinus writes:

"As far removed as is the [dead image] from the living face, so far is the [phenomenal] world removed from the living æon [the noumenal]. What then is the cause of the image? The majesty of the [living] face, [or person,] which exhibits the type [of the universe] to the painter, and in order that it [the universe] may be honoured by its name [—the name or real being of the majesty of the godhead]. For it is not the authentic [or absolute] nature which is found in the form; it is the name which completes the deficiency in the confection. The invisible nature of deity co-operates so as to induce faith in that which has been fashioned."

Here we have the same idea as in Fragment i., and presumably it was taken from the same Letter. The "painter" is of course the user of the creative forces of the phenomenal world, who copies from the types or ideas in the noumenal world of reality. He whom the Jews called God and Father, was said by Valentinus to be the "image and prophet of the true God," the word prophet meaning one who speaks for and interprets. The "image" is the work of Sophia or Wisdom, who is the "painter" who transfers the types from the noumenal spaces on to the canvas of the phenomenal world, and the "true God" or the "God of truth" is the creator of the noumenal world, which contains the types of all things. He is the god of life; the "image" is the god of death.

VALENTINUS. 305

"All things that come forth from a pair [or syzygy] are fullnesses (plērōmata), but all which proceed from a single [æon] are images."

This will be explained later on; it refers to the "fall" of Sophia from the æon-world, whereby the phenomenal universe came into existence.

The remarks of Clement which immediately follow are almost unintelligible; they deal with the coming of the "excellent" spirit, the infusion of the light-spark into man.

vi. From the Letter on the Community of Friends.

"Many of these things which are written in the public volumes, are found written in the Church of God. For those teachings which are common, are the words which proceed from the heart, the law written in the heart. This is the People of the Beloved who are loved by and love Him."

Concerning the People of the Beloved.

Clement assumes that Valentinus means by "public volumes" the Jewish writings and the books of the philosophers.

The "public volumes," however, for Valentinus included not only the works of the philosophers and the scriptures of the Jews, but also the scriptures of all other religions, and also the Christian documents in general circulation. He merely asserts that the only "common" or general truths are those pertaining to the Community of Friends, or Saints, who form the Church of God, the People of the Beloved. These truths come from the heart; he protests against the narrow view that can find truth in only one set of scriptures; and declares it is in all scriptures and philosophies, if one looks to the spirit and not the letter.

vii. A very doubtful Fragment from Eulogius of Alexandria writing at the end of the Sixth Century.

The Galileans. If this fragment can be accepted as genuine, we learn that the early Christians, whom Valentinus calls "the Galileans of the time of Christ," believed in the doctrine of two natures, whereas the Valentinians asserted that there was but one. This is quite credible, following on the lines of argument of Isidorus concerning the unit consciousness of the soul and its responsibility, and the teaching of Valentinus that Jesus "worked out" his own divinity.

viii. The Myth which Valentinus made.

Hippolytus (II.) inserts the following scrap of information in the midst of the lengthy description of the system of Marcus, which he copied from Irenæus:

The Wisdom of the "Little One." Valentinus says that he once saw a child that had only just been born, and that he proceeded to question it to find out who it was. And the babe replied and said it was the Logos." To this, says Hippolytus, Valentinus subjoined a "tragic myth," which formed the basis of his teaching. Have we here an incident from the prologue to one of Valentinus' treatises; and is the "tragic myth" Valentinus' modification of the great Sophia-mythus which was the *deus ex machinâ* of part of his cosmogony?

ix. From a Psalm.

Finally from the same source, *The Philosophumena*, we recover the following lines; it is probable that Hippolytus took them from the same treatise from which he derived the above information, and that the Psalm endeavoured to explain why the new-born babe was the Logos, why "this" is "That," as the Upaniṣhads have it, and all is one.

The Chain of Being.

> "All things depending in spirit I see;
> All things supported in spirit I view;
>   Flesh from soul depending;
>   Soul by air supported;
>   Air from æther hanging—
>   Fruits borne of the deep—
>   Babe borne of the womb."

Whether or not this exceedingly mystical Psalm was taken in the sense we have suggested above is merely problematical. Such mystic utterances could of course be interpreted from both the microcosmic and macrocosmic standpoints; and Hippolytus gives us what he asserts to be a Valentinian interpretation from the latter point of view.

The "flesh" is the Hylē (the Hebdomad of Basilides); the "soul" is that of the Demiurge (the "material" force of the ætheric spaces, the Ogdoad of Basilides); the Demiurge hangs from the Spirit, which from one point of view is the Great Limit or Boundary, separating the Plērōma, or world of reality, from the Kenōma or phenomenal universe, and from another is Sophia or Wisdom, in the Kingdom of the Midst. Thus the Demiurge hangs from Sophia; Sophia from the Great Boundary or Horos (a further differentiation of the Basilidian simple idea of the Great Firmament); Horos from the Plērōma, the Blessed Treasure of the æons; and this world of ideas, or Living Æon, from the Abyss or Great Depth, the Father, the God beyond being.

This is the Valentinian chain of being, the subordinate details of which are so abstruse and so complicated, that no one has hitherto been able to make any consistent scheme out of their chaotic and contradictory representations in the writings of the Fathers.

In the MS. of *The Philosophumena* the above fragment is prefixed by the disconnected word "Harvest." Hilgenfeld accordingly speaks of Valentinus "hymning the Great Harvest," which is a very grandiose conception, but an idea difficult to connect with the lines quoted.

Such is the poor sum total of our information as to what Valentinus actually taught himself—nine, or rather eight, shreds of fragments in all. Yet what strong, joyous words, bursting with life, in the midst of the dullness of the refutators' rhetoric.

To these fragments it might seem proper to append the account which Irenæus (cap. 11) copied from a former hæresiological writer. It is generally assumed that this more ancient authority was Justin Martyr; but whoever he may have been, he was a mere summarizer, and even at that early date in hæresiology (*cir.* 150), was struggling with the contradictory accounts he had heard of the "Valentinian" Gnosis. I, therefore, consider this source as no more worthy of special notice than the other summaries of general so-called Valentinian doctrine found in the writings of the Fathers. We have nothing certain to learn in it of the teaching of Valentinus himself, and that is the only search on which we are at present engaged.

Thus we take our farewell of the "great unknown" of Gnosticism, whose name was nevertheless the best known of all, whose influence was the most far-reaching, and whose doctrines, instead of being a cut-and-dried system of dead vocables, were so animate with life that the kaleidoscopic representations of them by his followers in the first place, and the puzzled and puzzling summaries by the Fathers of these protean representations in the second, have proved the despair of scholarship. The reason of this for the most part is that, in endeavoring to bring order into this chaos, words and terms have been followed as clues instead of ideas. Not only in the case of the Valentinian cycle of ideas, but also in every other phase of the Gnosis, these delusive guides have been generally followed as leaders out of the labyrinth. But the Adriadne's thread which takes us out of the maze is spun out of ideas, not of names. The Gnostics were ever changing their nomenclature; the god of one system might even be the devil of another! He who makes a concordance of names merely, in Gnosticism, may think himself lucky to escape a lunatic asylum; he, on the contrary, who seeks the idea behind the

The Ariadne's Thread out of the Maze.

name, will often find himself in a realm of great beauty and harmony of thought. Men like the Gnostics have ever had intuitions of a real state of being, of definite and precise realms of consciousness; yet each has caught but a glimpse of the reality, as all men must so long as they are imprisoned in a body. If the Gnostics exhausted the philosophy and religion of their time in striving to find a decent vestment for the naked truth, as they thought they saw it, who shall blame them? Though they contradict one another, in the view of the word-hunter, they do not contradict themselves for the follower of ideas. The idea is the key which opens the mysteries of the Gnosis, and those who refuse to use this living key must be content to have the treasury closed against them.

We shall now, before dealing with the followers of Valentinus, attempt, from the chaos of summaries, to sift out some of the leading ideas of the Valentinian cycle of the Gnosis. If we were to bring all these contradictory accounts together and treat them to a critical analysis, it is to be feared that the general reader, for whom these sketches are written, would either close our pages in despair; or, if he attempted to follow the details and the weighing of probabilities, be reduced to such a state of mental perturbation that he would forget all that has gone before, and be rendered totally unfit to comprehend what is to follow. Such technical work must be reserved for treatment elsewhere, meantime we will attempt, not to give an exposition of the system of "them of

Valentinus"—if indeed they ever had a single definite system—but merely to sketch some outlines of their ideas on æonology.

SOME OUTLINES OF ÆONOLOGY.

IN order to elevate our thought to a contemplation of the transcendent problems towards which the mind of these Gnostics was carried, we should refresh our memory with the sketch of the Basilidian system which has been given above. From the world of men, our earth, we must pass in thought through the sublunary spaces, visible and invisible; thence we must pass beyond the moon-firmament, the heaven, into the æthereal spaces—the star-worlds, and their infinite inhabitants, spaces and regions, orders and hierarchies—bounded at the utmost limits of space and time, by the Great Firmament, the Ring "Pass Not," which marks off the phenomenal universe from the universe of reality out of space and time. It is a Boundary everywhere and—no "where."

Towards the Great Silence.

Here we bid farewell to time and space, and reach the region of paradox, for mortal man has still to speak of it in terms of phenomenal things—calling it a region, although it is not a region; speaking of it as the Living Æon, though it transcends all life; hymning it as the Light-world, though its light is darkness to mortal eyes, because of the superabundance of its brilliancy.

This is the Plērōma, the world of perfection, of

perfect types and perfect harmony. The mind falls back from it, unable to comprehend, and yet the spirit within cries unto man with a voice that can brook no denial: "Onward still; beyond still, and beyond!" Then is there Silence; no words, no symbols, no thoughts can further avail. The mind is mute, the spirit is at peace, at rest in the Supreme Silence of contemplation, of union with the Divine, the Great Deep—Profundity, the within of things, that which permeates all, goes *through* all.

The Depth Beyond Being. Our Gnostics are said to have "begun" with this conception of Bythus, or the Abyss of Profundity; but this is a mistake. Basilides had already shown how impossible it was to name the God beyond all; are we to think that the Valentinians fell short of so obvious a truth? By no means; some of them taught of the Beyond the Deep, a hierarchy of Deeps; and curiously enough in the Codex Brucianus we meet with such hierarchies, and also find them assumed in the *Pistis Sophia* treatise. What absurdity, then, to seek a "beginning" in infinitude! Such a conception as a beginning was low down in the scale of being; we can speak of the "beginning" of some special phenomenal universe, but there is an infinitude of such universes, and infinitude has no beginning.

Beyond the Plērōma, or ideal type of all universes, there was—what? Silences more unspeakable than Silence, and Depths deeper than the Deep! How the Valentinians would have laughed at the notion of ascribing a monistic or dualistic theory to their intuition of what lay beyond Being, and of making this the basis of dividing them into an Eastern and Western school! Yet that is what Hippolytus (II.) and many modern critics have done.

Let us then leave the mystery in the Silence of that Depth beyond Being—a Silence which, as it were, shut off the Plērōma from the Depth beyond Being by a still higher Boundary than the Great Firmament. This highest Boundary was within the innermost depths of the Plērōma itself, the inward world, just as the Great Boundary was beyond the depths of the phenomenal external world. The idea connoted by the term "depth" takes thought away from all ideas of three dimensional matter, as we know it, and introduces it to the notion of "through" in every direction at the same time, inside and out as well.

We next have to treat of the "being" of the Plērōma of the æons. Every "being" in this "Fullness of Being" (Plērōma) was also, in its turn, a "fullness" or perfection, and the nature of the life of these "beings" was shown forth in their names. They were called æons, or "eternities," for they were out of time and space. Everything outside the Plērōma, that is to say, everything in the phenomenal universe, on the contrary, was an "image" or deficiency. The phenomenal world was therefore called by such names as the Kenōma or "Emptiness," the Image, etc.

The Æon-world.

It is, however, evident that until we reach the phenomenal world, no possible human language can serve us to express modes of being which transcend cosmogonic operations. And yet the hardihood of the

Gnostic genius had to find some method whereby it could adumbrate the manner of being of the æons, which were *ex hypothesi* out of time and space. Let us then turn our attention to one of the methods whereby this was attempted. Not that the Gnostics worked from below upwards, they received from above and brought it down into matter; in brief, their expositions were attempts to describe a *living symbol*, which is said to have been shown them in vision.

The Platonic Solids.

Now Pythagoras and Plato, and the instructors in the Mysteries, declared that physical matter was ultimately of a geometrical nature; that in all things "God geometrizes." Thus the five regular solids formed the summit of the geometrical knowledge of the Platonic school. It was because of the attention bestowed on these solids by this school, that posterity has called the five the Platonic Solids. The whole of the Elements of Euclid, says Proclus, were but an introduction to this science of the perfect solids. These polyhedra were believed to lie at the back not only of earth-formation, but of every genus, species, and individual in the material universe. It is strange that no subject in mathematics has been so neglected as that of the regular solids; but so it is, and the moderns laugh at such "puerilities" of the ancients.

For the re-discovery and elaboration of a part of this science within the last six years I must refer the "*doulx lecteur*" to the works of a young Spanish scientist, Señor Soria y Mata.

No one of course who is entirely ignorant of the

subject, will be able to comprehend fully the following general indications; but the nature of finger-posts is to point in certain directions, not to accompany the traveller along the road; and the "gentle reader" who requires such personal conducting must seek it in Señor Soria's admirable essays. For the present our work is simply to set up sign-posts; and so we return to our task.

But even supposing, some one may say, that the five solids (which are all variations of one in various combinations with itself) have some connection with the typical elements which build up the invisible molecular structure of physical matter, what has that to do with the Valentinian Gnostics? A great deal, we may answer. Marcus, one of the earliest followers of Valentinus, has some system of a kabalistic numbering assigned to him, and in connection with this Hippolytus (II.) declares that the whole of Valentinianism was based on the numbers and geometry of Pythagoras and Plato.

No further proof, however, is brought forward of this sweeping generality, and no scholar has so far supplied the missing link. It is, nevertheless, entirely credible that the æonology of the Valentinian School was based partly on such considerations. Let us then attempt to make a few suggestions on the subject, not from the numbering ascribed to Marcus, but from the living side of Pythagorean and Platonic mathematics, the "*mathēsis*" which was the same as the "*gnōsis*," and which is said to have been called even by Pythagoras himself, "the gnōsis of things that are."

It was then perhaps along this line of thought

A Living Symbolism. that some of the Gnostic thinkers sought for a living symbolism, which should adumbrate in some fashion the manner of being of the æons. From the region of definite polyhedrical matter, the ordering of which, though invisible to the eye, could yet be imagined in the mind, the symbolism could be pushed back a further stage—from the molecular to the atomic as we should say now-a-days. The regular solids were thus the eventuation in physical matter of certain systems of perfect equilibrium of "points" in space. These points were not pure mathematical abstractions, but actual centres of force, bearing certain relations to one another, equilibrated by a law of polarity or syzygy. This was the region of the atom. The atom was thought of as a living thing of force, a sphere, said by some to be a spherical ("conical") swirl, the most perfect figure, ever contracting and expanding, generative of all motions, while it is itself self-motive, and yet from another point of view "immovable," as pertaining to the "foundations of earth." It is smaller than the small as matter, yet greater than the great as energy.

It was the atom and its combinations, then, as we should now-a-days say, which the Valentinian Gnosis envisaged in its æonology. I do not, however, for a moment suggest that any Gnostic philosopher thought of the atom in the same way as a modern physicist does; I believe, on the contrary, that the most advanced of the Gnostics were shown this living symbol of world-formation in vision, and the various systems were efforts to explain such visions. Of course, any symbol is immensities removed from the reality, but the endeavour to imagine, or the privilege of being shown, the living type lying beyond the simplest types of physical matter-formation, is at any rate nearer the reality than any dead physical shape. Thus the atom and its simplest modes of differentiated being, may be taken as symbols of the æon-world, the Plērōma, the world of life and light, beyond time and space, the undecaying heart of the eternities.

The following view may then be of interest to students of symbolism, who as a rule confine their attention solely to plane figures, and thus deal as it were with the "shadows of the dead." For a plane figure is, so to speak, only a shadow of a dead solid; it is the living system of force behind or within the latter which is the first spark of life in the series. In order to see this more clearly, let us take a familiar symbol, the interlaced triangles or "Solomon's Seal." In solids this symbol is represented by two mutually interpenetrated tetrahedra; from this union come the cube and octahedron. The dodecahedron and icosahedron come from the mutual congress of five tetrahedra, a quintuplication. Thus we have our five regular solids. The fundamental type is the tetrahedron, and the force-system behind it consists of two pairs of atoms, or a double syzygy or couple in perfect equilibrium. The nature of the relationship of these atoms or spheres to each other, and of the interplay of their motions, is the mode of life or being of the symbol; and when this is learned, then the symbol becomes alive and thus the forces which the "shadow" of the "dead" solid symbolizes, are in the hand of the solver of the "mystery." One form of ancient magic, especially practised in Egypt, consisted of a most complicated extension of this idea, which wandered far beyond the limits of the geometrical symbols. Needless to say that the vast majority who practised the art, had not the slightest idea of the "reasons" for their performances. Magic for the general was never a rational thing. It consisted of an infinite number of "rules of thumb," and this side of it is consequently, and quite rightly, regarded by the present age of intelligent enquiry as a superstition.

<small>The "Fourth Dimension."</small> The intelligent student of symbolism will thus endeavour to free his mind from the limitations of three-dimensional space, and think within into the state of the so-called "fourth dimension." For it is only along this line of thought that there is any hope of the faintest conception of æonic being. As the matter is of the first importance for a student of Gnosticism, and at the same time one of great difficulty, the following line of thought may be suggested as a preliminary exercise. Think of an atom, or monad, as a sphere which generates itself, or swells out, from a point and refunds itself again into that point. This gives the simple idea of position. Take two of such spheres at the same moment of expansion, that is to say two equal spheres, and place them in mutual contact. This can be done in an infinite number of ways, so that they may be in any direction the one with the other.

Reduce these spheres in thought to mathematical

points, and we have the simplest idea of extension— one dimension. The two points are the extremities or boundaries of a line.

Next, take three similar spheres and bring them into mutual contact. They can be placed in any direction the one to the other. Reduce them in thought to points, and we have three points not in a straight line, lying in a plane surface, or superfices of two dimensions. Then take four such spheres and bring them into mutual contact. Reduce them in their turn to points, and their positions require space of three dimensions. Finally, take five such spheres and try to imagine how they can be brought into mutual contact, that is to say, how each one can touch all the rest. This cannot be imagined in three dimensions, and requires the conception of another "dimension"—something to do with the content of the spheres—the idea of "through." This does not seem to be so much a "fourth dimension" as an involution of perception, retracing the path we have so far followed.

For instance, three-dimensional space is for normal sight bounded by surfaces; those who have inner vision ("four-dimensional" sight) say that the contents of an object—*e.g.*, a watch—appear, in some incomprehensible way, spread out before them as on a surface. If this is so, then three-dimensional space, the fourth link in our chain, is the turning point, and hence consciousness turns itself inwards once more towards the point, which when reached will become the illimitable circumference, or plērōma of consciousness—the nirvāṇic "atom," so to say.

Let us now try to imagine how the Gnosis symbolized the ideal universe, the type of all universes—the primal atom or monad, its motions, and modes of self-differencing and self-emanation within itself. The object of their contemplation was identical with the world of ideas, or noëtic world, of Plato; the light-world of ancient Irān; the "eternal egg," or type, from which all universes come forth, of ancient Khem; the "resplendent germ," or *hiranya-garbha*, of the Upaniṣhads—all of which has been intuitively set forth in philosophical terms by Leibnitz in his *Monadology*.

The Eternal Atom.First, then, we have the conception of an infinite sphere of Light, Light which transcends the glory of the most brilliant sun, as that sun's glory transcends the flame of a rush-light; Light beyond thought. As yet there is naught but infinite Light; yet through it there is ever a something going, as it were from and to its centre, which is everywhere and nowhere, a breath ever outbreathing and inbreathing, an endless energy which nothing human can perceive or know. It is the Life-breath of the universe at the zero-point of being, to use terms familiar to some theosophical students.

We next proceed to what we must call a change of state; but we should remember that all the states we are attempting thus to symbolize, in reality exist *simultaneously*; and though in thought we are to follow out a kind of emanation or evolution, it is in reality an ever-existing infinite state of consciousness out of time and space.

In this ever-pulsating field of universal energy

(which is everywhere and nowhere), a something arises slightly less brilliant than the transcendent Light, another mode of motion as it were, which we may symbolize as an oval or egg-like swirling, ever swelling-out and in-drawing. Within this two "foci" are gradually developed, as it pulsates and swells. The inner periphery of the egg-envelope contracts in the midst through the action of the two foci, the symbols of equilibrium, of positive and negative, the law of syzygy or pairing. The two part asunder. Bythus and Ennœa, Profoundity and Thought, are the first syzygy of æons, now symbolized as two spheres. Being separate, in some mysterious fashion they are differently affected by the great out-breath and in-breath, yet each manifests the qualities of the other. One is positive, the other is negative, as it were, and these qualities are at once communicated to the whole of the great Light-sphere, for they are everywhere and nowhere at once. Polarity is thus stated to be a mode of being of the Plērōma; the law of syzygy is affirmed.

The Law of Syzygy.

But duality arising, multiplicity must follow; and not only multiplicity but universality. For the Plērōma must be simultaneously the type of the One, Many and All, and monotheism, polytheism and pantheism must each find its source therein.

In following out our symbolic imagery, however, we cannot think the whole at once. We try to conceive that whatever process we gain an intuition of by means of our symbols, takes place everywhere, always, and simultaneously with every other process and manner of being; but of this we can get no

x

mental image. We can only pass from one process to another by following out the behaviour of a single pair of our living symbols. To proceed then.

Thus we have spheres evolving, each positive-negative in itself, but positive or negative in its relationship to the other. In thought we will treat one as positive, the other as negative, and thus try to imagine the changes of mode. As the twin spheres in their turn expand and contract, when they touch, from the negative a "veil" or "mist" is shed forth and as it were "lines" the great Light-sphere.

The Law of Differentiation. The law of densification and perpetual differentiation is declared. At each contract the negative sphere becomes less light and more passive as it were, though in reality the "lowest" æon far transcends the most brilliant radiance in the universe. The negative light-sphere developes into progeny, differentiates its substance, impregnated by the positive light-sphere. That is to say, the Light-world is differentiated into "planes" of being; there are "veils" and "firmaments." But how many and of what kind?

I must refer the reader again to Señor Soria's essays on the polyhedric origin of species for the only possible series of physical systems of perfect equilibrium of spheres of equal diameter, from two upwards, if he would follow out this most interesting problem in greater detail and work out the matter for himself. For the moment it is sufficient to state that the first æonic hierarchy of the Valentinian Plērōma is said to have been an ogdoad, or group of eight, which was sometimes considered as a dual tetrad—in living symbols, the system of equilibrium behind two equally interpenetrated tetrahedra.

A point of interest which should not be overlooked, however, is to be noticed as following from the consideration of the ogdoadic mode of the Plērōma. The Bythus and Ennœa are no longer regarded as a single pair; Ennœa, the negative sphere, has produced offspring. She is now the type of "seven-robed" Nature, Isis; while Bythus is the Great Deep or "Water-whirl," Osiris, the æther. The negative sphere is now seven spheres (herself, and six like unto herself and the positive sphere)— that is, three pairs of æons. Here we have the type of the one sphere of sameness, and the seven spheres of difference, of the Pythagorean and Platonic World-soul. The Ogdoad and Hebdomad of Basilides have also here their types. *[The Three and the Seven.]*

Thus having declared the law of duality, or syzygy, we next find the law of triplicity asserted in the triad of syzygies into which the negative sphere is differentiated. These are the three great stages or spaces of the Plērōma, and the syzygies, or modes of polarity, of these phases were called Mind-Truth, Word-Life, and Man-Church, for reasons which are somewhat obscure, and to which we shall return later on.

We are next told of a dodecad and decad of æons which owe their existence to one or other of the syzygies of the ogdoad. The accounts of their genesis are entirely contradictory; sometimes also the decad is placed before the dodecad, and, seeing of course that ten naturally comes before twelve, the critics *[The Twelve and Ten.]*

have without exception preferred this order. The matter is at best purely conjectural in such a chaos, but experience leads us to choose the less likely as being the more correct account. What on earth should have induced some of the Valentinians to put the twelve before the ten if their symbolism had not necessitated such an order?

We shall therefore take the main phases of the Plērōma to be those symbolized by the ogdoad, the dodecad and the decad in turn; not that one came from the other in reality (they all existed together eternally), but because the living symbols are described in a dramatic myth, one of the variants of which we shall shortly present to the reader.

The ogdoad is a term connoting the operations of the living processes behind the symbol of two interpenetrated tetrahedra, and therefore includes all the permutations of their complementary progeny (the cube and octahedron). Thus the ogdoad was divided into a higher and lower tetrad, and in various other ways, including the one and the seven as described above; the one and the seven can be represented by the curious geometrical fact that if seven equal circles be taken, and six be grouped round the central one, each circumference respectively will be found to exactly touch two adjacent circles and the one in the middle, while the greater circle can be described round all seven. This is of course but the shadow of a symbol, and is only intended to serve as a mnemonic; but the fact is curious, and such natural facts were not so lightly regarded by the Platonists as they are by the moderns, especially when they had to do with the most perfect figures—circles and spheres, the natural symbols of perfections or plērōmata.

We have now come to a stage where the differentiation of the primal simplicity is to be represented by groups of twelve; the mode of being of the Plērōma is now the dodecad. It is a curious fact that if we were to imagine space filled with spheres all of equal diameter and in mutual contact, we should find that each sphere was surrounded with exactly twelve other spheres; moreover, if we should imagine the spheres to be elastic, and that pressure be brought to bear on one of such systems of twelve, on every side at once, the central or thirteenth sphere would assume a dodecagonal form—in fact, a rhombic dodecahedron. *The Dodecahedron.*

If we further remember that there is frequent mention of a "thirteenth æon," which has hitherto puzzled all the commentators; that the Pythagoreans and Platonists and Indian philosophers asserted that the dodecahedron was the symbol of the material universe; that we are assured by some who have psychic or clairvoyant vision to-day that the field of activity of the atom is contained by a rhombic dodecahedron; and that the "twelve" signs of the zodiac have hitherto remained a mere irrational hypothesis—then we may be inclined to think that there was good reason for insisting on the dodecad as an important phase of æonian being.

Moreover, each phase of the Plērōma is supposed to be positive to the succeeding phase. Thus the Plērōma as a whole is positive to the dyadic stage; in the dyadic stage, Bythus is positive to Ennœa, who becomes various and sevenfold. The sevenfold is positive to the dodecad stage, which consists of thirteen spheres.

If we think of the dodecad as the dodecahedron we shall be dealing with the phenomenal universe, and thus be without the Plērōma; here we are dealing with the living type behind, in the æon-world, that is to say the system of thirteen spheres which eventuate the dodecahedron in the physical world.

Each of these thirteen contains in itself the seven modes of being of the preceding phase, and thus, in every system of thirteen, there is in reality a multitudinous progeny. These are the children of that phase of being which we may call the multiplicity of sameness, *i.e.*, the atomic ocean of like contiguous spheres; and they in their turn undergo a change which will eventuate in a harmonious arrangement or perfection, to be finally denoted by the perfect number ten, the decad.

The Decad. How, then, do we get from the dodecad to the decad, from atomic matter to the perfect form? Perhaps somewhat in this way. Every sphere is living, moving in all ways at once, so to speak, and yet in another sense motionless. The types of external motion are up, down, right, left, back, front, and round—seven in all; to these we have to add in and out, and a motion that is no motion we can imagine. And thus we reach a new phase of being through the decad or ten, which begins, as it were, another series of motions on a higher plane (1, 2, 3, etc., and then 11, 12, 13, etc.).

The seven motions, or modes of life, in every

system of thirteen spheres, are simple in the great sphere which surrounds the thirteen—the fourteenth or boundary of the system; but in the subordinate thirteen spheres the modes of motion act and react on each other (for each subordinate sphere contacts so many others) and produce a number of other modes of a subordinate nature, namely (7 × 13 or) 91. If to these we add as rulers the seven simple rates of motion, in all we have 98 (91 + 7) different modes. To these we add the two higher modes, the in- and out-breathing, and in all we have 100. The one hundred is the perfection (10 × 10) of the perfect number (10). We shall see later on how the Gnostics, in one of their systems, in their perfecting of the Plērōma, found themselves compelled to add two æons, and so introduced Christ and the Holy Spirit into the myth of the Plērōma-drama.

Thus the hundred obtained along the line of development of the ogdoad and dodecad, by the addition of two new factors, or the operation of a new syzygy, led by another path of simplification to the ten, the number of consummation.

Now the number of root-æons in the Plērōma was said to be thirty (8 + 12 + 10), to which we may add Christ and the Holy Spirit—the representatives of the Bythus and Sigē (Silence) beyond the Plērōma —and finally the That beyond all, so getting thirty-three, the number of the Vaidic pantheon of thirty-three deities, the 8 Vasus, 12 Adityās and 10 Rudras, with a supreme Rudra at their head, and Heaven and Earth.

The number 100 also gives a hint whereby to

explain the ordering of the subordinate phases of the Plērōma, as found in the system attributed by Hippolytus (II.) to the Docetæ, where mention is made of the "thirty-fold, sixty-fold and one hundred-fold."

I do not for one moment suggest that these speculations were the basis of Gnostic æonology; I believe the Gnostics were "shown" their æon-lore in vision, and that they found analogies to what they were shown, in nature and in the science of the time. Pythagoras was also, I believe, shown the same truths and worked them out in mathematical symbols. The Gnostics were acquainted with the system of his followers—a system of which unfortunately only the merest fragments have reached us—and they doubtless pressed into their service his theological arithmetic and geometry to aid in their expositions; but this was only *one* means out of a number which they employed for the same purpose. But to continue with our æonology.

Chaos.

But how, out of the perfection of the Plērōma (for every one of the æons was a perfection or plērōma in its turn), was the imperfection, or deficiency, of cosmic matter to come, which should serve as the substance out of which the "images" or "creatures" of the universe were to be formed? So far the living symbol of the Plērōma has produced perfect spheres, all in pairs, a light and less light or "darker" globe; for the twelve and ten, just like the eight, consist of pairs. The various phases have been brought about by the light globes acting on the "darker" ones. But now a new change takes place. There is an interaction of "dark" globes; and the result is no longer a perfect sphere innate with motion, but an amorphous mass, in one sense *out of* the Plērōma, as being *lower* than it, or not of its nature. When this takes place, the whole system endeavours, as it were, to right itself, just as the organs and corpuscles of the human body do when anything goes wrong in it, for the Plērōma is the spiritual body of the Heavenly Man. But the various æons of themselves cannot effect their purpose, they can only act on the "formlessness" when they combine together. From every one of the thirty æons, as it were, there shoots forth a ray, and all the rays somehow or other, form a new æon or globe of light, which rounds off the amorphous mass, or "abortion," burns it into shape, enters into it, and finally carries it back to the rest.

This is the living symbol of the world-drama, and was worked out by the Gnostics in much mythological detail. To everything below the Plērōma, the Plērōma is one, a single thing, containing the powers of all the æons; it is the "living æon" and acts upon cosmic matter, which is shapeless, and so endows it with form and creates the universe. But this is only the "enforming according to essence"; there is also an "enforming according to knowledge," or consciousness, which pertains to the soteriological part of the drama.

The idea seems to have been that the "abortion," or chaos, was destitute of the life-swirl or vortex. The vortex is the finger of fire, as it were, or light-spark, shot forth by the light-æons, in their positive phases; the negative spheres cannot shape or fashion the abortion, but can only densify or materialize it; the mother-breath cools, the father-breath warms the plasm of the universe. This plasm is now, so to say, thrown out of the ideal world into the cosmic plane, or rather, let us say, from the cosmic plane into the plane of a star-system; for the human mind cannot grasp such immensities as those of the ideal world, and all we can do is to single out a finite example from the infinitudes of space. Anything thrown out of the great cosmic sweep and the life of the æons is, as it were, "crucified in space"; or rather that which is incarnated into it, leaves the plane of infinitude where it is one with the Father, and is "crucified." The Logos takes a body, and His body is the cosmos. The Heavenly Man is crucified in space. But this crucifixion is no shame, no disgrace; the cross is the body of the Heavenly Man, the universe; and the symbol which the wise have chosen for that mystery, is the figure of the Heavenly Man with arms outstretched pouring His life and love and light into His creatures. He is the source of all good to the universe, the perpetual self-sacrifice.

Far lower down in the scale of being there is another crucifixion, when the spirit is incarnated into the plane where there is male and female, and is thus cut off from the great life and motion of the Plērōma. The spirit in man is no longer consciously in the grand sweep of the Great Breath, the Nirvāṇic Ocean of Life.

But we must return to cosmic substance and its fashioning. This substance is so fine and rare and subtle, that it transcends all substance we know of; indeed the mother-substance of cosmos is of so marvellous a nature that the Gnostics called it Wisdom herself, the highest vesture with which the spirit could be clothed. That which gives Wisdom her first enformation, is the potency of all the æons, called the Common Fruit of the Plērōma.

We have now arrived at the beginning of the evolution of the cosmos, according to this scheme of universal philosophy. We must, however, if our imagination is to stand the strain, be more modest, and confine our attention to the beginning of a solar system instead of the origin of the cosmos. Cosmos.

The ætheric spaces destined to be the home of the future system are void and formless. From the fullness of potential energy, the Plērōma, there comes forth the stream of power, the spiral vortex—the Magna Vorago, or Vast Whirlpool, of Orpheus. It is the fiery creative power; there is as it were the purification of the spaces by fire. He enters into the formlessness, and becomes the thing which it lacked, the spiral life-force or primordial atom; He also fashions it without. The mother-substance becomes a sphere, irradiate with life, a whirling mass of stardust. The "atom" becomes the "flying serpent," the comet, which as it were first hovers over the mother-substance, the new-born system. It is the "serpent" and the "egg" again, the spermatozoön and ovum of the solar embryon.

We have now reached a stage where we have to deal with the differentiation of this nebula according to the types in the Divine Mind, in other words, the

Plērōma. It is at this point that the intuitions of antiquity and the most recent discoveries of modern science should meet face to face. This most desirable union of the past and the present is, I believe, not so distant an event as one might be led to suppose, but the present essay does not give us scope even to suggest a few indications of the subject. The matter is exceedingly technical, and we are not at present engaged on such a task, but are merely enabling the general reader to while away an hour or two among the Gnostics.

Mythology.

We will, therefore, break off here on the borderland between the æonology and cosmogony of the Valentinian circle of Gnosticism, and before going any farther give a specimen of their mythological treatment of the æon-process. As we have already remarked more than once, the accounts in the Church Fathers are inconsistent and in many details contradictory. We hope, however, that the sketch we have given above of the trend of ideas will throw some light on all accounts, but as we have not the space to give all, we must select one as a specimen; and the fact that Hippolytus (II.) seems to have had a Gnostic MS. in front of him (seeing that he invariably adheres more closely to his written authorities than any of his predecessors) shall guide us in our selection. Hippolytus, in his *Philosophumena*, may be quoting from a late writing compared for instance with the *Excerpts from Theodotus;* but his account is more or less a reflection of the way in which a Gnostic looked at the matter, while the *Excerpts* are most pitifully mutilated and misplaced. As for

Irenæus' summary, it is at best a sorry patchwork. Not, however, that the account of Hippolytus is not also a patchwork. It is manifestly patched together, nevertheless the main pattern is taken from some treatise in the private circulating library of the Valentinian school.

It may, however, before dealing with the account of Hippolytus, be of interest to give the reader some general idea of the important rôle played by the personified Wisdom in Gnostic mythology. As Wisdom was the end of the Gnosis, so the pivot of the whole Gnostic mythological drama was the so-called Sophia-Mythus. For whether we interpret their allegories from the macrocosmic or microcosmic standpoint, it is ever the evolution of the *mind* that the initiates of old have sought to teach us. The emanation and evolution of the world-mind in cosmogenesis, and of the human mind in anthropogenesis, is ever the main interest of the secret science.

<small>The Sophia-Mythus.</small>

The dwelling of Sophia, as the World-Soul, according to our Gnostics, was in the Midst, in the Ogdoad, between the upper or purely spiritual worlds, and the lower psychic and material worlds. Below the Ogdoad was the Hebdomad or Seven Spheres of psychic substance. Truly hath "Wisdom built for herself a House, and rested it on Seven Pillars" (*Prov.* ix. 1); and again: "She is in the lofty Heights; she stands in the Midst of the Paths, for she taketh her seat by the Gates of the Powerful Ones, she tarrieth at the Entrances [of the Light-World]" (*ibid.*, viii. 2), says the Wisdom in its Jewish tradition.

Moreover, Sophia was the Mediatrix between the upper and lower spaces, and at the same time projected the Types or Ideas of the plērōma into the cosmos. But why should Wisdom, who was originally of a pneumatic or spiritual essence, be in the Middle Space, an exile from her true Dwelling? Such was the great mystery which the Gnosis endeavoured to solve. Seeing again that this "Fall of the Soul" (whether cosmic or individual) from her original purity involved her in suffering and misery, the object which the Gnostic philosophers had ever before them, was identical with the problem of "sorrow" that Gautama Sākyamuni set himself to solve. Moreover, the solution of the two systems was identical in that they traced the "cause of sorrow" to Ignorance, and for its removal pointed out the Path of Self-knowledge. The Mind was to instruct the mind; "self-analysing reflection" was to be the Way. The material mind was to be purified, and so become one with the spiritual mind. In the nomenclature of the Gnosis this was dramatized in the redemption of the Sophia by the Christ, who delivered her from her ignorance and sufferings.

<small>The Mother of Many Names.</small>
It is not surprising, then, that we should find the Sophia in her various aspects possessed of many names. Among these may be mentioned: the Mother, or All-Mother; Mother of the Living, or Shining Mother; the Power Above; the Holy Spirit; again, She of the Left-hand as opposed to the Christos, Him of the Right-hand; the Man-woman; Prouneikos or Lustful one; the Matrix; Paradise; Eden; Achamōth; the Virgin; Barbēlō;

Daughter of Light; Merciful Mother; Consort of the Masculine One; Revelant of the Perfect Mysteries; Perfect Mercy; Revelant of the Mysteries of the whole Magnitude; Hidden Mother; She who knows the Mysteries of the Elect; the Holy Dove who has given birth to Twins; Ennœa; Ruler; and the Lost or Wandering Sheep, Helena, and many other names.

These terms refer to Sophia or the "Soul"—using the term in its most general sense—in her cosmic or individual aspects, according as she is above in her perfect purity; or in the midst, as intermediary; or below, as fallen into matter. But to return to:

HIPPOLYTUS' ACCOUNT OF ONE OF THE VARIANTS OF THE SOPHIA-MYTHUS.

"VALENTINUS and Heracleon and Ptolemæus and the entire school of these [Gnostics], disciples of Pythagoras and Plato and following their guidance, laid down the 'arithmetical science' as the fundamental principle of their doctrine.

"For them the beginning of all things is the Monad, ingenerable, imperishable, incomprehensible, inconceptible, the creator and cause of all things that are generated. This Monad is called by them the Father. Now as to its nature, there is a difference of opinion among them. For some declare . . . . that the Father is devoid of femininity, and without a syzygy, and solitary; *[The Father of all.]*

whereas others think it is impossible that the creation of all things should be from a single male principle, and so they are compelled to add to the Father of all, in order that He may be a Father, the syzygy Silence. But as to whether Silence is a syzygy or not, let them settle this dispute among themselves. . . ."

Hippolytus has missed the point as usual; there were Fathers for every plane, the monads or monadic state of being, and also Father-Mothers, the dyads or dyadic state of being, and as forth.

"In the beginning, says [the Gnostic whose MS. Hippolytus had before him], naught was that was created. The Father was alone, increate, without space, or time, or any with whom to take counsel, or any substantial nature capable of being conceived by any means. He was alone, solitary, as they say, and at rest, Himself in Himself, alone. But since He was creative, it seemed good to Him at length to create and produce that which was most beautiful and most perfect in Himself. For He was [now] no longer lover of solitariness. For He was all love, says [the writer of the MS.], but love is not love if there be nothing to be loved.

<small>The Parents of the Æons.</small>
"Therefore, the Father, alone as He was, emanated and generated Mind-and-Truth, that is to say, the dyad, which is Lady and Beginning, and Mother of all the æons they reckon in the Plērōma. And Mind-and-Truth, having been emanated from the Father, possessing the power of creation like His creative parent, in imitation of the Father, emanated Himself also Word-and-

Life. And Word-and-Life emanates Man-and-Church. And Mind-and-Truth, when He saw that His own creation had become creator in His turn, gave thanks to the Father of all, and made an offering unto Him of ten æons, the perfect number. For, says [the writer], Mind-and-Truth could not offer the Father a more perfect number than this. For it needs must have been that the Father who was perfect, should be glorified with a perfect number; now the 'ten' is a perfect number, for the first number of the series of multiplicity is perfect. [The 10 begins the series of multiplicity in the system of numeration with radix 10.] The Father, however, was more perfect still; for increate Himself, alone, by means of the first single syzygy, Mind-and-Truth, He succeeded in emanating all the roots of things created.

"And when Word-and-Life also saw that Mind-and-Truth had glorified the Father of all in a perfect number, Word-and-Life also wished to glorify His own father-mother, Mind-and-Truth. But since Mind-and-Truth was create and not possessed of perfect fatherhood, [or] the quality of parentlessness [ingenerability], Word-and-Life does not glorify his own father Mind with a perfect, but with an imperfect number. Thus Word-and-Life offers Mind-and-Truth twelve æons."

The reader need hardly be reminded that this summary of the variant of the myth has confused what we have supposed to have been the original order of the Ten and Twelve, as may be seen from the next paragraph but one of Hippolytus.

The Names of the Æons.

"So then the first created roots of the æons ... are as follows: Mind-and-Truth, Word-and-Life, Man-and-Church, ten from Mind-and-Truth, and twelve from Word-and-Life; eight and twenty in all. [The ten, consisting of five syzygies,] are called by the following names: Depthlike-and-Commingling, Unageing-and-Union, Self-productive-and-Bliss, Immoveable-and-Blending, Alone-begotten-and-Happiness."

In this nomenclature we have an attempt to shadow forth the positive and negative aspects of the father-motherhood (polarisation) of the creative mind, androgynous and self-generative. Hippolytus then continues:

"These are the ten æons which some derive from Mind-and-Truth, and others from Word-and-Life. Some again derive the twelve from Man-and-Church, and others from Word-and-Life; and the names they give these [six syzygies] are: Comforter-and-Faith, Father-like-and-Hope, Mother-like-and-Love, Everlasting and Understanding, Church-like-and-Happiness, Longed-for-and-Wisdom."

It is evident that this list has suffered damage in the hands of copyists; we can, however, make out some resemblance to the list of the "fruits of the spirit," in Paul's *Letter to the Galatians* (v. 22, 23), "love, joy, peace, long-suffering, gentleness, goodness, faith, mildness, temperance." The word translated "Happiness" is a different form from the "Happiness" of the decad, but both come from the same root. It is impossible to represent the difference in the present English we have at our disposal. We would also call the attention of the student to the term for the female aspect of the first and sixth syzygy—Faith-Wisdom (Pistis-Sophia). Epiphanius gives a totally different set of names for the æons—a set of "*nomina barbara*" which have so far proved the despair of every philologist, and with which, therefore, we need not trouble the general reader. The Greek terms, however, for the positive aspects of the six syzygies are probably in part reflections of the characteristics of the higher triad of æons, in part prototypes of the characteristics of the Holy Spirit. Mind-and-Truth, Word-and-Life, Man-and-Church, seem to appear in the terms Father-like and Mother-like, Comforter and Longed-for, Everlasting and Church-like; the female aspects of the higher triad being male aspects in the hexad. I believe that the names of the æons are probably doctrinal variants or attempts at translation of original Zoroastrian terms—of Hormuz and the Amshaspands and the rest of the Light-beings—and that the "*barbara nomina*" are a relic of these terms; the ideas and schematology of the æons, however, are demonstrably Egyptian. But to continue with our Hippolytus.

"Now, the twelfth of these twelve, and the last of the eight and twenty æons, female in nature, and called Wisdom (Sophia), beheld the number and power of the creative æons; she ascended [or returned] to the depth of the Father, and perceived that whereas all the rest of the æons, as being themselves create, created through a syzygy, the Father alone created without a syzygy. She, therefore, longed to imitate the Father and create by

The World-Mother.

herself without her consort (syzygy), and so achieve a work in nothing inferior to the Father; in ignorance that it is the increate alone, the absolute cause, and root, and breadth, and depth of the universal [creations], who has the power of creating by Himself alone, whereas Wisdom, being created and coming into being after a number of others, is thus incapable of possessing the power of the increate. For in the increate, says the writer, are all things together, whereas in the create the feminine has the power of emanating the essence [or substance], while the masculine possesses the power of enforming the essence emanated by the feminine. Wisdom, therefore, emanated the only thing which she could, namely, a formless essence, easy to cool down [into shape]. And this is the meaning, says he, of the words of Moses: 'The earth was invisible and unwrought' [according to the translation of the Seventy]. This, says he, is the Good [Land], the Celestial Jerusalem, into which God promised to lead the children of Israel, saying, 'I will lead you into a good land flowing with milk and honey.'

The Abortion.

"And thus ignorance arising in the Plērōma owing to Wisdom, and formlessness through the creature of Wisdom, tumult arose in ths Plērōma [from fear] lest the creations of the æons should in like manner become formless and imperfect, and destruction in no long time seize on the æons [themselves]. Accordingly they all betook themselves to praying the Father to put an end to Wisdom's grieving, for she was bewailing and groaning because of the 'abortion' which she had produced by herself—for thus they call it. And so the Father, taking pity on the tears of Wisdom and giving ear to the prayers of the æons, gives order for an additional emanation. For He did not Himself emanate, says the writer, but Mind-and-Truth emanated Christ-and-Holy-Spirit for the enforming and elimination of the abortion, and the relief and appeasing of the complaints of Wisdom. Thus with Christ-and-Holy-Spirit there are thirty æons."

Here we have the type of the dual world-creator and redeemer—Christ, the Logos, by whom all things were made, and the Holy Ghost, the Comforter.

"At any rate some of them think that the triacontad of æons is made up in this way, while others would unite Silence to the Father and add the [æons of the Plērōma] to them.

"Christ-and-Holy-Spirit, then, being additionally emanated by Mind-and-Truth, eliminates this formless abortion of Wisdom's, which she begat of herself and brought into existence without a consort, from among the universal æons, so that the perfect æons should not be thrown into confusion at the sight of its formlessness."

These passages throw great light on the term "only-begotten" ($\mu o\nu o\gamma \epsilon \nu \eta s$). Orthodoxly the phrase "only-begotten son" is taken to mean that Christ was the only son of the Father. Apologetic philology, moreover, has asserted that it means "the only one of his kind." In the list of the decad of æons given above, the male aspect of the last syzygy is called by this name, where I have translated it "alone-begotten." In the above passage,

The Term "Only-begotten."

the "abortion" of Wisdom is called by the same term, and I have translated it "which she begat of herself," there being no doubt that the term usually translated "only-begotten" means nothing of the kind, but "created alone," that is to say, created from one principle and not from a syzygy or pair. There are many instances of this meaning of the word, not only among the Gnostics, but also in the lines of Orphic and Egyptian tradition. Hippolytus then proceeds:

The Cross.
"Moreover, in order that the formlessness of the abortion should finally never again make itself visible to the perfect æons, the Father Himself also sent forth the additional emanation of a single æon, the Cross [or stock], which being created great, as [the creature] of the great and perfect Father, and emanated to be the guard and wall of protection [lit., paling or stockdale] of the æons, constitutes the Boundary of the Plērōma, holding the thirty æons together within itself. For these [thirty] are they which form the [divine] creation."

The word translated by "cross" in the N.T., means generally a stock or stake. As we learn from Grätz, it was the custom of the Jews, as a warning to others, to expose on a stake the bodies of those who were stoned, the cruel pain of the Mosaic penalty being in later times mitigated by a soporific draught of hyssop and other ingredients. The phrase "hanging on the tree" is thus comprehensible also. But, as previously remarked, for the Plērōma, we have to deal with living and not with dead symbols, and the cross-idea is thus transformed into the conception of a great wall (*sc.* sphere), by which the living Æon is "bounded"—if an infinite can be bounded by a finite—the prototype of the mystic Christ bound to or in the tree of the body.

The idea was simple, the expression of it in words exceedingly confused.

Thus Hippolytus writes:

"Now it is called the Boundary because it bounds off the deficiency (*hysterēma*) from the perfection (*plērōma*); again it is called the Partaker, because it partakes of the deficiency; and also the Cross [stake or stock], because it is fixed immovable and unchangeable [*lit.* without repentance or change of mind]; so that nothing of the deficiency should approach the æons within the Plērōma."

It is difficult to reconcile the various characteristics of this great boundary as given by Hippolytus. It is of course the Great Firmament or Limitary Spirit of Basilides, and the Last Limit of the *Pistis Sophia* treatise. It was there that the glorious "robe of power" had been left behind, when the Saviour descended for the regeneration of the cosmos without the Plērōma, and with which he was again clothed at his final initiation, after perfecting his task, as magnificently set forth in the opening pages of the MS. This is the Limit "against which none shall prevail," until the Day Be-with-us, the Day of Come-unto-us of the so-called *Book of the Dead* and the Askew Codex—the day of final initiation or perfectioning for the rare individuals who have made themselves worthy to become gods or christs (and thus a day which perpetually is), but for the

The Last Limit.

average mass of humanity the end of the world-cycle when all things pass into *pralaya*, as Indian philosophy calls it (and thus the final consummation of the present universe).

This "robe of power" is presumably the highest spiritual body, or *principium individuitatis*, which participates of the divine and human natures, that is to say, opens up the realms of the divine world to the man, and makes him a partaker of eternal being. Thus its living symbol is a ○, the reflection of the body, or self-limitation, of the sexless Heavenly Man, the Logos, whereby He limits Himself and crucifies Himself for the good of humanity. Lower down in the scale of being this becomes the dead symbol of the orthodox cross (+), the man of sex.

It is to be noticed that this Limit is due to the Father alone, and by its means He consummates and perfects the whole of the divine world of æons, which accordingly become one entity, the Living Æon, to every creation outside the Plērōma. But to continue with Hippolytus' summary:

"Without, then, this Boundary, Cross, or Partaker, is what they call the Ogdoad; this is the Wisdom-without-the-Plērōma, which Christ-and-Holy-Spirit, when they had been after-emanated by Mind-and-Truth, shaped and wrought into a perfect æon, so that she should finally become by no means inferior to any of those within the Plērōma. When, then, Wisdom-without had had shape given her, seeing that it was impossible that Christ-and-Holy-Spirit, in that they were emanated from Mind-and-Truth, should remain along with her outside the Plērōma, Christ-and-Holy-

Spirit ascended to Mind-and-Truth within the Boundary, to join the rest of the æons in their glorification of the Father.

"And since at length there was, as it were, the singleness of peace and harmony of all the æons within the Plērōma, it seemed good to them no longer to glorify the Father by means of their several syzygies, but also to hymn His glory by a [single] offering of fit fruits to the Father. The whole thirty æons accordingly agreed to emanate a single æon, the common fruit of the Plērōma, as the sign of their unity, unanimity and peace. And inasmuch as it is an emanation of all the æons unto the Father, they call it the Common Fruit of the Plērōma. Thus were the things within the Plērōma constituted.

The Mystic or Cosmic Jesus.

"And now the Common Fruit of the Plērōma had been emanated—Jesus (for this is His name), the great High Priest; when Wisdom-without-the-Plērōma, seeking after the Christ who had enformed her, and the Holy Spirit, was thrown into great terror, lest she should perish, now that He who had enformed and stablished her had withdrawn."

This operation of enforming Wisdom, or cosmic substance, is apparently the making of a boundary for the Ogdoad (the ætherial space) in its turn, following the law of similitude, and then fashioning the separated substance according to the types of the æons. This is dramatically set forth as follows:

"She mourned and was in great doubt, pondering on who was her enformer [the Christ]; who the Holy Spirit; whither had they departed; who prevented

The Grief of Sophia.

them from being with her; who envied her that fair and blessed vision. Plunged in such sufferings, she betook herself to praying and beseeching Him who had left her. Thereupon the Christ within the Plērōma and the rest of the æons took pity on her prayers, and sent forth out of the Plērōma the Common Fruit, to be Consort of Wisdom-without, and corrector of the passions which she suffered in seeking after the Christ.

"And so the Common Fruit coming forth from the Plērōma, and finding her afflicted by the four primal passions—namely, fear, grief, doubt and supplication—set right her sufferings; and in doing so He perceived that neither was it proper [on the one hand] that such passions, as being of the nature of an æon and peculiar to Wisdom, should be destroyed, nor [on the other] should Wisdom continue in such afflictions as fear and grief, supplication and doubt. Accordingly, inasmuch as he was so great an æon, and child of the whole Plērōma, He made the passions depart from her, and turned them into substantial essences; and fear he made into psychic essence, and grief into subtle matter [hylic essence], and doubt into elemental [dæmonian] essence, and conversion—prayer and supplication—He made into a path upwards, that is to say repentance and the power of the psychic essence which is called 'right.'"

Just as the passions in man are regarded as being of a material nature, so are the passions of the cosmic soul imagined as substantial essences by the dramatisers of the world-process in this scheme of universal philosophy.

We have now come to the stage of the Wisdom-drama which represents the constitution of the "sensible" world, as distinguished from the "intelligible," to use Platonic terms. But before we proceed with Hippolytus' summary, a few words of explanation may be added to guide the student through the maze of Gnostic technicalities.

The Sensible World.

The lower or fallen Wisdom is the prime substance, or World-mother, chaotically moved by four great impulses, her primal "afflictions" or "passions."

From her chaotic state she is rescued by the Divine Power from above, the synthesis of the powers of the intelligible or noëtic universe. Chaos becomes cosmos; un-order, order. The "passions" (fear, grief, doubt and supplication) are separated from her, and she is purified and remains above, while the passions contract into denser phases of substance, constituting the sensible universe. Above them broods the Power, the representative of the three highest planes (the intelligible universe or Plērōma) and of the One beyond, the Supreme Deity. This Divine Power is called the Common Fruit.

The four "passions" are separated from Sophia, and she remains as the substance of the highest of the lower planes. Fear and grief become the substances of the psychic and hylic (or physical) planes respectively. Doubt is regarded as a downward tendency, a path downward to even more dense and gross states of existence than the physical; while supplication (prayer, repentance, or aspiration) is regarded as a path upwards to the Heaven-world.

This is the power of the soul which is called "right," the tendency downwards into matter being called "left." We may now return to the consideration of our text.

Its Demiurge.

"The fabricative power [proceeds] from 'fear.' This is the meaning of the scripture, says the writer, 'The fear of the Lord is the beginning of Wisdom,' for it was the beginning of the sufferings of Wisdom. She [first] feared, then grieved, then doubted, and then flew for refuge to prayer and supplication. Moreover, he says, the psychic substance is of a fiery nature, and they call it [Middle] Space and Hebdomad and Ancient of Days. And whatever other statements of this kind they make concerning this [space], they [in reality] refer to the [cosmic] psychic substance, which they declare to be the fabricative power of the [physical] world. And it is of a fiery nature. Moses also, says the writer, declares, 'The Lord, thy God, is fire burning and consuming,' for thus he would have it written."

The action of the emotion of fear is said to contract and densify the aura or subtle envelope of man. The psychic plane is a contraction or densification of the mental, and the material again of the psychic.

"Now the power of fire, he says, is twofold; for there is a fire which is all-devouring and cannot be quenched and . . ."

A lacuna unfortunately occurs here; perhaps to be filled up by the words, "and another that is quenchable."

"According to this, then, the soul [that is, the psychic substance] is partly mortal [and partly immortal], being as it were a kind of mean. (It is [both] the Hebdomad [the sublunary space] and [also] the means of bringing the Hebdomad to an end.) For it is below the Ogdoad [the mind or spirit-substance]—where is Wisdom, the day of perfect forms [that is, the sun-space], and the Common Fruit of the Plērōma—but above the hylic matter [the earth-space], of which it is the fashioner [or demiurgic power]. If then the soul is made like unto the things above, it becomes immortal, and entereth into the Ogdoad, which is, he says, the Jerusalem above the heavens; whereas if it be made like to matter, that is to say the material passions, then it is destructible and perishes."

The next sentence has a wide lacuna, which I have endeavoured to bridge over as follows:

"As, therefore, proceeding from the psychic substance, [and not from an æon or plērōma], the first and greatest power [of the Sensible World] was an image, [and not a plērōma, namely the Workman (Demiurge); while the power proceeding from the material substance or 'grief' was] the Accuser (Diabolus), the ruler of this world.

"[The power, moreover, which proceeds] from the elemental [or dæmonian] substance, that is to say 'doubt,' is Beelzeboul.

"[And] Wisdom herself energises from above, from the Ogdoad, as far as the Hebdomad. [For] they say that the Workman knows nothing at all, but is, according to them, mindless and foolish, and knows not really what he does or works. Owing to his ignorance Wisdom energised and strengthened for him everything he made; and, though it was she who had done so, he imagined it was himself who had of himself achieved the fabrication of the universe, and so he began to say: 'I am God, and beside me there is no other.'

"Here then we have our Tetraktys according to Valentinus, 'a source of ever-flowing nature having roots,' and our Wisdom from which the whole creation is now constituted both psychic and material."

This is meant by Hippolytus to be ironical and a sneer both at Pythagoras and Valentinus. The four "passions" are of course very far from the Tetraktys proper; they are only a reflection of it on the lower planes.

"Wisdom is called 'Spirit,' and the Workman 'Soul'; while the Accuser (Diabolus) is the 'Ruler of this World' [Body], and Beelzeboul the 'Ruler of Dæmons' [Chaos]. Such is what they tell us.

"Moreover, basing all their teaching on mathematical considerations, as I have said before, they declare that the æons within the Plērōma emanate a new series of thirty other æons following the law of similitude, in order that the Plērōma should be finally grouped into a perfect number. For just as the Pythagoreans divided into twelve [? ten] and thirty and sixty—and have further subtleties on subtleties, as has been shown—in the same way these (Gnostics) also subdivide the creations within the Plērōma.

"The contents of the Ogdoad are also subdivided; and Wisdom (who is the mother of all living [the cosmic Eve] according to them) and the Common Fruit of the Plērōma (the Word) have emanated others who are the heavenly Angels, Citizens of Jerusalem Above, in the heavens. For this Jerusalem is Wisdom-without, and her bridegroom is the Common Fruit of the Plērōma." *"Words" or Minds.*

Some critics have preferred a reading which would make Wisdom and the Common Fruit emanate "seventy words"; but though this was the number of the nations among the Jews in contradistinction to the twelve tribes of Israel, for which reason also the "seventy" (standing for seventy-two) apostles were chosen after the "twelve," according to the historicizing narratives, I prefer to follow the reading of the Codex, as indeed I have done in every case.

"The Workman also emanated souls; for he is the substance of souls. According to them the former is Abraham, and the latter the children of Abraham." *Souls.*

(A nomenclature which would explain the otherwise very absurd expression "Abraham's bosom.")

"It was moreover from the material and elemental substance that the Workman made bodies for the souls. And this is the meaning of the saying, 'And God fashioned man, taking clay from the earth, and breathed into his person [*lit.*, face] the breath of life; and man became a living soul.'

"This [soul] is, according to them, the 'inner man,' called psychic when it dwells in the body of hylic matter, but material, destructible, imperfect, when [its vehicle is] formed of elemental substance."

352 FRAGMENTS OF A FAITH FORGOTTEN.

Hippolytus here seems to be summarising the otherwise very elaborate cosmogenesis and exegesis of the Valentinians into a few brief paragraphs, and the reader should never forget that the summary is made by an unfriendly hand. I have, however, thought it good to let the student see for himself that, even so, the Church Father could not eliminate all the meaning of the Gnostic writer.

Bodies.

"And this material man is, according to them, as it were, an inn or dwelling-place at one time of the soul alone, at another of the soul and dæmonian existences [elementals], at another of the soul and 'words' [or angels] which are 'words' sown from above — from the Common Fruit of the Plērōma and Wisdom—into this world, dwelling in the body of clay together with the soul, when dæmons cease to cohabit with her. And this is, says [the Gnostic writer], what was written in the scriptures [Paul's *Letter to the Ephesians*]: 'For this cause I bow my knees to the God and Father and Lord of our Lord Jesus Christ, that God may vouchsafe to you that Christ should dwell in your inner man'—that is to say, the psychic and not the bodily man—'that ye may be strong to know what is the Depth'—that is, the Father of the universals—'and what is the Breadth'—that is, the Cross, the Boundary of of the Plērōma—'and what is the Greatness'—that is, the Plērōma of the æons. Wherefore 'the psychic man,' says [Paul elsewhere in his first *Letter to the Corinthians*], 'does not receive the things of the Spirit of God, for they are foolishness to him'; and foolish, says [the Gnostic writer], is the power of the Workman, [that is, the power (or soul) sent forth by the Workman], for he himself was foolish and mindless, and thought that he was fashioning the world unaided, being ignorant that it was Wisdom, the Mother, the Ogdoad, who infused energy into him for the formation of the universe without his knowing it.

"All the Prophets and the Law, therefore, spake from the Workman, foolish know-nothings of a foolish God, according to the writer. For which cause, he writes, the Saviour says: 'All who came before me are thieves and robbers'; and the Apostle: 'The mystery which was unknown to former generations.' For none of the Prophets, says he, spake about any of the things of which we speak; they were at that time unknown. . . .

"When, therefore, the world-formation was ended future evolution was to consist of the unveiling [revelation] of the Sons of God—that is to say of the Workman—[the revelation] which had [hitherto] been hidden—in which, says he, the psychic man had been hidden, having a veil over his heart. When, therefore, the veil was to be raised and these mysteries revealed, Jesus [as the first example of the new evolution] was born through Mary, the virgin, according to the saying: 'Holy Spirit shall come upon thee'—Spirit is Wisdom—'and Power of Highest shall overshadow thee'—Highest is the Workman—'for that which is born of thee shall be called holy.' For he was not born of the Highest alone, like as men fashioned after the type of Adam owe their origin to the Highest alone, that is the Workman. Jesus, the new man, was of the Holy Spirit—that is to say

The New Man.

Wisdom—but of the Workman also, in order that the Workman might furnish the moulding and make-up of his body, but the Holy Spirit supply his essence or [substance], and so he might be a heavenly word, born from the Ogdoad through Mary."

That is to say, that Jesus was the type of the perfected man, who had transcended the necessity of rebirth, the cycle of generation. He was the manifestation of one of the Sons of God, who together make up the Divine Sonship. These sons are all 'words' or *logoi*, according to this nomenclature. The whole nature of such a man was said to be advanced one stage. Thus his body was made by the power which furnished other men's souls; his soul was of the same nature as the spirits of other men; and his spirit was a "word," the direct progeny of æons, partaker of the Plērōma.

The Mystic Body of the Christ.

"Now there is much investigation devoted by them to this subject, and it is the starting-point of schism and disagreement. Hence their doctrine is divided in twain, and one teaching is called the Anatolic, according to them, and the other the Italic. They [who get their teaching] from Italy, of whom are Heracleon and Ptolemæus, say that the body of Jesus was [originally] of psychic constitution, and, because of this, at his baptism the Spirit, like a dove, descended upon him—that is to say, the 'word' of the Mother from above, Wisdom—and united with his psychic [body], and raised him from the dead. This is, says the writer, the saying: 'He who raised Christ from the dead will vivify also your mortal bodies'— that is to say, psychic [bodies]. For the clay it was which came under the curse. 'For earth,' says [Moses], 'thou art, and unto earth shalt thou return.' Whereas those [who derive their teaching] from the East, of whom are Axionicus and Ardesianes [? Bardesanes], say that the body of the Saviour was spiritual. For the Holy Spirit — that is to say Wisdom—came upon Mary, and also the power of the Highest, the Workman's art, in order that that [substance] which had been given to Mary, might be fashioned.

"We may leave them, then, to investigate such matters by themselves, and [so too] anyone else who may like to carry on such investigations." The writer, moreover, goes on to say that, just as the imperfections on the plane of the æons within were corrected, so also were those on the plane of the Ogdoad, the Wisdom-without, set right, and further those on the plane of the Hebdomad were also corrected.

"(For the Workman was taught by Wisdom, that he was not God alone, as he thought, and beside him there was no other, but through Wisdom he learned to know the Better [Deity]. He received, [however, only] elementary instruction from her [became a catechumen], and the first initiation, and was [thus] taught the mighty mystery of the Father and the æons; and [thus] he could reveal it to no one else.)"

Soteriology.

The terms used denote that the Demiurge received instruction, but was not given the higher power or initiation, whereby he could become a teacher or initiator in his turn; he received the "*muēsis*," but not the "*epopteia*."

"(This is the meaning, according to the writer, of his words unto Moses: 'I am the God of Abraham, and the God of Isaac, and the God of Jacob, and the name of God I have not made known unto them'—that is to say, I have not declared the Mystery, nor explained who is God, but I kept to myself in secret the Mystery which I heard from Wisdom.)

"Since then the things above [in the Plērōma, Ogdoad and Hebdomad] had been set right, by the same law of succession the things here [on earth] were to meet with their proper regulation. For this cause Jesus, the Saviour, was born through Mary, that things here might be righted. Just as Christ was additionally emanated by Mind-and-Truth for the righting of the sufferings of Wisdom-without, that is to say the 'abortion'; so again did the Saviour, born through Mary, come for the righting of the sufferings of the soul."

The above will give the reader some general notion of the cycle of ideas in which these Gnostics moved. The exposition of the Gnostic writer has doubtless suffered much in the summarizing process to which it has been subjected; nevertheless, even if it had been given in full, it would have to be ascribed to a pupil and not to a master of the Gnosis such as Basilides or Valentinus. In order to obtain a more consistent and detailed exposition of the Valentinian cycle of ideas, it would be necessary first of all to analyse (1) the above account, (2) the contents of the *Excerpts from Theodotus*, and (3) the summary of the tenets of the followers of Ptolemy given by Irenæus in his opening chapters, and then re-formulate the whole. Hippolytus' account, however, is quite sufficient to acquaint the reader with the general outlines, and a more detailed exposition would be out of place in these short sketches.

We shall now give a brief outline of the teachings of the more prominent leaders of Gnostic thought in this period, and so we return to a consideration of "them of Valentinus."

Of Theodotus and Alexander we know nothing, and of Secundus only the fact that he divided the highest Ogdoad, within the Plērōma, into two Tetrads, a Right and Left,—though we are of course not to suppose that he originated such a fundamental notion.

We shall, therefore, confine our attention to Marcus, Ptolemæus, Heracleon and Bardesanes, brief notices of whom will bring our information derived from indirect sources—namely, the Patristic writings—to a conclusion.

Let us then turn to "them of Valentinus" and first treat of Marcus and his number-symbolism.

THE NUMBER-SYMBOLISM OF MARCUS.

Sources. A LONG section in Irenæus is our almost exclusive source for a knowledge of Marcus and his followers. Hippolytus and Epiphanius simply copy Irenæus and add nothing but new terms of condemnation, while our information from other sources is a question of lines and not of paragraphs. The unreliability of Irenæus as a chronicler of Gnostic views is already known to our readers, and in the case of Marcus and the Marcosians is more painfully patent than usual. It seems that some of the adherents of the school were to be found even among the rude populace of the Rhone valley, and the worthy Presbyter of Lyons was especially anxious to discount their influence. He begins the attack by retailing all the scandalous stories he can collect about Marcus, a man he had never seen, and who had not been nearer to the sheepfold of Lyons than Asia Minor, or at best Egypt!

Irenæus professes first of all to describe what took place at the initiation-ceremonies and secret rites of the Marcosians, and paints a graphic picture of charlatanry and debauchery, much to his own satisfaction. To all of these reports and descriptions, however, the Marcosians gave a most emphatic denial, and therefore we shall not at present trouble the reader with the Presbyter's statements on the subject, except to remark that he himself acknowledges that he depends entirely on hearsay, and to point out to the student that the account seems to be a very distorted caricature of the ceremonies, the ritual of which is partly preserved to us directly in the Askew Codex and one of the MSS. of the Codex Brucianus.

Irenæus next proceeds to give a *résumé* of a Marcosian MS. which had fallen into his hands. He apparently quotes some passages verbatim, but for the most part contents himself with a summary, so that we can by no means be sure what the writer of the document really said. The original of the document Irenæus ascribes to Marcus himself, whom throughout the whole section he apostrophises as a contemporary; it is, however, probable that this is merely rhetorical—as is the case with Hippolytus, who, thirty or forty years afterwards, in his opening paragraph, predicts that the result of his exposure of Marcus will be that "he *will now* desist [from his imposture]," although the body of the Gnostic doctor had long been laid in the grave.

Of Marcus himself we know nothing beyond the fact that he was one of the earlier pupils of Valentinus, or at any rate belonged to the earlier circle of Valentinian ideas. His date is vaguely placed somewhere about the middle of the second century; he is said to have taught in Asia Minor, and Jerome, two hundred years afterwards, states that he was an Egyptian.

To the student of Gnosticism who regards the Gnostic doctors as cultured men who made a brave effort to formulate Christianity as a universal philosophy, or rather as a divine science springing from the ground of a philosophy of religion, the attempt of Marcus to adapt the Hebrew number-letter

Number-letters.

system, devised by "kabalistic" Rabbis, to the Greek alphabet, and so work out a number-symbolism for the too abstruse æon-genesis and world-process of the Gnosis, is a point of great interest. It may, however, be that the Hebrews copied from the Greeks; or that both derived this method from Egypt.

As must be patent to everyone, the methods of symbolism of the Gnostics were very numerous; many attempts were made to convey to the physical consciousness some idea of the modes, not only of superphysical existence, but also of what was definitely stated to be suprarational being. That these attempts were all doomed to failure, as far as general comprehension was concerned, is no reason for us to deride the efforts made; that we have not even to-day, with all our elaborate mathematical formulæ, evolved a sufficient symbolism, is no reason for denying the possibility of such an achievement within certain limits in future ages.

Marcus attempted this gigantic task with insufficient means, it is true, with means too that appear to our prosaic minds to-day as fantastic and even worthless; nevertheless he was not without a tradition that to some extent justified his making the attempt.

The ancient religion of the Chaldæans was astronomical and mathematical; cosmogenesis and evolution were worked out in the symbolism of numbers. Every letter of the sacred language had a certain numerical equivalent, and thus words and sentences could be constructed which could be interpreted numerically, and be finally made explanatory of natural and celestial phenomena and processes. Since the sacred books of the "Mathematicians" are said to have been written with this definite object in view, the mathematical key given to the initiate into the ancient star-lore of Chaldæa, might thus open the door to the sacred science of nature and man as known to the seers of that ancient civilisation.

The Rabbis of the Jews, on their return from captivity, presumably brought with them some notions of this method of number-letters, and later on proceeded to turn it to account as a means, both of explaining away much that was distasteful to the cultured mind in their ancient traditions, and of reading into the old cosmogonic and patriarchal fables new and spiritual meanings, derived to a large extent from their contact with Oriental ideas during the years of captivity and subsequently. This method of mystical exegesis by number-letters was developed to a marvellous extent by the Hellenising tendencies of the cultured Rabbis among the Diaspora; and Egypt, and especially Alexandria, was one of the main centres of this peculiar learning. A relic of this number-system has come down to the present times with the tradition of the Kabalah. It is to be observed, however, that the Rabbis *adapted* the system to a heterogeneous library of works of various dates and many recensions, which were not originally composed with this end in view. True, they believed that every word and letter of the Law had been directly inspired by God, and thus contained a wonderful magical potency, but the relentless logic

Kabalism.

of modern Biblical research has to a large extent overturned this fond hypothesis, and their pious number-processes must now for the most part be regarded as the development of apologetic Rabbinism, and as legitimate only for such small parts of the documents as may have been composed in Babylon by scribes who were already versed in the Chaldaic method.

There is little doubt that Valentinus and his pupils were acquainted with all there was to learn at Alexandria of Rabbinical exegesis, in which the hopes of the Jews were more than ever centred after the destruction of the second temple in A.D. 70. They were also perfectly familiar with the Pythagorean number-philosophy, the symbolism of which no doubt had many resemblances to the number-books of the ancient Chaldeans. It is therefore but little surprising to find that one of them busied himself with adapting this ancient method of symbolism (if indeed it was not already native to Grecian tradition) to the Greek alphabet, in which the documents of the new faith, and, as they firmly believed, the new world-science, were now almost exclusively written. Needless to say, the Greek alphabet would not stand the strain; nevertheless it was a good exercise for a pupil of the Gnosis, and offered wide scope for the use of much ingenuity.

This exercise in correspondences was naturally no contribution to knowledge, but only a means of conveying knowledge otherwise acquired. It will, however, be of interest to give the reader a brief sketch of some of Marcus' ideas, as far as it is possible to recover them from the contemptuous summary of the Marcosian MS. by Irenæus in his polemic. They are also additionally interesting as showing intimate points of contact with the Coptic treatises we have so often referred to.

The source of the document's inspiration is ascribed to the Supernal Four, the highest hierarchy of the Plērōma, which however only reveals itself to mortals in its "feminine" form, for the world cannot bear the power and effulgence of its "masculine" greatness. The same idea is current in India. The God (Deva) uses his power, the Goddess (Shakti, Devī), as his means of communication with mortals; his own form no mortal can behold and live. The whole of what follows is based upon the Greek texts of Hippolytus (Duncker and Schneidewin) and Epiphanius (Dindorf) —who copied from the lost Greek text of Irenæus— and upon the oft-times unintelligent and barbarous Latin version of the Greek original of Irenæus (Stieren).

The MS. apparently opened with the following passage descriptive of the speaking forth of the Word of the Supernal Father.

"When first the Father, the not even the One, beyond all possibility of thought and being, who is neither male nor female, willed that His ineffability should come into being, and His invisibility take form, He opened His mouth and uttered a Word, like unto Himself; who, appearing before Him, became the means of His seeing what He himself was —namely Himself appearing in the form of His own invisibility."

The Great Name.

Now the utterance of the Great Name was on this wise. The Father spake the Word; the first note of His Name was a sound of four elements; the second sound was also of four elements; the third of ten; the fourth and last of twelve. Thus the utterance of the whole Name was of thirty elements and four sounds or groupings.

After the words "the first note of His Name was a sound of four elements," Irenæus has dragged into his summary a suggestion of his own, probably derived from some numerical exegesis of the Prologue to the fourth Gospel, which he had come across elsewhere in his heresy-hunt. Thus he evidently breaks into the thread of the summary with the interjected note, "namely $\dot{\alpha}\rho\chi\dot{\eta}$," the "Beginning" of the Prologue.

Further, each single element of the thirty has its own peculiar utterance, character, letters, configurations and images. But no element is acquainted with the form of the sound of which it is an element; in fact, so far from knowing its parent-sound, it pays no attention even to the utterance of its associate elements in its own sound-hierarchy, but only to its own utterance.

Thus uttering all that it knows, it thinks it is sounding forth the whole Name. For each of the elements, being a part of the whole Name, enunciates its own peculiar sound as the whole Word, and does not cease sounding until it arrives at the very last letter of the last sub-element in its own peculiar tongue.

Now the consummation or restitution of all things

THE NUMBER-SYMBOLISM OF MARCUS. 365

takes place when all these original elements, coming to one and the same letter or note, send forth one and the same utterance, a symbol of which was the chanting of the sacred word "Amen" in unison. It was these notes of the scale of the Primordial Harmony which were the means of giving form to the Living Æon, which transcended all idea of substance and generation. To such forms the Lord referred when speaking of "the angels who continually behold the face of the Father."

The ordinary spoken names for these elements are: æons, words, roots, seeds, plenitudes (plērōmata), fruits. The "spoken" names are distinguished from the "authentic" names, or *mysticæ voces*, many instances of the cypher-equivalents of which will be found in the Coptic Codices.

Now every divine element, with all its sub-sounds, notes, or letters, was contained in the phase of the Divine Being to which the symbolic name of Church had been given. The term "Church" (Ecclesia) means the "Calling Forth," the Heritage of the Elect, a substitute for an "authentic" name, which was only revealed to the initiated members of the school. The Church was the female aspect of the fourth and last syzygy, or pair, of the Tetrad, or Holy Four, the Lords of the Plērōma.

When the last note of the last sub-element of these supernal elements had uttered its own peculiar sound, the echo of it went forth, in the image of all these elements and sub-elements, and gave birth to another series; and it is this series which is the cause not only of the elements

The Echo of the Name.

of the world which we know, but also of those elements which have a prior existence to those of our world.

The last divine note itself, of which echo rang on echo downwards, was wafted upwards by its own parent-sound to complete and consummate the whole Name; while the echo descended to the parts below, and remained as though cast out of the Plērōma.

This parent-sound or element, from which the last note, containing potentially the utterance of the parent-sound, descended below, consisted of thirty letters or elements, and each of these contains other letters or elements, by means of which the name of each root-element is spelt, and so on infinitely. That is to say, the sub-elements as it were spell out the name, or manifest the power, of the main element; and the power or name of each sub-element in turn is manifested or spelt by other minor sub-elements, and so on infinitely.

Marcus brought home this grand idea to the minds of his pupils by pointing out an analogy in the Greek alphabet. Thus take any single letter, say Δ, delta; as soon as you name it, you have five letters, namely Δ delta, E epsilon, Λ lambda, T tau, A alpha. Again E, epsilon, is resolved into E epsilon, Ψ psi, I iota, Λ lambda, O omicron, N nu; and so on infinitely. The illustration is certainly graphic enough.

The Symbolic Body of the Man of Truth.

The Gnostic MS. then proceeded to describe a method of symbolizing the Great Body of the Heavenly Man, whereby the twenty-four letters of the Greek alphabet were assigned in pairs to the twelve "limbs." The Body of the Heavenly Man was the graphic symbol of the ideal economy, dispensation, or ordering of the universe, its regions, planes, hierarchies and powers.

This symbolic representation was called the schema or configuration of the one element (τό σχῆμα τοῦ στοχείου), and also the glyph (or character) of the figure (or diagram) of the Man of Truth, presumably the God of Truth of the Codex Brucianus, one of the treatises of which contains a whole series of diagrams of the various moments of emanation of the creative deity under this designation.

In the phrase "glyph of the figure" (ὁ χαρακτὴρ τοῦ γράμματος), the word γράμμα means either (i.) a letter of the alphabet, or (ii.) a note of music, or (iii.) a mathematical figure or diagram. The character, glyph, or configuration, would thus be the symbol or reflection of the super-spiritual Plērōma, regarded (i.) as the last letter of the four-lettered Great Name, or (ii.) as the last note of the Divine Harmony which is sung forth by the Supernal Logos or Word. To avoid complication and symbols of symbols, we have taken the word γράμμα in its third sense, in which it declares its consanguinity with the great art of systematising the elements and powers of nature, known in India as *tantra* ("systematising," "ordering.") Tāntrika is now a janus-faced art, white and black, and its main feature is the drawing of magical diagrams (*yantras*), to represent the configuration of the elements and powers which the operator desires to use.

I omit here all mention of Mark's diagram of the

body of the Heavenly Man, as the consideration of it would take up too much space in these short sketches.

Now the Word, the male energy of the middle pair or syzygy of the trinity (Mind-Truth, Word-Life, Man-Church) and the sum of the six, issued forth from the mouth of Truth. This Word is the Logos or Supreme Reason of all things, the self-generator of the universe, who bestows fatherhood ($\pi\alpha\tau\rho o\delta o\tau o\rho a$ $\lambda o\gamma o\nu$) on all things. On earth this Word becomes the name known commonly to all Christians, namely, Christ Jesus. But Jesus is only the sound of the name down here and not the power of the name. Jesus is really a substitute for a very ancient name, and its power is known to the "elect" alone of the Christians.

It is the six-lettered name. But even this is only a symbol; among the æons of the Plērōma it is manifold, and of another form and type, and this is known only to them who are akin to the Logos in their hearts, those whose angels or greatnesses are with Him for all time.

Now the twenty-four letters of the alphabet, attached to the various limbs of the Body of the Heavenly Man in the diagram, are the symbols, or images, of the emanations of the three powers which contain the sum total or Plērōma of the æonic elements above. And there is a further analogy to their nature in the alphabet. For there are nine consonants (or soundless letters), eight liquids (or semi-sounds), and seven vowels (or sounds).

The consonants symbolise the ineffable or soundless elements of Mind-and-Truth; the liquids, midway between the soundless letters and the sounds, typify the elements of Word-and-Life, which receive the emanation from the unmanifested above, and receive back the ascent from the manifested below; and the vowels represent the elements of Man-and-Church, for sound going forth through the Man enformed all things. For the echo of His voice investured them with form.

This reminds us of the elaborated division of the Platonic world of ideas into three spaces: (1) noëtic; (2) both noëtic and noëric; and (3) noëric. (See my essay on Orpheus).

Thus we have the series 9, 8, 7; and if we take 1 from 9 and add it to 7, we get 8, 8, 8—or Jesus, the six-lettered name ($\iota\eta\sigma o\hat{v}\varsigma$), the numerical values of the letters of which amount to 888. That is to say, He who had his seat with the Father (Mind), left his seat and descended, sent forth to the one from whom He was separated (the Church), to restore the divine creation to a state of equilibrium, in order that, the unities of the Plērōmas (or three phases of the Plērōma or ideal cosmos) being reduced to an equality, there might be a common product of a single power from all of them in all of them. Thus the 7 obtained the power of the 8, and the three spaces became equal in their numbers, namely, 3 eights, and these added together are 24.

The Numbers.

Now these three spaces or elements are each twofold (positive and negative), 6 in all, and these again fourfold, 24 in all, the reflection of the elements of the Unnameable, in dyads, triads and tetrads.

Moreover, if you would find the 6 among the 24

letters of the alphabet, which are only images of the real elements, you will find it hidden in the double letters Ξ (κϛ), Ψ (πϛ), Z (δϛ). Add this 6 to the 24 and we have again a symbol of the 30 æons of the Plērōma.

Gospel Exegesis.

With much ingenuity our Gnostics found these numbers and processes in the prologue to Genesis, and elsewhere in the Old Covenant library; we need not, however, follow them into this field of letter-numbering. But when we find that they treated the Gospel-legends also not as history, but as allegory, and not only as allegory, but as symbolic of the drama of initiation, the matter becomes of deep interest for the theosophical student.

Thus they said that the transfiguration-story was symbolic (ἐν ὁμοιώματι εἰκόνος) of the divine economy as manifested in the man seeking perfection; in other words, of a certain stage of initiation.

To make this further apparent, we will use terms already familiar to some of our readers.

After "six days," that is to say, in the seventh stage since the disciple first set his feet on the path, he ascended into the "mountain"—a graphic symbol for the higher states of consciousness.

He ascended the fourth and became the sixth. That is to say, he ascended with three and was joined by two, the Peter, James and John, and Moses and Elias of the familiar Gospel-narrative.

The "three" are the powers he had already won over the gross, subtle and mental planes—presumably the degrees of *srotāpanna*, *sakadāgamin* and *anāgāmin* in the Buddhist tradition. The "two" are the representatives of the spiritual and divine powers which welcome and support him, and thus he becomes sixth, or possessed of the spiritual consciousness, while still in the body,—the *arahat* stage.

It was this "six," said the Marcosians, which had descended and been detained in the Hebdomad, or region of the seven spheres of difference; the "six" being in reality of the same essence as the World-mother, the eighth encircling sphere of sameness, which is above or beyond these seven. The six (the *arahat*) being thus of the same essence as the World-mother (Wisdom) contains essentially in himself the whole number of all the elements or powers— a fact already typified in the stage symbolised in the baptism-myth by the descent of the dove. The dove is the Alpha and Omega (1 and 800) of the diagram, the first and last of the numbers, representing the head. Moreover the word for "dove" in Greek is περιστερά, and 80 (π) + 5 (ε) + 100 (ρ) + 10 (ι) + 200 (σ) + 300 (τ) + 5 (ε) + 100 (ρ) + 1 (α) = 801.

Again, it was on the "sixth day," the "preparation," that the divine economy, or order of things, manifested the "last man," the "man from heaven," for the new birth or regeneration of the "first man" or "man of the earth"; and further the passion began in the sixth hour and ended in the sixth hour, when the initiate was nailed to the cross. All of which was designed to indicate the power of creation (inception) and regeneration or rebirth (consummation), typified in the number 6, to those who were admitted to the mysteries of initiation, called by the Marcosian writer the "Sons of the Light," or

"Sons of the Man," for the Greek will carry both meanings.

For creation or descent is represented by the number 2, that is to say by dyads, and regeneration or ascent by the number 3, that is to say by triads, and $2 \times 3 = 6$.

The Creation of the Sensible World.

Now as to the creation of the sensible universe: the Logos, as creator, uses as his minister, or servant, the seven-numbered "greatness" (that is to say, the septenary hierarchy of the ideal universe, the Plērōma or Mind of the Logos, symbolized by the seven vowels), in order that the fruit of His self-meditated meditation may be manifested.

The creation of our particular universe (or solar system), however, is regarded as a fabrication, or building, according to a type in the Divine Mind. The creative fabricator or builder is, as it were, a reflection of the universal Logos, enformed by Him, but as it were separated or cut off, and thus remaining apart from or outside the Plērōma. It is by the power and purpose of the Divine Logos, that the demiurgic power, by means of his own emanation or life (the reflection of the Life of the Plērōma), ensouled the cosmos of seven powers, according to the similitude of the septenary power above, and thus was constituted the soul of the visible all, our cosmos. The demiurge makes use of this work as though it had come into existence through his own will alone; but the seven spheres of the world-soul (the cosmic life)—copies of the æonic spheres which no cosmic spheres can really represent—are in reality hand-maidens to the will of the Divine Life, the supernal Mother.

THE NUMBER-SYMBOLISM OF MARCUS. 373

Now the first of these seven spheres, or heavens, sounds forth the sound or vowel A, the second the E, the third the H, the fourth and midmost the I, the fifth the O, the sixth the Y, and the seventh and fourth from the middle the Ω. And all uniting together in harmony send forth a sound and glorify him by whom they were emanated (the system-logos or world-builder); and the glory of the sound is carried up to the Forefather of the Plērōma (the Divine Logos), while the echo of their hymn of glory is borne to earth, and becomes the modeller and generator of them upon the earth, that is to say the souls of men.

Irenæus now appears to have come to the end of the MS., and so proceeds to give the friend to whom he is writing, as many other details of Marcosian ideas as he has picked up from scraps of quotations or from hearsay,—"*quæ ad nos pervenerunt ex iis*" (c. xv.). He returns once more to a consideration of the eternal economy of the Plērōma, and to an exposition from which he has already quoted a scrap in another connection (c. xi. 3), as follows:

"Before all universes there is a source (or beginning) before the primal source, prior even to that state which is inconceivable, ineffable, unnameable, which I number as Noughtness. With this No-number consubsists a power to which I give the name Oneness. This Noughtness and Oneness, which are in reality one, emanated, although they did not really emanate, the intelligible (or ideal) source of all, ingenerable and invisible, to which speech gives the name of Monad (or Nought). *The Tetraktys.*

With this Monad consubsists a power of equal substance (ὁμοούσιος) with it, which I call One. These powers, Noughtness, Oneness, Nought and One, send forth the rest of the emanations of the æons.

"Noughtness" (lit., "monadity") is the root of the monad, the O or circle containing all the numbers—the no-number.

This passage shows the distinct influence of Basilides; but among the best critics opinions are divided as to whether it should be assigned to Marcus or Heracleon.

The names of this highest tetrad or tetraktys, however, are really incapable of representation in human speech; they are the "holy of holies," names known to the Son alone, while even He does not know what the Four really are, this final knowledge of the one reality being referred to the Father alone.

These names pertain to the "sacred language," specimens of which are given in the fragments from the *Books of the Saviour* attached to the *Pistis Sophia* document and in two of the treatises of the Codex Brucianus.

The substitutes for these names are: Ineffable (ἄρρητος) and Silence (σειγή), Father (πατήρ) and Truth (ἀλήθεια); the Greek words for which consist respectively of 7 and 5, and 5 and 7 letters, or twice 7 and twice 5, the 24 elements of the Plērōma.

So also with the substitutes for the names of the second tetrad: Word (λόγος) and Life (ζωή), Man (ἄνθρωπος) and Church (ἐκκλησία); the Greek names consisting respectively of 5 and 3, and 8 and 8 letters—in all 24.

Again the spoken or effable name of the Saviour, Jesus (ἰησοῦς), consists of 6 letters, while His ineffable name consists of 24. As stated above, the name = 888, and thus, by another permutation, = 24.

Similar number-permutations are also found in the letters of the word Christ.

But enough of this apparent forcing of an unwilling alphabet into the arms of a number-symbolism—perhaps the reader will say. The Marcosians, however, might in the first place plead in excuse the example of Philo and Alexandrine Judaism, which believed not only in the literal inspiration of the Hebrew text of the Old Covenant, but also that the Greek version of the so-called Seventy was written by the finger of God; and in the second, they might perhaps have said: The Greek names for the æons are but substitutes for other names which have these number-equivalents, and pertain to the secrets of our initiation.

The really scientific part of the system is the number-process as a natural symbolism of primeval evolution; it is not enough to label this Pythagoreanism and so dismiss it with a sneer, for all our modern physical science is based upon exactly the same considerations of measure and number.

Now the One contains in itself implicitly the three incomprehensibles, Noughtness, Oneness and Nought. *Theological Arithmetic.* Thus the One is the representative of the upper tetrad. And since all numbers come from the One, this tetrad is called the All-Mother, or Wisdom Above. From her proceeds as a daughter, the lower tetrad, the comprehensible numbers, the 1, 2,

3 and the 4, the Wisdom Below, which must be regarded as 8 potentially, seeing that the 1 manifests the unmanifestable One, the representative of the unmanifestable tetrad. The Wisdom below is thus reckoned as 8, or the ogdoad. But this ogdoad contains the decad, for $1+2+3+4=10$. And this decad by congress with the 8 makes 80, and by congress with the 8 and itself makes 800; so that the 8, or world-mother, is separated into three spaces, 8, 80, and 800, in all 888, which is the number of her enforming power or consort Jesus, the creative Logos from above, the $1+2+3$, or 6, the consort of the 4 or last number of the lower tetrad.

This enformation of the world-substance by means of the decad—by means of the creative 888 or "Jesus" —was the "enformation according to substance"; but there was another enformation of a higher kind, by means of the "Christ," the "enformation according to knowledge." This was the regeneration by means of the dodecad. Now $6 \times 2 = 12$; $(1+2+3) \times 2 = 12$; $10+2=12$; $8+4=12$.

The $8+4$ is the ogdoad with the first tetrad added to it; the $10+2$ is the decad with the twin powers of the upper and lower tetrads added to it; the $(1+2+3) \times 2$, or 6×2 is the doubling of the enforming power or its ascent into itself.

Jesus the Master.

These eternal types and processes were to be seen in nature and history. Thus in the case of the great Master, just as the world-soul was in ignorance before she was fashioned and regenerated, so were men in ignorance and error before the coming of the Great One, Jesus. He took flesh as Jesus, in order that He might descend to the perception of men on earth. And they who recognized Him ceased from Ignorance, and ascended from Death unto Life, His "Name," or Power, leading them unto the Father of Truth. For it was the will of the All-Father to put an end to Ignorance and destroy Death. And the ending of Ignorance is the Knowledge ($ἐπίγνωσις$) of Him (the Christ). For this reason a man was chosen by His will whose constitution was after the image of the power above (the lower tetrad), that is to say, sufficiently developed to act as a fit vehicle.

Now the lower tetrad is spoken of as Word and Life, Man and Church. And powers emanating from these four Holy Ones watch over the birth and mould the lower vehicles of the Jesus on earth. And this, it was said, was shown clearly in the allegorical scripture. "Gabriel" takes the place of the Word (Reason or Logos), the "Holy Spirit" that of the Life, the "Power of the Highest" that of the Man, and the "Virgin" that of the Church.

Again, at the baptism there descended upon the Jesus, thus perfectly constituted (or enformed according to substance), the dove, which soars again to heaven, its upward course completing the Jesus (or 6) and making him into the Christ (or 12), the enformation according to knowledge, or perfect illumination. And in the Christ subsists the seed of them who descend and ascend with Him. And the power of the Christ which descends is the seed of the Plērōma, containing in itself both the Father and the Son, and the unnameable power of Silence, the Mother, (which is only known through them), and the rest of the æons. Now this power of Silence, this Peace and Comfort, is the Holy Spirit. It was this Spirit which spoke through the mouth of Jesus in the Gospel-narratives, and proclaimed itself as Son of Man, and revealed the Father, descending on Jesus and becoming one with Him. It was this Saviour who put an end to death, by the removal of ignorance, and Jesus made Him known as his Father, the Christ.

Jesus is really the name of the man who was perfected in his lower nature (that is to say, the initiate); but because of its adaptability and formation the name has been given to the Man who was to descend into him (in other words, the Master). And he who was the vehicle of this Great One, had thus in him both the Man and Word and Father and the Ineffable, and Silence and Truth and Life and Church (for the Master is one who is at-one with these).

After three sections of abuse, Irenæus resumes the subject of Marcosian number-correspondences in cap. xvi.; but the reading of the key-passage which deals with the imperfections of the dodecad and the consequent "passion" of the cosmic soul and individual souls is so faulty that, as yet, I have been able to make nothing out of it.

The "Moving Image of Eternity."

With cap. xvii., however, the æonic types are traced in the economy of the cosmos. The two tetrads are shown in the four elements fire, water, earth, and air, and their four characteristics, hot, cold, dry, and moist. The decad is shown in the seven spheres, and the eighth which encompasses them, and in addition the sun and moon. This clearly shows that the "seven spheres" are not the "planets," of either astrology or astronomy. Finally the dodecad is shown in the so-called zodiacal circle.

Now the motion of these seven spheres is exceedingly rapid, whereas the eighth sphere, or heaven, is much slower than the motion of the seven mutually interpenetrating spheres, and as it were balances or checks their otherwise too rapid motion by pressure on their periphery; the result is that the whole mass takes some 30 years to pass through a sign, or a twelfth part, of the zodiacal belt. This retarding sphere was thus regarded as an image of the Great Boundary which surrounds the "Mother of thirty names" or Plērōma. Again, the moon encompasses its "heaven," the lower boundary, in 30 days; and the sun completes its cyclic return in 12 months. There are moreover 12 hours in every day, and each hour is divided into thirty parts, according to the 12 great divisions of the zodiac, each of which has again 30 sub-divisions, 360 in all; the earth again has 12 climates. All of which is doubtless to be referred to the tradition of the common source of the ancient Chaldæan and Egyptian religions.

For the world-fabricator, or time-spirit, when he desired to copy the infinite, æonian, invisible and timeless nature of Eternity, was not able to make a model of its abiding and eternal nature, seeing that he himself was the result of a deficiency in this eternal nature; so he represented Eternity in times and seasons, and numbers of many years, thinking by a manifold number of times to imitate its infinitude. Thus it was that truth abandoned him and he followed after a lie; and therefore when the times are fulfilled his work will come to an end.

Irenæus devotes his next three chapters (capp. xviii.-xx.) to what he has heard of the Marcosian interpretation of scripture. This is of little interest; but in chapter xxi. the Bishop of Lyons gives us some of the formulæ used by the school, and these are of greater interest, although the Marcosians denied their accuracy. Thus he says that the words of the baptismal consecration are as follows:

From the Marcosian Ritual.

"[I baptise thee] unto the Name of the unknown Father of the universals, unto Truth, the Mother of all, unto Him who descended on Jesus, unto the union, redemption, and communion of [thy] powers."

Next we have what purports to be the translation of a Hebrew invocation to the Christ; Irenæus gives the original Hebrew, but in such a woefully corrupt guise that it has baffled the ingenuity of the best of scholars.

"I invoke thee, O Light, who art above every power of the Father, Thou who art called Light and Spirit and Life; for Thou hast reigned in the body."

The formula of the rite of angelic redemption (the "angelic redemption" was the means whereby the candidate became one with his "angel" above), one of the higher degrees of Gnostic initiation, is then given:

"[I invoke] the Name hidden from every godhead and lordship, the Name of Truth, in which Jesus, the Nazarene, clothed himself in the zones (or girdles) of Light, [the Name] of the Christ, Christ the Living One, through the Holy Spirit, for angelic redemption."

Next follows the formula of the restoration or

restitution, the final consecration. They who solemnize the rite declare as follows:

"There is no separation between my spirit, my heart, and the Super-celestial Power. May I enjoy thy Name, O Saviour of Truth!"

And then the candidate replies:

"I am confirmed and redeemed; I redeem my soul from this æon (world) and all that cometh therefrom, in the name of IAŌ, who redeemed its soul, unto redemption in Christ, the Living One."

Then the assistants rejoin:

"Peace unto all on whom this Name doth rest!"

There were also prayers for the dead, and also formulæ for the soul in passing through the seven gates of the seven purgatorial spheres, of which the following are given by Irenæus as specimens:

"I am the son of the Father, of the Father who is beyond all existence [that is to say, generation, or *saṁsāra*, the sphere of rebirth] while I, His son, am in existence. I came [into existence] to see mine own and things not mine, yet not wholly not mine, for they are Wisdom's, who is [my] female [counterpart] and made them for herself. But I derive my birth from Him who is beyond existence, and I return again unto mine own whence I came forth."

And then they pass through the various planes of the purgatorial realms, and the powers of the regions make way before them. The final "apology" is made to the powers surrounding the world-fabricator, or demiurge, and runs as follows:

"I am a vessel more precious than the female power [lower Wisdom] who made you. Your mother knoweth not the root from which she came; but I know myself and know whence I am, and I invoke the incorruptible Wisdom [above], who is in the Father. She it is who is the Mother of your mother, the Mother who hath no mother, nor any male consort. But it was a female born from a female who made you, one who knoweth not her Mother, but thinketh herself to be alone [self-generated]. But I invoke her Mother to my aid."

And so he passeth on to his own, casting off his chains, that is to say, the soul, or lower nature.

It is evident that we have in the above an indication of the same range of ideas which we find worked out with such elaboration in the *Pistis Sophia* and Codex Brucianus treatises: the light-robe of the Master, the Living One, the invocations, apologies, prayers for the dead, baptism and chrism, all clearly distinguishable; all of which formed part of the great cycle of Gnostic initiations in known Valentinian circles. The degrees of this initiation were more and more secret as they became more real. Irenæus may have heard of some of the formulæ of the lower grades, but the higher grades could only be understood by the picked disciples of these very intellectual and highly mystical schools. The documents pertaining to the higher degrees seem never to have come into the hands of the Church Fathers.

PTOLEMY.

OF the life of Ptolemy, one of the oldest pupils of Valentinus, we know absolutely nothing. It was through some of the pupils of Ptolemy mainly that Irenæus (I. i.-viii.) become acquainted with a rough outline of some of the ideas of the developed Gnosticism of this line of tradition; but whether or not Ptolemy himself was alive when the Presbyter of Lyons wrote the opening chapters of his Refutation, somewhere about A.D. 185-195, it is impossible to say. Of the writings of Ptolemy two fragments alone have been preserved: an interpretation of the magnificent Proem of the Beginnings still extant in the Prologue to the fourth canonical Gospel (Iren., I. viii. 5), and a letter to a lady called Flora, quoted by Epiphanius (*Hær.*, xxxiii.).

Whether or not the teaching of Ptolemy had any essential differences from that of his master Valentinus, it is at present impossible to decide; and the copied statement of Tertullian (*Adv. Valent.*, 4) —that with Ptolemy the names and numbers of the æons were separated into personal substances external to Deity, whereas with Valentinus these substances had been included in the sum of the Godhead, as sensations, affections, and emotions—is perfectly unintelligible to the student of Gnosticism.

We will first consider the Letter to Flora, and then the interpretation of the Logos-doctrine Proem. The Letter to Flora gives the view which the Valentinian

The Letter to Flora.

tradition held concerning the world-process, the old Covenant theology, and the documents of the Jewish law.

Opinions, says Ptolemy, are divided; some holding the one extreme and contending that the Jews' Law came direct from God and the Father (the Logos); others maintaining the absolute contrary, and declaring that it emanated from the opposite power, the destroyer, the god of this world (the Accuser or Diabolos). Both of these extreme views are unwise. On the one hand, the Law is evidently imperfect, as may be seen from the crude ideas ascribed to God in some of the documents, ideas foreign to the nature and judgments of the God of the Christ; and on the other, the world-process cannot be the work of an unjust power, for the Saviour Himself declared that a house divided against itself cannot stand; and the "Apostle" long ago robbed of its sting the "baseless wisdom" (ἀνυπόστατον σοφίαν) of such liars, in the words, "all things were made by Him," the Logos, and not by a god of destruction.

Ptolemy, like the rest of the Valentinians, condemns as strongly such false gnosis as later the now-called "orthodox" Fathers, headed by Irenæus, condemned all gnosis. But at this time the phrase "knowledge falsely so called" was not a condemnation of all gnosis, for there still was an "orthodox" Christian gnosis, as Clement of Alexandria and others have so well shown.

Such views, then, are held only by those who are ignorant of the causative law; the one body of extremists being ignorant of the God of Justice (the framer of the kārmic law), the other of the All-Father, whom the Saviour was the first to know and proclaim to the Jews.

The Gnostics held a middle position between these extremes, the only possible one. Ptolemy thus proceeds to answer the doubts of Flora entirely in the spirit of what is now called the "Higher Criticism"; he lays down a position immediately self-evident to the cultured Gnostic genius, and said to be based on the words of Jesus, but only recovered by modern scholarship after many long centuries of obscurantism. *The "Higher Criticism."*

The law, as set forth in the Five Books ascribed to Moses, is not from one source, that is to say, not from God alone. In fact, three sources may be distinguished: (1) laws given by Moses under inspiration; (2) laws enacted by Moses himself; (3) laws added by the elders.

This division is borne out by the "Words of the Saviour"; for with regard to divorce He taught that it was permitted by Moses only because of the Jews' hardness of heart, whereas the Law of God from the beginning laid down that husband and wife should not be sundered. The law of Moses was simply an enactment of expediency, it was not the Law. Moreover, the traditions of the elders were equally not the Law. For the inspired Law taught that honour was *due* to father and mother; and Jesus had opposed this old truth of kārmic duty to the ignorant tradition of the elders, which taught that anything given to father or mother by the child was a *gift*—a phrase which Ptolemy quotes differently from the

BB

readings of either of the synoptic documents that still preserve it; namely, "whatsoever benefit thou receivest from me, is a gift to God."

Thus three distinct sources are to be distinguished, only one of which can be referred to what can in any sense be called revelation.

Again, as to the first division, this in its turn is resolvable into three elements: (1) a good element (the Decalogue), endorsed and completed by the teaching of Christ; (2) a bad element, which He set aside, the "eye for an eye" law of retaliation; and (3) the typical and symbolical rites, such as circumcision, the sabbath and fasting, which the Christ translated from their sensible and phenomenal forms into their spiritual and invisible meaning. This is borne out in a remarkable fashion by one of the newly discovered Sayings: "Jesus saith, Except ye fast to the world, ye shall in no wise find the Kingdom of God; and except ye sabbatize the sabbath, ye shall not see the Father." (See *Sayings of Our Lord*, Grenfell and Hunt; London, 1897).

Thus with regard to the third element, the Christ taught that the "offerings" to God were not to consist of incense and the slaughter of irrational animals, but of spiritual thanksgiving, and goodwill and good works to our neighbours; that circumcision was not of anything physical, but of the spiritual heart; that keeping the sabbath was resting from evil works; and in like manner fasting was from baser things, and not from physical food.

From what source, then, came the "inspiration" of Moses in establishing such observances? From a source midway between the world of men and the God over all; that is to say, from the intermediate realms, or world-soul, the fabricative power of this physical world. The source of Moses' inspiration was not the Perfect Deity of the Christ, but an inferior source, not good (for God alone is really good), nor evil (the power which opposes good alone being evil), but imperfect; the power of the adjuster or arbitrator. This source is inferior to the Perfect Deity; it is only conditionally righteous or just, and so inferior to the perfect righteousness and justice of God. The maker or soul of our world is generable, the creator of the divine creation ingenerable. But the world-maker is superior to the opposer, the world, whose substance is destruction and darkness, and whose matter is material and manifoldly divided. But the substance of the cosmic spaces of the ingenerable Father (the cosmic spaces, or "universals," as opposed to the "world," or our earth; the cosmic planes as distinguished from the terrestrial) is incorruptibility and self-existent Light, simple and one.

The Source of Moses' Inspiration.

The substance of these cosmic spaces is differentiated in an incomprehensible manner into two powers or aspects, soul enforming body; that is to say, the "planetary soul" enforming the "earth." This soul is an image of the ideal cosmos, and it is from one of its powers that Moses received his inspiration.

So far the sensible letter of Ptolemy to Flora; in which the Gnostic doctor, by his knowledge of the unseen world and understanding of the teaching of the Christ, intuitively applies a canon of criticism to the contents of the Pentateuch, which the best scholarship of our own century has taken a hundred years to establish intellectually.

We will now proceed to consider the interpretation which Ptolemy gave to the glorious Proem that now stands at the head of the fourth Gospel.

The Proem to the Fourth Gospel.

The Beginning is the first principle brought into being by God, and in it the Father emanated all things in germ, or potentially. This Beginning is called Mind, Son, and Alone-begotten (that is to say, brought forth by the Father alone).

The next phase of being was the emanation of the Logos (Reason or Word) in the first principle, the Beginning or Mind. This Logos in His turn contained in Himself the whole substance of the Æons, which substance the Logos enformed.

According to the Lexicon of the Alexandrian Hesychius, the philosophical meaning of the term Logos is "the cause of action" ($\dot{\eta}$ τοῦ δράματος ὑπόθεσις).

The opening words, therefore, treat of the divine hypostases.

"In the Beginning was the Logos, and the Logos was (one) with God, and the Logos was God. He was in the Beginning (one) with God." I translate the phrase πρὸς τὸν Θεὸν by the words "one with God," and not by the simple and familiar "with God," on the authority of Ptolemy (ἡ πρὸς ἀλλήλους ἅμα καὶ ἡ πρὸς τὸν πατέρα ἕνωσις), seeing that the simple English preposition "with" does not convey the sense of the Greek.

First of all there is a distinction made between the three, God, Beginning and Logos, and then they are at-oned, or identified; in order that first the emanation of the two from the one may be shown—of the Son (or Beginning or Mind) and of the Logos from the Father)—and then the identification or at-one-ment of the two with each other and with the Father may be indicated.

For in the Father and from the Father is the Beginning; and in the Beginning and from the Beginning is the Logos. Well said is it then, "In the Beginning was the Logos," for He was in the Son (or Mind).

"And the Logos was (one) with God." For the Beginning is one with God, and, consequently, the Logos is one. For what is of God, is God.

"All came into being through Him, and without Him nothing had being." That is, the Logos was the cause of the divine or æonic creation.

But "that which has its being in Him is Life"— the syzygy or consort of the Logos.

The Æons came into being *through* Him, but Life was *in* him. And she who is in Him, is more akin to Him than they who came into being through Him. For she is united to Him and bears fruit through Him.

"And the Life was the Light of men"—"men" signifying first of all the supernal Man and his spouse, the Church, for they were enlightened, or brought to light through Life. Thus far concerning the Plērōma or divine world.

The next verse, "The Light shineth in the

Darkness and the Darkness comprehended it not," refers to the sensible universe. For though the chaos of the sensible universe was made into cosmos by the passion of the Divine Æon, the sensible world knew Him not. And this Æon is thus Truth and Life, and "Word made flesh," in the cosmic process. It is the enlightened only who have "beheld His glory," the glory of the Alone-begotten Son, the Divine Æon or Plērōma, given unto Him by the Father, full of Grace (another name for Silence and Peace) and Truth.

And thus, said Ptolemy, distinct reference to the two tetraktydes—Father and Silence, Mind and Truth, Word and Life, Man and Church—is contained in the Proem.

Such was the nature of the exegesis of Ptolemy with regard to the Proem of the Logos-doctrine, and here we must reluctantly leave him, for we have no further information.

Irenæus' summary, in his opening chapters, of what he had picked up concerning the tenets of "them of Ptolemy," differs but slightly from the outlines of the æon-process and Sophia-mythus drama already familiar to our readers from the account of Hippolytus.

HERACLEŌN.

OF the life of Heracleon, whom Clement of Alexandria (*Strom.*, iv. 9) calls the "most esteemed of the school of Valentinus," we again know nothing except that he wrote certain Memoirs (ὑπομνήματα), containing a commentary on the fourth Gospel. The date of this commentary, the first on any book of the New Testament collection, is generally ascribed to the decade 170-180 A.D. The Gnostic Heracleon is thus the first commentator of canonical Christianity, and considerable fragments of his work have been preserved by Origen in his own Commentary on the so-called Johannine Gospel. These fragments were first collected by Grabe in his *Spicilegium*, reprinted by Massuet and Stieren in their editions of Irenæus, and by Hilgenfeld in his *Ketzergeschichte* (1884), and finally in 1891 re-edited from a new collation of all the eight known (only three having previously been collated) MSS. by Brooke in *Texts and Studies*, i. 4.

His Commentary on the Fourth Gospel.

In these fragments Heracleon assumes the "Valentinian" system as a basis; but it is kept in the background, and his exegesis is often endorsed by Origen.

The Gnostics were still in the Christian ranks, they were still members of the General Christian body, and desired to remain members; but bigotry finally drove them out because they dared to say that the teaching of the Christ contained a wisdom which transcended the comprehension of the majority.

The commentary of Heracleon, however, need not detain us, for it is, so to say, outside the circle of distinct Gnostic exegesis; it stands midway between it and General Christianity, and in almost the same position as the views of Clement and Origen.

BARDESANES.

Biography. WE will now treat of Bardesanes, "the last of the Gnostics," as Hilgenfeld calls him, and so bring to an end these rough sketches of the Christian theosophists, which we have endeavoured to reconstruct from the disfigured scraps of the originals preserved in Patristic literature.

Bardesanes was the "last of the Gnostics," in the sense of being the last who attempted to make any propaganda of the phase of the Gnosis we are dealing with, among the ranks of Common Christianity; for the Gnosis was still studied in secret for centuries, and often reappeared in the pages of history in other guises, *e.g.*, the so-called Manichæan movement; for "You may pitch out nature with a fork, still she will find a way home."

Bardesanes, or Bar-daisan (so called from the river Daisan (the Leaper), on the banks of which he was born), was born at Edessa, on July 11th, 155 A.D., and died, most probably in the same city, in 233, at the age of 78. His parents, Nuhama and Nahashirama, were rich and noble; and young Bardaisan not only received the best education in manners and learning which was procurable, but was brought up with a prince who afterwards succeeded to the throne as one of the Abgars; he not only shared the young prince's martial exercises, but in his youth won great fame for his skill in archery. He married and had a son, Harmonius.

At what age he embraced Gnostic Christianity is uncertain; but his eager spirit not only speedily converted his royal friend and patron, but induced the Abgar to make it the state religion, and thus (it is said) Bardesanes must have the credit of indirectly establishing the first Christian state. When Caracalla dethroned the Abgar Bar-Manu in 216, Bardesanes made manful defence of the Christian faith before the representative of the Roman Emperor, so that even Epiphanius is compelled to call him "almost a confessor."

Subsequently he went for a time to Armenia, where he composed a history based on the temple chronicles, which he found in the fortress of Ani, and translated it into Syriac. This Armenian history of Bardaisan was the basis of the subsequent history of Moses of Chorēnē. Bardaisan was also a great student of Indian religion, and wrote a book on the subject, from which the Platonist Porphyry subsequently quoted. But it was as a poet and writer on Christian theology and theosophy that Bardaisan gained so wide a reputation; he wrote many books in Syriac and also Greek, of which he was said to be master, but even the titles of most of them are now lost.

Writings.

His most famous work was a collection of 150 Hymns or Psalms on the model of the Psalm-collection of the second temple, as still preserved in the Old Covenant documents. He was the first to adapt the Syriac tongue to metrical forms and set the words to music; these hymns became immensely popular, not only in the Edessene kingdom but wherever the Syriac tongue was spoken.

Of the rest of his works we hear of such titles as *Dialogues against the Marcionites, The Light and the Darkness, The Spiritual Nature of Truth, The Stable and Unstable,* and *Concerning Fate*. Nothing of these has come down to us except a Syriac treatise, which was brought to the British Museum in 1843, among the Nitrian MSS. This MS. is entitled *Book of the Laws of Countries*, and purports to be a summary of Bardaisan's views on fate or karman, as set forth by one of his pupils. The Syriac text and an English translation were published by Cureton in 1855; and once more (as in the case of the discovery of the *Philosophumena* MS. and Basilides) the possession of an approximately first-hand source has revolutionised the old view, based on the hearsay of the Fathers generally, and of the polemic of Ephraim in particular. In fact, the latest view (that of Hort) tries to rob Gnosticism of Bardesanes, and carry him off into the fold of orthodoxy. As more is known and understood about the Gnostics, the same policy will no doubt be adopted in other cases; but surely since Orthodoxy has cursed Bardesanes throughout the ages, it might at least leave him the name derived from those of whom his master Valentinus learned his wisdom, and let him be Gnostic still.

But before considering Bardaisan's views on "fate," let us see whether we can abstract anything of value from the indirect sources. We are indebted for what we know mainly to Ephraim of Edessa, who wrote some 120 years later than our Gnostic. Of the temper of this saint when combatting a dead man who had done him no injury, and who had been so loved and admired by all who knew him, we may judge by the epithets he applied to Bardesanes, who (he avers) died "with the Lord in his mouth, and demons in his heart." Thus he apostrophizes Bardaisan as a garrulous sophist; of tortuous and double mind; outwardly orthodox, a heretic in secret; a greedy sheep-dog in league with the wolves; a faithless servant; a cunning dissembler practising deceit with his songs.

Indirect Sources.

In his zealous fury, however, Ephraim confuses Bardesanites, Marcionites and Manichæans, although Bardesanes strongly opposed the views of the former, and the religion of the latter was as yet unborn when the Gnostic doctor wrote. Ephraim's fifty-six Hymns against Heresies, for instance, the metre and music of which he appropriated from our Gnostic poet, are an indiscriminate polemic against not only Marcion, Bardaisan and Mani, but also against their disciples, the very different views of both teachers and pupils being hopelessly jumbled together.

The only clear traces of Bardaisan are four scraps from his Hymns, quoted in the last two Hymns of

Ephraim. The first three are as follows, in Hort's translation:

From his Hymns.

(1) "Thou fountain of joy
    Whose gate by commandment
    Opens wide to the Mother;
    Which Beings divine
    Have measured and founded,
    Which Father and Mother
    In their union have sown,
    With their steps have made fruitful."

(2) "Let her who comes after thee
    To me be a daughter
    A sister to thee."

(3) "When at length shall it be ours
    To look on thy banquet,
    To see the young maiden,
    The daughter thou sett'st
    On thy knee and caressest?"

The first fragment is generally referred to the idea of Paradise, which is usually placed above the third of the seven heavens, or in the midst of the seven spheres; it seems, however, rather to refer to the Ogdoad or space above the seven phases of psychic substance, the Jerusalem Above of the Valentinians.

The second fragment appears to be an address of the Divine Mother to the elder of her two daughters, the Wisdom above in the Plērōma and the Wisdom below in the Ogdoad, where is the spiritual Heaven-world.

The third fragment is most probably an address to the Divine Mother of all, the Holy Spirit, and refers to the consummation of the world-process, when the spiritual souls shall be taken from the Ogdoad into the Plērōma, and made one with their divine spouses at the Great Wedding Feast, in the Space of the Light-maiden, the Wisdom above.

The remaining fragment consists of only two lines, and is as follows:

(4) "My God and my Head
    Hast thou left me alone?"

This cry was ascribed to the lower Wisdom by the Valentinian school, both in the world-drama, when the world-substance invokes the aid of her consort, the æonic world-fashioner, and also in the soul-tragedy of the spirit fallen into matter, the sorrowing Sophia, as in the *Pistis Sophia* treatise.

Nothing more of a certain nature can be deduced from the polemical writings of Ephraim, and the only scrap of interest we can glean from other writers is a beautiful phrase preserved by the Syrian writer Philoxenus of Mabūg (about 500 A.D.): "The Ancient of Eternity is a boy"—that is to say, is ever young.

Let us now turn to Bardaisan's views on "astrology" and "fate," or, in other words, his conception of karman, and quote a few passages from Cureton's somewhat unintelligible translation of The

Book of the Laws of Countries (in his *Spicilegium Syriacum*, pp. 11, *sqq.*).

This dialogue was written by a pupil of our Gnostic, and Bardaisan is introduced as the main speaker; in fact, the pupils' only break in here and there with a short question for literary effect. We may be therefore fairly confident that we have in this treatise a faithful reproduction of the views, not only of Bardaisan on fate or karman, but also of the Gnostics of his school.

The following extracts from the speeches of Bardaisan will throw much light also on the astrological ideas in the *Pistis Sophia*.

"I likewise . . . know that there are men who are called Chaldæans, and others who love this knowledge of the art, as I also once loved it [before he met with the teaching of Valentinus], for it has been said by me, in another place, that the soul of man is capable of knowing that which many do not know, and the same men [*sic*] meditate to do; and all that they do wrong, and all that they do good, and all the things which happen to them in riches and in poverty, and in sickness and in health, and in defects of the body, it is from the influence of those Stars, which are called the Seven, they befall them, and they are governed by them. But there are others who say the opposite of these things,—how that this art is a lie of the Chaldæans, or that Fortune does not exist at all, but it is an empty name; and all things are placed in the hands of man, great and small; and bodily defects and faults happen and befall him by chance. But others say that whatsoever a man doeth, he doeth of his own will, by the Free-will that has been given to him, and the faults and defects and evil things which happen to him, he receiveth as a punishment from God. But as for myself, in my humble opinion, it appeareth to me that these three sects are partly true, and partly false. They are true, because men speak after the fashion which they see, and because, also, men see how things happen to them, and mistake; because the wisdom of God is richer than they, which has established the worlds and created man, and has ordained the Governors, and has given to all things the power which is suitable for each one of them. But I say that God, and the Angels, and the Powers, and the Governors, and the Elements, and men and animals have this power; but all these orders of which I have spoken have not power given to them in everything. For he that is powerful in everything is One; but they have power in some things, and in some things they have no power, as I have said: that the goodness of God may be seen in that in which they have power, and in that in which they have no power they may know that they have a Lord. There is, therefore, Fortune, as the Chaldæans say."

And that everything is not in our own Free-will, that is that Free-will is not absolute, is plainly visible in everyday experience. Fortune also plays its part, but is not absolute, and Nature also. Thus "we men are found to be governed by Nature equally, and by Fortune differently, and by our Free-will each as he wishes."

Karman.

Fortune and Nature.

"That which is called Fortune is an order of procession which is given to the Powers and the Elements by God; and according to this procession and order, intelligences [minds, egos] are changed by their coming down to be with the soul, and souls are changed by their coming down to be with the body; and this alteration itself is called the Fortune and the Nativity of this assemblage, which is being sifted and purified, for the assistance of that which by the favour of God and by grace has been assisted, and is being assisted, till the consummation of all. [Compare in the system of Basilides the 'benefitting and being benefitted in turn.'] The body, therefore, is governed by Nature, the soul also suffering with it and perceiving; and the body is not constrained nor assisted by Fortune in all the things which it does individually; for a man does not become a father before fifteen years, nor does a woman become a mother before thirteen years. And in the same manner, also, there is a law for old age; because women become effete from bearing, and are deprived of the natural power of begetting; while other animals which are also governed by their own Nature before those ages which I have specified, not only procreate, but also become too old to procreate, in the same manner as also the bodies of men when they are grown old do not procreate; nor is Fortune able to give them children at that time at which the body has not the Nature to give them. Neither, again, is Fortune able to preserve the body of man in life, without eating and without drinking; nor even when it has meat and drink, to prevent it from dying, for these and many other things pertain to Nature itself; but when the times and manners of Nature are fulfilled, then comes Fortune apparent among these, and effecteth things that are distinct one from another; and at one time assists Nature and increases, and at another hinders it and hurts; and from Nature cometh the growth and perfection of the body; but apart from Nature and by Fortune come sickness and defects in the body. For Nature is the connection of males and females, and the pleasure of the both heads [*sic*]; but from Fortune comes abomination and a different manner of connection and all the filthiness and indecency which men do for the cause of connection through their lust. For Nature is birth and children; and from Fortune sometimes the children are deformed; and sometimes they are cast away, and sometimes they die untimely. From Nature there is a sufficiency in moderation for all bodies; and from Fortune comes the want of food, and affliction of the bodies; and thus, again, from the same Fortune is gluttony, and extravagance which is not requisite. Nature ordains that old men should be judges for the young, and wise for the foolish; and that the valiant should be chiefs over the weak, and the brave over the timid. But Fortune causeth that boys should be chiefs over the aged, and fools over the wise; and that in time of war the weak should govern the valiant, and the timid the brave. And know ye distinctly that, whenever Nature is disturbed from its right course, its disturbance is from the cause of Fortune, because those Heads and Governors, upon whom that alternation is which is called

The Right and Left.

Nativity, are in opposition one to the other. And those of them which are called Right, they assist Nature, and add to its excellency whenever the procession helps them, and they stand in the high places, which are in the sphere, in their own portions; and those which are called Left are evil, and whenever they, too, occupy the places of height, they are opposed to Nature, and not only injure men, but, at different times, also animals, and trees and fruits, and the produce of the year, and the fountains of water, and everything that is in the Nature which is under their control. And on account of these divisions and sects which exist among the Powers, some men have supposed that the world is governed without any superintendence, because they do not know that these sects and divisions and justification and condemnation proceed from that influence which is given in Free-will by God, that those actions also by the power of themselves may either be justified or condemned, as we see that Fortune crushes Nature, so we can also see the Free-will of man repelling and crushing Fortune herself; but not in everything, as also Fortune itself doth not repel Nature in everything; for it is proper that the three things, Nature and Fortune and Free-will, should be maintained in their lives until the procession be accomplished, and the measure and number be fulfilled, as it seemed good before Him who ordained how should be the life and perfection of all creatures, and the state of all Beings and Natures."

Bardaisan thus makes Free-will, Fate, and Nature the three great factors of the kārmic law, all three being ultimately in the hand of God. Each re-acts on each, none is absolute. Nature has to do with body, Fate or Fortune with soul, and Free-will with spirit. None of them is absolute, the absolute being in God alone.

By a strange chance, however, one of the hymns of the great poet of Gnosticism has been preserved to us entire; it is now generally admitted that the beautiful "Hymn of the Soul," as it has been called, imbedded in the Syriac form of the apocryphal *Acts of Judas Thomas*, preserved in the British Museum codex, is almost undoubtedly from the stylus of Bardaisan. Nöldeke and Macke were the first scholars to call attention to the fact. (See Lipsius' *Die apokryphen Apostelgeschichten*, i. 299, *sqq.*, 1885). It is a beautiful legend of initiation, and was first translated by Wright (*Apochryphal Acts of the Apostles*, ii. 238—245; 1871); it has now quite recently (1898) been re-translated by Bevan, using Wright's version as a basis. Since the time of Wright so much work has been done on this "master-piece of religious poetry," as the Cambridge Reader in Arabic justly calls it, that the translation of the pupil is to be prefered to that of the teacher, and Professor Bevan's work must now be considered not only to have superseded Wright's, but to be the best on the subject.

The Hymn of the Soul.

The high probability of the Bardesantist origin of the poem is based on the following considerations: The three main accusations of the orthodox Father Ephraim against Bardaisan, who, he says, taught that there were Seven Essences (Īthyē), are: "(1) That he denied the resurrection and regarded the separation of the soul from the body as a blessing; (2) that he held the theory of a divine 'Mother' who in conjunction with 'the Father of Life' gave birth to a being called 'the Son of the Living'; (3) that he believed in a number of lesser 'gods,' that is to say, eternal beings subordinate to the supreme God.

"Now, it is remarkable," says Professor Bevan, "that these three 'heresies' all appear distinctly in the Poem before us. There can be no doubt that the Egyptian garb, which the prince puts on as a disguise and casts away as soon as his mission is accomplished, represents the human body. The emphatic declaration that the 'filthy and unclean garb' is 'left in their country' conveys an unmistakable meaning; it would be difficult, in an allegorical piece, to deny a material resurrection more absolutely."

Since Bardaisan, like all the great Gnostics, believed in reincarnation, such a conception as the resurrection of the same physical body must have been regarded by him as a gross superstition of the ignorant. Such a "proof" of identity of doctrine as is here brought foward could hardly occur to one who has realised the meaning of the doctrine of rebirth.

"The true clothing of the soul, according to the poet, is the ideal form which it left behind in heaven and will resume after death. [Only after the 'death unto sin'; the Light-robe is not for all.] As for the Father of Life, the Mother, and the Son of the Living, they here figure as the Father 'the King of kings,' the Mother 'the Queen of the East,' and the Brother 'the next in rank.' Finally the 'lesser gods' appear as 'the kings,' who obey the command of the King of kings."

If the student, in reading this masterpiece of Gnostic poesy, will bear in mind the beautiful Parable of the Prodigal Son, as preserved in the third Synoptic, he will be able to trace the basic similarity of ideas in the outer and inner traditions, and note how the inner expands and explains the outer.

I do not know on what authority this beautiful poem has been called the Hymn of the Soul; there is no authority in the text for the title, and the Gnostic poet had a far more definite theme in mind. He sang of the consummation of the Gnostic life, the crown of victory at the end of the Path; not of any vague generalities but of a very definite goal towards which he was running. He sang of the "wedding garment," the "robe of initiation," so beautifully described in the opening pages of the *Pistis Sophia*. Thus, then, in most recent translation runs what I will venture to call:

THE HYMN OF THE ROBE OF GLORY.

When I was a little child.
And dwelling in my kingdom, in my Father's house,
And in the wealth and the glories
Of my nurturers had my pleasure,
From the East,[1] our home,
My parents, having equipped me, sent me forth.
And of the wealth of our treasury [2]
They had tied up for me a load.
Large it was, yet light,
So that I might bear it unaided—
Gold of . . . [3]
And silver of Gazzak the great,
And rubies of India,
And agate (?) from the land of Kushān (?),
And they girded me with adamant [4]
Which can crush iron.
And they took off from me the bright robe,

[1] Either the Plērōma or Ogdoad, the spiritual realms. The following notes are all mine.

[2] A Gnostic technical term.

[3] Beth-'Ellāyē (Wright). It is highly probable that all the names of countries and towns, some of which Bevan has omitted as too doubtful, are substitutes for states or regions of the higher planes; the identification of some of them has entirely baffled scholars, and the identification of the rest is mostly unsatisfactory. No doubt Bardaisan, or his son Harmonius, or whatever Bardesanist wrote the poem, was familiar with the great caravan route from India to Egypt, and used this knowledge as a substructure, but the whole is allegorical. (Since writing this note some excellent work of interpretation on these lines has been done by German scholars. See Bibliography).

[4] A symbol, presumably, for the mind-body, or vesture.

Which in their love they had wrought for me,
And my purple toga,
Which was measured (and) woven to my stature.
And they made compact with me,
And wrote it in my heart that it should not be forgotten:
"If thou goest down into Egypt,[1]
And bringest the one pearl,[2]
Which is in the midst of the sea[3]
Hard by the loud-breathing serpent,[4]
(Then) shalt thou put on thy bright robe
And thy toga,[5] which is laid over it,
And with thy Brother,[6] our next in rank,[7]
Thou shalt be heir in our kingdom."
I quitted the East (and) went down,
There being with me two messengers,[8]
For the way was dangerous and difficult,
And I was young to tread it.
I passed the borders of Maishān,
The meeting place of the merchants of the East,
And I reached the land of Babel,
And I entered the walls of . . . [9]

---

[1] The body, a technical term common to many Gnostic schools.

[2] The Gnosis.

[3] Of matter, gross and subtle.

[4] Perhaps the elemental or animal essence in matter.

[5] Two of the higher vestures of the Self, of which there were three.

[6] The higher ego presumably.

[7] Next in rank to the Mother and Father.

[8] The powers that compel to rebirth presumably, the representatives of the Father and Mother.

[9] Sarbūg (Wright). These are apparently various planes or states.

I went down into Egypt,
And my companions parted from me.
I betook me straight to the serpent,
Hard by his dwelling I abode,
(Waiting) till he could slumber and sleep,[1]
And I could take my pearl from him.
And when I was single and alone,
A stranger to those with whom I dwelt,
One of my race, a free-born man,
From among the Easterns, I beheld there—
A youth fair and well-favoured.

. . . . *   *   *   *   *
*   *   *   *   *   *

*   * and he came and attached himself to me.
And I made him my intimate,
A comrade with whom I shared my merchandise.
I warned him against the Egyptians
And against consorting with the unclean;
And I put on a garb like theirs,
Lest they should insult (?) me because I had come
    from afar,
To take away the pearl,
And (lest) they should arouse the serpent against
    me.
But in some way or other
They perceived that I was not their countryman;
So they dealt with me treacherously.
Moreover they gave me their food to eat.
I forgot that I was a son of kings,
And I served their king;

---

[1] The serpent is presumably the passions, which inhere in the elemental essence.

And I forgot the pearl,
For which my parents had sent me,
And by reason of the burden of their . . .
I lay in a deep sleep.[1]
But all those things that befell me,
My parents perceived and were grieved for me;
And a proclamation was made in our kingdom,
That all should speed to our gate,
King and princes of Parthia
And all the nobles of the East.
So they wove a plan on my behalf,
That I might not be left in Egypt,
And they wrote to me a letter,
And every noble signed his name[2] thereto:
" From thy Father, the King of kings,
And thy Mother, the Mistress of the East,
And from thy Brother, our next in rank,
To thee our son, who art in Egypt, greeting!
Up and arise from thy sleep,
And listen to the words of our letter!

---

[1] Is it possible that in the above a real piece of biography has also been woven into the poem? I am inclined to think so. It may even be a lost page from the occult life of Bardaisan himself. Filled with longing to penetrate the mysteries of the Gnosis, he joins a caravan to Egypt and arrives at Alexandria. There he meets with a friend on the same quest as himself. Bardaisan first of all has the misfortune to fall into the hands of some sensual and self-seeking school of magic, and forgets for a time his real quest. Only after this bitter experience does he obtain the instruction he sought in the initiation of the Valentinian school. Of course this speculation is put forward with all hesitation, but it is neither an impossibility nor an improbability.

[2] Names are powers. Compare the beautiful "Come unto us" passages in the Song of the Powers of the *Pistis Sophia*, *pagg.* 17 *sqq.*

Call to mind that thou art a son of kings!
See the slavery—whom thou servest!
Remember the pearl
For which thou didst speed to Egypt!
Think of thy bright robe,
And remember thy glorious toga,
Which thou shalt put on as thine adornment,
When thy name hath been read out in the list of the valiant,
And with thy Brother, our [? next in rank],
Thou shalt be [? king] in our kingdom."
And my letter (was) a letter
Which the King sealed with his right hand,
(To keep it) from the wicked ones, the children of Babel,
And from the savage demons of . . .[1]
It flew in the likeness of an eagle,
The king of all birds;[2]
It flew and alighted beside me,
And became all speech.
At its voice and the sound of its rustling,
I started and arose from my sleep.
I took it up and kissed it,
And loosed its seal (?), (and) read;
And according to what was traced on my heart
Were the words of my letter written.
I remembered that I was a son of kings,
And my free soul longed for its natural state.
I remembered the pearl,

---

[1] Sarbūg (Wright).
[2] The descent of the Holy Ghost or spiritual consciousness.

For which I had been sent to Egypt,
And I began to charm him,
The terrible loud-breathing serpent.
I hushed him to sleep and lulled him to slumber;
For my Father's name I named over him,
And the name of our next in rank,
And of my Mother, the Queen of the East; [1]
And I snatched away the pearl,
And turned to go back to my Father's house.
And their filthy and unclean garb
I stripped off, and left it in their country, [2]
And I took my way straight to come
To the light of our home, the East.
And my letter, my awakener,
I found before me on the road,
And as with its voice it had awakened me,
(So) too with its light it was leading me

. . . .

Shone before me with its form,
And with its voice and its guidance,
It also encouraged me to speed,

* * * * * *

And with his (?) love was drawing me on.
I went forth, passed by . . .
I left Babel on my left hand, [3]
And reached Maishān the great,

---

[1] The names of Father, Son, and Holy Ghost, that is to say, the powers of the immortal principles in man.

[2] He left his body behind in trance, during the initiation.

[3] He goes to "the right" like all the initiates in the Orphic and other Mysteries.

The haven of the merchants,
That sitteth on the shore of the sea.

* * * * *

And my bright robe, which I had stripped off,
And the toga wherein it was wrapped,
From the heights of Hyrcania (?)
My parents sent thither,
By the hand of their treasurers,
Who in their faithfulness could be trusted therewith.
And because I remembered not its fashion—
For in my childhood I had left it in my Father's house—
On a sudden as I faced it,
The garment seemed to me like a mirror of myself. [1]
I saw it all in my whole self,
Moreover I faced my whole self in (facing) it.
For we were two in distinction,
And yet again one in one likeness.
And the treasurers also,
Who brought it to me, I saw in like manner,
That they were twain (yet) one likeness. [2]
For one kingly sign was graven on them,
Of *his* hands that restored to me (?)
My treasure and my wealth by means of them.
My bright embroidered robe,

---

[1] Compare the *logos*: "As any of you sees himself in a mirror, so let him see Me, in himself."—Resch, *Agrapha* (*Texte u. Untersuchungen*, Bd. v., Heft 4), 36 *b*, and *As Others saw Him*, p.88.

[2] The mystery of the syzygy; compare the story of the infancy in the *Pistis Sophia*.

THE HYMN OF THE ROBE OF GLORY.

Which . . . . . with glorious colours;
With gold and with beryls,
And rubies and agates (?)
And sardonyxes varied in colour,
It also was made ready in its home on high (?)
And with stones of adamant
All its seams were fastened;
And the image of the King of kings was depicted in full all over it,
And like the sapphire stone also were its manifold hues.
Again I saw that all over it
The motions of knowledge[1] were stirring
And as if to speak
I saw it also making itself ready.
I heard the sound of its tones,
Which it uttered to those who brought it down (?)
Saying, "I . . . ."[2]
Whom they reared for him (?) in the presence of my fathers,
And I also perceived in myself
That my stature was growing according to his labours.[3]
And in its kingly motions
It was spreading itself out towards me,[4]
And in the hands of its givers

---

[1] Gnosis; the robe in the *Pistis Sophia* contains all "knowledges" (γνώσις).

[2] "I am the active in deeds" (Wright).

[3] The "causal" body or vesture which constitutes the higher ego.

[4] "It poured itself entirely over me" (Wright)—the same simile as is used several times in the Askew Codex.

It hastened that I might take it.
And me too my love urged on
That I should run to meet it and receive it;
And I stretched forth and received it,
With the beauty of its colours I adorned myself
And my toga of brilliant colours
I cast around me, in its whole breadth.
I clothed myself therewith, and ascended
To the gate of salutation and homage;
I bowed my head, and did homage
To the Majesty[1] of my Father who had sent it
    to me,
For I had done his commandments,
And he too had done what he promised,
And at the gate of his princes
I mingled with his nobles;
For he rejoiced in me and received me,
And I was with him in his kingdom.
And with the voice . . .
All his servants glorify him.
And he promised that also to the gate
Of the King of kings I should speed with him,
And bringing my gift and my pearl
I should appear with him before our King.

Well may Professor Bevan call this glorious hymn a "master-piece of religious poetry"; it is not only magnificent as poetry, but priceless as a record of occult fact. What then have we not lost by the barbarous destruction of the Hymns of Bardaisan?

[1] This seems to be One different from the Father Himself, and the subject of the third and fourth lines from the end.

SOME TRACES OF THE GNOSIS IN THE UNCANONICAL ACTS.

FOREWORD.

JUST as there existed, prior to and alongside of the canonical Gospels, many other settings of the Sayings and Doings of the Lord, so there existed, prior to and alongside of the selected or canonical Acts, many other narratives professing to record the doings and sayings of the Apostles and Disciples of the Lord. Most of these originated in what are now called heretical circles, but were subsequently worked over by orthodox editors to suit doctrinal prejudices, and eagerly embraced by the Catholic Church. As Lipsius, the greatest authority on the subject, says: "Almost every fresh editor of such narratives, using that freedom which all antiquity was wont to allow itself in dealing with literary monuments, would recast the materials which lay before him, excluding whatever might not suit his theological point of view—dogmatic statements, for example, speeches, prayers, etc., for which he would substitute other formulæ of

The Gnostic Acts.

his own composition, and further expanding and abridging after his own pleasure, or as the immediate object which he had in view might dictate." (Art. "Apocryphal Acts of the Apostles," in Smith and Wace's *Dictionary*, incorporated into his exhaustive *Die apokryphen Apostelgeschichte*, 1883, etc.)

The main point of interest for us is that some of these edited and re-edited documents still preserve traces of their Gnostic origin; and Lipsius has shown that their Gnosticism is not to be ascribed to the third century Manichæism, as has been assumed by some, but to the general Gnosis of the second century.

<small>Catholic Over-working.</small>

There was a very wide circulation of such religious romances in the second century, for these formed the main means of Gnostic public propaganda. The technical inner teachings of Gnosticism the Church Fathers, as we have seen, assailed with misrepresentation and overwhelmed with ridicule; to these onslaughts the Gnostics made no reply, most probably because they were bound by their oaths of secrecy on the one hand, and on the other knew well that the doctrines of the inner life could not be decided by vulgar debate. The inner teachings of their Gospel were for those within; to the rest they were foolishness. But the Acts-romances, often no doubt based on actual occurrences of the inner life, were not of so difficult a character. They may seem vastly fantastic to modern criticism, but to every shade of Christianity in those early years they were entirely credible. These formed the intermediate link between the General Church and the inner teachings of Gnosticism, and they could not be disposed of by ridicule.

Another method had to be used. As Lipsius says: "Catholic bishops and teachers knew not how better to stem this flood of Gnostic writings and their influence among the faithful, than by boldly adopting the most popular narrations from the heretical books, and, after carefully eliminating the poison of false doctrine, replacing them in this purified form in the hands of the people."

Fortunately the "purification" has not been complete, and some traces of the "poison" are still to be found, as we hope to show our readers in the sequel.

It would be out of place in these short sketches to attempt a description of these Acts, or enter into a critical treatment of their sources; our only object is, to rescue from this mass of literature a few fragments which still preserve traces of old Gnostic teachings. The original works in which these teachings were first formulated, have disappeared; the tradition has been badly mutilated by many editors and scribes. Can it be that the new-found Coptic *Acts of Peter* may give us the translation of an original untampered-with text? *Early Collectors.*

The earliest collection of these Gnostic Acts is said to have been made by a certain Leucius (there are no less than eighteen variants of the name), or Leucius Charinus, who is said to have been a disciple of John; but of course no reliance can be placed on this latter assertion, unless "John" is taken for the writer of the Fourth Gospel, and not one of the original Twelve. At any rate the so-called Leucian Acts were early; in the opinion of Zahn this collection was made at a time when the Gnostics were not yet

DD

considered heretical, that is to say, prior to 150 A.D. However this may be, the Leucian Acts were a second century collection, for Clement of Alexandria was acquainted with them; they were also probably collected at Alexandria.

Another early collector of Gnostic Acts was a certain Linus, of whom nothing certain is known. He may probably have lived at Rome. The Abdias-collection is too late to be noticed in this connection.

For a full discussion of all these points, and an analysis of all the Gnostic fragments and references preserved in the Apocryphal Acts, I must refer the student to Lipsius' great work on the subject. We will now present the reader with the most important of these fragments, so that he may judge of their nature. Some of these Acts are untranslated in English; I use the most recent texts of Zahn, Bonnet and Lipsius.

FROM THE ACTS OF THOMAS.

WE have already given the reader the most important fragment preserved in the *Acts of Thomas*, or Judas Thomas; it is the beautiful Hymn of the Soul, composed in every likelihood by Bardesanes. If the *Acts of Thomas* had given us nothing else than this grand Gnostic Hymn of the Robe of Glory, their life would not have been preserved in vain. Fortunately, however, there is more to be gleaned from them. The following is a translation of the beautiful Ode to Sophia, as it is called.

A Hymn to Wisdom.

"The Maiden is Light's daughter; in her the King's radiance is treasured. Majestic her look, and delightsome; in radiant beauty she shineth.

"Like to spring flowers are her garments; from them streameth scent of sweet odours. Throned o'er her head the King sitteth, with food free from death feeding them at His table.

"Truth crowneth her head; Joy sports at her feet. She openeth her mouth as becomes her; all songs of praise she lets stream forth.

"Two and thirty are they who sing praises; . . . Her tongue is like the entrance veil, moved by them who enter in only.

"Her neck towereth step-like; the first world-builder did build it. Her hands suggest the band of blessed Æons, proclaiming them (?); her fingers point toward the City's Gates.

"Her bridal chamber ($\pi\alpha\sigma\tau\acute{o}s$) doth stream with light, and pour forth scent of balsam and sweet herbs, delicious scents of myrrh and savoury plants; with myrtle wreaths and masses of sweet flowers 'tis strewn within. Her bridal couch is decked with reeds (?).

"Her bridesmen are grouped round her; seven are they in number; she hath picked them herself. Seven, too, are her bridesmaids dancing before her.

"Twelve are they who serve and attend her; their eyes ever look for the Bridegroom, that He may fill them with light.

"For ever with Him will they be in joy everlasting; and will take their seats at that feast where the Great Ones assemble, and remain at that banquet of which the Eternal (αἰώνιοι) alone are deemed worthy.

"In kingly dress shall they be clad, and put on robes of light, and both shall joy in bliss and exultation, singing praise to the Father.

"For of His glorious radiance they've received; and at the sight of Him, their Lord, they have been filled with light. They have received from Him immortal food that knows no waste.

"They've drunk of wine that makes men thirst no more, nor suffer fleshly lust. So with the Living Spirit they glorify Truth's Father, and sing their praise to Wisdom's Mother."

Would that we had the original of this beautiful hymn, for even the faulty and distorted version that remains is beautiful. Can it be that we have here another of the Hymns of Bardaisan? In any case the hymn looks back to the sacred marriage of the Sophia with her Bridegroom the Christ, to which reference has already been made in our sketch of the Basilidian Gnosis.

In this marriage the cosmic Sophia was received back into the Light-world, and united with her heavenly spouse. This was to take place at the Great Consummation; but, mystically, it was ever taking place for those who united themselves with their Higher Selves. *Its meaning.*

As in the consummation of the universe the World-soul was reunited with the World-mind, so in the perfectioning of the individual the soul was made one with the Self within.

The Maiden is the daughter of the Plērōma of Light; she reflects the splendour of the Kings, the Lords of the Light-realm. Above her in the Light-realm sits throned the King of Glory, the Christos, who giveth the food of deathlessness to the Spiritual Souls (Pneumatics) who are worthy to be bidden to the Feast.

At this high initiation the whole Plērōma (the two and thirty Æons) sing songs of rejoicing that the victory is won. 'Tis only such perfected souls who can move Wisdom's tongue in praise to God; they alone can make the subtle substance of such lofty heights vibrate in songs of praise.

The following verse is difficult to understand, and doubtless does not preserve the original. The "City" is the Plērōma; the bride-chamber is the Pastos, the shrine, the holy place, where the initiation is given —the Jerusalem Above, identical perhaps with the City of which we read in the superior MS. of the Codex Brucianus.

Thither the purified soul is conducted by seven pairs or syzygies of powers. Rising aloft she takes with her the twelve, her servants, no longer her rulers as in the lower world, where she has so long been chained in the bonds of desire. The twelve are now her own purified powers, whereby the Light of the Christos is reflected. In the phrase, "both shall joy in bliss and exultation," of the third verse from the end, "both" refers to the reunited soul with its "Angel"—those Angels who always behold the Face of the Father.

This and much else does the hymn reveal to those who love the Gnosis, for many pages would not exhaust its full meaning.

Two Sacramental Invocations. But we must hasten on to the remaining fragments in the *Acts of Thomas*, and so present our readers with a translation of two interesting sacramental prayers or invocations in hymn-form. The first runs as follows:

"Come Thou Holy Name of Christ, Name above all names; come Power from above; come Perfect Mercy; come highest gift!

"Thou Mother of compassion, come; come Spouse of Him, the Man; come Thou Revealer of the mysteries concealed; Thou Mother of the seven mansions come, who in the eighth hath found Thy rest!

"Come Thou who art more ancient far than the five holy Limbs—Mind, Thought, Reflection, Thinking, Reasoning; commune with those of later birth!

"Come Holy Spirit, purge Thou their reins and heart!"

The second runs thus:

"Come highest Gift; Thou Perfect Mercy, come; Thou knower of the Chosen's mysteries, descend; Thou who dost share in all the noble striver's struggles, come!

"Come Silence, Thou Revealer of the mighty things of all the Greatness; come Thou who dost make manifest the hidden, and make the secret plain!

"Come Holy Dove, mother of two young twins; come Hidden Mother, revealed in deeds alone!

"Come Thou who givest joy to all who are at one with Thee; come and commune with us in this thanksgiving (eucharist) which we are making in Thy name, in this love-feast (agapē) to which we have assembled at Thy call!"

These sacramental invocations are to be referred to the same circle of ideas as the formulæ of the Marcosian Gnosis which we have already given.

A Note thereon.

The Name is not the name "Christos," but the Name or Power of the Christ, His *shakti* (to use a term of Indian theosophy) or syzygy.

The "one more ancient than the five limbs," is the Man, the spouse of the Sophia or Holy Spirit, the Christos. The five limbs are presumably the Pentad of the æons referred to in the new-found Gnostic *Gospel of Mary*, and the names of them are very similar to those mentioned in the "Simonian" system. They are one of the highest orderings of the limbs, or members, of the Heavenly Man, of which we read so much in the Bruce and Askew Codices.

"Those of later birth" are the neophytes awaiting the initiation of the "seal of perfection." The "mighty things of the whole Greatness" are the mysteries of the Plērōma.

The Holy Dove is again the Sophia or World-soul; according to the Gnosis of Bardaisan, she had two daughters. Ephraim, the bitter opponent of the Bardesanists, says that they were called Shame of the Dry and Image of the Water; whether these were really their names or not, they were presumably the productive World-earth and procreative World-water, the builders of the material world; in other words, the sublunary and terrestrial regions.

Before leaving the *Acts of Thomas* it may be interesting to give the reader a specimen of the stories with which such religious romances were filled. The Apostle Judas Thomas, or the Twin of Jesus, is fabled to have received India by lot for his apostolic sphere of work. Thomas at first does not wish to go, but is sold by Jesus, his master, to a trader from the East as a slave "skilled in carpentry." We take the following summary of the story from Salmon's *Introduction to the New Testament* (8th ed., 1897, pp. 337, 338).

The Palace that Thomas Built.
"When Thomas arrives in India, he is brought before the King, and being questioned as to his knowledge of masons' or carpenters' work professes great skill in either department. The King asks him if he can build him a palace. He replies that he can, and makes a plan which is approved of. He is then commissioned to build the palace, and is supplied abundantly with money for the work, which, however, he says he cannot begin till the winter months. The

King thinks this strange, but being convinced of his skill acquiesces. But when the King goes away, Thomas, instead of building, employs himself in preaching the Gospel, and spends all the money on the poor. After a time the King sends to know how the work is going on. Thomas sends back word that the palace is finished all but the roof, for which he must have more money; and this is supplied accordingly, and is spent by Thomas on the widows and orphans as before. At length the King returns to the city, and when he makes inquiry about the palace, he learns that Thomas has never done anything but go about preaching, giving alms to the poor, and healing diseases. He seemed to be a magician, yet he never took money for his cures; lived on bread and water, with salt, and had but one garment. The King, in great anger, sent for Thomas. 'Have you built me a palace?' 'Yes.' 'Let me see it.' 'Oh, you can't see it now, but you will see it when you go out of this world.' Enraged at being thus mocked, the King committed Thomas to prison, until he could devise some terrible form of death for him. But that same night the King's brother died, and his soul was taken up by the angels to see all the heavenly habitations. They asked him in which he would like to dwell. But when he saw the palace which Thomas had built, he desired to dwell in none but that. When he learned that it belonged to his brother, he begged and obtained that he might return to life in order that he might buy it from him. So as they were putting grave-clothes on the body, it returned to life. He sent for the King, whose love for him he knew, and implored him to sell him the palace. But when the King learned the truth about it, he refused to sell the mansion he hoped to inhabit himself, but consoled his brother with the promise that Thomas, who was still alive, should build him a better one, The two brothers then received instruction and were baptized."

FROM THE ACTS OF JOHN.

A Recently Published Fragment.

IN a recent volume of that most valuable series Texts and Studies (*Apocrypha Anecdota II.*, by M. R. James, 1897), there is a long fragment of *The Acts of John*, much of which has never been previously published. It has been rescued from a fourteenth century MS. preserved in Vienna. The original of these Acts is early, belonging as they do to the Leucian collection. Seeing that Clement of Alexandria quotes from them, we must assign the third quarter of the second century to them as the *terminus ad quem*. We have therefore before us an early document, our interest in which is further increased by the fact of its distinctly Gnostic nature.

The Rationale of Docetism.

Nearly the whole of the fragment consists of a monologue put into the mouth of John, in which is preserved for us a most remarkable tradition of the occult life of Jesus. The whole setting of the christology is docetic and the fragment is thus a most valuable addition to our knowledge on this interesting point of Gnostic tradition. Docetism was the rank growth of the legends of certain occult powers ascribed to the "perfect man," which were woven into the many christological and soteriological theories of the Gnostic philosophers; and also, as I believe, of a veritable historical fact, which has been obscured out of all recognition by the many historicizing narrations of the origins. After His death the Christ did return and teach His followers among the inner communities, and this was the part origin of the protean Gnostic tradition of an inner instruction. He returned in the only way He could return, namely, in a "psychic" or "spiritual" body; this body could be made visible at will, could even be made sensible to touch, but was, compared to the ordinary physical body, an "illusory" body—hence the term "docetic."

But just as the external tradition of the "Poor Men" was gradually transmuted, and finally exalted Jesus from the position of a prophet into the full power and glory of the Godhead itself, so the internal tradition extended the original docetic notion to every department of the huge soteriological structure raised by Gnostic genius. *The Acts of John* pertain to the latter cycle of tendencies, and "John" is the personification of one of the lines of tradition of the protean docetism, which had its origin in an occult fact, and of those marvellous teachings of initiation which became subsequently historicized, and which John sums up in the words: "I held firmly this one thing in myself, that the Lord contrived all things symbolically and by a dispensation toward men, for their conversion and salvation."

<small>The Evolution of Tradition.</small>

That the Christ was possessed of spiritual powers of a very high order is easy of belief to any student of occult nature. That he could appear to others in a *māyāvi-rūpa*, as it is called in India, and change its appearance at will, is quite possible of credit. But that the tradition of these and other such happenings should have been handed down without exaggeration and fantastic embellishment, would be entirely contrary to human experience in such matters.

<small>Mystic Stories of Jesus.</small>

Thus, then, we are told that at the calling of James and John, first of all James saw Jesus as a child, while John saw Him first as a man "fair and comely and of a cheerful countenance"; afterwards he saw Him as one "having a head rather bald, but a thick and flowing beard," while James asserted that He appeared "as a youth whose beard was newly come."

Moreover, another peculiarity which John remarked, was that His eyes never closed. Strangely enough, this is one of the signs of a "god" given in the Hindu scriptures. Many changes of appearance did John remark, sometimes as of "a man small and uncomely, and then again as one reaching to heaven"—a fact quite credible when related of a pupil in sympathetic contact with the powerful "presence" or "glory" of a Master. But stranger still, when John lay upon his breast, "sometimes it was felt of me to be smooth and tender, and sometimes hard, like stones." Moreover, when Jesus was in prayer and contemplation, there was seen in Him "such a light as it is not possible for a man that useth corruptible speech to tell what it was like."

The following naïve story will at the end bring a smile to the face of the reader, but at the same time it will give the student of hidden nature proof that the legend is not based entirely on the imagination, but pertains to the domain of occult fact, if at any rate the many similar legends, current in India, concerning the touch of yogins when in certain states of ecstasy are at all to be credited. (The quotations are for the most part from Dr. James' translation).

"Again in like manner he leadeth us three up into the mountain, saying 'Come ye to Me.' And we again went: and we beheld Him at a distance praying. Now therefore I, because He loved me, drew nigh unto Him softly as though He should not see, and stood looking at His back. And I beheld Him that He was not in any wise clad with garments, but was seen of us naked thereof, and not in any wise as a man; and His feet whiter than any snow, so that the ground there was lighted up by His feet; and His head reaching unto heaven, so that I was afraid nd cried out; and He turned and appeared as a man of small stature, and took hold of my beard and pulled it and said unto me, 'John, be not unbelieving, and not a busybody.' And I said unto Him, 'But what have I done, Lord?' And I tell you, brethren, I suffered great pain in that place where he took hold upon my beard for thirty days.

"But Peter and James were wroth because I spake with the Lord, and beckoned unto me that I should come unto them, and leave the Lord alone. And I went, and they both said unto me, 'He that

The Christ speaks with Jesus.

was speaking with the Lord when he was upon the top of the mount, who was He? for we heard both of them speaking.' And I, when I considered His great grace and His unity which hath many faces, and His wisdom which without ceasing looked upon us, said, 'That shall ye learn if ye inquire of Him.'

"Again, once when all of us His disciples were sleeping in one house at Gennesaret, I alone, having wrapped myself up, watched from under my garment what He did; and first I heard Him say, 'John, go thou to sleep,' and thereupon I feigned to be asleep; and I saw another like unto Him come down, whom also I heard saying unto my Lord, 'Jesus, do they whom thou hast chosen still not believe in thee?' And my Lord said unto Him, 'Thou sayest well, for they are men.'"

Here, in my opinion, is the direct tradition of an inner fact which led to the subsequent great doctrinal distinction between Jesus and the Christ in Gnostic Christianity. The Christ was the Great Master; Jesus was the man through whom He taught during the time of the ministry.

An Early Form of one of the Great Miracles.

Interesting again is the simple story that when Jesus and His disciples were each given a loaf by some well-to-do householder, Jesus would bless the loaf and divide it among them, and each was well satisfied with his portion, and thus "our loaves were saved whole"—an incident credible enough to any student of occultism, and supplying a basis on which the gorgeous oriental imagination could easily in time construct the legend of the feeding of the five thousand. Such incidents were all that the writer deemed advisable to tell to the uninitiated; there were many more of a nature too sacred or too far from credibility to be revealed to the outer circles.

"Now these things, brethren, I speak unto you for the encouragement of your faith toward Him; for we must at present keep silence concerning His mighty and wonderful works, inasmuch as they are mysteries and peradventure cannot at all be either uttered or heard."

Next follows the "Hymn" which was sung before He was taken by "the lawless Jews." The disciples are described as holding one another's hands so as to make a ring round Jesus, who stands in the midst, and to each line He sings, they intone in chorus the sacred word "Amen." It is evidently some echo of the Mysteries, and the ceremony is that of a sacred dance of initiation. The Hymn stands at present in a very confused and mutilated form, and the rubrics have almost entirely disappeared. I have therefore permitted myself a few conjectures; in some passages, however, the confusion is so great that it is impossible to venture on a suggestion. In the following C. stands for the candidate, I. for the initiator (the Christ), and A. for the assistants.

A Ritual from the Mysteries.

    C. "I would be saved."
    I. "And I would save."
    A. "Amen."
    C. "I would be loosed."
    I. "And I would loose."

A. " Amen."
C. " I would be pierced."
I. " And I would pierce."
A. " Amen."
C. " I would be born."
I. " And I would bring to birth."
A. " Amen."
C. " I would eat."
I. " And I would be eaten."
A. " Amen."
C. " I would hear."
I. " And I would be heard."
A. " Amen."

" I would be understood, being all understanding (mind)."

A. " Amen."
C. " I would be washed."
I. " And I would wash."
A. " Amen."

" (Grace [*i.e.*, the Sophia] dances.)"
" I would pipe ; dance all of you."
A. " Amen."
" The Ogdoad plays to our dancing. Amen."
" The Dodecad danceth above [us]. Amen."
        [The reading of this line is hopeless.]
" He who danceth not, knoweth not what is being done."

C. " I would flee."
I. " I would [have thee] stay."
A. " Amen."
C. " I would be robed [in fit garments]."
I. " And I would robe [thee]."

A. "Amen."
C. "I would be at-oned."
I. "And I would at-one."
A. "Amen."
"I have no house, and I have houses. Amen."
"I have no place, and I have places. Amen."
"I have no temple, and I have temples. Amen."
I. "I am a lamp to thee who beholdest Me."
A. "Amen."
I. "I am a mirror to thee who perceivest Me."
A. "Amen."
I. "I am a door to thee who knockest at Me."
A. "Amen."
I. "I am a way to thee, a wayfarer."
A. "Amen."
I. "Now respond thou to my dancing."

"See thyself in Me who speak; and when thou hast seen what I do, keep silence on My mysteries."

"(Dancing.) Observe what I do, for thine is this passion (suffering) of the Man which I am to suffer (perform)."

[Here probably followed a mystery-drama of the crucifixion and piercing.]

"Thou couldst never [alone] have understood what I suffer. I am thy Word (Logos—Highest Self). I was sent by the Father."

"When thou didst look on My passion, thou didst see Me as suffering; thou stood'st not firm, but wast shaken completely. . . ."

"Thou hast Me for a couch, rest thou upon Me."

"Who am I? That shalt thou know when I depart."

"What I am now seen to be, that I am not; but what I am thou shalt see when thou comest."

"If thou hadst known how to suffer, thou wouldst have had the power not to suffer."

"Know then suffering and thou shalt have the power not to suffer."

"That which thou knowest not, I myself will teach thee."

"I am thy God, not that of thy betrayer."

C. "I would be brought into harmony with holy souls."

I. "In Me know thou the Word of wisdom."

The Doxology.

So run the mutilated fragments of this most interesting relic of inner Gnostic ritual; in the version of *The Acts of John* from which we are quoting, this so-called Hymn begins and ends with the following doxology, to each line of which the disciples, "going round in a ring," are said to answer back "Amen."

"Glory to Thee, Father. Amen!

"Glory to Thee, Word; glory to Thee, Grace. Amen!

"Glory to Thee, Spirit; glory to Thee, Holy One; glory to Thy glory. Amen!

"We praise Thee, O Father; we give thanks to Thee, O Light, wherein dwelleth no darkness. Amen!"

If we had only a description of the "drama," the "things done," as well as of the "things said," at this most instructive ceremony, much light might be thrown on the meaning of the "passion" of the Christ as it was originally understood. When, moreover, we reflect that most precious fragments of this hidden part of earliest Christendom are being discovered almost yearly, it is not too wild a hope that some tattered leaf may give us further light. That, however, the " mystery of the cross," the mystic crucifixion, was understood by the Gnostics in a fashion far different from the literal historic narrative, is abundantly proved by these same Johannine Acts.

When the Lord was hung upon the "bush of the cross," He appeared unto John, who had fled unto the " Mount of Olives."

"Our Lord stood in the midst of the cave and filled it with light and said, 'To the multitude below, in Jerusalem [? the Jerusalem Below—the physical world], I am being crucified, and pierced with lances and reeds, and gall and vinegar is given Me to drink; to thee now I speak, and hearken to My words. 'Twas I who put it in thy heart to ascend this mount, that thou mightest hear what disciple must learn from Master, and man from God.'

The Mystery of the Cross.

"And having thus spoken, He showed me a cross of light set up, and about the cross a great multitude, and therein one form and one likeness; and on the cross another multitude, not having one form, and I saw the Lord Himself above the cross, not having any shape, but only a voice; and a voice not such as was familiar to us, but a sweet and kind voice and one truly of God, saying unto me: 'John, it is needful that one should hear these things from Me; for I have need of one who will hear. This cross of light is sometimes called the Word by Me for your sakes, sometimes Mind, sometimes Jesus, sometimes Christ, sometimes Door, sometimes Way, sometimes Bread, sometimes Seed, sometimes Resurrection, sometimes Son, sometimes Father, sometimes Spirit, sometimes Life, sometimes Truth, sometimes Faith, sometimes Grace.

"'Now these things it is called as toward men; but as to what it is in truth, as conceived of in itself and as spoken of to thee—it is the marking off (delimitation) of all things, the firm necessity of those things that are fixed and were unsettled, the harmony of Wisdom. And whereas it is Wisdom in harmony (or fitly ordered), there are on the Right and Left Powers, Principalities, Sources, and Dæmons, Energies, Threats, Wrath, Accusers, Satan, and [Below] the Lower Root from which hath proceeded the nature of the things in genesis.

"'This, then, is the cross which fixed all things apart by Reason, and marked off the things that come from genesis, the things below it, and then compacted all into one whole.

"'This is not the cross of wood which thou wilt see when thou hast descended; nor am I He that is upon the cross, whom now thou seest not but only hearest a voice.

"'By the others, the many, I have been thought to be what I am not, though I am not what I was. And they will [still] say of Me what is base and not worthy of Me.

"'As, therefore, the Place of Rest is neither seen nor spoken of, much more shall I, the Lord of that Place, be neither seen nor spoken of.

"'Now the multitude of one aspect that is about

the cross is the lower nature, and those whom thou seest on the cross, if they have not one form, it is because not yet hath every Limb of Him who came down been gathered together. But when the upper nature shall be taken up, and the race which is repairing to Me, in obedience to My voice; then that which [as yet] hears Me not, shall become as thou art, and shall no longer be what it now is, but above them [of the world], even as I am now. For so long as thou callest not thyself Mine, I am not what I am. But if hearing thou hearkenest unto Me, then shalt thou be as I am, and I shall be what I was, when I have thee as I am with Myself. For from this thou art. Pay no attention, then, to the many, and them outside the mystery think little of; for know that I am wholly with the Father and the Father with Me.

The Interpretation thereof.

"'Nothing therefore of the things which they will say of Me have I suffered; nay, that suffering also which I showed unto thee and unto the rest in the dance, I will that it be called a mystery. For what thou seest that did I show thee; but what I am that I alone know, and none else. Suffer me then to keep that which is Mine own, and that which is thine behold thou through Me, and behold Me in truth that I am, not what I said, but what thou art able to know, for thou art kin to Me.

"'Thou hearest that I suffered, yet I suffered not; that I suffered not, yet did I suffer; that I was pierced, yet was I not smitten; that I was hanged, yet was I not hanged; that blood flowed from Me, yet it flowed not. In a word those things that they say of Me, I had not, and the things that they say not, those I suffered. Now what they are I will shadow forth (riddle) for thee, for I know that thou wilt understand.

"'See thou therefore in Me the slaying of a Word (Logos), the piercing of a Word, the blood of a Word, the wounding of a Word, the hanging of a Word, the passion of a Word, the nailing [? fixing or joining] of a Word, the death of a Word. And by a Word I mean Man. First, then, understand the Word, then shalt thou understand the Lord, and thirdly the Man, and what is His passion.'"

The Initiation of the Cross.

It is evident that we have here the tradition of the inner schools as to the great mystery of initiation called the Cross. The Cross is apparently three limbed, having a right, a left, and a lower arm, like the Egyptian tau. On it the body of the candidate presumably was bound, and in trance his soul ascended the mountain of initiation, the "height" within. Here he meets the Master, but only hears His voice; not yet can he see Him as He is, for all his limbs are not yet gathered together, the perfect Osiris is not formed in him, but will be at a higher stage, when he is at-oned with the Christ.

How beautiful are these echoes from the old teaching, and what light they throw on things otherwise entirely incomprehensible! It was these inner experiences of the soul which were the life and strength of the Gnosis, experiences in which the complex systems that "the tongue of flesh" endeavoured to enunciate with such labour, received illumination and light—"sweet, joyous light," as the Shepherd of

Hermes the Thrice-greatest has it. Well now can we imagine the significance of the greeting among such scholars of the hidden way as: "The mystery of that which hangs 'twixt heaven and earth be with you."

Of the idea of the Little and Great Man, the lower and higher selves, in such circles of initiation we hear elsewhere from *The Gospel of Eve* (Epiph., xxvi. 3), describing one of these visions on the Mount.

The Higher and Lower Selves.

"I stood on a lofty mountain and saw a mighty Man, and another, a dwarf, and heard as it were a voice of thunder, and drew nigh for to hear; and it spake unto me and said: 'I am thou and thou art I; and wheresoever thou art I am there, and I am sown (or scattered) in all; from whencesoever thou willest thou gatherest Me, and gathering Me thou gatherest Thyself."

The "dwarf" presumably corresponds to the "man of the size of a thumb in the æther of the heart" of the Upaniṣhads; as yet he is smaller than the small, but as the spiritual nature develops he will become greater than the great, and grow into the stature of the Heavenly Man—the Supreme Self.

As to the scattering and collecting of the Limbs, there is a passage cited by Epiphanius (*ibid.*, 13) from *The Gospel of Philip*, which throws some further light on the subject. It is an apology or defence to be used by the soul in its ascent to the Heaven-world, as it passes through the middle spaces, and runs as follows:

"I have recognised myself and gathered myself together from all sides. I have sown no children to the Ruler [the lord of this world], but have torn up his roots; I have gathered together my limbs that were scattered abroad, and I know thee who thou art."

So much for what we can glean from the text of the latest published fragment of these most instructive Acts; from the already known texts there are several other fragments of interest. The following is a prayer of praise put into the mouth of John at the sacred feast prior to his departure from life. It is addressed to the Christ.

A Prayer of Praise to Christ.

"What praise, what offering, what thanksgiving, shall we, in breaking bread, speak of but Thee alone? We glorify Thy Name [*i.e.*, Power] which hath been spoken by the Father; we glorify Thy Name which hath been spoken through the Son; we glorify the Resurrection shown unto us through Thee; we glorify Thy Seed, Word, Grace, Faith, Salt, True Pearl ineffable, Treasure, Plough, Greatness, Net, and Diadem, Him who hath been called for our sakes the Son of Man, Truth, Rest, and Gnosis, Power, Statute, Frankness, Hope, Love, Freedom, and Going-for-refuge to Thee. For Thou alone art the one Lord, the Root of Deathlessness, and Source of Incorruptibility, Seat of the Æons. All these hast Thou been called for us, that we invoking Thee by them, may know that as we are we never can embrace Thy Greatness, greatness that can alone be contemplated by the Pure, for it is imaged in Thy man alone."

The same phrase, "Thy man," is found in the beautiful treatise of Hermes Trismegistus known as *The Secret Sermon on the Mountain:* "Thou art the God; Thy man thus cries to Thee through fire, air, earth; through water, spirit, through these Thy creatures." But indeed the whole of the so-called Poimandrēs collection of the Trismegistic literature comes from the same source as the Gnosis.

The high ideal of the Gnostic life, and the lofty level to which these strivers after the sinless state aspired, are amply shown in the farewell address to his disciples, put in the mouth of John by the Gnostic composer or compiler of the Acts.

"Brothers and fellow-servants, co-heirs and co-partners in the kingdom of the Lord, ye know how many powers the Lord hath granted you through me—how many wonders, healings how many, how many signs, what gifts [of the Spirit], teachings, guidings, reliefs, services, glories, graces, gifts, bestowings of faith, communions—how many ye see with your own eyes given unto you, how many that neither these eyes of yours can see, nor these ears hear! Stand ye, therefore, fast in Him, in every deed remembering Him, knowing wherefore the mystery of the dispensation towards men is being worked out. John's Farewell Address to his Community.

"The Lord Himself exhorteth you through me: 'Brethren, I would be free from grief [on your behalf], from violence, plottings, punishments.'

"For He knoweth the violence that comes from you, He knoweth the dishonour, He knoweth the plotting, He knoweth the punishment that comes through them who obey not His commandments.

"Let not then our Good God be grieved, Him the compassionate, merciful and holy, the pure and spotless one, the one and only one, unchangeable, of speckless purity, who knows not guile or wrath, higher and loftier than any attribute that we can name or think, Jesus our God.

"May He be glad of us as citizens of a well-ruled state; may He rejoice at our living in purity; may He have rest by our reverent behaviour; may He be free from care by our continence; may He be delighted by our dwelling in brotherhood; may He laugh with joy at our prudence; may He rejoice at our love for Him.

"These things do I say unto you, hastening to the end of my appointed task, which has been brought to an end for me by the Lord. For what else can I say to you? Ye have the pledges of our God; ye have the sureties of His goodness; ye have His presence which can never leave you. If then ye sin no more, He doth forgive you all that ye have done in ignorance; but if, having once known Him and having received of His mercy, ye turn back into such paths then shall your former sins be put to your charge, and ye shall have neither portion nor mercy before Him."

Immediately on this there follows the last prayer of John to the Christ on behalf of his brethren.

John's Last Prayer.

"Thou who hast woven this wreath by Thy weaving, Jesus, Thou who hast united these many blossoms into that sweet flower of Thine whose scent can never fade, Thou who hast sown these Words, protector of Thine own, healer who heal'st for naught, Thou only one who ever doest good, stranger to arrogance, Thou only merciful, the friend of man, Thou only saviour, righteous one, who ever seest all things and art in all and always ever-present, God, Jesus, Christos, Lord, who with Thy gifts and Thy compassion dost screen [all] them who hope on Thee, Thou who dost right well know all those that do us wrong and who blaspheme Thy holy Name, Thou only Lord, watch o'er Thy servants and protect them; yea, Lord, do this!"

The rest of the prayer has also a strong Gnostic colouring, but sufficient has already been quoted to give the reader some idea of the lofty thoughts which animated such communities of the early days.

But before leaving *The Acts of John* we cannot refrain from presenting the reader with the best known story that has crept into their compilation. It is strange that, where there is so much beauty, this particular story should have been singled out for most frequent quotation, and that many theological students know nothing else of the contents of these instructive documents but "The Story of John and the Bugs." But so it is, and we give it as a specimen of the many legends that were current among the people, and also because it is not deficient in humour, an uncommon commodity in the circles of the pious. We take the account from Salmon's summary. (*Op. supra cit.*, p. 350).

Once on a time John and his companions were a-journeying for apostolic purposes. "On their journey the party stopped at an uninhabited caravanserai. They found there but one bare couch, and having laid clothes on it they made the Apostle lie on it, while the rest of the party laid themselves down to sleep on the

The Story of John and the Bugs.

floor. But John was troubled by a great multitude of bugs; until after having tossed sleepless for half the night, he said to them in the hearing of all: 'I say unto you, O ye bugs, be ye kindly considerate; leave your home for this night, and go to rest in a place which is far from the servant of God.' At this the disciples laughed, while the Apostle turned to sleep, and they conversed gently, so as not to disturb him. In the morning, the first to awake went to the door, and they saw a great multitude of bugs standing. The rest collected to view, and at last St. John awoke and saw likewise. Then (mindful rather of his grateful obligation to the bugs than of the comfort of the next succeeding traveller) he said: 'O ye bugs, since ye have been kind and have observed my charge, return to your place.' No sooner had he said this, and risen from the couch, than the bugs all in a run rushed from the door to the couch, climbed up the legs, and disappeared into the joinings. And John said: 'See how these creatures, having heard the voice of a man, have obeyed; but we, hearing the voice of God, neglect and disobey; and how long?'"

FROM THE ACTS OF ANDREW.

FROM *The Acts of Andrew* the following Address to the Cross is of great interest, when compared with what has been already quoted from *The Acts of John* and with the rest of the Gnostic ideas on the subject. For the Gnostics the Cross was a symbol of cosmic processes as well as of the crucifixion of the soul in matter and of its regeneration, and it is to be regretted that our information is so fragmentary. The following Address put into the mouth of Andrew has been worked over by Catholic scribes, but the underlying material is plainly to be derived from the Gnostic circle of ideas.

Address to the Cross.

"Rejoicing I come to thee, thou Cross, the lifegiver, Cross whom I now know to be mine; I know thy mystery, for thou hast been planted in the world to make fast things unstable.

"Thy head stretcheth up into heaven, that thou mayest symbol forth the heavenly Logos, the head of all things. Thy middle parts are stretched forth, as it were hands to right and left, to put to flight the envious and hostile power of the evil one, that thou mayest gather together into one them [*sci.*, the limbs] that are scattered abroad. Thy foot is set in the earth, sunk in the deep, that thou mayest draw up those that lie beneath the earth and are held fast in the regions beneath it, and mayest join them to those in heaven.

"O Cross, engine, most skilfully devised, of

salvation given unto men by the Highest; O Cross, invincible trophy of the conquest of Christ o'er His foes; O Cross, thou life-giving tree, roots planted on earth, fruit treasured in heaven; O Cross most venerable, sweet thing and sweet name; O Cross most worshipful, who bearest as grapes the Master, the true vine, who dost bear too the Thief as thy fruit, fruitage of faith through confession; thou who bringest the worthy to God through the Gnosis and summonest sinners home through repentance!"

FROM THE TRAVELS OF PETER.

The Descent of Man.

To the above may be added the final speech put into the mouth of Peter, in the romance of his Travels, or Circuits (Tours). It is found in the fragment of of the Linus-collection, called *The Martyrdom of Peter.* The legend says that Peter insisted on being crucified head downwards, and the reasons for this strange proceeding are given as follows in the faulty Latin translation.

"Fitly wert Thou alone stretched on the cross with head on high, O Lord, who hast redeemed all of the world from sin. I have desired to imitate Thee in Thy passion too; yet would I not take on myself to be hanged upright. For we, pure men and sinners, are born from Adam, but Thou art God of God, Light of true Light, before all æons and after them; thought worthy to become for men Man without stain of man, Thou hast stood forth man's glorious Saviour. Thou ever upright, ever raised on high, eternally above! We, men according to the flesh, are sons of the first man (Adam), who sunk his being in the earth, whose fall in human generation is shown forth. For we are brought to birth in such a way, that we do seem to be poured into earth, so that the right is left, the left doth right become; in that our state is changed in those who are the authors of this life. For this world down below doth think the right what is the left; this world in which Thou, Lord, hast found us like the Ninevites, and by Thy holy preaching hast Thou rescued those about to die."

"The authors of this life" presumably refer to the powers that bring the man to birth. The Jonah-myth was a type of the initiate, who, after being three days and three nights in the "belly of Sheol" or Hades, preached to those in Nineveh, the Jerusalem Below, that is to say, this world.

But for the brethren there was a still further instruction as to the meaning of the Mystic Cross.

"But ye, my brothers, who have the right to hear, lend me the ears of your heart, and understand what now must be revealed to you—the hidden mystery of every nature and the secret spring of every thing composed. For the first man, whose race I represent by my position, with head reversed, doth symbolize his birth into destruction; for that his birth was death and lacked the life-stream. But of His own compassion the Power Above came down into the world, by means of corporal substance, to him who by a just decree had been cast down into the earth, and hanged upon the Cross, and by the means of this

The Mystic Redemption of the Cross.

most holy calling [the Cross], He did restore us and did make for us these present things (which had till then remained unchanged by men's unrighteous error) into the Left, and those that men had taken for the Left into eternal things. In exaltation of the Right He hath changed all the signs into their proper nature, considering as good those thought not good, and those men thought malefic most benign. Whence in a mystery the Lord hath said: 'If ye make not the Right like as the Left, the Left like as the Right, Above as the Below, Before as the Behind, ye shall not know God's kingdom.' This saying have I made manifest in me, my brothers; this is the way in which your eyes of flesh behold me hanging. It figures forth the way of the first man.

"But ye, beloved, hearing these words and by conversion of your nature and changing of your life perfecting them, even as ye have turned you from that way of error where ye trod, unto the most sure state of faith, so keep ye running and strive towards the peace of that which calls you from above, living the holy life. For that the way on which ye travel there is Christ. Therefore with Jesus, Christ, true God, ascend the Cross; He hath been made for us the one and only Word. Whence also doth the Spirit say: 'Christ is the Word and Voice of God.' The Word in truth is symbolized by that straight stem on which I hang. [As for the Voice—] since that voice is a thing of flesh, with features not to be ascribed unto God's nature, the cross-piece of the cross is thought to figure forth that human nature which suffered the fault of change in the first man, but by the help of God-and-man, received again its real mind. Right in the centre, joining twain in one, is set the nail of discipline, conversion and repentance."

The Latin translation is very faulty and often obscures the Greek original, but enough of the meaning has been preserved to show the general drift of the thought. The first quotation is one of the sayings from *The Gospel according to the Egyptians*; the source of the second is not known. Compare also the changing of the Right and Left with the conversion of the spheres in the opening pages of the *Pistis Sophia* treatise.

Other speeches and innumerable isolated phrases, which still preserve traces of the Gnosis, could be cited from the existing remains of the uncanonical Acts, but sufficient has been written to give the reader an idea of the extensive popular literature of this kind which emanated from Gnostic circles in the early years, and to show him that very different ideas prevailed among those who were in touch with the inner tradition, from those of that exclusively historical view which eventually gained the upper hand.

Afterword.

Whether or not these ideas throw light on the Christ's teaching, each must decide for himself. That, however, they were ideas put forward by men vastly nearer the time of the origins than ourselves—by men whose whole lives were devoted to the Christ, striving by every means to purify themselves, and to experience in themselves the truths of the unseen world and realize the teachings of the Master—is amply manifest.

FF

THE GNOSIS ACCORDING TO ITS FRIENDS.

Sempiterna Lux! Nec divitias nec honores peto; me modo Divinæ Lucis radio illumines!

From *An Essay of Transmigration in Defence of Pythagoras* (London, 1692).

SOME GREEK ORIGINAL WORKS IN COPTIC TRANSLATION.

THE ASKEW AND BRUCE CODICES.

So far we have endeavoured to recover some fragments of flotsam and jetsam from the pitiful wreck of the Gnosis, wrought by the hands of its bitterest foes, the orthodox Church Fathers; we will now try to give the reader some rough idea of the contents of some Gnostic treatises, which have been preserved to us in Coptic translation by the hands of its friends.

We have to consider the contents of three precious documents known as the Askew, Bruce, and Akhmīm Codices, the last of which was only discovered in 1896. We shall reserve the Akhmīm Codex for later notice, since little is so far known of it, and so give our immediate attention to the Askew and Bruce Codices.

The Askew Codex was bought by the British Museum from the heirs of Dr. Askew at the end of the last century (presumably a little prior to 1785). The MS. is written on vellum in Greek uncials, in the Upper Egyptian

The Askew Codex.

dialect, and is not in roll but in book-form. It consists of 346 quarto pages, and for the most part is in an excellent state of preservation; a few leaves only are missing. The Codex is a copy and not an original; and the original was a translation from the Greek. The general contents consist of a treatise to which custom has given the name *Pistis Sophia*, owing to a heading in the middle of the general narrative, added by another hand. The treatise has no superscription or subscription, and though there is a long incident in it dealing with the passion and redemption of the Sophia, other parts of equal length might just as well be called *The Questions of Mary*, as Harnack has suggested, and Matter long prior to him. The Codex also contains a short inset and a lengthy appendix entitled *Extracts from the Books of the Saviour*. For a further description I must refer the reader to the Introduction of my translation.

The Bruce Codex.

The Bruce Codex was brought to England from Upper Egypt in 1769 by the famous Scottish traveller Bruce, and bequeathed to the care of the Bodleian Library, Oxford. It is written on papyrus, in Greek cursive characters, in the Upper Egyptian dialect, and consists of seventy-eight leaves, in book-form. Its leaves are in a most terrible state of disorder and dilapidation, and many are missing. A scientific examination of the Codex reveals the fact that it consists of two distinct MSS., containing the remains of at least two distinct Gnostic works and some fragments. The superior MS., of better material and finer handwriting, contains a treatise of great sublimity, but without a title, the first and last pages being lost. The other MS. contains fragments of at least two separate books, and preserves the title *The Book of the Great Logos according to the Mystery*. This is taken by Schmidt to be the general title, and to comprise two parts which he calls respectively the *First* and *Second Book of Ieou*.

The contents of these treatises are of such a marvellous and complex nature, that I despair of giving the general reader any adequate conception of them. The student may, however, form some idea of the task by reading my translation of the *Pistis Sophia* treatise and the *Extracts from the Books of the Saviour;* but even this will give him no adequate conception of the complexity of the contents of the Codex Brucianus, of which, unfortunately, there is as yet no English translation.

Translations.

In 1891 Amélineau published a text and French translation of the Bruce Codex with a brief introduction; but his text was based on Woide's copy of the Codex made a century ago, and the French *savant* had no idea that he was dealing with two distinct MSS., whose leaves were jumbled up in inextricable confusion.

In 1892 Dr. Carl Schmidt, having with admirable patience collated the copies of the Codex made by Schwartze and Woide with the original at Oxford, and with still greater acumen and industry separated the two MSS. and placed their respective leaves in order, published a critical text, with a German translation and a voluminous commentary.

In the following *résumé*, with regard to the Codex

456 FRAGMENTS OF A FAITH FORGOTTEN.

The Difficulty of the Subject.

Brucianus, I shall follow Schmidt's translation and not Amélineau's. Schmidt is by far the most competent authority in the field, and no praise is too high a tribute to pay this most distinguished Coptic scholar for his unwearied patience. I have before me a rough translation of the whole of Schmidt's voluminous work, and have spared no pains to make myself acquainted with his labours; but, even with his help, I feel as yet a very tyro in the Gnosticism revealed in these treatises. For, though Schmidt throws light on many points, innumerable problems are still left untouched; in fact, with all his admirable scholarship and infinite research, he is entirely baffled on just those very points which seem to have been of greatest interest to the composers or compilers of these Gnostic documents.

When, in 1896, I published a translation of the *Pistis Sophia* I had intended to follow it up with a commentary; but I speedily found that in spite of the years of work I had already given to Gnosticism, there were still many years of labour before me, ere I could satisfy myself that I was competent to essay the task in any really satisfactory fashion; I have accordingly reserved that task for the future. Meantime, in the present short sketches nothing more is attempted than a very tentative summary, so that the general reader may obtain some notion of the contents of our Coptic Gnostic treatises; my only excuse for breaking silence being that there is absolutely nothing as yet in English on the contents of the Bruce Codex.

We will, then, first of all attempt a summary of the contents of the so-called *Pistis Sophia* treatise; then a summary of the *Extracts from the Books of the Saviour*, inserted in and following after this treatise in the Askew Codex. This will be followed by a summary of the fragments contained in the inferior MS. of the Bruce Codex. I shall venture, however, to transpose Schmidt's main order, and place what he calls *The Second Book of Ieou* before what he calls *The First*, for the general subjects of his first group of fragments seem to me to follow the subjects of his second, rather than the contrary. It is quite true that the beginning of his second division starts on the *verso* of the papyrus leaf, the *recto* of which contains the end of the other; but this only assures us the correct position of two adjacent fragments. That the numerous other fragments are always arranged in their proper sequence is by no means quite certain, though I frankly confess I so far see no more satisfactory ordering of the chaos myself.

That we have among these fragments part of the original contents of *The Books of Ieou* mentioned in the *Pistis Sophia* seems highly probable, but that we can assign our fragments definitely to Books I. and II. is not so certain. The whole will therefore in our summary stand under the general title, *The Book of the Great Logos according to the Mystery*, without further distinction, including both the introductory matter and also the leaves surrounded by a border, which Schmidt adds as an appendix. But it must be understood that this is a tentative arrangement. There may be several treatises to which the fragments of the inferior MS. of the Bruce Codex ought to be assigned for anything we know to the contrary.

This will be followed by the fragments of the untitled treatise contained in the superior MS.

The purpose that has guided me in this general arrangement is, as far as possible, to place the contents of these Coptic translations roughly in such a sequence that the reader may be led from lower to higher grades of the Gnosis. I am perfectly aware that higher mysteries (the three Spaces of the Inheritance) are spoken of and explained in the *Pistis Sophia* treatise than in the rest of the matter, but they are not revealed. In *The Book of the Great Logos* and in the *Extracts from the Books of the Saviour* some of the mysteries are given, and the disciples are made to see face to face. I therefore place the summary of the *Pistis* first, though it was probably composed last.

SUMMARY OF THE CONTENTS OF THE SO-CALLED PISTIS SOPHIA TREATISE.

THE treatise begins by informing us that Jesus, after rising from the dead, had spent eleven years with His disciples, instructing them. So far, however, He had taught them the mysteries of the inner world up to a certain point only, apparently up to the outermost realms of the Light-world only, and yet even so far with omissions of many points which they were as yet incapable of understanding. But so wonderful had been the instruction imparted that the disciples imagined that all had been revealed to them, and that the First Mystery—the Father in the likeness of a dove—was the end of all ends and the gnosis of all gnoses. They did not know that this First Mystery was the lowest of a vast series of still higher mysteries.

The Teaching of the Eleven Years.

It came to pass, therefore, in the twelfth year, that the disciples were assembled with the Master on the Mount of Olives, rejoicing that they had, as they thought, received all the fullness. It was the fifteenth day of the month Tybi, the day of the full moon. Jesus was sitting apart, when, at sunrise, they beheld a great light-stream pouring over Him, so that he became lost to view in the ineffable radiance which stretched from earth to heaven. The light was not one radiance, but its rays were of every kind and type; and in it the Master soared aloft into heaven, leaving the disciples in great fear

The Mystic Transfiguration and Ascent in the Twelfth Year.

and confusion as they silently gazed after Him. From the third hour of the fifteenth day until the ninth hour of the morrow (thirty hours) the Master was absent; and during this time there was a shaking of all the regions and great confusion and fear, while songs of praise came forth from the interior of the interiors.

The Master returns to His Disciples.
On the ninth hour of the morrow they saw Jesus descending in infinite light, more brilliant far than when He had ascended; the light was now of three degrees, glory transcending glory. The disciples were dismayed and in great fear, but Jesus, the compassionate and merciful-minded, spake unto them, saying: "Take courage, it is I; be not afraid." At their prayer Jesus withdraws His great light into Himself, and appears in His familiar form once more, and the disciples come to worship, and ask Him, saying: "Master, whither didst thou go? or on what ministry wentest thou? or wherefore are all these confusions and shakings?"

The Master, now speaking as the glorified Christ, bids them rejoice, for that now He will tell them all things "from the beginning of the truth to the end thereof," face to face, without parable, for that authority has now been given Him by the First Mystery to reveal these things unto them.

Of the Mystic Incarnation of the Twelve.
For this cause is it that He hath again been clothed in the vesture of light, the robe of glory, which he had left with the First Mystery, in the lowest spaces of the supernal Light-realm. He hath received it in order that He may speak to human kind and reveal all the mysteries, but

first of all to the Twelve. For the Twelve are His order, whom He hath chosen from the beginning, before He came into the world. He chose twelve powers, receiving them from the hands of the twelve Saviours of the Light-treasure, and when He descended into the world cast them, as light-sparks, into the wombs of their mothers, that through them the whole world might be saved. It is by reason of these powers that they are not of the world, for the power in them is from Him, a part of Himself.

So too another of His powers was in John the Baptizer with water for the remission of sins; not only so, but the soul of John was the soul of Elias reborn in him. These things had He explained before, when He said: "If ye will receive it, John the Baptist is Elias, who, I said, was for to come"; but they had not understood. *That the Soul of Elias is born in the Baptist.*

Into Mary, His mother, also He had implanted a power higher than them all, "the body which I bore in the height," and also another power instead of the soul, and so Jesus was born. It was He Himself who had watched over the birth of His disciples, so that no soul of the world-rulers should be found in them, but one of a higher nature. *Of His own Incarnation.*

And the Master continued in His conversation and said unto them: "Lo, I have put on My vesture, and all power hath been given Me by the First Mystery. Yet a little while and I will tell you the mystery of the plērōma and the plērōma of the plērōma; I will conceal nothing from you from this hour, but in perfectness will I perfect you in the whole plērōma, and all perfection, and every mystery; which things, *Concerning the Robe of Glory.*

indeed, are the perfection of all perfections, the plērōma of all plērōmas, and the gnosis of all gnoses, which are in My vesture. I will tell you all mysteries from the exterior of the exteriors, to the interior of the interiors. Hearken, I will tell you all things which have befallen Me.

"It came to pass, when the sun had risen in the regions of the east, that a great stream of light descended in which was My vesture, the same which I had laid up in the four-and-twentieth mystery, as I have said unto you. And I found a mystery in My vesture, written in these five words which pertain to the height: Zama, Zama, Ōzza, Rachama, Ōzai. And this is the interpretation thereof:

"The Mystery which is beyond the world, that whereby all things exist: It is all evolution and all involution; It projected all emanations and all things therein. Because of It all mysteries exist and all their regions."

The Hymn of Welcome "Come unto us."

Hereupon the Master recites the hymn of praise and welcome sung by the powers at His investiture on the Great Day "Come unto us"—the day of this supreme initiation, when all His Limbs are gathered together. "Come unto us, for we are Thy fellow-members (or limbs). We are all one with Thee. We are one and the same, and Thou art one and the same. This is the First Mystery, who hath existed from the beginning in the Ineffable, before He came forth; and the Name thereof is all of us. Now, therefore, we all live together for Thee at the last limit, which also is the last mystery from the interior. That also is part of us. Now, therefore, we have sent Thee Thy vesture, which, indeed, is Thine from the beginning, which Thou didst leave in the last limit, which also is the last mystery from the interiors, until its time should be fulfilled, according to the commandment of the First Mystery. Lo, its time being fulfilled, I give it Thee.

"Come unto us, for we all stand near to clothe Thee with the First Mystery and all His glory, by commandment of the same, in that the First Mystery gave us two vestures to clothe Thee, besides the one we have sent Thee, since Thou art worthy of them, and art prior to us, and came into being before us. For this cause, therefore, the First Mystery hath sent for Thee through us the mystery of His glory, two vestures."

The hymn proceeds to explain how that the first vesture hath in it the whole glory of all the names of all the mysteries of all the orders of the spaces of the Ineffable; that the second contains the whole glory of all the names, or powers, of all the mysteries, or emanations, of the orders of the twin spaces of the First Mystery; that the third vesture contains all the glory of the powers of the emanations of all the spaces and sub-spaces below these supernal realms as far as the earth. The hymn then continues:

The Three Vestures of Light.

"Lo, therefore, we have sent Thee this [third] vesture, without any [of the powers] knowing it from the First Statute downward; because the glory of its light was hidden in it [the First Statute], and the spheres with all their regions from the First Statute downwards [knew it not]. Make haste, therefore;

clothe Thyself with this vesture. Come unto us; for ever, until the time appointed by the Ineffable was fulfilled, have we been in need of Thee, to clothe Thee with the two [remaining] vestures, by order of the First Mystery. Lo, then, the time is fulfilled. Come, therefore, to us quickly, in order that we may clothe Thee, until Thou hast accomplished the full ministry of the perfections of the First Mystery, the ministry appointed for Thee by the Ineffable. Come, therefore, to us quickly, in order that we may clothe Thee, according to the commandment of the First Mystery; for yet a little while, a very little while, and Thou shalt come to us, and shalt leave the world. Come, therefore, quickly, that Thou mayest receive the whole glory, the glory of the First Mystery."

The Journey into the Height. Thereupon, on hearing the hymn of the powers, the Master said, He donned the lowest robe of glory, and, changed into pure light, soared upwards and came to the lower firmament. And all the powers of that firmament were in great confusion because of the transcendent light; and on seeing the mystery of their names or powers inscribed in it, leaving their ranks, they bowed down and worshipped, saying: "How hath the Lord of the plērōma changed us without our knowing!" And they all sang together to the interior of the interiors a hymn of praise in harmony.

And so He passed upwards and inwards to the First Sphere above the firmament, shining with a radiance forty-and-nine times as great as before, and the gates were opened and He entered the mansions of the Sphere, and the powers were changed and worshipped, and sang hymns of rejoicing as before.

Thence upward and inward he passed to the Second Sphere, shining with a light nine-and-forty times still more intensified, and the powers of that sphere did as them beneath them, and bowed and worshipped and sang hymns to the interior of the interiors.

Still continuing His triumphal flight, He soared still higher within, to the Space of the Twelve Æons, shining with radiance forty-and-nine times still further increased. And all the orders and rulers of the Æonic Space were amazed. Those of them called the Tyrants, under their great leader Adamas, in ignorance fought against the light; but in vain, for they only expended their strength one against the other, and fell down and became "as the inhabitants of the earth who are dead and who have no breath in them"—that is to say, deprived of the light-spark, like the unknowing among men.

And He took from them a third of their power, that they should no more prevail in their evil doings; so that if men should invoke them for evil in the magic practices which the transgressing Angels brought down from above, they should not be able to work their will as heretofore. *The Master Robs the Æons of a Third of their Light.*

And so He changed the Fate-Sphere, over which they are lords. For by order of the First Statute and First Mystery, they had been set, by Ieou, the Overseer of the Light, all facing the Left, accomplishing their influences. But now they were changed so that for six months they faced the Left and for six months the Right.

The Questions of Mary.

Hereupon, the Master having invited questions and interpretations of the mysteries He has revealed, Mary Magdalene, who is throughout represented as the most spiritual by far of all the disciples, comes forward, and being granted permission to speak, interprets a passage from Isaiah by the light of the new teaching. The passage begins with the words: "Where, then, O Egypt, where are thy diviners and ordainers of the hour?"—and among other things Egypt is said to mean the "inefficacious matter (*hylē*)."

Mary is commended for her intuition, and in reply to her further questioning, the Master explains that all their power has not been taken from these Rulers of the Fate, by the third robe of glory, but only a third of it; so that if the ordainers of the hour chance on the Fate or the Sphere turning to the Left, they will say what is to take place; but if they chance on it turning to the Right they will not be able to prophesy, for He has changed all the influences. But those who know the mysteries of the magic of the Thirteenth Æon will accomplish them perfectly, for He has not taken away the power in that Space, according to the command of the First Mystery.

Why the Rulers have been robbed.

In reply to a question by Philip, it is explained that this conversion of the spheres has been effected to aid the salvation of souls; otherwise the number of perfected souls would have been kept back from its accomplishment, that is to say, of those who shall be counted in the heritage of the height, by means of the mysteries, and shall dwell in the Light-treasure. The power of the Rulers is in the matter of the world which they make into souls. By the victory of the Master a third of this power has been taken from them, and converted to a higher substance.

In answer to Mary's further questioning, it is further explained how this third part of their power was taken away. It always had been that their power, as it became purified, was gathered back to the higher world by Melchisedec, the Great Receiver or Collector of Light, it being continually liberated by the spheres being made to turn more rapidly, that is to say by the quickening of evolution owing to the influx of Light. The substance of the Rulers is graphically described as "the breath of their mouths, the tears of their eyes, and the sweat of their bodies"—the matter out of which souls are made.

But as their power was gradually taken from them, their kingdom began to be dissolved; the Rulers therefore began to devour their own matter, so that it should not be made into souls of men and so be purified, and in every way strove to delay the completion of the number of perfect souls—the crown of evolution. So it came to pass that they fought against the great soul of the Master as He passed through them, and so He changed them and their configurations and influences, "and from that hour they have not had the power to turn towards the purgation of their matter to devour it."

"I took away a third part of their power; I changed their revolution; I shortened their circles, and caused their path to be lightened, and they were greatly hurried, and were thrown into confusion in their path; and from that hour they have no more had the power of devouring the matter of the purgation of the brilliancy of their light."

The Shortening of the Times.

Thus had He shortened their times and hastened evolution. "For this cause I said unto you before, 'I have shortened the times because of my Elect.'" The "Elect" (Pneumatics) are the perfect number of souls who shall receive the mysteries; indeed had not the times been shortened, "there would not have been a single material (hylic) soul saved, but they would have perished in the fire which is in the flesh of the Rulers."

The Heaven-journey continued.

After these explanations the Master continues the narrative of his heaven-journey. All the great powers of the Æonic Spaces, when they saw what had happened to their Tyrants, adored and sang hymns to the interior of the interiors. And so He passed inward to the veils of the Thirteenth Æon. Here, outside this Space, He found Pistis Sophia, sitting alone, mourning and grieving because she had not been brought into the Thirteenth Æon, her proper region in the height. She was grieving because of the sufferings brought upon her by Arrogant, one of the three Triple Powers. But when she saw the radiant light-vesture of the Master, containing the whole glory of her mystery, the mystery of the Thirteenth Æon, she began to sing a song to the light which is in the height, which she had seen in the veil of the Treasure of Light. And as she sang, the veils of the Thirteenth Æon were drawn apart, and her syzygy, and her two-and-twenty fellow-emanations within the Æon, making together four-and-twenty emanations who came forth from the Great Invisible Forefather and the two other great Triple Powers of that Space, gazed upon the light of His vesture.

Hereupon follows the mystic story of the sufferings of Pistis Sophia. In the beginning she was in the Thirteenth Æon with her companion Æons. By order of the First Mystery, she gazed into the height and saw the light of the veil of the Treasure of Light, and desired to ascend into that glorious realm, but could not. She ceased to do the mystery of the Thirteenth Æon and ever sang hymns to the Light she had seen. *The Myth of Pistis Sophia.*

Hereupon the Rulers in the Twelve Æons below hated her, because she had ceased to do their mystery —the mystery of intercourse or sexual union—and desired to go into the height and be above them all.

And Arrogant, the disobedient one, that one of the three Triple Powers of the Thirteenth Æon who refused to give the purity of his light for the benefit of others, but desired to keep it for himself and so be ruler of the Thirteenth Æon, led the onslaught against her. Arrogant is apparently the conservative power of the "matter" of this Space. He joined himself to the number of the Twelve Æons and fought against the Sophia. He sent forth a great power from his light and other powers from his matter, the reflections of the powers and emanations above, into Chaos; and caused the Sophia to look down into the lower regions, that she might see this power and imagine *The Enmity of Arrogant.*

it was the real Light to which she aspired. And so in ignorance she descended into matter, saying: "I will go into that region, without my consort, to take the light, which the Æons of Light have produced for me, so that I may go to the Light of lights, which is in the Height of heights."

The Fall into Matter.

Thus pondering she went forth from the Thirteenth Æon and descended into the Twelve; but they pursued her, and so she gradually descended to the regions of Chaos, and drew nigh to the light-power which Arrogant had sent below, to devour it. But all the material emanations of Arrogant surrounded her, and the light-power of Arrogant set to work to devour all the light-powers in the Sophia; "it expelled her light and swallowed it, and as for her matter they cast it into Chaos." This light-power of Arrogant is that Ialdabaôth "of which," says the Master, "I have spoken to you many times."

And so Sophia was greatly weakened and beset and "cried out exceedingly, she cried on high to that Light of lights which she had seen in the beginning, in which she had trusted [hence is she called Pistis (Faith) Sophia], and began to sing songs of repentance," whereby she might be converted or taken back to the Light.

The lengthy incident of the Pistis Sophia occupies pp. 42-181 of the Coptic translation, and her thirteen repentances and songs of praise are a mystical interpretation of a number of the Psalms of the Second Temple collection and of five of the Odes of Solomon.

To attain to the knowledge of the Light, the

human soul (as the world-soul before it) has to descend into matter *(hylē)*. Hence the Sophia, desiring the Light, descends towards its reflection, from the Thirteenth Æon, through the Twelve, into the depths of Chaos or Unorder, where she seems in danger of entirely losing all her own innate light or spirit, being continually deprived of it by the powers of matter. Having descended to the lowest depths of Chaos, she at length reaches the limit, and the path of her pilgrimage begins to lead upward to spirit again. Thus she reaches the middle point of balance, and still yearning for the Light, rounds the turning point of her cyclic course, and changing the tendency of her thought or mind or nature, recites her penitential hymns or repentances. Her chief enemy is the false light—presumably the counterfeit spirit of which we shall hear later on—the desire-nature, which is assisted by four-and-twenty material powers, the reflections of the supernal projections, powers or co-partners of the Sophia, the whole looked at from without making an ordering into forty-nine. *The Descent of the Soul.*

The Sophia first utters seven repentances. At the fourth of these, the turning point of some sub-cycle of her pilgrimage, she prays that the *image* of the Light may not be turned from her, for the time is come when "those who turn in the lowest regions" should be regarded—"the mystery which is made the type of the race." *Its Repentance and Redemption.*

At the sixth the Light remits her transgression; *viz.*, that she quitted her own region and fell into Chaos. This perhaps refers to the dawning of the consciousness of the higher ego in the lower personality. But as yet the command has not come from the First Mystery to free her entirely from Chaos. This may refer to the higher illumination when the consciousness of the true spiritual soul is obtained.

Therefore at the conclusion of her seventh repentance, where she pleads that she has done it all in *ignorance*, through her *love* for the Light, Jesus, her syzygy (without the First Mystery) raises her up to a slightly less confined region in Chaos, but Sophia still *knows not* by whom it is done.

It is only at the ninth stage that the First Mystery partly accepts her repentance and sends Jesus in the form of the Light to her help, so that she recognises it.

Her next four hymns are sung *knowingly* to the Light, and are of the nature of thanksgiving, and of declaration that justice will shortly overtake her oppressors, while at the same time she prays to be delivered wholly from her "transgression"—the lower desire-nature.

<small>The Degrees of Purification.</small>

After the thirteenth repentance, Jesus again, of himself, without the First Mystery, emanated a brilliant power of light from Himself, and sent it to aid Sophia, to raise her still higher in Chaos, until the command should come to free her entirely. There are, therefore, as it seems, three degrees of purification from the chaotic elements of the lower nature.

Next follows a description of the light-powers, which are to be closely compared with the description of the three vestures of glory in the opening pages of the Codex.

Then, while Sophia pours forth hymns of joy, the power becomes a "crown to her head," and her *hylē* (or material propensities) begins to be entirely purified, while the spiritual light-powers which she has succeeded in retaining during her long combat, join themselves with the new vesture of light which has descended upon her.

The Light-Crown.

Then is the law fulfilled, and the First Mystery in His turn sent forth another great light-power, which joined with that already emanated by the Light, and it became a great light-stream. This stream was nothing else than the First Mystery Himself looking without, coming forth from the First Mystery looking within.

When all this is accomplished the Sophia is completely purified, and her light-powers are re-established and filled with new light, by their own co-partner of light, that syzygy without whom Sophia in the beginning had thought to reach the Light of lights, unaided, and so fell into error.

But all is not yet over; the final victory is not yet won. For the higher she rises the stronger are the powers or projections sent against her; they proceed to *change their shapes*, so that she now has to struggle against still greater foes, which are emanated and directed by the subtlest powers of cosmos.

Thereupon Sophia is not only crowned but entirely surrounded with the light-stream, and further supported on either hand by Michael and Gabriel, the "sun" and "moon." The "wings of the great bird" flutter, and the "winged globe" unfolds its

The Final Victory.

pinions, preparatory to its flight. Thus the last great battle begins.

The First Mystery looking without directs her attack against the "cruel crafty powers, passions incarnate," and makes the Sophia tread underfoot the basilisk with seven heads, destroying its *hylē*, "so that no seed can arise from it henceforth," and casting down the rest of the opposing host.

Thereupon Sophia sings triumphant hymns of praise on being set free from the bonds of Chaos. Thus is she set free and *remembers*.

Still the great Self-willed one and Adamas, the Tyrant, are not yet entirely subdued, for the command has not yet come from the First Mystery looking within. Therefore does the First Mystery looking without seal their regions and those of their rulers "until three times are accomplished," presumably until the end of the seven cycles or ages, of which the present is said to be the fourth, when the perfect number of those of humanity who reach perfection will pass into the interplanetary *Nirvāṇa* —to use a Buddhist term. This *Nirvāṇa*, however, is a state out of time and space, as we know them, and therefore can be reached *now* and *within* by very holy men who can attain the highest degree of spiritual contemplation. Then shall the Gates of the Treasure of the Great Light be opened and the heights be crossed by the pilgrim.

An otherwise unknown Story of the Infancy.

In the course of the many interpretations of scripture given by the disciples and women disciples, Mary, the Mother of Jesus ("my mother according to matter, thou in whom I dwelt"), who is also one of the women disciples, receives permission to speak and tells a quaint story of the Infancy, otherwise entirely unknown.

And Mary answered and said: "My Master, concerning the word which Thy power prophesied through David, to wit, 'Mercy and truth are met together, righteousness and peace have kissed each other; truth hath flourished on the earth, and righteousness hath looked down from heaven'—Thy power prophesied this word of old concerning Thee.

"When Thou wert a child, before the Spirit had descended upon Thee, when Thou wert in the vineyard with Joseph, the Spirit came down from the height, and came unto me in the house, like unto Thee, and I knew Him not, but thought that He was Thou. And He said unto me, 'Where is Jesus, my Brother, that I may go to meet Him?' And when He had said this unto me I was in doubt, and thought it was a phantom tempting me. I seized Him and bound Him to the foot of the bed which was in my house, until I had gone to find you in the field—Thee and Joseph, and I found you in the vineyard; Joseph was putting up the vine poles.

"It came to pass, therefore, when Thou didst hear me saying this thing unto Joseph, that Thou didst understand, and Thou wert joyful and saidest, 'Where is He, that I may see Him? Nay [rather] I am expecting Him in this place.' And it came to pass, when Joseph heard Thee say these words, that he was disturbed.

"We went together, we entered into the house,

we found the Spirit bound to the bed, and we gazed upon Thee and Him, and found that Thou wert like unto Him. And He that was bound to the bed was unloosed; He embraced Thee and kissed Thee, and Thou also didst kiss Him; ye became one and the same being."

At the end of the story of the Sophia, Mary asks: "My Master and Saviour, how are the four-and-twenty Invisibles [the co-powers of Sophia]; of what type, of what quality; or of what quality is their light?"

<small>Of the Glory of Them of the Thirteenth Æon.</small>

And Jesus answered and said unto Mary: "What is there in this world which is comparable to them; or what region in this world is like unto them? Now, therefore, to what shall I liken them; or what shall I say concerning them? For there is nothing in this world with which I can compare them; nor is there a single form to which I can liken them. Indeed, there is nothing in this world which is of the quality of heaven. But, Amen, I say unto you, every one of the Invisibles is nine times greater than the Heaven [the lower firmament], and the Sphere above it, and the Twelve Æons all together, as I have already told you on another occasion.

"[Again] there is no light in this world which is superior to that of the sun. Amen, Amen, I say unto you, the four-and-twenty Invisibles are more radiant than the light of the sun which is in this world, ten thousand times, as I have told you before on another occasion; but the Light of the Sun *in its true form*, which is in the space of the Virgin of Light, is more radiant than the four-and-twenty, . . . ten thousand times more radiant."

The Master promises further, when he takes them through the various spaces of the unseen world, to bring them all finally into the Twin Spaces of the First Mystery, as far as the supreme Space of the Ineffable, "and ye shall see all their configurations as they really are, without similitude."

"When I bring you into the region of the rulers of the Fate-Sphere, ye shall see the glory in which they are, and compared with their greatly superior glory, ye will regard this world as the darkness of darkness; and when ye gaze down on the whole world of men, it will be as a speck of dust for you, because of the enormous distance by which [the Fate-Sphere] will be distant from it, and because of the enormous superiority of its quality over it." {The Scale of Light.}

And so shall it be in ever increasing glory of light with each higher space, the lower appearing as a speck of dust from its sublimity, as they are taken through the Twelve Æons, the Thirteenth Æon (or the Left), the Midst, the Right (*sci.*, of the cosmic cross), the Light-world, and the Inheritance of Light within it.

Then Mary asks: "Master, will the men of this world who have received the mysteries of light be higher in Thy Kingdom than the emanations of the Treasure of Light?" {The Perfect shall be Higher than the Emanations of Light in the Kingdom.}

And in answer the Master explains the ordering and nature and functions of these great emanations, and how that, at the final time of the completion of the æon and the ascension of the plērōma, these all shall have a higher place in His Kingdom; but this time has not yet come. But high above all of them the souls of men who have received the mysteries of light, shall take precedence.

The "Last" shall be "First."

And Mary said: "Master, my indweller of light hath ears, and I comprehend every word which Thou speakest. Now, therefore, O Master, concerning the word which Thou hast spoken, to wit, 'All the souls of human kind which shall receive the mysteries of light, shall in the Inheritance of Light take precedence of all the Rulers who shall repent, and all them of the region of those who are on the Right, and the whole space of the Treasure of Light'; concerning this word, my Master, Thou hast said unto us aforetime, 'The first shall be last and the last shall be first,' that is, the 'last' are the whole race of men who shall be first in the Light-kingdom; so also they that are [now] in the space of the height are the 'first.'"

The Three Supernal Spaces of the Light.

The Master then continues in His conversation and tells them of the glorious beings and spaces, of which He will treat in detail in His further teaching, up to the inner Space of the First Mystery, but of those within these supernal spaces He will not treat in the physical consciousness, for "there is no possibility of speaking of them in this world"; nay, "there is neither quality nor light which resembleth them, not only in this world, but also no comparison in those of the Height of Righteousness." He, however, in lofty language describes the greatness of the five

Great Supporters of the outer Space of the First Mystery, above or within which is the inner Space of the First Mystery, and above all the Space of the Ineffable.

To these supernal realms of the Inheritance shall come those who have received the light-mysteries, and each shall occupy the space according to the mystery he has received, a higher space or a lower according to the degree of the mysteries he has received; each shall have the power of going into all regions of the Inheritance below him, but not of ascending higher. *The Inheritance of Light.*

"But he who shall have received the complete mystery of the First Mystery of the Ineffable, that is to say, the twelve mysteries of the First Mystery, one after another, ... shall have the power of exploring all the orders of the Inheritance of Light, of exploring from without within, from within without, from above below, and from below above, from the height to the depth, and from the depth to the height, from the length to the breadth, and from the breadth to the length; in a word, he shall have the power of exploring all the regions of the Inheritances of Light, and he shall have the power of remaining in the region which he shall choose in the Inheritance of the Light-kingdom. *The Mystery of the First Mystery.*

"Amen, I say unto you, this man, in the dissolution of the world, shall be King over all the orders of the Inheritance of Light; and he who shall have received the Mystery of the Ineffable, that man is Myself. *The Gnosis of Jesus, the Mystery of the Ineffable.*

Hereupon follows a magnificent recital of the perfect Gnosis of such a one, for:

"That Mystery knoweth why there is darkness, and why light."

And so on, in great phrases describing the wisdom of the supreme Mystery, who knows the reason of the existence of all things: darkness of darkness and light of light; chaos and the treasure of light; judgment and inheritance of light; punishment of sinners and rest of the righteous; sin and baptisms; fire of punishment and seals of light; blasphemies and songs to the light; and so on through many pairs of opposites, ending with death and life.

But the recital of the greatness of the supreme Gnosis is not yet ended, for the Master continues: "Hearken, therefore, now further, O My disciples, while I tell you the whole Gnosis of the Mystery of the Ineffable."

It is the Gnosis of pitilessness and compassion; of destruction and everlasting increase; of beasts and creeping things, and metals, seas, and earth, clouds and rain, and so on working downwards from man into nature and upwards through all the supernal realms.

The Disciples lose Courage in Amazement at the Glories of the Gnosis.

But the disciples are amazed at the glories of the Gnosis of this greatest Mystery and lose courage. And Mary said: "O Master, if the Gnosis of all these things is in that Mystery, who is the man in this world who shall be able to understand that Mystery and all its gnoses, and the manner of all the words which thou hast spoken concerning it?"

And the Master said: "Grieve not, My disciples,

concerning the Mystery of that Ineffable, thinking that ye will not understand it. Amen, I say unto you, that Mystery is yours, and every one's who shall give ear unto you, and shall renounce the whole world, and all the matter therein, who shall renounce all the evil thoughts that are therein, and shall renounce all the cares of this æon.

"Now, therefore, will I tell you: Whosoever shall renounce the whole world and all therein, and shall submit himself to the Divinity, to him that Mystery shall be far more easy than all the mysteries of the Kingdom of Light; it is far simpler to understand than all the rest, and it is far clearer than them all. He who shall come to a knowledge of that Mystery, hath renounced the whole of this world and all its cares. For this cause have I said unto you aforetime: 'Come unto Me all ye that are oppressed with cares and labour under their weight, and I will give you rest, for My burden is light and My yoke easy.'" *The Highest Mystery is the Simplest of them All.*

Let them not be dismayed at the vast complexity of the emanation of the plērōma and the world-process, "for the emanation of the plērōma is its Gnosis." Let but the Christ be born in their hearts by their forsaking the delights of the world, and they shall grow into the being of the plērōma and so possess all its Gnosis.

The Master then continues His description of the Gnosis of the Mystery of the Ineffable, resuming it at the point where He had broken off, and leading them higher and higher into the supernal heights through space after space, and hierarchy after hierarchy, of stupendous being and its emanation, *Concerning the One Word of the Ineffable.*

up to the Mystery itself, the First Mystery who knoweth why He came forth from the Last Limb of the Ineffable. All this, which He now recites simply, naming the great spaces and their indwellers, He promises to explain at length in His further teaching.

"Now, therefore, it is the Mystery of the Ineffable which knoweth why all of which I have spoken unto you hath come into existence; of a truth all this hath existed because of Him. He is the Mystery which is in them all; He is the emanation of them all, the re-absorption of them all, and the support of them all.

"This Mystery of the Ineffable is in all those of which I have spoken, and of which I shall speak in treating of the emanation of the plērōma. He is the Mystery which is in them all, and He is the One Mystery of the Ineffable. And the Gnosis of that which I have said unto you, and of what I have not yet spoken unto you, but of all of which I shall speak when treating of the [full] emanation of the plērōma, and the whole Gnosis of each of them, one after another, that is to say, why they exist—all this is the One Word (Logos) of the Ineffable."

"The Mystery of the Ineffable is the One and Only Word, but there is another [Word] on the Tongue of the Ineffable; it is the rule of the interpretation of all the words which I have spoken unto you."

It is then explained how that he who receives this One and Only Word, when he comes forth from the body of the matter of the Rulers, becomes a great light-stream, and soars into the height; he stands in no need of apology or symbol, for all powers bow down before the vesture of light in which he is clothed, and sing hymns of praise, and so he passes upwards and onwards, through all the Inheritances of Light, and higher still until he becometh one with the Limbs of the Ineffable. "Amen, I say unto you, he shall be in all the regions during the time a man can shoot an arrow."

The Glory of Him who Receives the Mystery.

Hereupon follows a recital of the greatness of such a soul. Beginning with the words, "Though he be a man in the world, yet is he higher than all angels, and shall far surpass them all," it recites in the same form all the grades of the supernal hierarchies of beings from angels upwards, and ends as follows:

"Though he be a man in the world, yet is he higher than the whole region of the Treasure, and shall be exalted above the whole of it.

"Though he be a man in the world, yet shall he be King with Me in My Kingdom. He is a man in the world but a King in the Light.

"Though he be a man in the world, yet is he a man who is not of the world.

"Amen, I say unto you, that man is Myself, and I am that man."

And at the great consummation all such men "shall be fellow-kings with Me, they shall sit on My right hand and on My left in My Kingdom.

"Amen, I say unto you, these men are Myself, and I am these men."

There then follows apparently an interpolation consisting of a quotation from some now unknown Gospel: "Wherefore have I said unto you aforetime, 'In the place where I shall be, there also will be my twelve ministers, but Mary Magdalene and John the virgin shall be higher than all the disciples.'

Of the Thrones in the Light-Kingdom.

"And all men who shall receive the Mystery in that Ineffable shall be on My left hand and on My right, and I am they and they are Myself.

"They shall be your equals in all things, and yet your thrones shall be more excellent than theirs, and My throne shall be more excellent than yours and [than those of] all men who shall have found the Word of that Ineffable."

And Mary thinks that this must be the end of all things and the Gnosis of all gnoses, and so protests: "Master, surely there is no other Word of the Mystery of that Ineffable, nor any other Word of the whole Gnosis?"

There are other Logoi.

The Saviour answered and said: "Yea, verily; there is another Mystery of the Ineffable and another Word of the whole Gnosis." Nay, a multitude of Words, He might have added.

Then Mary asks whether those who do not receive the Mystery of the Ineffable before they die, will enter the Light-kingdom. The Master answers that every one who receives a mystery of light, any one of them, shall after death find rest in the Light-world appropriate to his mystery, but no one who has not become a Christ will know the Gnosis of the whole plērōma, for "in all openness I am the Gnosis of the whole plērōma."

The Degrees of the Mysteries.

So he who receives the first mystery of the First Mystery shall be King over the spaces of the First Saviour in the Light-realm, and so on up to the twelfth.

And Mary asks: "Master, how is it that the First Mystery hath twelve mysteries, whereas the Ineffable hath but one Mystery?"

The answer is that they are really one Mystery; this Mystery is ordered into twelve, and also into five, and again into three, while still remaining one; they are all different aspects or types of the same Mystery.

The two higher mysteries of the three not only ensure the possessor of them, when he leaves the body, his appropriate lot in the Inheritance, but they further bestow boons with regard to others. If a man "perform them in all their configurations, that is to say when he shall have created those mysteries for himself," they give the power of further enabling him to protect one who is not a participator in the Words of Truth, after his death, so that he shall not be punished. Of course such a man cannot "be brought into the Light until he have performed the whole polity of the light of those mysteries, that is to say, the strict renunciation of the world"; but he will be sent back again into "a righteous body, which shall find the God of Truth and the higher mysteries." *The Boons they Grant.*

But as for the highest mystery of all, "whosoever shall receive the Mystery which is in the whole Space of the Ineffable, and also all the other sweet mysteries which are in the Limbs of that Ineffable, *The Limbs of the Ineffable.*

of which I have not yet spoken unto you, both concerning their emanation, and the manner in which they are constituted, and the type of each of them as it is—I have not told you why It is called the Ineffable, or why It lies stretched out with all Its Limbs, or how many Limbs there are therein, or what are all Its regulations; nor will I say this unto you immediately, but only when I come to speak of the emanation of the [whole] plērōma; [then] will I tell you every detail, one by one, for It hath emanated together with Its own Word, just as it is in Itself, together with the sum total of all its Limbs, which belong to the regulation of the One and Only One, the changeless God of Truth—in the region, therefore, of which each shall receive the mystery in the Space of that Ineffable, there shall he inherit up to the region which he shall have received, [as far as] the whole region of the Space of that Ineffable; nor shall he give explanation throughout the regions, nor apology nor symbol, for [such souls] are without symbol and have no receivers."

So also for the second Space below this, the Space of the First Mystery looking within; such souls require no apology.

But for the third Space, the Space of the First Mystery looking without, each region has its receiver, explanation, apologies, and symbols, of all of which the Master will speak in due course.

The Thousand Years of Light.

"But when the plērōma is completed, that is to say, when the number of perfect souls shall be reached, and the Mystery shall be accomplished according to which the plērōma is the plērōma, I shall pass a thousand years, according to the years of Light, reigning over all the emanations of the Light and the whole number of perfect souls who shall have received all the mysteries."

Now "a day of the Light is a thousand years in the world, so that thirty-six myriads of years and a half a myriad of years of the world make a single year of the Light."

The glories of the Light-kingdom with its three Realms and Kings is then described.

"Now the mysteries of these three Inheritances of Light are exceedingly numerous. Ye shall find them in the two great Books of Ieou." The higher ones He will reveal unto them; "but as for the rest of the lower mysteries, ye have no need thereof, but ye shall find them in the two Books of Ieou, which Enoch wrote when I spoke with him from the Tree of Knowledge, and from the Tree of Life, which were in the Paradise of Adam." *The Books of Ieou.*

Hereupon Andrew is in great amazement, and cannot believe that men of the world like themselves can have so high a destiny reserved for them, and can reach such lofty heights. "This matter, then, is hard for me," he says.

When Andrew had said these words, the spirit of the Saviour was moved in Him, and He cried out and said: "How long shall I bear with you, how long shall I suffer you? Do ye still not know and are ye ignorant? Know ye not and do ye not understand that ye are all Angels, all Archangels, Gods and Lords, all Rulers, all the great *Ye are Gods.*

Invisibles, all those of the Midst, those of every region of them that are on the Right, all the Great Ones of the emanations of the Light with all their glory; that ye are all, of yourselves and in yourselves in turn, from one mass and one matter, and one substance; ye are all from the same mixture. . . .

"The great Light-emanations have not at all [in reality] undergone sufferings, nor changes of region, nor have they at all torn themselves asunder, nor poured themselves into different bodies, nor have they been in any affliction.

Of Souls in Incarnation.
"Whereas, ye others, ye are the purgations of the Treasure, ye are the purgations of the region of them that are on the Right, ye are the purgations of all the invisibles and all the rulers; in a word, ye are the purgation of all of them. And ye have been in great afflictions and great tribulations, in your pourings into different bodies in this world. And after all these afflictions which came from yourselves, ye have struggled and fought, renouncing the whole world and all the matter that is in it; and ye have not held your hands in the fight, until ye found all the mysteries of the Kingdom of Light, which have purified you, and transformed you into refined light, most pure, and ye have become pure light itself. . . .

"Amen, I say unto you, the race of human kind is of matter. I have torn myself asunder, I have brought unto them the mysteries of light, to purify them, for they are the purgations of all the matter of their matter. . . .

"Now the Light-emanations have no need of any

mystery, for they are pure; but the human race hath need of purification, for all men are purgations of matter. . . .

"For this cause, therefore, preach ye to the whole human race, saying, 'Cease not to seek day and night, until ye have found the purifying mysteries'; and say unto them, 'Renounce the whole world, and all the matter therein', for he who buyeth and selleth in this world, he who eateth and drinketh of his own matter, who liveth in his own cares and all his own associations, amasses ever fresh matter from his matter, in that the whole world, and all that is therein, and all its associations, are exceedingly material purgations, and they shall make enquiry of every one according to his purity."

The Preaching of the Mysteries.

This is followed by a long instruction on the nature of the preaching of the disciples to the world when the Master shall have gone unto the Light.

"Say unto them, 'Renounce the whole world and the matter that is in it, all its cares, all its sins, in a word, all the associations that are in it, that ye may be worthy of the mysteries of light, and be saved from all the torments which are in the judgments.'"

The Burden of the Preaching.

They are to renounce mourning, superstition, spells, calumny, false witness, boasting and pride, gluttony, garrulity, evil caresses, desire of avarice, the love of the world, robbery, evil words, wickedness, pitilessness, wrath, reviling, pillage, slandering, quarrelling, ignorance, villainy, sloth, adultery, murder, hardness of heart and impiety, atheism, magic potions, blasphemy, doctrines of error,—that they may escape the torments of fire and ice and other graphic horrors of an elaborate hell, capped by the torments of the Great Dragon of the inexorable Outer Darkness, reserved for the greatest of sins, where such absolutely unrepentant souls "shall be without existence until the end" of the æon; they shall be "frozen up" in that state.

The Boundary Marks of the Paths of the Mysteries.

Thus far for the negative side, the things to be abandoned; but for the positive, the things to be done, they are to: "Say unto the men of the world, 'Be ye diligent, that ye may receive the mysteries of light, and enter into the height of the Kingdom of Light.'"

They are to be gentle, peacemakers, merciful, compassionate, to minister unto the poor and sick and afflicted, be loving unto God, and righteous, and live the life of absolute self-renunciation.

"These are all the boundary marks of the paths of them that are worthy of the mysteries of light."

Unto such and such only are the mysteries to be given; the absolute condition is that they make this renunciation and repent.

"It is because of sinners that I have brought these mysteries into the world, for the remission of all the sins which they have committed from the beginning. Wherefore have I said unto you aforetime, 'I came not to call the righteous.'"

The After-death State of the Uninitiated Righteous.

The question now arises as to good men who have not received the mysteries, how will it be with them after death?

"A righteous man who is perfect in all righteousness," answers the Master, yet who has not received the mysteries of light, on going forth from the body, is taken charge of by the Receivers of Light—as distinguished from the Receivers of Wrath. "Three days shall they journey round with that soul in all the creatures of the world," and pass it through all the elements of the judgments, instructing it therein, and then it shall be taken to the Virgin of Light and sealed with an excellent seal that it may be carried into a righteous body of the æons, so that it may in its next birth find the signs of the mysteries of light and inherit the Kingdom of Light for ever.

So with a man who has only sinned twice or thrice, he shall be sent back into the world according to the type of the sins he hath committed; "I will tell you these types when I shall come to explain the emanation of the plērōma" in detail.

"But Amen, Amen, I say unto you, even though a righteous man have not committed any sin at all, it is impossible to take him into the Kingdom of Light, because the sign of the Kingdom of the Mysteries is not with him." He must have gnosis as well as righteousness.

Of Those who Repent and again Fall Back.

The question next arises as to the sinner who has repented, and received the mysteries, and then has fallen away, and again repented, provided he be not a hypocrite; "Wilt Thou or not that we remit his transgressions unto seven times, and give him the mysteries again?"

The Saviour answered and said: "Remit ye his sin not only unto seven times, but Amen, I say unto you, remit ye it unto him many times seven times, and each time give ye him the mysteries from the beginning, the mysteries which are in the first Space from the exterior; perchance ye will win the soul of that brother, so that he may inherit the Kingdom of Light. . . .

The Added Glories of the Saviours of Souls.

"Amen, I say unto you, he who shall give life unto a single soul, and shall save it, in addition to his own proper light in the Kingdom of Light, he shall further receive an additional glory for the soul which he shall have saved, so that he who shall save a host of souls, in addition to his own proper glory in the Glory, he shall receive a host of additional glories for the souls which he shall have saved."

Nay, they shall not only give the lower mysteries, but the higher mysteries as well, provided always the man sincerely repent and is not a hypocrite; all mysteries up to the three highest mysteries of the First Mystery, "for the First Mystery is compassionate and merciful-minded."

Concerning the Irreconcilables.

"But if that man again transgresseth, and is in any kind of sin, ye shall not remit his sin again from that hour, nor any more accept his repentance; let him be for you a stumbling-block and transgressor.

"For Amen, I say unto you, these three mysteries shall witness against his last repentance for him from that hour. Amen, I say unto you, the soul of that man shall have no more probation for the world of the height henceforth from that hour, but it shall dwell in the habitation of the Dragon of the Outer Darkness."

In all of this the disciples have no choice; if they know a man is sincere, and not a hypocrite or merely curious to know what kind of things the rites of the mysteries are, they must give him these mysteries and not withhold them, even if he be one who has never received any of the lower mysteries; for should they hide them from him, they will be subject to a great judgment.

Beyond the giving of these three higher mysteries they have no power, for they have not sufficient knowledge.

But the case of a man who has fallen away after receiving the highest mysteries they can give, is not entirely hopeless; it is, however, in the hands of the First Mystery and the Mystery of the Ineffable alone. *Of the Infinite Compassion of the Divine.*

These alone can accept repentance from such a man, and grant him the remission of his sins, for these Mysteries are "compassionate and merciful-minded, and grant remission of sins at any time."

The question is now raised, Supposing they give the mysteries in error to those who are hypocrites and who have deceived them and have afterwards made a mock of the mysteries "mimicking us and making forgeries of our mysteries," what then are they to do? *Of those who Mimic the Mysteries.*

In this case they are to appeal to the First Mystery, saying: "The mystery which we have given unto these impious and iniquitous souls, they have not performed in a manner worthy of Thy mystery, but they have [merely] copied [what we did]; give back [therefore] that mystery unto us, and make them for ever strangers to Thy Kingdom."

In that hour the mysteries such impious souls

have received, shall return to them, and such people can receive pardon from no one save only the Mystery of the Ineffable.

In the case of the unbelieving friends and relatives of those who have received the mysteries, the latter may by their prayers and invocations procure a better lot in the after-death state for their relatives and friends, so that they may be sent back into conditions favourable for their receiving the mysteries in another life.

Can the Pains of Martyrdom be Avoided.

It is then asked whether the mysteries will save the disciples from the pains of martyrdom. "For they are in exceeding great number who persecute us because of Thee, and multitudes pursue us because of Thy name, so that if we be submitted to the torture, we shall utter the mystery, that we may immediately depart from the body without suffering pain."

The answer is not clear; every one who has accomplished the first (*i.e.*, highest) of the three higher mysteries, in life, when the time comes to leave the body, shall soar into the Kingdom of Life without need of apology or sign. But it is not said that the pains of martyrdom can be avoided.

The Mystery of the Resurrection of the Dead.

But they will be able to help others, for "not only ye, but all men who shall achieve the mystery of the resurrection of the dead, which healeth from demonian possessions, and sufferings, and every disease, [which also healeth] the blind, the lame, the halt, the dumb, and the deaf, [the mystery] which I gave unto you aforetime—whosoever shall receive of these mysteries and achieve them, if he ask for any thing whatever hereafter, poverty or riches, weakness or strength, disease or health, or the whole healing of the body, and the resurrection of the dead, the power of healing the lame, the blind, the deaf, and the dumb, of every disease and of every suffering—in a word, whosoever shall achieve this mystery, if he ask any of the things which I have just said unto you, they shall at once be granted unto him."

Hereupon the disciples cried out together in transport: "O Saviour, Thou excitest us with very great frenzy because of the transcendent height which Thou hast revealed unto us; and Thou exaltest our souls, and they have become paths on which we travel to come unto Thee, for they came forth from Thee. Now, therefore, because of the transcendent heights which Thou hast revealed unto us, our souls have become frenzied, and they travail mightily, yearning to go forth from us into the height to the region of Thy Kingdom." *The Transport of the Disciples.*

The Master continues His teaching, saying that the rest of the mysteries which have been committed unto them they may give to others, but not the mystery of the resurrection of the dead and the healing of disease, "for that mystery pertaineth to the rulers, it and all its namings." This they are to retain as the sign of their mission, so that when they do such wonder-deeds, "they will believe on you, that ye preach the God of perfection, and will have faith in all your words." *That this Mystery is to be kept Secret.*

The next point of instruction taken up is the question: "Who constraineth a man to sin?" This opens up the whole subject of the constitution of man, and gives rise to a very interesting exposition of Gnostic psychology.

The Constitution of Man.

When the child is first born, the "light-power," "soul," "counterfeit spirit," and "body," are all very feeble in it. "None of them hath sense enough as yet for any work, whether good or evil, because of the exceeding great weight of oblivion."

The babe eateth of the delights of the world of the Rulers; the power absorbeth from the portion of the power which is in the delights, the soul from the portion of the soul in the delights, the counterfeit spirit from the portion of evil in the delights, and the body from the unperceptive matter in the delights.

There is also another factor called the "destiny," which remains as it came into the world and takes nothing from the delights.

So, little by little, all these constituent elements in man develop, each sensing according to its nature. "The power senseth after the light of the height; the soul senseth after the region of mixed righteousness, which is the region of the Mixture (*sci.*, of Light and Matter); and the counterfeit spirit seeketh after all vices, and desires, and sins; but the body hath no power of sensing unless it be an impulse to gain strength from matter."

The power is evidently the higher mind, the soul the lower mind, and the counterfeit spirit the animal nature.

"The power within impelleth the soul to seek after the region of light and the whole Godhead;

whereas the counterfeit spirit draggeth down the soul, and persistently constraineth it to commit every kind of iniquity and mischief and sin, and persisteth as something foreign to the soul, and is its enemy, and maketh it commit all these sins and evils"—bringing them into operation against the soul because of what it has done in the past; moreover, for the future, "it spurreth on the Workmen of Wrath to bear witness to all the sin which it will constrain the soul to commit. And even when the man sleepeth by night or by day, it plagueth him in dreams with the desires of the world, and causeth him to long after all the things of this world. In a word, it bindeth the soul to all the actions which the Rulers have decreed for it, and is the enemy of the soul, causing it to do what it would not." This it is which constraineth a man to sin. *The Evil Desire which Constraineth a Man to Sin.*

The "destiny" is that which leadeth the man to his death. Then come the Receivers of Wrath to lead that soul out of the body.

"And for three days the Receivers of Wrath travel round with that soul through all the regions, taking it through all the æons of the world; and the counterfeit spirit and destiny accompany that soul, but the power withdraws itself unto the Virgin of Light." *The Cycle of the After-death State of the Sinner.*

The soul is then brought down into Chaos, and the counterfeit spirit becometh the receiver of that soul, and haunteth it, rebuking it in every punishment because of the sins which it hath caused it to commit; it is in exceeding great enmity to the soul.

The soul then rises higher, still always haunted

by the counterfeit spirit, until it comes to the Ruler of the Way of the Midst between the lower firmament and the earth-surface. Here it is still subjected to the punishments of its counterfeit spirit, according to its "destiny."

It is then brought by the counterfeit spirit to the "light of the sun,"—the Way of the Midst being apparently the sublunary regions—and taken to the Judge, the Virgin of Light, according to the commandment of Ieou, the First Man; and "the Virgin of Light sealeth that soul and handeth it over to one of her receivers, and will have it carried into a body, which is the record of the sins which it hath committed."

"Amen, I say unto you she will not suffer that soul to escape from transmigrations into bodies, until it hath given signs of being in its last cycle according to its record of demerit."

And of the Initiated Righteous.
In the case of a righteous soul, however, and one that hath received the higher mysteries of light, "when the time of that soul is come for its passing from the body, then the counterfeit spirit followeth after that soul, and also the destiny. They follow after it in the way whereby it shall pass into the height.

"And before it goeth far into the height, it uttereth the mystery of the breaking of the seals and all the bonds of the counterfeit spirit, whereby the Rulers bind it to the soul"; and so they cease to impede the soul, and the destiny departeth to its own region, to the Rulers of the Way of the Midst, and the counterfeit of the spirit to the Rulers of the Fate-

Sphere. And so it becometh a glorious light-stream and passeth up to its inheritance, for "the receivers of that soul, who pertain to the light, become wings of light for that soul," and will be a vesture of light for it. Such a soul requires no seals or apologies.

But one that hath received the lower mysteries only, requires such apologies and seals, all of which the Master promises to give them in His detailed exposition of the emanation of the plērōma. For the present He simply states what spaces have to be traversed and what are the rulers.

Mary compares some of the statements with former sayings, including one which the Master spake "unto us aforetime by the mouth of Paul our brother." She further interprets the saying, "Agree with thine enemy whilst thou art in the way with him, lest at any time thine enemy deliver thee to the judge, and the judge deliver thee to the officer, and the officer cast thee into prison; thou shalt not come out thence till thou hast paid the uttermost farthing," as referring to the Judge, the Virgin of Light, and the recasting of the soul into another body, for that no soul is free from transmigration until it gives signs of being in its last cycle. *"Agree with thine Enemy."*

Mary next enquires as to the nature of the mysteries of the baptisms which remit sins, and the Master replies:

"The counterfeit spirit beareth witness to every sin which the soul hath committed; not only doth it bear witness concerning the sins of the souls, but it sealeth every sin that it may be stamped on the *The Stamping of the Sins on the Souls.*

soul, so that all the rulers of the punishments of sinners may know that it is the soul of a sinner, and may be informed of the number of sins which it hath committed, by the number of the seals which the counterfeit spirit hath stamped upon it, so that they may chastise it according to the number of sins which it hath committed. This is the fashion in which they treat the soul of the sinner.

The Burning Up of the Sins by the Fires of the Baptism Mystery.

"Now, therefore, when a man receiveth the mysteries of the baptisms, those mysteries become a mighty fire, exceedingly fierce, wise, which burneth up sins; they enter into the soul secretly and devour all the sins which the counterfeit spirit hath implanted in it.

"And when the fire hath purified all the sins which the counterfeit spirit hath implanted in the soul, the mysteries enter into the body occultly, that the fire may secretly pursue after the pursuers and cut them off with the body. They chase after the counterfeit spirit and the destiny, to separate them from the power and the soul, and place them with the body, so that the counterfeit spirit, the destiny, and the body may be separated into one group, and the soul and power into another. And the mystery of baptism remaineth between the two, and separateth the one from the other, in order that it may cleanse them and make them pure, that the soul and power may not be fouled in matter."

It is then further explained that all the twelve and other mysteries of the First Mystery and of the Ineffable are still higher than the mysteries of the

THE PISTIS SOPHIA. 501

baptisms; but all of this will be explained in a further teaching.

Mary gives interpretations of passages of scripture by the light of the new teaching, the opportunity being offered by a recapitulation of some of the points by the Master, with enquiry as to whether they have well understood. Especially is the unending compassion of the highest Mysteries insisted upon.

"If even a king of to-day, a man of the world, granteth boons unto them who are like unto him, if he moreover granteth pardon unto murderers, and them that are guilty of intercourse with males, and other horrible and capital crimes; if, I say, it is in the power even of one who is a man of the world to act thus, much more then have that Ineffable and that First Mystery, who are lords of the whole plērōma, power over everything to do as they will, and grant remission of sin unto every one who shall have received the Mystery. *The Infinite Forgiveness of Sins.*

"Again, if even a king of to-day investeth a soldier with a royal mantle, and sendeth him to foreign regions, and the soldier there committeth murders and other grave offences worthy of death, and yet they are not brought home to him, because he weareth the royal mantle, how much more, then, [is it the case with] them who are mantled in the mysteries of the vestures of that Ineffable, and those of the First Mystery who are lords over all them of the height and all them of the depth!"

Thereupon the Master makes trial of Peter, to see whether he is compassionate, in the case of a woman who had fallen away after receiving the mystery of baptism, and Peter comes out of the trial successfully.

But Delay not to Repent.

It is then explained that the lot of a man who has received the mysteries and fallen away and not repented, is far worse than that of the impious man who has never known them. As to those who are indifferent, thinking they have many births before them and need not hasten, the Master bids the disciples:

"Preach ye unto the whole world, saying unto men: 'Strive together that ye may receive the mysteries of light in this time of stress, and enter into the Kingdom of Light. Put not off from day to day, and from cycle to cycle, in the belief that ye will succeed in obtaining the mysteries when ye return to the world in another cycle.'

For at a Certain Time the Gates of the Light will be shut.

"Such men know not when the number of perfect souls [shall be filled up]; for when the number of perfect souls shall be completed, I will then shut the Gates of the Light, and from that time none will be able to come in thereby, nor will any go forth thereafter, for the number of perfect souls shall be [completed], and the mystery of the First Mystery be perfected—[the mystery] whereby all hath come into existence, and I am that mystery.

"From that hour no one shall any more enter into the Light, and none shall come forth, in that the time of the number of perfect souls shall be fulfilled, before I set fire to the world, that it may purify the æons, and veils, the firmaments and the whole world, and also all the matters that are still in it, the race of human kind being still upon it.

"At that time, then, the faith shall show itself forth more and more, and also the mysteries in those days. And many souls shall pass through the cycles of transmigrations of body and come back into the world in those days; and among them shall be some who are now alive and hear Me teach concerning the consummation of the number of perfect souls, [and in those days] they shall find the mysteries of light, and shall receive them. They shall mount up to the Gates of Light, and shall find that the number of perfect souls is complete, which is the Consummation of the First Mystery and the Gnosis of the Plērōma; they will find that I have shut the Gates of Light, and that from that hour no one can come in or go forth thereby.

"Those souls then will cry within through the Gates of Light, saying: 'Master, open unto us.' And I will answer unto them, saying, 'I know not whence ye are.' And they will say unto Me, 'We have received the mysteries, and we have fulfilled all Thy doctrine; Thou didst teach us on the high ways.' And I will answer unto them, saying, 'I know not who ye are, ye who have practised iniquity and evil even unto this day. Wherefore go [hence] into the Outer Darkness.' Forthwith they will depart to the Outer Darkness, where there is weeping and gnashing of teeth."

"I know not whence ye are."

Mary then asks as to the type of the Outer Darkness and the number of the spaces and regions of punishment; and then follows an elaborate description of the space-dragon of this Outer Darkness, whose tail is in its mouth, and its twelve

The Dragon of Outer Darkness.

dungeons, with their authentic faces and names of the rulers, of the doors and angels that watch at them, and what souls pass into the Dragon and how; it is explained how the names are all contained in one another, and what are the torments and degrees of the fires. Thereupon follows the teaching how the souls of the uninitiated may be saved, and how finally the Mystery will save even those who have no more chance of rebirth.

It is further explained how the initiated become light-flames and streams of light. Mary pleads for them who have neglected the mysteries; and the efficacy of the names of the twelve rulers of the dungeons is explained, and how that the souls who know the names escape from the Dragon and are taken to Ieou, and their subsequent fate.

The Draught of Oblivion. Then comes fresh instruction as to the Rulers of the Fate and the Draught of Oblivion—"the seed of iniquity, filled with all manner of desire and all forgetfulness . . .; and that deadly draught of oblivion becometh a body external to the soul, like unto the soul in every way, and its perfect resemblance, and hence they call it the counterfeit spirit."

The manner of the fashioning of a new soul is then described, and how the power is inbreathed into it; this is set forth generally, and more detailed information is promised on a future occasion.

The Parents we are to Leave. It is further explained that the saying, "He who shall not leave father and mother and follow after Me," refers to the "parents" or fashioners of the soul and counterfeit spirit, and not our earthly parents, far less the parents of the light-power within—the Saviour and His mysteries.

Further information is also given as to the counterfeit spirit and its elemental builders, three-hundred and sixty-five in number; the embryonic stages of incarnation; the kārmic compulsion of the parents — the father and mother of the physical body; the occult process of gestation; the mode of incarnation of the various constituent elements in man; occult physiognomy; the nature of the destiny and how a man comes by his death; and various other questions of a like nature. And then the Saviour continues:

Of the Books of Ieou again.

"Now, therefore, for the sake of sinners have I torn myself asunder and come into the world, to save them, and also because it is necessary that the righteous, who have never done evil, and have never committed sin, should find the mysteries which are in the Books of Ieou, which I made Enoch write down in Paradise, when I spake to him from the Tree of Knowledge, and from the Tree of Life, and which I made him deposit in the rock of Ararad; and I set Kalapataurōth, the Ruler that is over Skemmut, on whose head is the foot of Ieou—the latter surroundeth all the Æons and the Fate-Sphere—I set [then] this Ruler to preserve the Books of Ieou from the flood, and [also] lest any of the Rulers out of enmity should destroy them. These [books] will I give unto you, when I have finished telling you the emanation of the plērōma."

But few only will comprehend the higher mysteries. "I tell you that there will be found one in a thousand and two in ten thousand for the consummation of the mysteries of the First Mystery."

<small>The Christ the First of this Humanity to Enter the Light.</small>

Before the coming of the First Mystery no soul of this humanity had fully entered into the Light; none of the prophets or patriarchs had as yet entered into the Light, but they will be sent back into righteous bodies and so find the mysteries and inherit the Kingdom.

The treatise brings itself to an end with the following paragraphs:

"Mary answered and said: 'Blessed are we before all men because of these great [truths] which Thou hast revealed unto us.'

"The Saviour answered and said unto Mary and all His disciples: 'I will also reveal unto you all the grandeurs of the height, from the interior of the interiors to the exterior of the exteriors, that ye may be perfect in every gnosis, and in every plērōma, and in every height of the heights, and every deep of the depths.'

<small>'Tis He who holds the Keys of the Mysteries.</small>

"And Mary answered and said to the Saviour: 'Now we know, O Master, freely, surely, plainly, that Thou hast brought the keys of the mysteries of the Kingdom of Light, which remit the sins of souls, that they may be cleansed, and be transformed into pure light, and be brought into the Light.'"

SUMMARY OF THE EXTRACTS FROM THE BOOKS OF THE SAVIOUR.

THE first extract occurs on pp. 252—254 of the Askew Codex, and runs as follows:

"And they that are worthy of the mysteries which lie in the Ineffable, that is to say, those that have not emanated—they are prior to the First Mystery. To use a similitude and correspondence of speech that ye may understand, they are the Limbs of the Ineffable. And each is according to the dignity of its glory, the head according to the dignity of the head, the eye according to the dignity of the eye, the ear according to the dignity of the ear, and the rest of the Limbs (or Members) [in like fashion]; so that it is manifest that 'there are many members, but only one body.' Of this I speak to you in a paradigm, a correspondence, and a similitude, but not in the reality of its configuration; I have not revealed the [whole] word in truth. *The Immanent Limbs of the Ineffable.*

"But the Mystery of the Ineffable and every Limb which is in It—that is to say, they that dwell in the Mystery of the Ineffable and they that dwell in [that Ineffable]—and also the three Spaces which follow after them, according to the mysteries, in truth and verity, all that [is Myself]. I am the Treasure of all of them, apart from which there is no treasure, apart from which there is no individuality in the world; but there are other words [? *logoi*], other mysteries, and other regions. *The Christ is the Ineffable.*

The Gnosis of the Christ.

"Now, therefore, Blessed is he [among men] who hath found the mysteries of the Space towards the exterior. He is a God, who hath found the words [? *logoi*] of the mysteries of the second Space in the midst. He is a Saviour and free of every space who hath found the words of the mysteries, the words of the third Space towards the interior. He is the very Plērōma itself (or more excellent than the universe)—the object of desire of all who are in that third Space—who hath found the Mystery in which they [all] are, and in which they are [all] set. Wherefore is he equal to [all of them]. For he hath found also the words [? *logoi*] of the mysteries, which I have set down for you in a similitude, namely, the Limbs of the Ineffable. Amen, I say unto you, he who hath found the words of these mysteries in the Truth of God [? the God of Truth], that man is chief in the Truth, he is its peer, because of these words and mysteries. The universe verily oweth its being to these words and mysteries. For which cause he who hath found the words of these mysteries, is equal to the Chief [of all]. It is the gnosis of the Gnosis of the Ineffable concerning which I speak unto you this day."

The second series of extracts is far longer and comes at the end of the Codex, occupying pp. 357—390. It begins with the words:

The Initiation of the Disciples on the Mount.

"It came to pass, therefore, after they had crucified Jesus, our Master, that He rose from the dead on the third day. And the disciples came together unto Him and besought Him, saying: 'Master, have mercy upon us, for we have left father and mother, and the whole world, and have followed Thee.'"

We are at once introduced to an atmosphere of ceremonies and invocations. Jesus stands by the Sea of the Ocean, surrounded by his disciples, male and female, and makes invocation with solemn prayer, saying: "Hear me, O Father, Father of all fatherhood, Boundless Light!" The prayer consists of the mystic vowels and formulæ interspersed with "authentic" names.

The disciples are grouped round Him, the women disciples stand behind, all clad in white linen robes; Jesus stands at an altar and with His disciples turns to the four quarters, invoking three times the name IAŌ. The interpretation of which is: "I, The plērōma hath gone forth; A, They shall return within; Ō, There shall be an end of ends."

This is followed by a mystic formula, which is interpreted as: "O Father of every fatherhood of the boundless [light-spaces], hear Me because of My disciples, whom I have brought into Thy presence, that they may believe in all the words of Thy truth; grant unto them all things for which I have cried unto Thee, for I know the Name of the Father of the Treasure of Light."

Then Jesus, whose mystery-name is Aberamenthō, invokes the Name of the Father of the Treasure, saying: "Let all the mysteries of the rulers, authorities, archangels, and all the powers and all the works of the Invisible Gods [their three mystery-names being

The First Veil is Drawn Aside.

given] withdraw themselves and roll themselves onto the right."

Thereupon all the lower regions speed to the west, to the left of the disk of the sun and of the moon.

The disk of the sun is symbolically described as a vast dragon with its tail in its mouth, mounted on seven powers, and drawn by four others figured as horses. The car of the moon is figured as a ship, its helms, or steering oars, being two dragons, male and female; it is drawn by two oxen, and steered by a babe on the poop, and at the prow is the face of a cat.

They enter the Way of the Midst.

And Jesus and His disciples soar aloft into the aërial regions, the Way of the Midst, and come to the first order of the Way of the Midst.

The Ordering of the Fate-Sphere is Described.

Here the disciples are instructed on the nature of this space and its rulers. They are told that above them there are Twelve Æons, six being ruled by Adamas and six by Iabraōth. The six under Iabraōth have repented and practised the mysteries of light, and have therefore been carried by Ieou, "the father of My father," to a pure atmosphere near the light of the sun. The six under Adamas have refused the mysteries of light, and persisted in the mystery of intercourse, or sexual union, and procreated rulers and archangels, and angels, workmen, and decans. They have accordingly been bound by Ieou in the Fate-Sphere. There are now three hundred and sixty of this brood, and again eighteen hundred ($1800 = 360 \times 5$) in each æon. Over them Ieou has set five other Great Rulers, called in the world of human kind by these names: Kronos, Arēs,

Hermēs, Aphroditē, and Zeus. Their incorruptible mystery-names and their genesis is also given.

Zeus is the head of the four, for Ieou reflected "that they had need of a helm to steer the world and the æons of the spheres." Zeus is good, and passes three months in the revolutions of the remaining four ruling powers, "so that every ruler in which he cometh is freed from his iniquity." The peculiarity of Zeus is that he has two æons for his habitation.

All this refers to the ordering of the Fate-Sphere; but Mary, who is also in these Extracts represented as the chief questioner, desires to be informed as to why the aërial Ways of the Midst, in which they are, and which lie below the Fate-Sphere, are "set over great torments." She beseeches the Saviour to have mercy upon them, "lest the receivers carry off our souls to the judgments of the Ways of the Midst."

The Master in answer promises to give them the mysteries of all gnosis: the mystery of the Twelve Æons of the Rulers, their seals, their numbers, and the manner of invocation to enter into their regions; in like manner the mystery of the Thirteenth Æon (the Left); the mystery of the Baptism of them of the Midst; the mystery of the Baptism of them of the Right; and the great mystery of the Treasure of Light.

All Mysteries up to those of the Light-Treasure are Promised them.

"I will give unto you all the mysteries and every gnosis, that ye may be called the Sons of the Plērōma, perfect in every gnosis and every mystery. Blessed indeed are ye beyond all men who are on the earth, for the Sons of Light have come in your time."

In these Ways of the Midst are further bound

by Ieou three hundred and sixty of the brood of Adamas, and five great rulers are further established over them, in a sort of reflection of the space above. The authentic names, types, and sub-hierarchies of these five are given. It is explained how all is ordered by Ieou, who is the providence of all the rulers and gods and powers which are in the matter of the Light of the Treasure, and by Zorokothora (Melchizedec), the legate of all the light-powers which are purified among the Rulers. These two great Lights descend at appointed seasons, to gather together the pure radiance of the light from those they have cleansed among the Rulers; this is done when the number and time of their task come to pass. But when the great Lights withdraw again, then the Rulers again rebel because of the "wrath of their iniquity," and march against the light-powers of the souls, and "hurry off all the souls that they can harry and ravish, to destroy them in the smoke of their darkness and their evil fire."

The Punishments of the Ways of the Midst.

The times that souls must pass in each of these regions of punishment of the five dæmonial hierarchies are given, and how these times are brought to an end. To take the first as an example: "It cometh to pass after these years, when the sphere of the Little Sabaōth (that is to say, Zeus) revolveth so as to come into the first æon of the Sphere, which is called in the world the Ram of Bubastis (that is to say, Aphroditē); when, then, she [Aphroditē] shall have come into the seventh house of the Sphere, which is the Balance, [it cometh to pass that] the veils between them of the Right and

The Duration of the Punishments.

them of the Left are drawn aside, and there glanceth forth from the height, among them of the Right, the Great Sabaōth, the Good, [lord] of the whole world and of all the Sphere. But before he glanceth forth, he gazeth down on the regions of Paraplēx [the ruler of the first dæmonian hierarchy], that they may be dissolved and perish, and that all the souls which are in her torments may be brought forth and again led into the Sphere, for they are perishing in the torments of Paraplēx."

And so for the other four of the five, with appropriate modifications. It appears that Ieou and Melchisedec are powers behind or symbolized by the sun and moon.

"These then are the operations of the Ways of the Midst concerning which ye have questioned Me."

And when the disciples had heard this, they bowed down and adored Him, saying: "Save us, O Master, have mercy upon us, that we may be preserved from these malignant torments which are prepared for sinners. Woe unto them! woe unto the children of men! for they are like the blind feeling in the darkness, and seeing not. Have mercy upon us, O Master, in the great blindness in which we are, and have mercy upon the whole race of human kind; for they lie in wait for their souls, as lions for their prey, to tear them in pieces and make food for their torments, because of the forgetfulness and ignorance in which they are. Have mercy, therefore, upon us, O Master, our Saviour, have mercy upon us, preserve us from this great stupor!"

The Disciples Pray for Mercy to Sinners.

Jesus said unto His disciples: "Have courage, fear not, for ye are blessed; nay, I will make you lords over all these, and place them in subjection under your feet. Ye remember that I have already said unto you before My crucifixion: 'I will give unto you the keys of the kingdom of the heavens.' Now again I say unto you, I will give them unto you."

They Enter an Atmosphere of Exceeding Great Light.

When Jesus had thus spoken, He chanted an invocation in the Great Name, and the regions of the Ways of the Midst were hidden from view and Jesus and His disciples remained in an atmosphere of exceeding great light.

Jesus said unto His disciples: "Come unto Me." And they came unto Him. He turned towards the four angles of the world; He uttered the Great Name over their heads, and blessed them and breathed on their eyes. Jesus said unto them: "Look up, and mark what ye see!"

The Vision of the Baptism Mysteries.

And they raised their eyes unto the height and saw a great light, exceedingly brilliant, which no man in the world could describe.

He said unto them a second time: "Look into the light, and mark what ye see!"

They said: "We see fire and water, and wine and blood."

Jesus, that is to say Aberamenthō, said unto His disciples: "Amen, I say unto you, I have brought nothing into the world when I came, save this fire and water, this wine and blood. I brought down the water and fire from the region of the Light of light, from the Treasure of Light; I brought down the wine and the blood from the region of Barbēlō.

EXTRACTS FROM BOOKS OF THE SAVIOUR. 515

And shortly after My Father sent unto Me the Holy Spirit in the form of a dove.

"The fire, the water, and the wine are for cleansing all the sins of the world; the blood I had as a sign of the body of human kind, and I received it in the region of Barbēlō, the great power of the Divine Invisible [? the Thirteenth Æon]; while the Spirit draweth all souls and bringeth them into the region of Light."

This is the "fire" He came to "cast on the earth" according to a former saying; this the "living water" the Samaritan woman should have asked for; this the "cup of wine" in the eucharist; this the "water" that came from His side.

"These are the mysteries of the light which remit sins"—that is to say, their names merely.

After this Jesus again gives the command that the powers of the Left return to their own region, and the disciples find themselves once more on the Mount of Galilee. *They Return to Earth.*

Hereupon Jesus celebrates the mystic eucharist and the first Baptism of Water, with ceremonies and invocations almost identical to those in the Codex Brucianus. The disciples enquire further as to the nature of the Baptism of Incense [? Fire], the Baptism of the Holy Spirit, and the Spiritual Chrism, and ask that the "Mystery of the Light of Thy Father" be revealed to them. *The Celebration of the Mystic Eucharist.*

Jesus said unto them: "As to these mysteries which ye seek after, there is no mystery which is higher than them. They will bring your souls into the Light of lights, into the regions of Truth *The Mysteries that are to be Revealed.*

and Righteousness, into the region of the Holy of all Holies, into the region where there is neither female nor male, nor form in that region, but only Light, unceasing, ineffable.

"No mystery is higher than the mysteries ye seek after, save only the mystery of the Seven Voices and their Nine-and-Forty Powers and Numbers; and the Name which is higher than them all, the Name which sums up all their names, all their lights, and all their powers."

The Punishments of Sinners in the Lower Regions and the Evil Bodies they Receive when Reborn.

Here follows a lacuna, and the text is resumed in the middle of a totally different subject. It treats of the punishment of him that curseth, of the slanderer, of the murderer, of the thief, of the contemptuous, of the blasphemer, of him who hath intercourse with males, and of a still fouler act of sorcery, the mention of which stirs the infinite compassion of the Master to wrath and denunciation.

The few remaining pages of the Codex are taken up with a description of the after-death state of the righteous man who has not received the mysteries; a man must suffer for each separate sin, but even the greatest of sinners, if he repent, shall inherit the Kingdom. The time favourable for the birth of those who shall find the mysteries is described.

The Cup of Wisdom.

As for the righteous man who has not been initiated, in his next birth he shall not be given the draught of oblivion, but "there cometh a receiver of the little Sabaōth, the Good, him of the Midst; he bringeth a cup full of intuition and wisdom, and also prudence, and giveth it to the soul, and casteth the soul into a body which will not be able to fall asleep and forget, because of the cup of prudence which hath been given unto it, but will be ever pure in heart and seeking after the mysteries of light, until it hath found them, by order of the Virgin of Light, in order [that that soul] may inherit the Light for ever."

The Extracts end with the disciples again beseeching Jesus to have mercy upon them; and the whole Codex is terminated by the note of a scribe describing the preaching of the apostles: *The Note of a Scribe.*

"They went forth three by three to the four points of heaven; they preached the Glad Tidings of the Kingdom in the whole world, the Christ being active with them in the words of confirmation and the signs and wonders which accompanied them. And thus was known the Kingdom of God in all the land and in all the world of Israel, [and this] is a testimony for all the nations which are from the east even unto the west."

SUMMARY OF THE FRAGMENTS OF THE BOOK OF THE GREAT LOGOS ACCORDING TO THE MYSTERY.

The Book of the Gnoses of the Invisible God.

THE first page is headed with the beautiful words: "I have loved you and longed to give you Life," and is followed by the statement: "This is the Book of the Gnoses (pl.) of the Invisible God"; it is the Book of the Gnosis of Jesus the Living One, by means of which all the hidden mysteries are revealed to the elect. Jesus is the Saviour of Souls, the Logos of Life, sent by the Father from the Light-world to mankind, who taught His disciples the one and only doctrine, saying: "This is the doctrine in which all Gnosis dwelleth."

This is evidently an introduction written by an editor or compiler; immediately after there begins a dialogue between Jesus and the disciples.

Jesus saith: "Blessed is the man who crucifieth the world and doth not let the world crucify him."

The Hidden Wisdom.

He then explains that such a man is he who hath found His Word, and fulfilled it according to the will of the Father. The apostles beg the Master to tell them this Word, for they have left all and followed Him; they desire to be instructed in the Life of the Father.

Jesus answers that the Life of His Father consists in their purifying their souls from all earthly stain, and making them to become the Race of the Mind, so that they may be filled with understanding, and by

His teaching perfect themselves, and be saved from the Rulers of this world and its endless snares. Let them then hasten to receive the Gnosis He is to impart—His Word—for He is free from all stain of the world.

The disciples break into praises of the Master—as the Light shining in the daylight—who hath enlightened their hearts until they receive the Light of Life, by means of the Gnosis which teacheth the hidden wisdom of the Lord.

Jesus saith: "Blessed is the man who knoweth this [Word] and hath brought down the Heaven, and borne the earth and raised it heavenwards; and it [the Earth] becometh the midst, for it is a 'nothing.'" *A Dark Saying is Explained.*

The Heaven is explained as being the invisible Word of the Father. They who know this—(who become children of the true Mind)—bring down Heaven to Earth. The raising of Earth to Heaven is the ceasing from being an earthly intelligence, by receiving the Word of these Gnoses (pl.) and becoming a Dweller in Heaven. Thus will they be saved from the Ruler of this World, and he will become the midst (that is to say, perhaps, that they will be above the Ruler and no longer subject to him as heretofore; he will be a "nothing" to them, that is to say, have no effect on them). Nay, the evil powers will envy them because they know Him, that He is not of this world and that no evil cometh from Him. But as for those who are born in the flesh of unrighteousness (and are not children of the Righteous Race, those of the second birth), they have no part in the Kingdom of the Father.

The Flesh of Ignorance.

Thereupon the disciples are in despair, for they have been born "according to the flesh" and have known Him only "according to the flesh." But the Master explains that not the flesh of their bodies is meant, but the flesh of unrighteousness and ignorance."

The disciples ask to be instructed in the nature of ignorance (ἄγνοια, the opposite of gnosis, γνῶσις), and the Master tells them that, to understand this great mystery, they must first put on His virginity and righteousness, and His robe (of glory), and seek to understand the teaching of the Word, whereby they will learn to know Him in the Fullness (Plērōma) of the Father.

The apostles answered and said, "Lord Jesus, Thou Living One, teach us the Fullness and it sufficeth us."

Here unfortunately the text breaks off and pages are lost; nowhere in the MS. is a direct continuation to be found.

Taking Schmidt's *Second Book of Ieou* first, we are introduced to the following narrative.

The Mysteries of the Treasure of Light.

Jesus bids the twelve disciples and also the women disciples to surround Him, and promises to reveal to them the great mysteries of the Treasure of Light, which no one in the Invisible God knows (that is to say, no one even of the powers of the Thirteenth Æon—the Æon which surrounds or is beyond or within the Twelve Æons—over which the Invisible God is ruler). If these mysteries are consummated, neither the Rulers of the Twelve Æons nor those of the Invisible God can endure them nor comprehend them, for they are the great mysteries of the interior of the interiors of the Treasure of Light. When these are consummated, the Receivers of the Light-treasure come and take the soul from the body, and bear it through all inferior spaces into the Light-treasure. Yea, the sins of that soul, whether conscious or unconscious, are blotted out, and the soul becomes pure Light. And not only does the purified soul pass through all inferior spaces, but also within into the Light-realm, ever inward, within all its spaces, orders, and powers, to the space of the Uncontainables in the innermost space of the Light-treasure.

These mysteries are to be guarded with utmost secrecy, and revealed to none who are unworthy; neither to father nor mother, to sister nor brother, nor to any relative; neither for meat nor drink, neither for woman nor gold nor silver, nor anything in this world. Beyond all to no sorcerer, those who practise certain most foul rites, whose God is the son of the Great Ruler, Sabaōth Adamas—the enemy of the Kingdom of Heaven, the chief of the six non-repentant Rulers. The mystery-name of this power is given and its monstrous form described. *To be Revealed to the Worthy Alone.*

Those alone are worthy of the mysteries of the Light-treasure (the emanation of the Unapproachable God) who have abandoned the whole world and all that pertains thereto, its gods and powers, and have centred their whole faith in the Light, giving ear to one another, and submitting themselves the one to the other, as do the children of the Light.

Now inasmuch as the disciples have left father

The Lesser Mysteries.

and mother and brethren and all their possessions, and have followed Him and fulfilled His commandments, Jesus promises that He will reveal to them the mysteries as follows: The mystery of the Twelve Æons and their Receivers, and the mode of their invocation, so that the disciples may pass through their spaces; the mystery of the Invisible God (the Thirteenth Æon) and his Receivers (them of the Left), etc.; of them of the Middle, etc.; of them of the Right. But before all He will give them the mysteries of the three Baptisms—the Baptism of Water, the Baptism of Fire, and the Baptism of the Holy Spirit. Moreover He will give them the Mystery of Withdrawing the Malice or Naughtiness ($\kappa\alpha\kappa\iota\alpha$) of the Rulers, and thereafter the Mystery of the Spiritual Chrism.

The Good Commandments.

But they must remember that, when they in turn give these mysteries to others, they must command them not to swear falsely, nor even to swear at all; neither to fornicate nor commit adultery; neither to steal nor covet other men's goods; neither to love silver nor gold, nor invoke the names of the seventy-two evil Rulers or of their angels for any purpose; not to rob, nor to curse, nor calumniate falsely, nor to rail, but to let their yea be yea and their nay nay; in a word, they must fulfil the good commandments.

The disciples remind Jesus that His first promise had been that they should be given the mysteries of the Treasure of Light, the greater, which are above these lower mysteries of which He has spoken.

Seeing then that the disciples have not only

abandoned all things in the world and kept all the commandments, but have further now followed Him for twelve years, Jesus assures them that He will further give them the mysteries of the Light-treasure, to wit: The mystery of the Nine Guardians of the three Gates of the Light-treasure and the way of their invocation, so that they may pass through their spaces; the mystery of the Child of the Child, etc.; of the Three Amens; of the Five Trees; of the Seven Voices; the will (?mystery) of the Forty-nine Powers; the mystery of the Great Name of all names, that is of the Great Light which contains, or is beyond, the Treasure of Light. The master-mysteries of the Light-treasure are those of the Five Trees and of the Seven Voices and of the Great Name. There is, however, yet another supreme Mystery, which bestows upon a man all the rest—the Mystery of the Forgiveness of Sins; this Mystery transmutes the soul into pure light, so that it may be received into the Light of lights.

The Greater Mysteries.

Such souls have already inherited the Kingdom of God while still on earth; they have their share in the Light-treasure and are immortal Gods; and at death, when they leave the body, all the Æons disperse and flee to the west, to the left, until their souls arrive at the Gates of the Light-treasure. And the Gates are opened to them, and the Wardens give them their seals and their Great Name. So they pass within successively through the various Orders, where they receive the successive seals and master-words—within into the Five Trees and Seven Voices; yea, still farther

The Powers they Confer.

within, to the Orders of the Parentless, to the spaces of their inheritance—the Order of the Thrice-spiritual; until they reach the space of the Ieou, the Lord over the whole Treasure—the middle Treasure; thence ever within to the inner Treasures—the spaces of the interior of the interiors, the within of the within, to the Silences, to Peace Eternal, in those Everlasting Spaces.

All of these mysteries Jesus promises to give to His disciples, that they may be called "Children of the Fullness (Plērōma) perfected in all mysteries."

The Master then gathers His disciples, men and women, round Him with the words: "Come all of you and receive the three Baptisms, ere I tell you the mystery of the Rulers!"

The Mystic Rite of the Baptism of the Water of Life.

He bids them go to Galilee and find a man or woman in whom the greater part of evil (or the superfluity of naughtiness) is dead, that is to say, who has ceased from intercourse or sexuality (συνουσία), and receive from such a one two jars of wine and bring them to the place where He is, and also two vine branches.

They do so, and the Master sets forth a place of offering (θυσία), placing one wine-jar on the right and one on the left, and strews certain berries and spices round the vessels; He then makes the disciples clothe themselves in white linen robes, puts a certain plant into their mouths, and the number of the Seven Voices and also another plant in their hands, and ranges them in order round the sacrifice.

Jesus then spreads a linen cloth, and on it places a cup, and bread or loaves according to the number of the disciples; He surrounds this with olive-branches, and also puts wreaths of olive-branches on the heads of His disciples. He next seals their foreheads with a certain seal (the diagram of which, authentic name, and interpretation of it—also in the secret cypher—are given).

The Master then turns with his disciples to the four corners of the world, and the disciples are commanded to set their feet together (an attitude of prayer). He then offers a prayer which is prefixed with an invocation in the mystery-language, interspersed with triple Amens, and continues as follows:

"Hear Me, My Father, Father of all fatherhood, Boundless Light, who art in the Treasure of Light! May the Supporters [or Ministers ($παραστάται$)] come, who serve the Seven Virgins of Light who preside over the Baptism of Life! [The mystery-names of the Supporters are here given.] May they come and baptize My disciples with the Water of Life of the Seven Virgins of Light, and wash away their sins and purify their iniquities, and number them among the heirs of the Kingdom of Light! If now Thou hast heard Me and hast had pity on My disciples, and if they have been numbered among the heirs of the Kingdom of Light, and if Thou hast forgiven their sins and blotted out their iniquities, then may a wonder be done, and Zorokothora come and bring the Water of the Baptism of Life into one of these wine-jars!"

The wonder takes place, and the wine in the right-hand jar becomes water; and Jesus baptizes them, and gives them of the sacrifice, and seals them with the seal (? of the Supporters), to their great joy.

The Baptism of Fire.

This is the Baptism of Water; we are next given a description of the Baptism of Fire. In this rite the vine-branches are used; they are strewn with various materials of incense. The eucharist is prepared as before, and the rest of the details are almost identical; the number of the Seven Voices is again used, but the seal is different.

The prayer is longer than the preceding one, but all to the same purpose; the supernal baptizers are no longer the Ministers of the Seven Virgins, but the Virgin of Life, herself, the Judge; she it is who gives the Water of the Baptism of Fire. A wonder is asked for in "the fire of this fragrant incense," and it is brought about by the agency of Zorokothora, a name now interpreted as Melchizedec. What the nature of the wonder was, is not stated. Jesus baptizes the disciples, gives them of the eucharistic sacrifice, and seals their foreheads with the seal of the Virgin of Light.

The Baptism of the Holy Spirit.

Next follows the Baptism of the Holy Spirit. In this rite both the wine-jars and vine-branches are used; the details are otherwise very similar, the number of the Seven Voices being again employed. The supernal givers of the Baptism are not mentioned, but as the final sealing after the rite is with the seal of the Seven Virgins of Light, we may suppose that they are the givers of the Baptism. A wonder again takes place, but is not further specified.

After this we have the Mystery of Withdrawing

the Evil of the Rulers. There is here no mention of the eucharist, but in other respects the ceremonial is very similar, and consists of an elaborate incense-offering. The number is that of the First Amen and the seal is very elaborate. The prayer asks that Sabaōth Adamas and all his chiefs may come, and take away their (the Rulers') evil or naughtiness from the disciples. At the end of it the disciples are sealed with the seal of the Second Amen, and the Rulers have no longer any power over them; they have now become immortal, and can follow Jesus into all spaces whither they would go.

The Mystery of Withdrawing the Evil of the Rulers.

Jesus having now given the disciples the mysteries of the Baptisms, the mode of invoking the powers, their numbers, seals, and authentic names, promises to give them the apologies (defences or formulæ), whereby they will now be able to enter into the interior of the spaces or realms of these powers, and pass through them.

So far as they have been taught, they will be enabled, when out of the body, to pass through the realms apparently of the six Æons which have not repented, those of Sabaōth Adamas; these with all their rulers and indwellers will disperse before them. But on reaching the six great Æons (those apparently of Iabraōth, who repented and believed in the Light), they will be detained until they receive the Mystery of the Forgiveness of Sins.

The Powers the Lesser Mysteries Confer.

The Mystery of the Forgiveness of Sins is said to have its being in the interior of the interior of the Treasures of Light; it is the perfect salvation of the soul. He who receives it is more excellent than all the gods and powers of the twelve Æons of the Invisible God (the Ruler of the Thirteenth Æon). This Mystery is the Great Mystery of the Unapproachable God; it is the perfection of all mysteries, making the soul all-perfect.

The Mystery of the Forgiveness of Sins.

It is this Mystery which will enable the disciples to pass into the Æons of the Invisible God—that is, the spaces that no physical eye can see, beyond the elements of water, fire, and air (or æther) — the baptismal mysteries of which have been already given.

The Power it Confers.

But with the aid of the rite of the Mystery of the Forgiveness of Sins all the Æons will withdraw to the west, to the left, as veils before the eyes, up to the twelfth, which will then be so purified by the Light of the Light-treasure, that all the ways by which the disciples will have ascended will be purified; and moreover the exterior of the Light-treasure (the exterior being the Space of the Thirteenth Æon) will be revealed, and they will see Heaven from below. It will be at this point that Jesus will give them the apologies, seals, and numbers of the Mystery with their interpretations. And when they have received these and go out of the body, they will become pure light and soar upwards into the Light-treasure.

And then the Guardians of the Gates of the Treasure will open to them, and they will pass upwards and ever inwards through the following spaces, the powers therein rejoicing and giving them their mysteries, seals, and names of power: the Orders of the Three Amens, of the Child of the Child, of the Twin Saviours, of the Great Sabaōth, of the Great Iaō the Good, of the Seven Amens, of the Five Trees, of the Seven Voices; the Orders of the Uncontainables, of the Impassables; the Orders of those who are before and beyond (in time and space) the Uncontainables and Impassables; the Orders of the Unstainables, and of those who are before and beyond them; the Orders of the Immovables, and of those who are before and beyond them; the Orders of the Parentless, and of those that are before them; the Orders of the Five Impressions, of the Three Spaces, of the Five Supporters, of the Thrice-spiritual, of the Triple Power, of the First Precept (or Statute), of the Inheritance, of the Silences and of Peace, of the Veils which are drawn before the Great King of the Light-treasure, unto the Great Man himself, the King of the whole Light-realm, whose name is Ieou.

<small>The Ordering of the Light Treasures.</small>

These spaces and orderings are also mentioned in the *Pistis Sophia* treatise, but I have omitted them in the summary in order not to confuse the reader. The subject is exceedingly difficult, and no one has so far succeeded in reconstructing in detail the elaborate scheme of the Gnosis presupposed by the compiler or compilers of our treatises, owing in a great measure to the fragmentary state of the Codex Brucianus on the one hand and to the insufficient data of the Askew Codex on the other.

Still upwards and inwards are they to soar to the Space of the Great Light which surrounds or transcends the outer Treasure of Light itself. Ieou

<small>The Great Light.</small>

is there too, he is the Great Light; this is the Second or inner Light Treasure. The guardians will open the Gates and they will pass into the Orders of the Triple Powers of the Second Light Treasure; thence inwards to the twelfth Order of the twelfth Great Power of the emanation of the True God. There are twelve Great Powers with twelve Chiefs in each of their Orders (of which the authentic names are given). These Twelve will stand apart in this Space and invoke the True God with this "Name" (? prayer), saying:

<small>Invocation to the True God.</small>

"Hear us, O Father, Father of all fatherhood! [Here follows a sentence in the mystery-language containing four of the vowels each seven times repeated—with the interpretation: That is to say, Father of all fatherhood, for the All hath come out of the Alpha, and will return to the Ōmega when the consummation of all consummations will take place.] We will now invoke Thy imperishable Names that Thou mayest send forth Thy great Light-power, and that it follow these Twelve Uncontainables [that is to say, the twelve disciples], for they have verily received the Mystery of the Forgiveness of Sins, and therefore are they not to be held back from approaching Thy Light-Treasure."

Thereon the True God will send forth his Light-power; it will shine forth from behind the disciples, and cause all the Treasures of the Second Light-realm to withdraw, and they will reach the Space of the True God.

Then will the True God in turn invoke the

Unapproachable God, that is to say the One and Only One, and He will send forth a Light-power out of Himself, into the Space of the True God, and the disciples shall be perfected in all fullness and be made into an Order in that Treasure. They shall sing hymns of praise to the Unapproachable God, for, while still in the body, they have received the Mystery of the Forgiveness of Sins, and attained to the Space of the True God.

Invocation to the Unapproachable.

The disciples hereupon ask to be given this Great Mystery; the Master promises that He will give it; but before receiving it, they must be told the mystery of the Twelve (supernal) Æons, their seals, names, and apologies. These are given, seal-diagrams, names, numbers, and apologies; the last being in the form "Make way [mystery names], ye Rulers of the first (second, etc.) Æon, for I invoke [other mystery names—these being superior names of the Light-treasure]."

The Mystery of the Twelve Æons.

The sixth (? seventh) Æon is called the Little Midst, for it belongs to the six Æons which have believed on the Light; the Rulers of these Æons have a little good in them.

In the twelfth Æon is the Invisible God and Barbēlō and the Ingenerable God. The Invisible God is in a space alone in the twelfth Æon with veils drawn before him, and in that Æon are many other gods called the great rulers of the Æons, though servants of the Invisible God, Barbēlō and the Ingenerable God.

In the thirteenth Æon is the Great Invisible God, the Great Virginal Spirit (? Barbēlō) and the four and twenty emanations of the Invisible God. The mystery-names of these four and twenty are given, and also the invocation of the higher names of the Light-treasure in which are contained a series of triple ōmegas four times repeated, and a series of triple ētas four times repeated. The names of these emanations are said to be their names "from the beginning."

The Thirteenth Æon.

Yet higher in the fourteenth Æon is a second Great Invisible God, and another Great God called the "Great Just One" (χρηστός); he is a power of the three Light-rulers which are within all the Æons, but without the Treasure of Light. Here also are numbers of emanations. The powers of this Æon will try to detain the disciples in order that they may perform the mysteries of Jesus in those spaces, and so these powers themselves receive further powers from the powers of the Light-treasure. The disciples, however, are given the proper seals, numbers, and apologies, so that the powers shall withdraw.

The Fourteenth Æon.

Now the three Great Rulers that are within all these Invisibles (i.e., the emanations of the Thirteenth and Fourteenth Æons), but without the Treasure of Light, are called the Triple-powered Gods, and are above all others.

The Three Great Rulers.

They themselves have received the mysteries of the Treasure of Light, for when the First Power came forth (from the Light-kingdom) they first of all remained in it (the Power), and when they emerged from it the Kingdom of Light was preached to them. "I gave them," says the Master, "the mysteries which I have given unto you, but I have not given them the Mystery of the Forgiveness of Sins. . . . Therefore now I say unto you that I, when I shall separate all the Æons, will give to these three Rulers of the Light, who are in the last [highest] of all the Æons, the Mystery of the Forgiveness of Sins, because they have believed in the Mystery of the Light-realm."

No one can pass beyond them till he have received the Mystery of the Forgiveness of Sins; but, continues the Master, they are not to fear on this account, for there is no place of punishment in those spaces, for their indwellers received the Mysteries (? of Baptism).

The seals, names, and apologies of these powers are then given, and here unfortunately the text breaks suddenly off, and we come to the end of Schmidt's *Second Book of Ieou*.

Taking now Schmidt's *First Book* we next come to a description of the middle Light-world, and its Ruler, the True God, the Demiurgos, above whom are the Treasures of the Plērōma of the Father. Jesus is still the narrator. The subject is one of immense complexity, with infinite emanations, treasures (*i.e.*, storehouses of riches and fullness), spaces, orders, and hierarchies, with diagrams and symbols, and hosts of (to me) absolutely unintelligible "authentic" names, which are said to be "in the language of my Father." The authentic name of the supernal Demiurgos is translated as the True God or God of Truth, and is given in Greek transliteration as

Concerning Ieou the Emanator of the Middle Light-world.

Ieou, which Schmidt transliterates into German as Jeû.

The Tetragrammaton. I would suggest that Ieou is a transliteration of the four-lettered mystery name of the creator according to Semitic and Chaldæan tradition, the tetragrammaton of the Kabalah. Theodoret tells us that the Samaritans pronounced this name Iabe (Iave) and the Jews Iaō. Since the sixteenth century, by adding the vowels of Adonai to the unpronounceable Y H V H, it has been pronounced Jehovah. It is now generally written Yahweh; but there is no certainty in the matter, beyond the fact that Jehovah is absolutely wrong. Ieou or Iaō are probably attempts in Greek transliteration at the same Semitic name, which contained letters totally unrepresentable in Greek; Yahoo or Yahuwh perchance, the name hidden in Iacchus (Yach), still further corrupted into Bacchus by the Greeks. Iacchus was the mystery-name of the creative power in that great mystery tradition; Bacchus was the name in the popular cult. But to continue with our summary.

Jesus, the Living One, has apparently taken his disciples with Him through the inner spaces of the unseen world, and brought them to the plane of this True God, from which He gives the mystic instruction on the creative dispensation of the universe, in the Realm of Light.

He first shows them Ieou in his own nature, as a simple emanation from the Ineffable Treasures of the Father, before he has in his turn sent forth emanations by the command of the Father. A strange combination of letters and signs is said to be the

BOOK OF THE GREAT LOGOS. 535

"name" of this God "according to the treasures which are outside this region"—that is to say, either the planes below or sub-planes of that plane.

Next follows a diagram—a square surrounding a circle, within which is another square containing three lines; this diagram is said to be the type of the treasures over which Ieou will rule, and it is also the type of Ieou himself before he emanated. *The Type of the Treasures.*

But out of Ieou are to come a host of emanations, through the command of the Father, who are in their turn to become fathers of treasures; each of these fathers is also to be called Ieou. This ordering is effected by Jesus as the Logos; but the True God is the father of all of these fathers or fatherhoods, for he is a direct emanation from the Father, and through him and from him all subsequent emanation will proceed. Further, from each of the subordinate Ieou's, through the command of the Father, will proceed other hosts to fill the treasures, and they shall be called Orders (or hierarchies) of the Treasures of Light. Myriads of myriads will arise out of them. We are therefore in the Light-kingdom.

We are next given a diagram which is said to be the type of the True God before he emanated, that is to say when the subsequent emanations lay potential within him. The diagram is like an egg, with a smaller egg or nucleus within it containing three lines or strokes. The upper circumferences, or shells, of both the egg and the nucleus are lacking, as though to represent the creative Light-beam from the Father streaming into them. *The Type of the True God Ieou.*

The Mystic Diagrams.

It is very probable, therefore, that in these diagrams squares may represent treasures or the substance-side, while circles may represent gods or the energy-side—but these can interchange, for the substance of one plane or phase becomes the energy of the plane below. The three strokes seem to represent the potential triad or trinity latent in all manifestation, and this triad acting within the tetrad of the squares produces the infinite ordering into twelves or dodecads. We should also recollect that in all probability we have only a very faulty reproduction of these diagrams, for we have to take into account the translating and copying and re-copying by ignorant scribes.

The three lines are said to be the three Voices, which Ieou will send forth when he is ordered "to praise the Father," that is to say, to emanate, for this is how the creative song of praise is sung.

Cosmic Embryology.

Next we have a diagram of the first moment of this emanation; it is curious to notice that the symbols used closely resemble a spermatozoon and ovum. Within a square is a small circle with its diameter produced, so that it very well represents the head and tail of a spermatozoon; the ovum consists of three concentric circles, the innermost of which has a diameter and is of the same size as the head of the spermatozoon, which has also a similar diameter; there are thus two of the lines or strokes or Voices still latent, and only one is so far manifest.

Following this comes a diagram the upper half of which apparently repeats the preceding diagram, and the lower half consists of six concentric circles with a point in the centre. The latter is called the seal ($\chi\alpha\rho\alpha\kappa\tau\acute{\eta}\rho$) upon the face or forehead of Ieou, and is said to be the type of the treasures. This emanation from the True God is caused by the streaming into the True God of a Light-power from the ineffable treasures above, in response to an invocation of Jesus as the Logos, calling upon the Name of His Father. The Light-power is called the "Little Idea," presumably to signify that though it has power to energize all creation, it is but little compared to the real "Greatnesses" or Ideas in the Divine Mind.

The Seal on the Forehead of Ieou.

What follows is beyond my power of summarizing. We have diagrams of a series of twenty-eight Ieou's, before the text again breaks suddenly off. What was the full number in the original is now impossible to say; Schmidt supposes thirty. The diagrams appear to have been very carelessly copied, but present certain general characteristics. The upper part generally consists of six squares, one within the other; within the smallest square is the word Ieou, and the special mystery-name of the Ieou or treasure for which the diagram stands. These names are generally placed over a small oblong figure (or two lines), which are said to stand for the "root" of the spaces or regions in which the particular Ieou is placed. Above and below, cutting through the top and bottom sides of the six squares, are two parallel lines, which are said to denote the paths whereby one must travel if he would enter into the space of the father of the treasure. These paths

General Characteristics of the Diagram.

where they cross the sides of the square are marked by Greek letters, alphas, which are said to stand for the curtains or veils which are drawn before the father. Above each diagram of squares we find again the three lines or strokes, which are now said to be the three Gates or Doors of each treasure. Each treasure has twelve orders, the authentic names of the Heads of each of which are appended, together with the authentic names of the three Guardians or Watchers of the Gates.

The lower half of each diagram consists of the seal upon the forehead of the Ieou; these seals are mostly circles with varying contents, but it is exceedingly difficult to trace any connection between them.

The Twelve, the Order of Jesus. Between the second and third Ieou diagram is another figure differing entirely from the rest of the series; as to its meaning I have no notion. It is followed by these words of Jesus: "From these orders I will take Twelve and range them for Myself, that they may serve Me." This probably refers to the prototypes of the souls of the disciples which Jesus chooses for Himself before their incarnation, as we learn from the *Pistis Sophia*.

With the twenty-eighth diagram the text breaks off suddenly; and the next subject we meet with, according to Schmidt's ordering of the leaves, is a hymn which Jesus sings to the First Mystery.

After printing this fragment in this place, Schmidt came to the conclusion that these pages must be separated, and treated as fragments of another work, on the ground that they could not be brought into organic unity with the rest.

We are now in the lower space or plane of the Thirteen Æons, each of which has its father or creator, its Ieou, with rulers, and subordinate powers, called decans and liturgi, signifying servants, ministers, or workmen. There are thirteen praise-givings, one for each Æon, but the text of the first four is missing. The general tenour of each petition is as follows:

Hymn to the First Mystery sung in the Thirteen Æons.

"Give ear unto me, while I sing Thy praises, O Thou First Mystery, who didst shine forth in his mystery [i.e., the mystery of that particular Æon]; it was Thy Light which caused Ieou to order this Æon and establish therein its rulers, ministers, and workers. [Then follows the "imperishable name" of the Æon.] Save all my Members (Limbs), which since the foundation of the world have been scattered abroad in all the rulers, ministers, and workmen of this Æon, and gather them all together and receive them into the Light!"

The final petition is concluded by a threefold Amen.

The peculiarity of the praise-giving with regard to the Thirteenth Æon consists in the fact that it is treated apparently as a separate plane or space. By command of the First Mystery the Ieou of this space brought into existence the space of the four and twenty invisible emanations, with all their rulers, gods, lords, archangels and angels, their ministers and workmen; further to this space of the Thirteenth Æon are assigned the "three gods." Moreover, by command of

The Thirteenth Æon.

the First Mystery the six Rulers under Iabraōth, who have believed in the Light-kingdom, are set just below this Thirteenth Æon in a space of pure air, the six unrepentant Rulers being apparently assigned to the lower impure atmosphere.

With regard to the scattering of the Limbs, we may remind the reader of Epiphanius' quotation from *The Gospel of Philip:* "I have recognised myself and gathered myself together from all sides. I have sown no children to the Ruler [the lord of this world], but have torn up his roots; I have gathered together my limbs that were scattered abroad, and I know thee who thou art."

The Sixty Treasures.

We are now introduced to a new subject. Jesus is taking His Order, the twelve disciples, through the Treasures of the Middle Light-world, and giving them the seals, numbers, and authentic names whereby these Treasures can be entered and passed through. There are sixty of these Treasures, but our narrative begins only in the the fifty-sixth, for all the intervening pages are lost. From what we are here told I am inclined to think that there were also sixty diagrams of the Ieou's, and not thirty only as Schmidt supposes. Fundamentally there were presumably twelve main treasures, but each apparently was regarded from five different standpoints, each view-point being called an order or ordering. There was thus a twelve-fold ordering, and a five-fold ordering as well, all immanent in the God "who dwells in the Middle of the universe," that is to say, in Ieou, the God of the Middle Light-world. Of the five, two are called the exterior, two the interior, and one the middle order.

Each treasure is said to be surrounded by six regions or spaces, represented by the squares of the diagrams. By a use of the seals (a series of very curious diagrams), numbers, and names, the Guardians, Orders, and Veils are said to disperse and the innermost space of the father of the treasure is reached, and so the secret of his authentic name is revealed. Moreover within each treasure is a Door or Gate, and without three Gates; each of the outer Gates has three Guardians, but the inner gate has but one, presumably the father of the treasure himself.

On the conclusion of this exposition, the disciples ask how all these spaces and their fatherhoods have come into being. Jesus replies that it is because of the "Little Idea," which the Father has left behind and not withdrawn into Himself; all else of the Father He has withdrawn into Himself. "It was in this Little Idea that I streamed forth, having My being in the Father; I burst forth and freed Myself therefrom. I shone forth and it emanated Me, the first emanation therefrom, its perfect likeness and image. When it had emanated Me I stood before it." This was the First Voice.

The Little Idea.

Again it shone forth and emanated, sending forth the Second Voice—all these spaces, which came forth one after another.

The Third Voice streamed forth and emanated the rulers of all these spaces.

It is He, Jesus, the First Voice, the first emanation, who has gathered together His own Order—the Twelve, and taken them through all the spaces, that they may serve Him; He has given them the powers whereby they may pass through all these spaces within, to the innermost space of the ruler of them all, the True God.

<small>The Name of the Great Power.</small>

The disciples then remind Jesus that He had promised to give them the one master-name, whereby every space could be traversed without the wearisome repetition of each of the separate names—the Name that was the key to unlock every gate in every treasure. Is this, they ask, the Great Name of the Father?

The Christ (the first mention of this title) replied: "Nay, but the Name of the Great Power that is in all the spaces."

He then gives them this authentic name—apparently a sentence in cypher, interspersed with the triple repetition of the seven vowels. It is to be said in the Space of the True God, in the "space of the interiors which belongs to the space of the exteriors." The name must be invoked, turning to the four corners of the treasure, and then followed by the request that all the paths to the fatherhood be left free to the disciple, "for I have invoked the Great Name of the God of all the spaces." Then will all the veils be withdrawn, and all the rulers disperse; they will withdraw "into their own form."

"Lo, now," continued the Master, "I have told you the [master-name]; guard it, and do not repeat it continually, so that all the spaces may not be disquieted because of the glory therein."

Hereupon Jesus commands His disciples to follow Him, and goes yet farther within, into the seventh treasure; this cannot apparently be the seventh treasure of the sixty, but must be some other ordering. Here He commands them to surround Him, and answer Him with a threefold Amen for every praise-giving, as He sings a hymn of praise to the Father because of the emanation of the treasures.

Hymn to the Unapproachable God Sung in the Seventh Treasure.

The Father is addressed first by the Ineffable Name, symbols of which are given; then as "God, My Father," and then as the "Unapproachable One." The form of each praise-giving begins with the words: "I praise Thee, Thou Unapproachable God, for that Thou didst shine forth in Thyself," and ends with the question: "For what now is Thy will, but that all this should be, O Unapproachable God?"

The subject of the hymn is that God has withdrawn Himself into Himself, into His Truth, save only one Little Idea, the space of which He has left as the shining Light-world, shining within the Father. It is a radiance of the Father within Himself, according to His will. This Light is Jesus, the one emanation of the Father through His will. Jesus is the perfect likeness and whole image of God. The second emanation brings into being the spaces which surround the Father. The third emanation is the bringing into being the powers and rulers of the Light-spaces, which are called Treasures. Moreover all these powers are energized by a Great Power emanated by the Father, so that they are called True Gods, that is, Gods in Truth (presumably as distinguished from the Gods of the vulgar pantheons). It is this Power that energizes not only in the various fathers of the treasures, but also in the subordinate powers.

Thus also are emanated the Guardians or Watchers and the sixty fatherhoods, one for each treasure. These sixty are called the " Orders of the Five Trees." It is also this Power which has brought into existence the seals and the great name. This same Power is further called the [First ?] Mystery and the Light-image surrounding the Father.

<small>The Great Logoi according to the Mystery.</small>

These Light-spaces are called the Spaces of the " Great Logoi according to the Mystery," in whom is the glory of the Father. This leads us to suppose that the " Great Logos " of the title of the treatise is the same as the First Mystery, the Great Power, and therefore identical with Jesus. The Great Logoi are also called Ieou's. The hymn then continues :

" I praise Thee, O Unapproachable God, for that Thou didst shine forth in Thyself ; Thou hast emanated Thy One and Only Mystery, Thou who art an unapproachable God even for these Logoi. Thou art an unapproachable among them, in this Great Logos according to the Mystery of Ieou, the father of all Ieou's, which is Thyself;—yet what is else Thy one and only will but that we should draw nigh Thee in them, O God that none can approach, to whom nevertheless we have drawn near in this Great Logos according to the Mystery of Ieou ? "

I am inclined to think that " Logos " is here used in two meanings. It generally means Reason or

Word; here it seems to mean also Sermon, Discourse, or Teaching.

The hymn ends with praises in which the Father is again said to have withdrawn, or inbreathed, Himself entirely into His Universal Likeness and Idea, with the single exception of the Little Idea, leaving it as a means whereby His boundless Riches, universal Glory, and mighty Mysteries might be manifested. The Great or Universal Idea and the Little Idea are thus seen to correspond in the ideal spiritual world to the ideas of the macrocosm and microcosm. And so ends this remarkable hymn, with a final triple Amen. *The Universal Idea.*

The two remaining fragments are put by Schmidt in an appendix. The first fragment is part of a hymn of praise, each praise-giving of which begins with the words:

"Give ear unto me, while I sing Thy praises, Thou Mystery before all Uncontainables and Impassables, who didst shine forth in Thy Mystery, in order that the Mystery that is from the beginning should be completed." *Hymn to the [? First] Mystery.*

The contents of the hymn are as follows, the imperishable names being added after each technical term:

The Mystery shining forth became Water of the Ocean. The Earth in the midst of the Ocean became purified. The whole vast matter of the Ocean became purified—that is to say, the Sea and all species existing therein. Through its shining forth it sealed the Sea and all that are therein, for the power that is in them was in disorder (? chaos) against the existing order (? cosmos).

The hymn here breaks off suddenly, and we have
The Way of the Midst. a description of the passing of the soul through the regions of the dæmonian powers, and of the imperishable names of the "mystery of their fear," whereby the soul can escape from their clutches. These are the spaces of the orders of the various great ministers of the Great Powerful Ruler in the Way of the Midst; and the names of these ministers, recoverable from this scrap, are the same as the Rulers of the Way of the Midst as given in the *Extracts from the Books of the Saviour.* This Great Powerful Ruler is further described as "he who is filled with wrath." He is the successor of the Ruler of the Outer Darkness, of that space which changes all forms. He is spread out on the Way of the Midst, so that he may carry off the souls like a robber.

The leaves on which these fragments are found differ from the rest of the MS. in that they are surrounded by single-lined borders.

SELECTIONS FROM THE UNTITLED APOCALYPSE OF THE CODEX BRUCIANUS.

THE beginning is lost, and the leaves that are left us plunge into the midst of a description of the supernal beings and spaces as follows:

"He [the God beyond Being] established Him, that they might strive towards the City in which is their Image. In this City it is that they move and live; it is the House of the Father, and the Vesture of the Son, and the Power of the Mother, and the Image of the Fullness (Plērōma). He is the First Father of the All; He is the first Being; He is the King of the Intangibles. It is He in whom the All moves. It is He in whom He gave it (the All) Form. This is the self-produced and self-generated Space; this is the Depth of the All. He is the Great One whose real being is deeper than the Depth. He it is to whom the All did come. The All was silent before Him and spake not to Him, for unspeakable and incomprehensible is He. He is the first Source; He it is whose Voice hath gone forth into all spaces. He is the first Tone, whereby the All doth sense and comprehend. He it is whose Limbs (Members) make a myriad of myriads of Powers, each one of which comes from them. *[The First Being.]*

"The second space came into being, which is to be called Demiurge, and Father, and Logos, and Source, and Mind, and Man, and Eternal, and Limitless. This is the Pillar (or Support); He is the Overseer. He, too, is Father *[The Second Being.]*

of the All; He it is upon whose Head the Æons form a wreath, shooting forth their rays. The Outline of His Face is beyond all possibility of knowing in the outer Worlds—those Worlds which ever seek His Face, desiring to know it, for His Word has gone forth into them, and they long to see Him. The Light of his Eyes penetrates the Spaces of the Outer Plērōma, and the Word which comes forth from his Mouth penetrates the Above and Below [of the Outer Worlds]. The Hair of His Head is the number of the Hidden Worlds, and the Outline of his Face is the type of the Æons. The Hairs of his Face are the number of the Outer Worlds, and the out-spreading of his Hands is the manifestation of the Cross; the out-spreading of the Cross is the ninefold, on the Right and the Left.

The Supernal Cross.

"The source of the Cross is the Man whom no man can comprehend. He is the Father; He is the Source from which the Silence wells; He it is who is desired in every Space. He is the Father from whom came forth the Monad like a light-spark, in comparison with which (Monad) all Worlds are as [? darkness]; for it is the Monad which has moved all things in their out-shining. And they have received Gnosis, and Life, and Hope, and Peace, and Love, and Resurrection, and Faith, and Rebirth, and the Seal. These are the ninefold which have come from the Father of those who are without beginning, from Him who is Father and Mother to Himself alone, whose Plērōma surrounds [that is transcends] the Twelve Depths.

The Twelve Depths.

THE UNTITLED APOCALYPSE.

"1. The first Depth is the All-source from which all Sources have come.

"2. The second Depth is the All-wise One from which all Wise ones have come.

"3. The third Depth is the All-mystery from which all Mysteries have come.

"4. The fourth Depth is the All-gnosis from which all Gnosis hath come.

"5. The fifth Depth is the All-holy from which all Holiness hath come.

"6. The sixth Depth is the Silence from which all Silence hath come.

"7. The seventh Depth is the Gate which hath no substance, from which all Substances have come.

"8. The eighth Depth is the Forefather from whom all Forefathers have come.

"9. The ninth Depth is the All-father-Self-father, in which all Fathers exist,—He being the only father they have.

"10. The tenth Depth is the All-power from which all Powers have come.

"11. The eleventh Depth is that in which is the First Invisible, from which all Invisibles have come.

"12. The twelfth Depth is the Truth from which all Truth hath come.

"This [the second space, as a Monad, which surrounds the Depths], is the Truth which embraces them all; this is the Image of the Father; this is the Truth of the All; this is the Mother of all [their] Æons; this it is which surrounds all Depths. This is the Monad which is incomprehensible or unknowable; this it is which has

The Primal Source.

no Seal (or Mark), in which are all Seals; which is blessed for ever and ever. This is the eternal Father; this the ineffable, unthinkable, incomprehensible, untranscendible Father; this it is in which the All became joyous; it rejoiced and was joyful, and brought forth in its joy myriads of myriads of Æons; they were called the 'Births of Joy,' because it (the All) had joyed with the Father. These are the Worlds from which the Cross upsprang; out of these incorporeal Members did the Man arise.

The Unmanifested.

"This is the Father and the Source of All, whose Members are gathered together and completed. All Names have come from the Father—whether such Names as Ineffable, or Unknowable, or Incomprehensible, or Invisible, or Single, or Solitary, or Power, or All-power, or whether all those Names which are named in silence alone—all of them come from the Father, whom all the outer Worlds behold as the stars of the firmament in the night. As men desire to see the sun, so do the outer Worlds desire to see the Father, because of his invisibility which is round about Him. For ever to the Æons doth He give Life, and through His Word hath the Indivisible [? Atom] learnt to know the Monad; and by His Word hath the holy Plērōma come into being.

The Manifested, the Plērōma.

"This is the Father, the second Demiurge; through the Breath of His Mouth Forethought made the that-which-is-not. The that-which-is-not arose through the will of Him, for He it is who commands the All to come into being. In this wise hath He made the holy Plērōma: four Gates, and in it (the Plērōma) are four Monads, a Monad for each Gate, and six Supporters for each Gate, making four and twenty Supporters, and four and twenty myriads of Powers for each Gate; and nine Ennads for every Gate, and ten Decads for every Gate, and twelve Dodecads for every Gate, and five Pentads of Powers for every Gate, and an Overseer who hath three faces—an ingenerable, a true, and an ineffable face, for every Gate.

"One of his faces looks without the Gate to the outer Æons, and the other looks on Setheus, and the third looks upwards—to the Sonship in each Monad [*i.e.*, the one Sonship contained in the four Monads], where [*i.e.*, above] is Aphrēdōn with his twelve Righteous Ones. There [above] is the Forefather; in that space is Adam [the Man] who belongs to the Light, and his three hundred and sixty-five Æons, and there is the Perfect Mind, [all three] surrounding a Basket [? network, representing a conical swirl of forces or atoms] that knows no death. *Three-faced and Two-faced Space.*

"The ineffable face of the Overseer looks within to the Holy of Holies—that is, to the Boundless one, he being the head of the Holy Place (Shrine). He has two faces; one opens to the space of the Depth and the other opens to the space of the Overseer who is called the 'Child.' And there is there [within] a Depth which is called the 'Light' or the 'Shining One,' in which is hidden an Alone-born (μονογενής), who manifests three Powers and is mighty in all Powers.

"He [the Alone-born] is the Indivisible; He it is who is never divided; it is for Him that the All has opened [? divided] itself, for to Him belong all the Powers."

The above passages, taken in order from the first pages, according to Schmidt's arrangement of the leaves, will give the reader some idea of the nature of the unabridged contents of this apocalyptic treatise. For the rest we must content ourselves with a translation of some of the more intelligible or striking passages.

The View of the Commentator. The original seer seems to have endeavoured to describe his vision of the inner spaces from different points of view, or rather to have seen the same mystery from various points of view, or aspects, in a series of visions. Interspersed we find the comments of another writer. The first indubitably clear instance of this is a passage of which unfortunately sad havoc has been made by the Coptic translator. The commentator tells us that the subject is very difficult, nay that it is utterly impossible to describe those things with the "tongue of flesh"; nevertheless he does not think that any one could succeed any better than has the original seer, or those who spoke or wrote through him. These spaces and beings are more excellent than the intellectual powers in man, and therefore it is impossible for any one to understand them, unless he have the good fortune to meet with a "kinsman" of those higher ones—that is to say, a "relative of the mystery"—one who has learned the mystery, that is to say, has experienced these states of consciousness;

and even then the Mystery of the Father cannot be expressed in its reality, as has been stated by even such advanced seers as Marsanēs and Nicotheus, former seers of the Gnosis; all the Perfect have seen Him, and have sung His praises each as best he could, but they have all failed to reveal Him. And a little later, in commenting on the "Metropolis of the Alone-begotten," the same writer quotes from another Master of the Gnosis, who, when he had understood, said: "Through Him is That-which-really-is and That-which-really-is-not, through which the Hidden-which-really-is and the Manifest-which-really-is-not exists." The Gnostic from whom this sentence is quoted is called Phōsilampēs; but the ideas are so identical with those of Basilides, that I cannot but think Phōsilampēs is merely some cryptonym of the school for this teacher.

Marsanēs, Nicotheus, and Phōsilampēs.

The Logos and His creative powers and self-emanation is the subject of much of our treatise. To take one instance out of many:

"This is Setheus, who dwells in the Shrine as a King and God. He is the Logos-Creator; it is He who commandeth the All to work. He is the Creative Mind according to the command of God, the Father; whom the creature adores as God, and as Lord, and as Saviour, and is subject to Him; at whom all things stand in wonder because of His grace and beauty; for whose head the inner universe forms a crown, and the outer is set under His feet, while the middle universe surroundeth Him, praising Him and saying:

The Creative Logos.

"'Holy, holy, holy is He, the [here follow the seven vowels each three times repeated]; that is to say: Thou art the Living One among the living; Thou art the Holy One among the holy; Thou art Being among beings; Thou art Father among the fathers; Thou art God among the gods; Thou art Lord among the lords; Thou art Space among the spaces.'

"Thus too do they praise Him: 'Thou art the House and Thou art the Dweller in the House.' And yet again do they praise and address the Son hidden in Him: 'Thou art, Thou art the Alone-begotten, Light, Life, and Grace.'"

We are told of the descent of the Light-spark or Light-stream from on high, and how it finally reaches matter.

The Descent of the Light-spark.
"Then the Veils were opened and Light penetrated to Matter below, and to those which possessed no form and no likeness; and thus have they gained for themselves the likeness of the Light. Some indeed rejoiced that the Light had come to them, and that they had become rich; others wept, because they had become poor, and what was theirs had been taken away from them. Thus came Grace in that which had come forth. And captivity was taken captive and praised the Æons who had received the Spark in themselves. And Guardians were sent them . . .; they gave help to those who had believed in the Light-spark."

The Spiritual Atom.
"And this [the Light-spark] is the Indivisible, which led the struggle for the universe; and all things were bestowed upon him, through Him who is exalted above all things; and the immeasurable

Depth was bestowed upon him, together with the countless fatherhoods that are therein."

In the field of its being is the God-bearing or God-generating Land. And the powers of him who is crowned with this Light-wreath, sing praises to the King, the Alone-begotten, the Logos, saying:

"Through Thee have we won fame, and through Thee have we seen the Father of all, and the Mother of all things hidden in all spaces, the Conceiver of all æons. She is the Conceiver of all gods and all lords; she is the Gnosis of all invisibles. Thy Image is the mother of all Uncontainables and the power of all Impassables. . . . Through Thy Image we saw Thee, fled to Thee, stood in Thee, and received the unfading wreath, which has been known through Thee. Praise to Thee, for ever and ever, O Thou Alone-begotten One. Amen!"

Hymn to the Logos.

Of such a one we learn: "He became a body of light and penetrated into the æons of the Indivisible, until he reached the Alone-begotten, who is in the Monad [the Father] who dwells in silence alone. And they [his powers] received the Grace of the Alone-begotten, that is to say His goodness, and he received the eternal wreath. He [the Logos] is the Father of all the Light-sparks; His is the chief of all immortal bodies; this is He for whose sake resurrection is granted to these [immortal] bodies."

The Christ.

Higher and higher grades of being are described, and we hear of the Perfected One "who has received the Grace of the Unknowable, and thereby such a Son-ship as the Plērōma could not endure, because of the superfluity of its light and the brilliancy which was in Him."

The Glorified of the Logos. Still higher soars the intuition of the Gnostic seer, and we read further of the Logos-Demiurgos, "with whom is a host of powers having wreaths (or crowns) on their heads. Their crowns send forth rays; the brilliancy of their bodies is as the life of the space into which they are come; the word (logos) that comes out of their mouth is eternal life, and the light that comes forth from their eyes is rest for them; the movement of their hands is their flight to the space out of which they are come, and their gazing on their own faces is knowledge of themselves; the going to themselves is a repeated return, and the stretching out of their hands establishes them; the hearing of their ears is the perception in their heart, and the union of their limbs is the in-gathering of the dispersion of Israel; their holding to one another is their fortification in the Logos. . . .

The At-onement. "And the whole at-onement was accomplished of the Creator-Logos with those who had come forth from the re-ordering which had been brought to pass. And they became all One, as it is written: 'They became all One in the One and Only One.'

"Then the Logos-Creator became Divine Power, and Lord, and Saviour, and Christ [or Righteous—χρηστὸς frequently occurring throughout the MS. for χριστός], and Good, and Father, and Mother. He it is whose labour has succeeded; He was honoured and became the Father of them who believed. He became the Lord and the Mighty One."

In this consummation, all things are ordered anew for the Victor. "To Him is given the first fruits of the sacrifice of the Sonship, whereby He is given power to become thrice-powerful. And He received the vow of the Sonship, because the universe has been sold [? into slavery]; and He received the struggle [task] which was entrusted to Him. He raised up the whole purity of matter and made it into a World, an Æon, and a City, which is called 'Immortality' and 'Jerusalem.' And it is also called the 'New Earth,' and 'Self-sufficing,' and 'Perfect Freedom.' That Land is a god-bearing and a quickening land."

Soteriology.

The Wreath and Robe of the glorified is sung of. "This is the Wreath of which it is written: 'It was given to Solomon on the day of the joy of his heart.'

"The first Monad has sent Him an ineffable Vesture, which is all Light, and all Life, and all Resurrection, and all Love, and all Hope, and all Faith, all Wisdom, and all Gnosis, and all Truth, and all Peace. . . . And in it is the universe, and the universe has found itself in it, and known itself therein. And it gave them all light in its ineffable Light, myriads of myriads of powers were given it, in order that it should raise up the universe once for all.

The Ineffable Vesture.

"It [? the Monad] gathered its vestures to itself, and made them after the fashion of a veil, which surrounds it on all sides, and poured itself over them, and raised up all, and separated them all according to orders and laws and forethought.

"And that-which-is separated itself from that-which-is-not, and that-which-is-not is the evil which has manifested itself in matter. And the Vesture-power separated that-which-is from that-which-is-not, and called that-which-is 'eternal' (æonian), and that-which-is-not 'matter'; and it divided in the midst that-which-is from that-which-is-not, and laid between them veils and purifying powers in order that they might cleanse and purge them."

The Purification of the Lower Nature.

The future work of the Glorified is further described: "And myriads of myriads of glories and angels and archangels and ministers were given Him to serve Him—those of matter. And authority over all things was given Him, and He created for Himself a mighty Æon, and in it laid a vast Plērōma, and in it a mighty Sanctuary, and all the powers He had received He placed in them. And He rejoiced in them, as He brought forth His creatures once again, according to the commandment of the Father who is hidden in silence, who sent Him these treasures. And the crown of Fatherhood was given Him, for He (the Father) has established Him as father of those who arose after Him [namely, His disciples, the disciples of the Master].

The World-Saviour.

"And He cried out and said: 'My children, with whom I travail until the Christ is formed in you'; and again He cries: 'Yea, I would set beside a holy virgin an only husband Christ.'

"So when He had seen the Grace with which the hidden Father had endowed Him, He himself desired to lead back the universe to the hidden Father, for

His [the Father's] will is this, that the universe should return to Him.

"And they [those who repented] fled before the matter of the [lower] æon, abandoning it, and soared upward to the Æon of Him who is father to Himself alone, and took the vow on themselves which was vowed for them by Him who says: 'He who hath forsaken father and mother, brother and sister, wife and child, and possessions, and will take up his cross and follow Me, he will receive the promises which I have vowed to him; and I will give such the mystery of the hidden Father, for they have loved what is His and have fled from him who has pursued them with force.' *The Promise.*

"So he gave them Glory, Joy, Jubilation, Gladness, Peace, Hope, Faith, Love, and Truth imperishable. This is the ninefold which is given unto them who have fled from matter. And they have become blessed and perfect, and have recognized the True God, and known the mystery which is given to the Man, for which cause He hath revealed Himself until they saw Him, for He [the True God] is in truth invisible; for their sakes hath He revealed in words His Logos, so that they might know Him and become gods and perfect."

Still speaking of the First-born and His glories, the cosmic powers of His spiritual vesture are again described:

"They gave Him a Vesture to consummate everything in Him. And in it are all bodies: the body of fire, the body of water, the body of ether, the body of earth, the body of air, the body of *The Powers of the Light-vesture.*

the angels, the body of the archangels, the body of the powers, the body of the mighty ones, the body of the gods, and the body of the lords; in one word, in it are all bodies, so that none may prevent Him from going upwards and downwards to the under-world.

"He is the First-born to whom the Inner and the Outer have promised everything He may desire. He it is who hath separated all matter; and as He hath poured Himself over it, 'like a hen which spreadeth her wings over her chickens,' so hath the First-born prepared matter and raised up myriads and myriads of species and kinds. And when the matter had grown warm, it set free the multitude of powers which are His; and they sprang up like herbs, and were separated according to kinds and species. And He gave them the law—to love one another, and to honour God, and praise Him, and seek for Him, who He is, and what He is, and to wonder at the place whence they have come out, for it is narrow and difficult, and not to return thither again, but to follow Him who hath given them the law.

The Mothers of Men.

"And He raised them out of the darkness of matter, which is their mother, and told them what Light is, for they had not yet known of the Light, whether it existed or not. Then He gave them the commandment never to injure one another, and went from them to the Mother of the universe, beside the Father, that they might [in turn] give laws to those who have come out of matter."

And the powers of the Mother sing a hymn to the Son, praising the One and Only One, and saying:

"Thou alone art the Boundless; Thou alone the Depth; Thou alone the Unknowable; Thou art He for whom all seek, and yet [unaided] find Thee not, for no one can know Thee against Thy will, and no one can praise Thee against Thy will. Thy will alone is it which became space for Thee, for no one can contain Thee, for Thou art the space of all. I pray Thee give orderings to those of the world, and regulations to my offspring according to Thy will. And grieve not my offspring, for no one is ever grieved by Thee; yet no one hath ever known Thy counsel. Thou art He of whom they all, both inner and outer, stand in need, for Thou alone art uncontainable, and Thou alone art beyond all vision, and Thou alone art beyond all substance; Thou who alone hast given seals [distinguishing marks or characteristics] to all creatures, and manifested them in Thyself.

The Song of Praise of the Mother Above.

"Thou too art Creator of those which have not yet manifested themselves. Thou alone knowest these; we know them not. Thou alone indicatest them to us, that we [the powers] may pray Thee for her [the Mother Sophia's] sake to manifest them to us, for we can know them through Thee alone. Thou alone hast exalted Thyself to the host of hidden worlds, that they might know Thee; it is Thou who hast given them to know Thee, that Thou hast brought them to birth in Thy incorporeal body, and Thou hast taught them

The Hidden Worlds.

that Thou hast begotten the Man in Thy self-born Mind, and in Thy Reflection and Conception.

The Man. "He is the Man begotten of Mind, to whom Reflection gave form. Thou hast given all things to the Man. He weareth them like these garments, and putteth them on like these vestures, and wrappeth Himself with the creation as with a mantle. This is the Man whom the universe prays to learn to know. Thou alone hast commanded the Man that he should manifest himself, that Thou shouldst be known through him, that Thou hast begotten him. Thou hast manifested Thyself according to Thy will. Thou art He to whom I pray, Thou Father of all fatherhood, God of all gods, Lord of lords—the 'I' who implores Him that He may order my forms and offspring, that I may prepare joy for them in Thy name and in Thy power."

[The hymnody becomes confused as the mystic identifies himself with the Sophia.]

"Thou One and Only King, Thou who changest not, give me a power, and I will cause my offspring to know Thee, that Thou art their Saviour."

The infinite Light-spark descends on the Sophia; the world-ordering is consummated in the world-drama; the purification of the inner nature achieved in the individual soul.

The Lord of Splendour. "And the Lord of Splendour descended and separated the matter and divided it into two parts and into two regions; and He gave boundaries to each region, regions that come from one father and one mother. And they who had fled to Him adored

Him; He gave them the place on His right, and bestowed on them eternal life and deathlessness. And He called the right the 'Place of Life,' and the left the 'Place of Death'; the right the 'Place of Light' and the left the 'Place of Darkness'; the right the 'Place of Rest' and the left the 'Place of Suffering.' And He drew boundaries and veils between them, so that they should not perceive each other, and placed watchers at the veils. And He gave to them who worshipped Him many honours, and exalted them above those who resisted and opposed Him. And He extended the space on the right into countless spaces, and made them into many orders, many æons, many worlds, many heavens, many firmaments, many regions, many places, many spaces; and He established laws for them and gave them regulations. 'Be steadfast in My word and I will give you eternal life, and send you powers; and I will strengthen you in spirits of power, and give you authority according to your will. And no one shall hinder you in what ye desire; and ye will beget for yourselves æons, worlds, and heavens, in order that the mind-born spirits may come and dwell therein. And ye will be gods, and will know that ye come from God, and will see Him that He is God in you, and He will dwell in your æon.' *His Promise to them who Believe.*

"These words said the Lord of the universe to them, and disappeared from them, and hid Himself from them.

"And the births of matter rejoiced that they had been remembered, and were glad that they had come out of the narrow and difficult place, and prayed to the hidden Mystery:

The Prayer of the Earth-born.

"'Give us authority that we may create for ourselves æons and worlds, according to Thy word, upon which Thou didst agree with Thy servant; for Thou alone art the changeless one, Thou alone the boundless, the uncontainable, self-thought, self-born, self-father; Thou alone art the unshakeable and unknowable; Thou alone art silence, and love, and source of all; Thou alone art virgin of matter, spotless; whose race no man can tell, whose manifestation no man can comprehend.

"'Hear me, in sooth, Father imperishable, Father immortal, God of the hidden worlds, Thou only Light and Life; Thou the only invisible, ineffable, unstainable, invincible; Thou alone prior to all existence! Hear our prayer, with which we pray Him who is hid in all places; Hear us and send us spirits incorporal, that they may dwell with us and teach us of those things that Thou hast promised us; that they abide in us and we may be bodies for them. For Thy will is this, that this may be; may it be! Give law to our work and establish it, according to Thy will and according to the statute of the hidden æons, and regulate us of Thyself, for we are Thine!'"

The Powers of Discrimination are Given Them.

In answer to this prayer it is described how that the mysteries (*sci.*, of baptism and the rest) were given to those who repented; these mysteries being in grades of purification, whereby the man rises to higher grades of consciousness, by the purity of his inner vehicles, which correspond with certain states or regions.

"And He hearkened to them and sent out separating powers, which know the statute of the hidden æons. He sent them out according to the command of the hidden ones, and established orderings, according to the ordering of the height and according to the hidden statute. They began from below upwards, so that the building might be duly erected in all its courses.

"He created the air-world as a resting-place for those who had come forth [from matter], so that they might abide there until the establishing of those beneath them; thereafter the true dwelling-place [?]; within this the place of repentance; within this the ætherial reflections [? of the mansions of the Inheritance]; within these the self-born reflections. At that place they baptize themselves in the Name of the Self-born, who is God over them; and powers are established there beside the spring of the Water of Life. . . .

<small>The Ladder of Purification.</small>

"Within these is the Pistis Sophia and the pre-existing and ætherial Jesus with his twelve æons."

The names of the powers in the last two spaces are given, but unfortunately a lacuna follows in the MS., and the following leaves are damaged in numerous places. Still higher and higher spaces are described as the purified souls mount the Great Ladder.

The Heavenly Man, and the Lord of the Plērōma, is sung of: "The Father has sealed Him as His Son in their interior, in order that they should learn to know Him in their interior. And the Name moved them in their interior, so that they saw the Invisible Unknowable. And they praised the One and Only

<small>The Son of God.</small>

One, and Conception, and the Mind-born Logos, praising the three, who are one, for through Him they became supersubstantial. And the Father took their whole likeness and made it into a City or into a Man; He limned the universe in His likeness—that is to say, all these powers. Each one of them knew Him in this City; all began to sing myriads of songs of praise of the Man or the City of the Father of the universe. And the Father has taken his glory and made it into a Vesture without for the Man. . . . He created his body in the type of the holy Plērōma."

Hereupon follows the whole configuration of the Limbs of the Heavenly Man. The rest of the MS. is taken up with a Hymn to the Light quoted from some other Gnostic hymn-maker, introduced by the words "he says," and runs as follows:

Hymn to the Light. "I praise Thee, O Father of all fathers of the Light; I praise Thee, O boundless Light more excellent than all the boundless ones; I praise Thee, O uncontainable Light surpassing all uncontainables; I praise Thee, O ineffable Light, before all ineffables."

And so on through an infinity of praise-givings, frequently of great beauty, until the MS. breaks off suddenly in the middle of a sentence.

NOTES ON THE CONTENTS OF THE BRUCE AND ASKEW CODICES.

THE attentive reader will have already perceived that the contents of the *Pistis Sophia* treatise, of the *Extracts from The Books of the Saviour*, and of the fragments given under the title *The Book of the Great Logos according to the Mystery*, are closely related together; they indubitably belong to the same school. The result of the researches of Schmidt into this very interesting question may be most clearly seen in his reply to Preuschen's criticism on his work, a copy of which was kindly sent me by Schmidt himself. (See *Zeitschrift für wissenschaftliche Theologie*, Pt. iv., 1894.) Schmidt here sums up his position, bringing together the results of his researches.

The Kinship of the Titled Treatises.

If I might myself venture a general opinion on so difficult and abstruse a subject, I would say that all the three compilations we are considering, belong not only to the same school, but also to one and the same effort at syntheticizing and reformulation. It is evident that each of them contains older materials, and it is almost certain that the writer of the *Pistis Sophia* was acquainted with the material of the Extracts of the Ieou and Baptism expositions. The far more difficult question is the relationship of the Extracts to *The Book of the Great Logos*, and the most difficult question of all is the school and authors to which to assign them.

Date.

So far there is nothing absolutely proved as to date, except that the compilers of these documents had access to the same Sayings-material as the compilers of the Canonical Gospels; the *terminus a quo* may, therefore, be placed somewhere about the end of the first quarter of the second century. But the curious phrase used in introducing a quotation from the Pauline Letters ("Thou didst say unto us aforetime by the mouth of Paul our brother") shows such complete indifference to the Canonical *Acts* account, that it argues an early date. Because of the complex nature of the contents, however, they have been ascribed by some to the third century; but this does not seem to me to be sufficient reason for so late a date, when we consider the complex nature of the new-found pre-Irenæic Gnostic work, and the exceedingly abstruse character of the contents of the superior untitled MS. of the Codex Brucianus, the contents of which Schmidt places well in the second century.

Authorship.

Some of the materials are undoubtedly very old indeed, but it is the compilation-problem that at present engages us. I think that all three were compiled by the same group, or even by the same writer (though the latter will seem a very rash hypothesis to some). It is evident that the treatises pertain to the most intimate centre of Gnosticism, familiar with the inmost traditions, the most secret documents, and the practical inner experiences of the school. It matters not whether you call this stream of the Gnosis, "Ophite," "Barbēlō-Gnostic," "Gnostic, or "Valentinian"; such names could have meant little for the compiler or compilers of these documents.

Now it is evident that the *Extracts* and part of *The Book of the Great Logos* are both based on the same original. It is true that the text of the Baptism extract of the Askew Codex differs slightly from the text of the same rite in the Bruce Codex, but they are probably translated by different hands, and both translators used great freedom in their version, and were often puzzled how to put the Greek into Coptic, as is evident in many passages.

A certain reformulation of the Gnosis is, then, referred to as *The Books of the Saviour* or *The Book of the Great Logos*; perhaps the original Greek document or documents had no title, and it was the copiers, or the Coptic translators and scribes, who added these titles. The *Pistis Sophia* treatise, however, refers to a work called *The Two Books of Ieou*, and further adds that they were given by the Saviour to Enoch and preserved from the Flood.

_{The Titles.}

Now it seems to me that if these references in the *Pistis* are not interpolations, *The Two Books of Ieou* cannot be identical with the common document in the *Extracts* and *The Book of the Great Logos*, but that this document was an overworking and reformulation of these two Books. *The Books of Ieou* belonged presumably to some ancient tradition, probably Egyptian, containing a host of symbols and seals, pass-words and mystery-names, and much else which were referred to what Manetho calls "the Egypt before

_{The Books of Ieou.}

the Flood" (the Egypt of the "First Hermes" or Agathodæmon), the traditions of which were equated with the Semitic traditions by Jewish and Christian Gnostic circles. I have dealt with this subject at length in my work on the Trismegistic literature.

The Probable Author.

I believe, then, that the common document in the *Extracts* and *The Book of the Great Logos* was not the actual *Books of Ieou* referred to in the *Pistis Sophia*, but that it contained the substance of the Ieou Books, worked up by a Gnostic writer into a new form. I further suggest that this writer was the same as the author of the *Pistis Sophia* treatise, who reformulated the *Books of Ieou* in the light of the Gnosis of the Living Master. These things, however, do not seem to have been done in order; they were more probably the various attempts at some consistent synthesis of the old wisdom, attempts which in all probability did not satisfy the writer. They were presumably the results of a long life of labour, and may have been several times revised or recast. Who can say in our present ignorance of all historical data?

The Obscurity of the Subject.

And if it be asked: Who could have made such an attempt? I can find no answer, on reviewing the whole list of known Gnostic writers, than that Valentinus alone could in any way have attempted it. But that this can ever be proved beyond cavil I have no hope, for we know practically nothing of him and his writings; we only know of his great reputation, and of his attempted reformulation of the Gnosis. Indeed so-called Valentinianism helps us not at all in this speculation;

on the contrary, if we are to believe in any way the indications of the Church Fathers, "they of Valentinus" seem to have formulated things somewhat differently, and their ideas form only a small worked-in part of the great syntheses with which we have been dealing. But the information of the Church Fathers is very defective, and they seem for the most part to have dealt with the semi-popular phase of Gnosticism. Such abstruse subjects and such inner teachings as our Codices contain, could not possibly have been circulated publicly; they were meant for "disciples." It is true that the *Pistis* is in parts in a far more popular form, but if it had been widely circulated; it is strange that no mention of so marvellous an exposition should remain.

I, however, put forward this speculation with all hesitation; it means a totally different reading of Valentinianism, a reading from within and not from without. Our ideas on Gnosticism have, however, been so often of late revised by new discoveries, that it may still be hoped that some new find may yet throw a clear light on this (at present) entirely obscure problem.

In the Introduction to my translation of the *Pistis Sophia*, I find that I have stated my conclusions somewhat more crudely than I should now do. I will, therefore, in repeating what I there said as to the probable story of the adventures of the contents of the Askew Codex, slightly modify some expressions.

The original Greek treatise which is now called the *Pistis Sophia* may, then, probably

The Original Pistis Sophia Treatise.

have been compiled by Valentinus in the latter half of the second century, perhaps at Alexandria. By "compiled" I mean that this Apocalypse or Gospel, or whatever its title may have been, was not invented from first to last by Valentinus; the framework of the narrative, the selection of texts and ideas from other scriptures, Hebrew, Christian, Egyptian, Chaldæan, Greek, etc., and the adaptation of the nomenclature, were his share of the task.

The Coptic Translation.

Of this original doubtless several copies were made, and mistakes may have crept in. One of these copies was presumably carried up the Nile and translated into the vernacular, Greek being but little understood so far up the river. The translator was evidently not a very accurate person; moreover his knowledge of the subject was so imperfect that he had to leave many of the technical terms in the original, and doubtless made guesses at others. It is also probable that some things were added and others subtracted on the score of orthodoxy. The wearisome length of the Psalms, for instance, which Pistis Sophia recites in her repentances, followed by the shorter Salomonic Odes, leads one to suppose that the compiler originally quoted only a few striking verses from each psalm, and that the later and more orthodox translator, with that love of wearisome repetition so characteristic of monkish piety, whether of the East or the West, added the other less apposite verses, with which he was very familiar, while he was compelled to leave the Salomonic Odes as they stood, owing to his lack of acquaintance with the originals.

Moreover, the translator must have translated or possessed a translation of other similar documents, which he or a later scribe styles *The Books of the Saviour*, and from them he extracted what he considered to be passages apposite to the subject in hand, and appended them to the *Pistis* translation. These Books also, in my opinion, came from the literary workshop of Valentinus. The Books of the Saviour.

The whole MS. of the Coptic translator seems to have been copied by some ignorant copyist, who made many mistakes of orthography. It was copied by one man as a task, and hurriedly executed; and I would suggest that two copies were then made and occasionally a page of one copy substituted for a page of the other; and, as the pages were not quite exact to a word or phrase, we may thus account for some puzzling repetitions and some equally puzzling lacunæ. This copy was conjecturally made towards the end of the fourth century. The Copyist.

What was the history of the MS. after this date is impossible even to conjecture. Its history must, however, have been exciting enough for it to have escaped the hands of fanatics—both Christian and Mohammedan. During this period some of the pages were lost.

The contents of the inferior MS. of the Bruce Codex presumably had somewhat similar adventures, may even have come from the same distributing Coptic centre.

It would be entirely out of place in these short

sketches to enter on a critical investigation into the nature of the æonology, cosmology, soteriology, christology, and eschatology of these documents, and attempt to trace their modifications. The evolution of the universe is according to a certain order, but its involution seems to change that order; the soteriology modifies the æonology and cosmology. It is, in my opinion, because of this, rather than for any other reason, that the scheme underlying the *Extracts* and *The Book of the Great Logos* is said to be an "older form" than that underlying the *Pistis* treatise.

<small>The Scheme presupposed in these Treatises.</small>
The scheme underlying the *Pistis Sophia* has been industriously analysed by Köstlin and revised and corrected by Schmidt, who has also endeavoured to trace the modification of the general scheme underlying the *Extracts* (hitherto erroneously called the Fourth Book of *Pistis Sophia*) and *The Book of the Great Logos*, and of the scheme presupposed in the *Pistis Sophia*, — modifications brought about by the revelation of the new glories of the three Spaces of the Inheritance in the last treatise.

As the general outlines of the scheme underlying the *Pistis Sophia* may be of service to the reader, we will give it here, but it should be understood that it represents only one configuration of the cosmic mystery, at a certain moment of time, or in a certain phase of consciousness.

The Ineffable.

The Limbs of the Ineffable.

I. The Highest Light-world, or The Kingdom of Light.
    i. The First Space of the Ineffable.

ii. The Second Space of the Ineffable, or the First Space of the First Mystery.
   ii. The Second Space of the First Mystery.
II. The Higher (or Middle) Light-world.
   i. The Treasure of Light.
   ii. The Place of the Right.
   iii. The Place of the Midst.
III. The Lower Light- or Æon-world (The Mixture of Light and Matter).
   i. The Place of the Left.
      1. The Thirteenth Æon.
      2. The Twelve Æons.
      3. The Fate.
      4. The Sphere.
      5. The Rulers of the Ways of the Midst.
      6. The Lower Firmament.
   ii. The World of Men.
   iii. The Under-world.
      1. Amenti.
      2. Chaos.
      3. Outer Darkness.

We now come to a brief consideration of the superior MS. of the Bruce Codex. Here also we must rule out of place any attempt to grapple with an exposition of the system presupposed by the compiler or compilers, in spite of the following opinion and high appreciation of Schmidt, who in his Introduction (pp. 34 and 35) writes:

"What a different world on the contrary meets us in our thirty-one leaves! We find ourselves in the pure spheres of the highest Plērōma,

An Appreciation of the Untitled Treatise.

see step by step this world, so rich in heavenly beings, coming into existence before our eyes; each individual space with all its inmates is minutely described, so that we can form for ourselves a living picture of the glory and splendour of this Gnostic heaven. The speculations are not so confused and fantastic as those of the *Pistis Sophia* and our two *Books of Jeû*; here everything is in full harmony and logical sequence. The author is imbued with the Greek spirit, equipped with a full knowledge of Greek philosophy, full of the doctrine of the Platonic ideas, an adherent of Plato's view of the origin of evil—that is to say Hylē (Matter). Here it is not Christ who is the organ of all communications to the disciples; it is not Jesus who is God's envoy, and the redeemer and bringer of the mysteries; but we possess in these leaves a magnificently conceived work by an old Gnostic philosopher, and we stand astonished, marvelling at the boldness of the speculations, dazzled by the richness of the thought, touched by the depth of soul of the author. This is not, like the *Pistis Sophia*, the product of declining Gnosticism, but dates from a period when Gnostic genius like a mighty eagle left the world behind it, and soared in wide and ever wider circles towards pure light, towards pure knowledge, in which it lost itself in ecstasy.

"In one word, we possess in this Gnostic work as regards age and contents a work of the very highest importance, which takes us into a period of Gnosticism, and therefore of Christianity, of which very little knowledge has been handed down to us."

While cordially agreeing with Schmidt in his last paragraph, and in his high appreciation of the sublimity of the contents of this MS., we must venture to differ from him as to the clearness and logical order of the contents as at present preserved to us. If all is so clear and in such logical sequence, it is surprising that Schmidt has made no attempt to explain the contents. Many and many an hour have I puzzled over the contents of his translation and tried to get them into order, but I have as yet always failed. The result of my study, however, has led me to differ from Schmidt's assumption that the work is by a single author.

Not to be attributed to a Single Author.

My present conclusion, which is of course put forward as entirely tentative, is that the underlying matter was originally in the form of an apocalypse, a series of visions of some subtle phase of the inner ordering and substance of things. I would suggest that these visions were not in an ordered sequence, but were written down, or taken down, at different times as the seer described the inner working of nature from different points of view. The original writer was clearly, as it seems to me, an adherent of the Basilidian Gnosis, imbued with its teaching and nomenclature; but he had his own illumination as well, and, seeing some of the things of which he had been taught, in high enthusiasm and inspired confidence, he sang of the greater things by analogy

The Apocalyptic Basis.

with the lower he had seen—even these lower being so glorious that he could not express them as they really are.

<small>The Over-working.</small>
These apocalyptic visions were elaborately expanded and annotated and welded into a unity (the first part being cosmogonical, and the second soteriological) by a writer of great knowledge and wide reading, who was not only familiar with all the Gnostic literature of his time, but also had seen the things for himself; he laboured to make a consistent treatise with the apocalyptic material, on which he set a very high value, as a basis; but he often did not succeed, and clearly states that it is impossible for any "tongue of flesh" to tell of such sublime mysteries.

I am strongly persuaded that the overwriting of this apocalypsis belongs to the same circle of literary activity of which we have been already treating. In it I think we have another specimen of the attempts to re-edit and syntheticize the Gnosis, of which the main attempt is associated with the activity of Valentinus. As to the history of the Greek original, it parallels presumably that of the *Pistis Sophia* original. It was probably translated about the same time, and had adventures of a somewhat similar nature.

THE AKHMĪM CODEX.

WE have now to lay before our readers what little information is at present available with regard to the latest find in Gnosticism. Ten years ago, Dr. Carl Schmidt informed me that he had hopes of bringing out a work on the subject (including presumably a text and translation) in some two years; but unfortunately his anxiously-awaited labours have not yet seen the light. We are, therefore, entirely dependent upon the report of the important communication made by him to the Royal Prussian Academy of Sciences (*Kgl. preuss. Acad. d. Wissenschaften*) published in the Transactions, and dated July 16th, 1896.

Schmidt's communication, entitled A "Pre-irenæic Gnostic Original Work in Coptic" ("*Ein vorirenaeisches gnostisches Original-werk in koptischer Sprache*"), proves the enormous importance of the happy discovery. His paper is of course exceedingly technical and learned, but the following summary will give the reader a general idea of a subject which at present can only appeal to a very limited number of specialists, but which ought in time to be familiar to all serious students of Christian theosophy.

In January, 1896, Dr. Rheinhardt procured at Cairo, from a dealer of antiquities from Akhmīm, this precious papyrus MS., which he asserted had been discovered by a fellah in a niche in a wall. The MS. is now in the Berlin Egyptian Museum, each leaf being carefully protected with glass.

The MS. and its Contents.

Unfortunately the MS. is not entirely perfect; it contained originally seventy-one leaves—six of which are now missing; each page contains about eighteen to twenty-two lines. The writing is of extraordinary beauty, and points to the fifth century.

After a short preface, the MS. bears the superscription *Gospel according to Mary*, and on p. 77 the subscription *Apocryphon of John*; immediately on the same page follows the title *Wisdom of Jesus Christ*, and on p. 128 the same subscription; the next page begins without a title, but at the end of the MS. we find the subscription *Acts of Peter*.

The MS. therefore contains three distinct treatises, *The Gospel of Mary* and *The Apocryphon of John* being the same piece.

The Gospel of Mary. The first work begins with the words: "Now it came to pass on one of these days, when John the brother of James — the sons of Zebedee — had gone up to the temple, that a Pharisee, named Ananias (?), came unto him and said unto him: 'Where is thy Master, that thou dost not follow him?' He said unto him: 'From whence He came thither is He gone (?).' The Pharisee said unto him: 'With deceit hath the Nazaræan deceived you, for he hath . . . you and made away with the tradition of your fathers.' When I heard this I went away from the temple to the mountain unto a solitary place, and was exceedingly sorrowful in heart and said: 'How now was the Saviour chosen; and wherefore was He sent to the world by His Father who sent Him; and who is His Father; and what is the formation of that æon to which we shall go?'"

While he is sunk in these thoughts, the heavens open, and the Lord appears to him and to the disciples, in order to resolve his doubts. The Saviour then leaves them, and again they are sorrowful and weep. They said: "How can we go to the heathen and preach the gospel of the kingdom of the Son of Man? If they have not received Him, how will they receive us?"

Then Mary arose, and, having embraced them all, spake unto her brethren: "Weep not, and be not sorrowful, nor doubt, for His grace will be with you all and will overshadow you. Let us rather praise His goodness that he hath prepared us, and made us to be men."

Peter requests her to proclaim what the Lord had revealed to her, thus acknowledging the great distinction which the Lord had always permitted her above all women. Thereupon she begins the narrative of an appearance of the Lord in a dream; unfortunately some pages are here missing.

Hardly has she finished, when Andrew rises, and says that he cannot believe that the Lord has given such novel teachings. Peter also rejects her testimony and chides her. And Mary in tears says unto him: "Peter, of what dost thou think? Believest thou that I have imagined this only in myself, or lied as to the Lord?"

And now Levi comes forward to help Mary, and chides Peter as an eternal quarreller. How the dispute went on we cannot determine, as two pages are missing. On p. 21 a new episode begins and continues to the end of the first treatise without a break.

The Lord appears again to John, and John

immediately repairs to his fellow-disciples and relates what the Saviour had revealed unto him.

Schmidt suggests that the original title was *The Apocalypse* or *Revelation*, and not *The Apocryphon of John*.

The Wisdom of Jesus Christ.

The book of the *Wisdom of Jesus Christ* begins with the words: "After His resurrection from the dead His twelve disciples and seven women disciples had gone into Galilee to the mount which . . . for they were in doubt as to the hypostasis of the All . . . as to the mysteries and holy economy. Then did the Saviour appear unto them not in His prior form but in the invisible spirit. His form was that of a great angel of light, His substance indescribable, and He was not clothed in flesh that dieth, but in pure, perfect flesh, as He taught us on the mountain in Galilee which was called . . . He said: 'Peace be unto you; My peace I give unto you.'" And they were all astonished and were afraid.

And the Lord bids them lay all their questions before Him; and the several disciples bring forward their doubts and receive the desired replies.

The Acts of Peter are likewise of Gnostic origin, and belong to the great group of apocryphal stories of the Apostles. This third document treats of an episode from the healing-wonders of Peter.

Irenæus Quotes from the Gospel of Mary.

The importance of the whole MS. is, not only that it hands down to us three hitherto unknown Gnostic writings, but especially that it gives us a work which was known to Irenæus, our first important "authority" on Gnosticism among the Fathers—

a work from which he made extracts, but without giving the sources of his information or quoting the title of the book. This work is *The Gospel of Mary*.

Irenæus begins the last section of his first Book (29-31) with the words: "And besides these, from among those whom we have before mentioned as followers of Simon, a multitude of Barbēlō-Gnostics hath arisen, and they have shown themselves as mushrooms from the ground."

In cap. 29 he treats mostly of a group of so-called Barbēlō-Gnostics, with regard to whom he gives the contents of one of the books they used, a teaching which we do not find put forward by either the earlier or later hæresiarchs. Theodoret (I. 13) among the rest of the Refutators alone knows of this teaching, and he simply copies Irenæus.

This source is our *Gospel of Mary*; and we can now for the first time control Irenæus point by point, and see how little the Church Father succeeded or could succeed in reproducing the exceedingly complicated systems of the Gnostic schools. A few examples will be sufficient to establish this point abundantly.

Irenæus begins his exposition with these words: "Some of them suppose a certain never-ageing Æon in a Virginal Spirit, whom they name Barbēlō. Where they say is a certain unnameable Father."

An Examination of his Statements.

This "Father of All" is characterized in our new document (p. 22) as the Invisible; as Pure Light, in which no one can see with mortal eyes; as Spirit, for no one can imagine how He is

The Father.

formed; the Everlasting, the Unspeakable; the Unnameable, for no one existed before Him to give Him a name. Of Him it is said: "He thinketh His Image alone and beholdeth it in the Water of Pure Light which surroundeth Him. And His Thought energized and revealed herself, and stood before Him in the Light-spark; which is the Power which existed before the All, which Power hath revealed itself; which is the perfect Forethought of the All; the Light, the Likeness of the Light, the Image of the Invisible; that is, the perfect Power, the Barbēlō, the Æon perfect in glory—glorifying Him, because she hath manifested herself in Him and thinketh Him. She is the first Thought, his Image; she becometh the First Man; that is, the Virginal Spirit, she of the triple Manhood, the triple-powered one, the triple-named, triple-born; the Æon which ages not, the Man-woman, who hath come forth from His Forethought."

The Mother.

According to this, the "Father of the All" stands at the head of the system, the "Invisible." After Him comes His "Image," that is, the "Barbēlō," the "perfect Power," the "unageing Æon" of Irenæus.

By thinking of His Image, His Thought reveals herself in the Light-spark, that is, in Barbēlō.

Irenæus gives all this in a short, incomprehensible abstract as follows: "And that He was fain to manifest Himself to the same Barbēlō. And that Thought came forth and stood before Him, and asked for Foreknowledge."

Our text then proceeds: "And Barbēlō besought Him to give unto her Foreknowledge. He nodded,

The Pentad.

and when He had thus nodded assent, Foreknowledge manifested herself and stood with Thought, that is Forethought, and glorified the Invisible and the perfect Power, the Barbēlō, for that through her she had come into existence.

"Again this Power besought that Incorruptibility be given unto her. He nodded, and when He had thus nodded assent, Incorruptibility manifested herself and stood with Thought and Foreknowledge, glorifying the Invisible and Barbēlō, in that through her she had come into existence.

"For their sakes she besought that Everlasting Life be given them. He nodded, and when He had thus nodded assent, Everlasting Life manifested herself, and they stood and glorified Him and Barbēlō, because through her they had come into existence in the manifestation of the Invisible Spirit.

"This is the pentad of the Æons of the Father, that is, the First Man, the Image of the Invisible; that is, Barbēlō, and Thought, and Foreknowledge, and Incorruptibility and Life Everlasting."

At the request of Barbēlō, also, the Invisible causes to come forth after Thought the three following feminine Æons, according to Irenæus; "Thought asked for Foreknowledge; Foreknowledge also having come forth, again upon their petition came forth Incorruptibility; then afterwards Life Eternal; in whom Barbēlō rejoicing, and looking forth into the greatness, and delighted with her conception, generated into it a Light like unto it; her they affirm to be the beginning of the enlightening and generation of all things; and that the Father seeing this Light anointed it with His goodness to make it perfect; and this they say is the Christ."

The Decad. In this passage without doubt Irenæus had before his eyes the words: "He is the decad of the Æons, that is, He is the Father of the ingenerable Father. Barbēlō gazed into Him fixedly . . . and she gave birth to a blessed Light-spark. Nor doth it differ from her in greatness. This is the Alone-begotten, who hath manifested himself in the Father, the self-generated God, the first-born Son of the All, the pure Light-spirit. Now the Invisible Spirit rejoiced over the Light, which had come into existence, which had first of all manifested itself in the first Power — that is, His Forethought — in Barbēlō. And He anointed him with His goodness, that he might be made perfect."

This Alone-begotten is consequently identical with the Light or the Christ. Irenæus offers us here no enlightenment, and further on he only gives us the sentence: "Therefore the First Angel, who stands near the Alone-begotten," etc.

The Alone-begotten asks for Mind to be given him; when this has been done, he praises, as Mind, the Father and Barbēlō.

Irenæus continues: "And this, they say, is Christ; who again requests, as they say, that Mind may be given to help him; and then came forth Mind; and after these the Father sends forth the Word."

In this place Irenæus has omitted a stage and quite forgotten the third male Æon, namely, Will. Our MS. gives us the following:

"The Invisible Spirit willed to energize. His Will energized and revealed itself and stood with the Mind and the Light praising Him. The Word followed the Will, for through the Word hath Christ created all things."

With this the upper Ogdoad is shut off from the Decad, the lower æon proceeding from separate pairs. Next we have the Self-begotten from Thought, the Word, of whom it is written: "Whom He hath honoured with great honour, because he came forth from His first Thought. The Invisible hath set him as God over the All. The True God gave him all powers, and made the Truth that is in Him subject unto him, that he might think out the All."

The Christ.

Irenæus reproduces this as follows: "Then afterwards, of Mind and the Word, they say, was sent forth the Self-begotten, to represent the Great Light, and that he was highly honoured, and all things made subject unto him. And the Truth was sent out also with him, and that there is a conjunction of the Self-begotten and Truth."

(It is impossible at present to attempt to analyze the system from the above fragments; it may, however, be suggested that the treatise is here exposing the three root-phases, or moments of emanation, of the Plērōma, or ideal world: (a) the In-generable, (b) the Self-generable, and (c) the Generable—the Father, the Logos, the All. The Gnosis, however, is more elaborate than any other known system, and its idealistic intuitions of primal processes know no limits.)

588   FRAGMENTS OF A FAITH FORGOTTEN.

From the Light of the Christ and the Incorruptible proceed forth four great Lights to surround the Self-begotten. Their names are Harmozel, Ōroiael, Daveithe and Eleleth. From Will and Everlasting Life proceed four others: Charis, Synesis, Aisthesis and Phronesis. Irenæus writes:

"And from the Light which is Christ, and Incorruptibility, four Luminaries were sent forth to surround the Self-begotten; and that from Will again and Life Everlasting, four such emanations were sent forth to minister under the four Luminaries, which they call Grace (Charis), Free-will (Thelesis), Understanding (Synesis), and Prudence (Phronesis). And that Charis for her part was conjoined with the great and first Luminary; and this they will have to be the Saviour, and call him Harmogen; and Thelesis with the second, whom also they call Raguel; and Synesis with the third, whom they name David; and Phronesis with the fourth, whom they name Eleleth."

This passage is of interest in many ways. We learn the correct names; we notice that three of them (Eleleth, Daveithe, Ōroiael) are also to be found in the Codex Brucianus, and thus we establish the relation of this important Codex with the first piece in our MS.

The Egyptian Origin of the Treatise. These proofs are sufficient to establish the point that *The Gospel of Mary* was composed before A.D. 180, and that the Greek original, from which the Coptic translation was made, was earlier than Irenæus. In the opinion of Dr. Schmidt, the work originated in Egypt. The School which used it was the same as that designated by

Irenæus as the Barbēlō-Gnostics, or, as they usually called themselves, simply the Gnostics; this School was further subdivided into many single denominations, whose names and teachings Epiphanius has given us in detail. Among them were circulated many books under the name of Mary; thus Epiphanius (*Hær.*, xxvi. 8) speaks of *The Questions of Mary*, both *The Great* and *The Little*, and even in xii. of *The Genealogy of Mary*. Celsus had previously also met with this School, and perhaps was acquainted with our work, for he informs us that some heretics derive their origin from Mary and Martha, and gives the well-known diagram of the so-called Ophites. Yet more; our original work shows us that Irenæus "copied" from our book only up to a certain place; and in I. 30, he used a second work of the same School which had fallen into his hands.

So far Dr. Schmidt, whose interesting communication is followed by a note of Professor Harnack. Harnack gives his opinion as follows:

"This find is of the first importance to primitive Church history; not only because we have one (or perhaps three) original Gnostic works of the second century — (is the *Wisdom of Jesus Christ* possibly the famous work of Valentinus?)—but kind fate has also added to our debt that Irenæus has quoted from one of the three treatises. We are thus for the first time in a position to control by the original the presentation of a Gnostic system as rendered by the Church Father. The result of this examination shows, as we might

The Opinion of Harnack.

have expected, that owing to omissions, and because no effort was made to understand his opponents, the sense of the by no means absurd speculations of the Gnostics has been ruined by the Church Father. Another fact—which can only with the greatest difficulty be extracted from the writings of their opponents—is that the system treats of a psychological process within the first principle, which the Gnostics desired to unfold. Tertullian certainly says once (*Adv. Valent.*, iv.): 'Ptolemæus, the pupil of Valentinus, split up the names and numbers of the æons into personified "substances," external to deity, whereas Valentinus himself had included these in the very summit of the godhead as the impressions of sensation and feeling'—but which of the Church Fathers has given himself the trouble thus to understand the speculations of Valentinus and of the other Gnostics?

"According to Hippolytus (*Philos.*, vi. 42), the followers of the Gnostic Marcus complained of the misrepresentation of their teaching by Irenæus; the followers of our newly discovered book could also have complained of the incomprehensible fashion in which Irenæus had represented their teachings.

"Thus, we had previously known a Gnostic work which probably originated in Egypt in the second century, only through an epitome of it by a Gallic bishop about the year 185, and now we find it again in a Coptic translation of the fifth century—verily a paradoxical method of transmission!"

If, however, the last chapters of Book I. of Irenæus are copied from the lost Syntagma of Justin or some other earlier work, as the best critics have previously maintained, then the original of our new document has a considerably earlier date than Schmidt or Harnack assign to it in the above Transaction.

The student of Gnosticism will at once perceive that the importance of the new find cannot be overestimated. The new documents throw light not only on the Codex Brucianus, but also on the system of the *Pistis Sophia*. We have now these three original sources on which to base our study of Gnostic theosophy; and there is hope that at last something may be done to rescue the views of the best Gnostic doctors from obscurity, and from the environment of pious refutation in which they have been previously smothered. The task of the sympathetic student should now be to find appropriate terms for the technicalities of the Gnosis, place the various orders of ideas in their proper relation, and show that the method of the Gnosis, which looked at the problems of cosmogony and anthropogony from above, may be as reasonable in its proper domain as are the methods of modern scientific research, which regard such problems entirely from below. We should not forget that men like Valentinus were theosophists, engaged on precisely the same studies as their brethren the world over. The greatest cosmogonies of the world are of the same nature as Gnostic cosmogenesis, and a study of these will convince us of the similarity of source. Gnostic anthropogenesis has many points of similarity with general theosophical ideas, and Gnostic psychology is in a great measure borne out by recent research. The

Gnostic technical terms are no more difficult of comprehension than those found in other theosophical writers; and there is an exact parallel between the varying use made of such terms by different writers on the Gnosis and the misrepresentation of the views of the Gnostics by the Church Fathers, and the various meanings given to like terms by other theosophical writers and the misrepresentation of such writers by their critics. The Gnostics were themselves partly to blame for their obscurity, and the Church Fathers were partly to blame for their misrepresentation. In brief, the same standard of criticism has to be applied to the writings of the Gnostics as the discriminating student has to apply to all such literature. It is true that to-day we speak openly of many things that the Gnostics wrapped up in symbol and myth; nevertheless our real knowledge on such subjects is not so very far in advance of the great doctors of the Gnosis as we are inclined to imagine; now, as then, there are only a few who really know what they are writing about, while the rest copy, compare, adapt, and speculate.

SOME FORGOTTEN SAYINGS.

IN the early centuries of Christianity there were in circulation many traditions, legends, and religious romances, called Memoirs, Acts, and Gospels, which contained Sayings-of-the-Lord or Logoi. These Logoi or Logia were oracles, or oracular utterances, couched in the same language and of much the same tenour as the prophetic utterances of the members of the Schools of the Prophets, which were introduced by the solemn formula, "Thus saith the Lord," when recorded in the books of the Old Covenant of the Jewish race.

In course of time certain of these traditional, legendary and mythical settings of the Logoi were declared to be alone historical, and a canon of orthodox tradition was evolved from the second half of the second century onwards. I use the term "mythical" in its best sense, that is to say, stories embodying in a designed symbolic fashion the teachings of the mysteries, concerning the nature of God, the universe and the human soul.

As only a few out of the many writings were selected, a large number of Logoi was thus rejected. The latest collection of these rejected Logoi has been made by Resch, and was published in 1889 in Gebhardt and Harnack's series of *Texte und Untersuchungen,* under the title of *Agrapha: Äussercanonische Evangelienfragmente.*

Rejected Logoi.

Some of these extra-canonical fragments are variants of the familiar canonical Sayings, and are of interest mainly for the reconstruction of one of the root-sources from which the synoptic compilers drew their information. A few have been preserved in the Pauline Letters. Others are entirely unfamiliar to those who are only acquainted with the canonical selection of the books of the New Covenant, generally called the New Testament. These Logoi are of special interest to students of the origins, and I therefore append a selection of them translated from Resch's text.

It may be mentioned that some of these Logoi have been worked into a religious novel by a Jewish writer, under the title *As Others Saw Him*, published in 1895, at London, by William Heinemann.

Be merciful that ye may obtain mercy; forgive that it may be forgiven unto you; as ye do so shall it be done to you; as ye give so shall it be given unto you; as ye judge so shall ye be judged; as ye do service so shall service be done to you; with what measure ye mete, with the same shall it be measured to you in return.

Wisdom sendeth forth her children.

He who is near Me is near the fire; and he who is far from Me is far from the kingdom.

If ye observe not the little [*sci.*, mystery], who will give you the great?

They who would see Me and reach My kingdom need must attain Me with pain and suffering.

Good must needs come, but blessed is he by whom it cometh; in like manner also evil must needs come, but woe unto him by whom it cometh.

The weak shall be saved by the strong.

Guard the mysteries for Me and for the sons of My house.

Cleave to the holy ones, for they who cleave to them are made holy.

The fashion of this world passeth away.

[Fashion—that is, configuration ($\sigma\chi\hat{\eta}\mu a$), for there are other worlds and other phases of this world].

As often as ye eat this bread and drink this cup make proclamation of My death and confession in My resurrection and ascension until I come [to you].

[A variant gives the saying in the third person, and speaks of the "death of the Son of the Man," the Logos. The Master promises to return to His disciples at the time of the performance of a certain holy rite.]

Be ye mindful of faith and hope, through whom is born that love to God and man which giveth life eternal.

There is a mingling that leadeth to death, and there is a mingling that leadeth to life.

Beholding a certain man working on the Sabbath, He said unto him: Man, if thou knowest what thou doest thou art blessed; but if thou knowest not, thou art accursed and a transgressor of the law.

Why do ye wonder at the signs? I give unto you a mighty inheritance which the whole world doth not contain.

When the Lord was asked by a certain man, When should His kingdom come, He saith unto him: When two shall be one, and the without as the within, and the male with the female, neither male nor female.

Call not any one "Father" on earth, for on earth

there are rulers [only]; in heaven is the Father from whom is every descent [that is, "blood descent from a father" (πατριά)] both in heaven and on earth.

Grieve not the Holy Spirit which is in you, and put not out the Light which hath shone forth in you.

As ye see yourselves in water or mirror, so see ye Me in yourselves.

As I find you, so will I judge you.

Seek for the great [mysteries] and the little shall be added to you; seek for the heavenly and the earthly shall be added to you.

Be ye approved money-changers, rejecting the bad and retaining the good.

Keep thy flesh pure.

Because of the sick I was sick; because of the hungry I was ahungered; because of the thirsty I was athirst.

Not rendering evil for evil, or railing for railing, or fist for fist, or curse for curse.

Love hideth a multitude of sins.

There are false christs and false teachers who have blasphemed the Spirit of Grace, and have spit forth its gift of grace; these shall not be forgiven either in this æon or in the æon to come.

[Grace is the "power above," the power of the Logos which makes a man a "christ." Charis or Grace is the consort of the Logos, His power or shakti. The false "christs" are those who have been "initiated" and broken their vows. The æon is a certain time-period.]

For the Heavenly Father willeth the repentance of the sinner rather than his chastisement.

For God willeth that all should receive of His gifts.

Keep that which thou hast, and it shall be increased into more.

Behold, I make the last as the first.

I am come to end the sacrifices, and if ye cease not from sacrificing, the wrath shall not cease from you.

[Woe unto him] who hath made sad the spirit of his brother.

And never rejoice unless ye see your brother [also] happy.

He who hath wondered shall reign, and he who hath reigned shall rest.

[This is a dark saying; it has been compared to the phrase of Plato: "There is no other beginning of philosophy than wondering"—that is to say, regarding the works of the Deity with wonder and reverence. This is the beginning of philosophy, or gnosis, and the end of it makes the man king of himself, and thus master of gods and men; thus is he at peace.]

My mother, the Holy Spirit, even now took me by one of the hairs of my head and carried me to the great mountain Tabor.

[The hairs of the head may perhaps symbolise the *nāḍi's*, as they are called in the Upaniṣhads, by which the soul goes forth from the body; the mountain is the way up to the spiritual regions.]

He who seeketh me shall find me in children from seven years [onwards]; for hidden in them I am manifested in the fourteenth period (æon).

[This may refer either to the higher ego or light-spark from the Logos, or to certain degrees of initiation, the initiated having to become as "little children."]

When Salome asked how long should death hold sway, the Lord said unto her: So long as ye women bring forth; for I came to end the works of the female. And Salome said unto Him: I have then done well in not bringing forth. And the Lord answered and said: Eat of every pasture, but of that which hath the bitterness [of death] eat not. And when Salome asked when should those things of which she enquired be known, the Lord said: When ye shall tread upon the vesture of shame, and when the two shall be one, and the male with the female neither male nor female.

["Shame" is presumably the same as the "mingling" in one of the Logoi quoted above. To tread on the vesture of shame is to rise above the animal nature.]

Pray for your enemies; blessed are they who mourn over the destruction of the unbelievers.

I stood on a lofty mountain, and saw a gigantic man and another, a dwarf; and I heard as it were a voice of thunder, and drew nigh for to hear; and He spake unto me and said, I am thou and thou art I; and wheresoever thou mayst be I am there. In all am I scattered, and whencesoever thou willest, thou gatherest Me; and gathering Me thou gatherest Thyself.

[Here again we have the mountain of initiation. The initiate beholds the vision of the Heavenly Man, the Logos, and of himself, the dwarf; of the Great

Man and the little man, the light-spark which sits in the heart.]

May thy Holy Spirit come upon us and purify us!

[From a very ancient version of the Lord's Prayer, instead of the clause "Thy kingdom come."]

Possess nothing upon the earth.

Though ye be gathered together with me in My bosom, if ye do not My commandments, I will cast you forth.

Gain for yourselves, ye sons of Adam, by means of these transitory things which are not yours, that which is your own, and passeth not away.

For even among the prophets after they have been anointed by the Holy Spirit, the word of sin has been found among them.

[That is to say, after they have been made "christs" ($\mu\epsilon\tau\grave{a}$ $\tau\grave{o}$ $\chi\rho\iota\sigma\theta\hat{\eta}\nu\alpha\iota$ $\alpha\grave{v}\tau o\grave{v}\varsigma$ $\grave{\epsilon}\nu$ $\pi\nu\epsilon\acute{v}\mu\alpha\tau\iota$ $\dot{a}\gamma\acute{\iota}\wp$). The "word of sin" means apparently erroneous prophetical utterances.]

If a man shall abandon all for my name's sake, at the second coming he shall inherit eternal life.

["For my name's sake" signifies the power of the Great Name which the Master used in his public preaching; the second coming is the descent of the Christ-spirit upon the candidate at his initiation. "Eternal life" is the life of the æons or spiritual existences, whose lives are an eternity.]

If ye make not the below into the above and the above into the below, the right into the left and the left into the right, the before into the behind [and the behind into the before], ye shall not enter into the kingdom of God.

[That is to say, ye shall not enter into the central point and so pass into the spiritual region.]

I am to be crucified anew.

I recognised myself, and gathered myself together from all sides; I sowed no children for the ruler, but I tore up his roots, and gathered together [my] limbs that were scattered abroad; I know thee who thou art, for I am from the realms above.

[This is the apology, or defence, of the soul of the initiate as it passes through the realms of the unseen world, each of which is in charge of a ruler, the minister of Death. As the Logos gathers together his children (the light-sparks, the limbs of his body), and takes them home into his bosom, so does the ego collect its limbs and becomes the Osirified.]

What ye preach with words before the people, do ye in deeds before every man.

Thou art the key [who openest] for every man, and shuttest for every man.

[This saying is put in the mouth of the disciples; in the direct formula it would read, "I am the key," &c.]

The Oxyrhynchus Papyrus.

Numerous other Logoi could be added from Gnostic literature, especially from the contents of the Coptic Codices; but enough has been given to show the reader that much of the Sayings-material has been rejected and forgotten. How precious some of this matter was, has been lately shown by a recent discovery. The ancient papyrus-fragment discovered on the site of Oxyrhynchus by Grenfell and Hunt, in 1897, preserves for us the most primitive form of the Logoi known to us. Of the six decipherable Sayings it contains, one is familiar to us, two contain new matter and important variants, and three are entirely new. If the proportion of now unknown to known sayings was as high in the rest of the MS. as in the solitary leaf which has reached us, then we have indeed lost more by the Canon than we have gained.

The new-found Sayings run as follows, omitting the one already familiar to us:

Jesus saith: Except ye fast to the world, ye shall in no wise find the Kingdom of God; and except ye sabbatize the Sabbath, ye shall not see the Father.

Jesus saith: I stood in the midst of the world, and in flesh was I seen of them, and I found all drunken, and none found I athirst among them. And My soul grieveth over the souls of men, because they are blind in their heart and see not. . . .

Jesus saith: Wheresoever there be two, they are not without God; and wherever there is one alone, I say, I am with him. Raise the stone, and there thou shalt find Me; cleave the wood, and there am I.

[The first part of this saying is exceedingly imperfect; I have followed Blass's conjectures. See Taylor's *Oxyrhynchus Logia,* Oxford; 1899].

Jesus saith: A prophet is not acceptable in his own country, neither doth a physician work cures upon those that know him.

Jesus saith: A city built on the top of a high hill and stablished can neither fall nor be hid.

Jesus saith: Thou hearest with one ear (but the other thou hast closed).

Since the publication of the first edition of this

work the rubbish heaps of ancient Oxyrhynchus have yielded yet another battered scrap of papyrus containing material from a similar collection of sayings, the decipherable portions of which run as follows in Grenfell & Hunt's edition (*New Sayings of Jesus*; London, 1904):

These are the . . . words which Jesus the Living (One) spake to . . . and Thomas, and He said unto (them): Every one who hearkeneth to these words shall never taste of death.

Jesus saith: Let not him who seeketh . . . cease until he findeth, and when he findeth he shall wonder; wondering he shall reign, and reigning shall rest.

Jesus saith: (Ye ask? Who are these) that draw us (to the kingdom if) the kingdom is in Heaven? . . . the fowls of the air, and all beasts that are under the earth or upon the earth, and the fishes of the sea (these are they that draw) you; and the Kingdom of Heaven is within you; and whosoever shall know himself shall find it. (Strive therefore?) to know yourselves, and ye shall be aware that ye are the sons of the . . . Father; (and?) ye shall know that ye are in (the City of God?), and ye are (the City?).

Jesus saith: Everything that is not before thy face and that which is hidden from thee shall be revealed to thee. For there is nothing hidden which shall not be made manifest, nor buried which shall not be raised.

CONCLUSION.

O Light of God, adorable! we worship Thee, that Thou may'st pour Thy light into our minds!

          Based on the Gāyatrī.

AFTERWORD.

READER, if you have read so far, you may have journeyed with me or have been taken by some other way; but if you have come so far upon the road, then it seems—to me at least—as though we had journeyed together to some region of light. We have for some short hours been privileged to enjoy converse with those who loved and love the Master. With their words still ringing in our ears, with the life of their love still tingling in our veins, how can we venture to speak ill of them? "Come unto Me, ye weary!" In such a light of love, how shall we find the heart to condemn, because they went out unto Him with all their being? Reading their words and looking upon their lives, I, for my part, see the brand "Heresy," writ so large upon their horizon for many, disappearing into the dim distance, and instead behold the figure of the Master standing with hands of blessing outstretched above their heads. I do not know why this side of earliest Christianity has been allowed to be forgotten. Doubtless there was a purpose served by its withdrawal; but to-day, at the beginning of the twentieth century, in the greater freedom and wider tolerance we now enjoy, may not the veil again be lifted? The old forms need not return—though surely some of them have enough of beauty! But the old power is there, waiting and watching, ready to clothe itself in new forms, forms more lovely still, if we will but turn to Him who wields the power, as He really is, and not as we limit Him by our sectarian creeds.

How long must it be before we learn that there are as many ways to worship God as there are men on earth? Yet each man still declares: My way is best; mine is the only way. Or if he does not say it, he thinks it. These things, it is true, transcend our reason; religion is the something in us greater than our reason, and being greater it gives greater satisfaction. To save ourselves we must lose ourselves; though not irrationally, if reason is transcended. If it be true that we have lived for many lives before, in ways how many must we not have worshipped God or failed to do so? How often have we condemned the way we praised before! Intolerant in one faith, equally intolerant in another, condemning our past selves!

What, then, think ye of Christ? Must He not be a Master of religion, wise beyond our highest ideals of wisdom? Does He condemn His worshippers because their ways are diverse; does He condemn those who worship His Brethren, who also have taught the Way? As to the rest, what need of any too great precision? Who knows with the intellect enough to decide on all these high subjects for his fellows? Let each follow the Light as he sees it—there is enough for all; so that at last we may see "all things turned into light—sweet, joyous light." These, then, are all my words, except to add, with an ancient Coptic scribe, "O Lord, have mercy on the soul of the sinner who wrote this!"

BIBLIOGRAPHIES.

As nothing which may really be called a bibliography of the subject exists, I append an attempt at a preliminary contribution towards a full Bibliography of Gnosticism. Every work (and article) of importance is (I am almost certain) included, and I think that the list of work done on the Coptic Gnostic writings may be said to be fairly complete; there is, however, a certain number of articles in periodicals and publications of learned societies (French especially) which is still to be added, though I do not think that this number is large. I might have added more references to Encyclopædias, but the vast majority of articles in such publications is of very little value. I have divided the General Bibliography into: (i.) Early Works; (ii.) Critical Studies prior to 1851; (iii.) Works subsequent to the Publication of the Text of the Philosophumena in 1851. Division i. contains works generally of very little value; Division ii. suffers from ignorance of the contents of Hippolytus' Philosophumena, the text of which was first published by Miller at Oxford in 1851. Its contents may be said to have revolutionized the study of Gnosticism. I have also kept apart the Bibliography of the work done on the Coptic Gnostic writings, which will, I believe, in the future still further revolutionize our ideas on the Gnosis. I have made a remark or two on the most popular sources of information in English, but have refrained from all other notes as out of place in so general a work as the present.

GENERAL BIBLIOGRAPHY.

Early Works.

1569. Marcossius (G. P.). De Vitis, Secretis, et Dogmatibus omnium Haereticorum . . . Elenchus alphabeticus. Coloniæ.

1659. Macarius (I.). Abraxas seu Apistopistus quæ est antiquaria de Gemmis basilidianis Disquisitio et cet. Antverpiæ.

1664. Siricius (M.). Simonis Magi Hæreticorum omnium Patris Pravitates et cet. Giessæ.

1667. Michaelis (?). Dissertatio de Indiciis Philosophiæ gnosticæ Tempore LXX., in Syntagma comment. Gœttingæ. Pt. 2, pp. 269 ff.

1690. Ittig (T.). T. Ittigii . . . de Hæresiarchis Ævi apostolici et apostolico primi, seu primi et secundi a Christo nato Seculi, Dissertatio. Lipsiæ. 2 pts. 1690—96. 2 ed. Lipsiæ 1703 (append. 1696 ed.).

1709. Ittig (T.). Dissertationis Ittigianæ de Hæresiarchis . . . adversus Catalecta F. Lotharii Mariæ a Cruce . . . Defensio. Lipsiæ,

1710. Strunz (F.). Friderici Strunzii Historia Bardesanis et Bardesanistarum et cet. Wittenburg.

1710. Massnet (R.). Prolegomena to his edition of Irenæus. Paris.

1734. Beausobre (I. de). Histoire critique de Manichée et du Manichéisme. Amsterdam. 2 vols. 1734, 1739. Vol. ii., pp. 1—142. Dissertation on Basilides, Marcion and Bardesanes as precursors of Mani.

1739. Mosheim (J. L. v.). Institutiones christianæ majores. Helmstadi. Vol. i., pp. 376 ff. An able dissertation on the Dositheans.

1750. (?). Mosheim (J. L. v.). Geschichte der Schlangenbrüder. Helmstädt (?). Not in British Museum.

1753. Mosheim (J. L. v.). De Rebus christianis ante Constantinum magnum Commentarii. Helmstadtii.

1756. Schumacher (J. H.). Erläuterung der Lehrtafel der Ophiten. Wolfenbüttel. Not in British Museum.

1773. Tittmann (C. C.). Tractatus de Vestigiis Gnosticorum in N. T. frustra quæsitis. Lipsiæ.

1790. Münter (F. C. C. H.) Versuch über u. s. v. (Essai sur les Antiquités ecclésiastiques du Gnosticisme). Anspach. Quoted by Amélineau in his Essai. Not in British Museum.

1795. Schelling (F. W. J. V.). De Marcione Epistolarum paulinarum Emendatore. Tübingen. Not in British Museum.

Critical Studies prior to 1851.

1818. Lewald (E. A.). Commentatio ad Historiam

Religionum veterum illustrandam pertinens de Doctrina gnostica. Heidelberg.

1818. Neander (J. A. W.). Genetische Entwickelung der vornehmsten gnostischen Systeme. Berlin.

1819. Hahn (A.). Bardesanes gnosticus Syrorum primus Hymnologus. Commentatio historico-theologica. Lipsiæ.

1819 (?) Hahn (A.). Dissertatio de Gnosi Marcionis. Not in British Museum.

1820. Bellermann (J. J.). Ueber die Gemmen der Alten mit dem Abraxasbilde. Berlin (?). Not in British Museum.

1820. Bellermann (J. J.). Ueber die Abraxas-Gemmen. Berlin. 3 programmes, 1820-1822.

1821. Fulder (?). Art. De Carpocratianis, in Ilgen's Historisch-theologische Abhandlungen der Gesellschaft zu Leipzig. Not in British Museum.

1821. Hahn (A.). Antitheses Marcionis. Königsberg. Not in British Museum.

1823. Hahn (A.). Evangelium Marcionis ex Auctoritate veterum Monumentorum. Könisberg.

1823. Giesler (J. C. L.). Crit. of Neander, in Allgemeine Literatur-Zeitung. Halle. Nr. 104, pp. 835—38.

1825. Neander (J. A. W.). Antignostikus. Geist des Tertullianus und Einleitung in dessen Schriften mit archäologischen und dogmen-historischen Untersuchungen. Berlin. 2 ed., 1849.

1825. Neander (J. A. W.). Allgemeine Geschichte der christlichen Religion und Kirche. Hamburg. 6 vols., 1825—52. Eng. Trans. (General History of the Christian Religion and Church) by Rose (H. J.) London. 2 vols., 1831—41; Terry

(J.) from 2nd ed. London. 9 vols., 1847—55; new ed. (Bohn). London. 2 vols., 1890. Vol. ii., "The Gnostic Sects," pp. 1—195.

1828. Matter (A. J.). Histoire critique du Gnosticisme et de son Influence sur les Sectes religieuses et philosophiques des six premiers Siècles de l' Ère chrétienne. Paris. 3 vols. 2 ed. revised, 1843. There is a German translation by Dörner.

1829. Burton (E.). An Enquiry into the Heresies of the apostolic Age (Bampton Lectures). Oxford.

1830. Giesler (J. C. L.). Art. in Theologische Studien und Kritiken. Hamburg. Pp. 395 ff.

1831. Möhler (J. A.). Versuch über den Ursprung des Gnosticismus. Tübingen. Also in his Gesammelten Schriften. Regensberg. 1839—40. Vol. i., pp. 403 ff.

1834. Neumann (C. F.). Art. Marcion's Glaubenssystem mit einem Anhange über das Verhältnis der Lehre Mani's zum Parsismus, dargelegt von Esnig, aus dem Armenischen übersetzt. Zeitschrift für die historische Theologie. Leipzig. Vol. i., pp. 71—78.

1834. Windischmann (W.). Art. on Esnig, in Bayerischen Annalen für Vaterlandskunde und Literatur. Munich (?). No. for Jan. Not in British Museum.

1835. Baur (F. C.). Die christliche Gnosis, oder die christliche Religions-Philosophie in ihrer geschichtlichen Entwiklung. Tübingen.

1839. Hildebrand (?). Philosophiæ gnosticæ Origines. Berlin. Not in British Museum.

1841. Simson (A.). Art. Leben und Lehre Simons

des Magiers. Zeitschr. f. d. histor. Theolog. Leipzig. Vol. iii., pp. 18 ff.

1841. Scherer (?). De Gnosticis qui in N. T. impugnari dicuntur. Strassburg. Not in British Museum.

1843. Norton (A.). The Evidences of the Genuineness of the Gospels. Vol. i., Boston, 1837; vol. ii., 1843; 2 ed., London, 1847. The whole of vol. ii. is devoted to the Gnostics.

1846. Grätz (H.). Gnosticismus und Judenthum. Krotoschin.

1847. Migne (J. P.). Dictionnaire des Hérésies, des Schismes, des Auteurs et des Livres jansénistes, des Ouvrages mis à l'Index, des Propositions condamnées par l'Église, et des Ouvrages condamnées par les Tribunaux français. Paris. 2 vols.

Works Subsequent to the Publication of the Text of the Philosophumena in 1851.

1852. Volkmar (G.). Das Evangelium Marcions. Text und Kritik mit Rücksicht auf die Evangelien des Martyrers Justin, der Clementinen und der apostolischen Väter. Leipzig.

1852. Jacobi (J. L.). Basilidis Philosophi gnostici Sententias ex Hippolyti Libro nuper reperto et cet. Berlin.

1852. Matter (A. J.). Une Excursion gnostique en Italie. Strasbourg.

1853. Le Vaillant de Florival (P. E.). French translation of Esnig. Paris. Not in British Museum.

1853. Baur (F. C.). Das Christenthum und die christliche Kirche der drei ersten Jahrhunderte. Tübingen. 2 ed., 1860.

1854. Hase (C. H.). Kirchengeschichte. Leipzig. 1854
—1877. On Basilides in the 7th to the 10th ed.
1855. Gundert (?). 3 Arts. in Zeitschrift fur die lutheranische Theologie. 1855, pp. 209 ff. ; 1856, pp. 37 ff., 443 ff. Name not mentioned in British Museum catalogue.
1855. Volkmar (G.). Art. Die Kolarbasus-Gnosis, in Zeitsch. f. d. histor. Theolog. Leipzig. Vol. iv., pp. 608 ff.
1855. Volkmar (G.). Die Quellen der Ketzergeschichte bis zum Nicänum kritisch untersucht. Erstes Band: Hippolytus und die römischen Zeitgenossen; oder die Philosophumena und die verwandten Schriften nach Ursprung, Composition und Quellen untersucht. Zürich.
1855. Uhlhorn (G.). Das basilidianische System mit besonderer Rücksicht auf die Angaben des Hippolytus. Göttingen.
1856. Hilgenfeld (A.). Art. Das System des Gnostikers Basilides. Theolog. Jahrbücher. Tübingen. Vol. i., pp. 86—121.
1856. Baur (F. C.) Art. Das System des Gnostikers Basilides und die neuesten Auffassungen desselben. Theologische Jahrbucher. Tubingen. Vol. i., pp. 121—162.
1857. Harvey (W. W.). Sancti Irenæi Libri quinque adversus Hæreses. Cambridge. 2 vols. Preliminary Observations on the Gnostic System, vol. i., pp. i.—cli.
1860. Möller (E.W.). Geschichte der Kosmologie in der griechischen Kirche bis auf Origenes mit Specialuntersuchungen uber die gnostischen Systeme. Halle.
1860. Noack (L.). Art. Simon der Magier. Psyche :

Zeitschr. f. d. Kentniss d. mensch. Seelen- und Geistesleben. Leipzig. Vol. iii, pp. 257—325.

1860. Lipsius (R.A.). Art. Der Gnosticismus. Ersch und Gruber's Allg. Encykl. Leipzig. Vol. lxxi., pp. 223—305. Also separately published at Leipzig.

1860. Baxmann (R.). Art. Die Philosophumena und die Peraten, eine Untersuchung aus der alten Häresiologie. Zeitschr. f. d. histor. Theolog. Leipzig. Vol. ii., pp. 218—257.

1861. Baxmann (R.). Art. Die häratische Gnosis. Zeitschr. f. christl. Wissenschaft u. christl. Leben. Berlin. 1861. Pp. 214—227.

1862. Hilgenfeld (A.). Art. Der Gnosticismus und die Philosophumena mit besonderer Rücksicht auf die neuesten Bearbeitungen von W. Möller und R. A. Lipsius. Zeitschr. f. wiss. Theol. Jena. Vol. iv., pp. 400—464.

1863. Merx (E. O. A.). Bardesanes von Edessa, nebst einer Untersuchung über das Verhältiss der clementinischen Recognitionen zu dem Buche der Gesetze der Länder. Halle.

1863. Renan (J. E.). Histoire des Origines du Christianisme. Paris. 8 vols. 1863—83. See vols. v., vi., vii.

1863. Lipsius (R. A.). Art. Ueber die ophitischen Systeme. Zeitschr. f. wiss. Theol. Jena. vol. iv., pp. 410—457.

1864. Lipsius (R. A.). Art. on Ophite Systems. Zeitschr. f. wiss. Theol. Jena. Vol. i., pp. 37—57.

1864. Hilgenfeld (A.). Bardesanes der letze Gnostiker. Leipzig.

1864. Gruber (J. N.). Die Ophiten. Historische Inaugural-Abhandlung. Würzburg.

1865. Lipsius (R. A.). Zur Quellenkritik des Epiphanios. Wien.

1867. Lipsius (R.A.). Art. Ueber die Zeit des Markion und des Herakleon. Zeitschr. f. wiss. Theol. Jena. Vol. i., pp. 75 ff.

1867. Lipsius (R.A.). Rev. on the original (not in British Museum) of the following. Literarische Centralblatt für Deutschland. Leipzig. Nr. xxvi.

1868. Hofstede de Groot (P.). Basilides am Ausgang des apostolischen Zeitalters als erste Zeuge für Alter und Autorität neutestamentlicher Schriften, inbesodere des Johannes-Evangelium u. s. w. Leipzig. German trans. from the Dutch.

1868. Hilgenfeld (A.). Art. Der Magier Simon. Zeitschr. f. wiss. Theol. Jena. Vol. iv., pp. 357—396.

1868. Fabiani (E.). Notizie di Simon Mago, tratte dai così detti Filosofumeni. Rome and Turin.

1869. Lipsius (R. A.). Art. Gnosis. Schenkel's (D.) Bibel-Lexikon. Leipzig. 5 vols., 1869—75.

1871. Heinrici (G.). Die valentinianische Gnosis und die heilige Schrift. Berlin.

1872. Lipsius (R. A.). Die Quellen der römischen Petrussage kritisch untersucht. Kiel.

1873. Lipsius (R. A.). Rev. on Heinrici's Valentinianische Gnosis. Protestantische Kirchenzeitung. Berlin. Nr. 8., pp. 174—186.

1873. Harnack (A.). Zur Quellenkritik der Geschichte des Gnosticismus. Leipzig.

1873. Berger (P.). Études des Documents nouveaux

fournis sur les Ophites par les Philosophumena. Nancy.

1873. Revillout (E.). Vie et Sentences de Secundus d' après divers Manuscrits orientaux, les Analogies de ce Livre avec les Ouvrages gnostiques. Extrait des Comptes rendus des Séances de l' Académie des Inscriptions et Belles-Lettres. Paris.

1874. Harnack (A.). Art. Zur Quellenkritik der Geschichte des Gnosticismus. Zeitschr. f. d. histor. Theol. Gotha. Pt. ii., pp. 143—226. Continuation of above.

1874. Harnack (A.). De Apellis Gnosi monarchica. Leipzig (?). Not in British Museum.

1875. Hilgenfeld (A.). Art. Der Gnostiker Appelles. Zeitschr. f. wiss. Theolog. Jena. Vol. i., pp. 51—75.

1875. Mansel (H. L.). The Gnostic Heresies of the first and second Centuries. London. A posthumous work edited by Lightfoot, consisting of notes of Lectures delivered in 1868.

1875. Lipsius (R. A.). Die Quellen der ältesten Ketzergeschichte neu untersucht. Leipzig.

1876. Hückstadt (E.). Art. Ueber das pseudo-tertullianische Gedicht adv. Marcionem. Zeitschr. f. wiss. Theolog. Jena. Vol. i., pp. 154 ff.

1876. Harnack (A.). Art. Beiträge zur Geschichte der marcionitischen Kirchen. Zeitschr. f. wiss. Theolog. Leipzig. Pt. i., pp. 80—120.

1876. Ludemann (M.). Art. Literarisches Centralblatt. No. xi. Not in British Museum.

1877. Jacobi (J. L.). Art. Gnosis. Herzog's Real Encyclopädie. Leipzig. 2 ed., 18 vols.,

1877—1888. American ed. New York and Boston. 1882—1883.

1877. Möller (E. W.) Art. Simon Magus. Herzog's R. E. (as above).

1877. Jacobi (J. L.). Art. Das ursprüngliche basilidianische System mit eingehender Rücksicht auf die bisherigen Verhandlungen. Zeitschr. f. Kirchengesch. Gotha. Vol. i., pp. 481—544.

1877. Smith (W.) and Wace (H.). A Dictionary of Christian Biography. London. 4 vols. 1877—1887. Contains an article on every important teacher of the Gnosis, and short notices of many of the principal technical terms by Hort, Salmon, and Lipsius.

1878. Hilgenfeld (A.). Art. Der Basilides des Hippolytus, in Zeitschr. f. wiss. Theolog. Jena. Vol. ii., pp. 228—250.

1879. Tulloch (J.). Art. Gnosticism. Encyclopædia Britannica. London. 9th ed. Very short and unworthy of the subject; the sole source from which the general reader in England gets his information.

1879. De Pressensé (E. de). Art. Gnosticisme. L'Encyclopédie des Sciences religieuses protestantes. Paris.

1880. Ménendez y Pelayo (M.). Historia de los Heterodoxos Españoles. Madrid. 3 vols.

1880. Hilgenfeld (A.) Art. Der Gnostiker Valentinus und seine Schriften. Zeitschr. f. wiss. Theol. Jena. Vol. iii., pp. 280—300.

1880. Meyboom (H. U.). Marcion en de Marcioniten. Leyden.

1880. Joël (M.). Blicke in die Religionsgeschichte zu Anfang des zweiten christlichen Jahrhunderts.

Breslau. 2 vols. 1880, 1883. Excurs ii. Die Gnosis. Vol. i., pp. 103—170.

1880. Hilgenfeld (A.). Art. Der Gnostiker Valentinus und seine Schriften, in Zeitschr. f. wiss. Theolog. Leipzig. Pt. iii., pp. 280—300.

1881. Kaufmann (G.). Die Gnosis nach ihrer Tendenz und Organization. Zwölf Thesen. Breslau.

1881. Hilgenfeld (A.). Art. Cerdon und Marcion. Zeitschr. f. wiss. Theolog. Leipzig. Pt. i., pp. 1—37

1881. Hilgenfeld (A.). Art. Revised Text of Letter of Ptolemy to Flora. Ibid., p. 214.

1881. Harnack (A.). Art. Tatian's Diatessaron und Marcion's Commentar zum Evangelium bei Ephraem Syrus. Zeitschr. f. Kirchengesch. Gotha. Pt. iv., pp. 471—505.

1881. Funk (F. X.). Art. Ist der Basilides der Philosophumena Pantheist? Theol. Quartalschrift. Tübingen. Vol. ii., pp. 277 ff.

1881. Funk (F. X.). Art. Ueber den Verfasser der Philosophumena. Theol. Quartalschrift. Tübingen. Vol. iv., pp. 423—464.

1883. Hilgenfeld (A.). Art. Valentiniana. Zeitschr. f. wiss. Theolog. Jena. Vol. iii., pp. 356—360.

1884. Giraud (?). Ophitæ, Dissertatio de eorum Origine, Placitis et Fatis. Paris. Not in British Museum; referred to by Carl Schmidt, who had, however, not met with a copy.

1884. Hilgenfeld (A.). Die Ketzergeschichte des Urchristenthums. Leipzig. Summing up the results of his previous researches.

1885. Zahn (T.). Art. Die Dialoge des Adamantinus (for Marcion). Zeitschr. f. Kirchengesch. Gotha. Vol. ix., pp. 193 ff.

1885. Salmon (G.). Art. The Cross-references in the Philosophumena. Hermathena. Dublin. Pp. 389 ff.

1887. King (C.W.). The Gnostics and their Remains, ancient and mediæval. London. 2 ed. 1st ed., 1864, very much smaller and containing no reference to the Pistis Sophia.

1887. Amélineau (E.). Essai sur le Gnosticisme égyptien ses Développements er son Origine égyptienne. Annales du Musée Guimet. Paris. Vol. xiv.

1888. Harnack (A.). Art. Valentinus. Encyclopædia Britannica. London. 9th edition. A longer article than Tulloch's on the whole of Gnosticism.

1888. Zahn (T.). Adopts Salmon's Philosophumena theory. Geschichte des N. T. Kanons. Erlangen. Vol I. i. p. 24, n. 2.

1889. Usener (H.). Religionsgeschichtliche Untersuchungen. Th. i. Das Weihnachtsfest. Bonn.

1889. Harnack (A.). Crit. on above. Theologische Literaturzeitung. Leipzig. Nr. viii., pp. 199—211.

1889. Hönig (A.). Die Ophiten. Ein Beitrag zur Geschichte des jüdischen Gnosticismus. Berlin.

1889. Harnack (A.). Crit. of Amélineau's Essai. Theolog. Literaturztg. Leipzig. Nr. ix., pp. 232 ff.

1890. Stähelin (H.). Die gnostischen Quellen Hippolyts in seiner Hauptschrift gegen die Häretiker Texte und Untersuchungen. Leipzig. Vol. vi., pt. 3.

1890. Harnack (A.). Sieben neue Bruckstücke der Sillogismen des Apelles. Text. u. Unter. Leipzig. Vol. vi., pt. 3.

1890. Kurtz (J. H.). Lehrbuch der Kirchengeschichte.

Leipzig. 11th ed., 1890. English trans. by Macpherson (J.). Church History. London. 3 vols., 1888—1890. Vol. i., pp. 98—125.

1891. Blunt (J. H.). Dictionary of Sects, Heresies, ecclesiastical Parties and Schools of religious Thought. London. New ed. Very unsatisfactory.

1891. Brooke (A. E.). The Fragments of Heracleon newly edited from the MSS. with an Introduction and Notes. Cambridge. Texts and Studies. Vol. i., No. 4.

1892. Mead (G. R. S.). Simon Magus. An Essay. London.

1893. Harnack (A.). Geschichte der altchristlichen Litteratur bis Eusebius. Leipzig. 2 vols.

1894. Anrich (G.). Das antike Mysterienwesen in seinem Einfluss auf das Christentum. Göttingen. Der Gnosticismus in seinem Zusammenhang mit dem Mysterienwesen. Pp. 74—105.

1894. Harnack (A.). Lehrbuch der Dogmengeschichte. Freiburg i. B. u. Leipzig. 3 vols., 3rd ed. 1st ed., 1886. Die Versuche der Gnostiker u. s. w. Vol. i., pp. 211—253.

1894. Harnack (A.). History of Dogma. English trans. by various hands. London. 7 vols. The Attempts of the Gnostics to create an Apostolic Dogmatic and a Christian Theology; or the Acute Secularising of Christianity. Vol. i., pp. 222—265.

1894. Kunze (J.). De Historiæ Gnosticismi Fontibus novæ Quæstiones criticæ. Leipzig.

1894. Harnack (A.). Rev. of Kunze's thesis. Theolog. Literaturztg. Leipzig. Pp. 506 ff.

1895. Amélineau (E.). Le nouveau Traité gnostique de Turin. Paris.
1895. Anz (W.) Zur Frage nach dem Ursprung des Gnostizismus. Texte u. Untersuch. Leipzig. Vol. xv.
1897. Nau (F.). Une Biographie inédite de Bardesane l'Astrologue. Paris.
1897. Bevan (A. A.). The Hymn of the Soul [attributed to Bardesan] contained in the Syriac Acts of St. Thomas. Texts and Studies. Cambridge. Vol. v., No. 3.
1898 Friedlander (M.). Der vorchristliche jüdische Gnosticismus. Göttingen.
1899. Nau (F.). Bardesane l'Astrologue : Le Livre des Lois des Pays. Paris.
1899. Burkitt (F. C.). The Hymn of Bardaisan, rendered into English. London.
1900. Mead (G. R. S.). Fragments of a Faith Forgotten. Some Short Sketches among the Gnostics, mainly of the First Two Centuries. A Contribution to the Study of Christian Origins. London.
1900. Preuschen (E.). Die apokryphen gnostichen Adamschriften aus dem Armenischen übersetzt.
1900 (?). Kreyenbühl. Das Evangelium der Wahrheit. 2 vols. Vol. ii. 1905 (?). Not in British Museum.
1901. Waitz (H.). Das pseudotertullianische Gedicht adversus Marcionem. Ein Beitrag zur Geschichte der altchrist. Literatur sowie zur Quellenkritik des Marcionitismus. Darmstadt.
1902. Liechtenhan (R.). Art. Die pseudepigraphe

Literatur der Gnostiker. Zeitschr. f. d. neutest. Wissenschaft. Giessen. Fascc. iii., xiv.

1903. Hoffmann (G.). Zwei Hymnen der Thomasakten. Zeitschr. f. d. neutest. Wissenchaft. Giessen. Vol. iv., pp. 273—309.

1903. De Faye (E.). Introduction à l'étude du Gnosticisme au IIe et IIIe Siècle. Paris.

1904. Waitz (W.). Die Pseudoklementinen Homilien u. Rekognitionen. Texte u. Untersuchungen. Leipzig. N. F. Bd. x. Hft. 4.

1904. Hilgenfeld (A.). Art. Der Königssohn und die Perlen. Ein morgenländischer Gedicht. Zeitschr. f. wissenschaft. Theologie. Leipzig. Vol. xlviii., (N. F. xii.). Hft. ii., pp. 229—241.

1904. Preuschen (E.). Zwei Gnostische Hymnen. Giessen.

1905. Harnack (A.). Ed. The Letter of Ptolemy to Flora. Cambridge.

1905. Krüger (G.) Art. Das Taufbekentniss der römischen Gemeinde als Niederschlag des Kampfes gegen Marcion. Zeit. f. d. neutest. Wiss. Heft i.

1906. Mead (G. R. S.). Thrice-Greatest Hermes. Studies in Hellenistic Theosophy and Gnosis. Being a Translation of the Extant Sermons and Fragments of the Trismegistic Literature, with Prolegomena, Commentaries and Notes. London. 3 vols.

THE COPTIC GNOSTIC WORKS.

The student will find critical notices on most of the following works in the Introduction to my translation of the Pistis Sophia.

1770. Art. in Brittische theolog. Magazin (?). See Köstlin infra. I can find no trace of this in the British Museum.

1773. Woide (C. A.). Art. in Journal des Savants. Paris.

1778. Woide (C. A.). Art. in Cramer's (J. A.) Beyträge zur Beförderung theologischer und andrer wichtigen Kentnisse. Kiel und Hamburg. Pp. 82 ff.

1799. Woide (C. A.). Appendix ad Editionem Novi Testamenti græci e Codice ms. Alexandrino et cet. Oxonii. P. 137.

1812. Münter (F. C. C. H.). Odæ gnosticæ Salomon tributæ, thebaice et latine. Prefatione et Adnotationibus philologicis illustratæ. Hafniæ.

1838. Dulaurier (É.). Art. in Le Moniteur. Paris. Sep. 27.

1843. Matter (J). Histoire critique du Gnosticisme. See General Bibliog. above. 2 ed. Vol. ii., pp. 41 ff., 350 ff. Dörner's German trans., vol. ii., pp. 69 ff., 163 ff.

1847. Dulaurier (É.). Art. Notice sur le Manuscript copte-thébain, intitulé La Fidèle Sagesse; et sur la Publication projetée du Texte et de la Traduction française de ce Manuscript.

Journal asiatique. Paris. 4th series. Vol. ix., juin, pp. 534—548.

1851. Schwartze (M. G.) Pistis Sophia, Opus gnosticum Valentino adjudicatum, e Codice manuscripto coptico londinensi descriptum. Text and Latin translation (1853) by Schwartze, ed. by Petermann (J. H.). Berlin.

1852. Bunsen (C. C. J.). Hippolytus und seine Zeit. Anfänge und Aussichten des Christenthums und der Menschheit. Leipzig. Vol. i., pp. 47, 48. Hippolytus and his Age. London. Vol. i., pp. 61, 62.

1853. Baur (F. C.) Das Christenthum und die christliche Kirche der drei ersten Jahrhunderte. Tübingen. Notes pp. 185, 186 and 205, 206.

1854. Köstlin (K. R.). Art. Das gnostische System des Buches Pistis Sophia. Theolog. Jahrbücher. Tübingen. Vol. xiii., pp. 1—104, 137—196.

1856. Migne (J. P.). Le Livre de la fidèle Sagesse. An anonymous translation in Migne's Dictionaire des Apocryphes. Paris. Vol. i. append., pt. ii., coll. 1181—1286.

1860. Lipsius (R. A.). Gnosticismus. Leipzig. Pp. 95 ff., 157 ff. See Gen. Bibliog.

1875. Wright (W.). The Palæographical Society. Facsimiles of MSS. and Inscriptions. Oriental Series. Ed. by W. W. London. Plate xlii.

1877. Jacobi (J. L.). Art. Gnosis. Herzog's Theolog. Real Encycl. See Gen. Bibliog.

1887. King (C. W.). The Gnostics and their Remains. Contains a translation of a number of pages of P. S. See Gen. Bibliog.

1887. Lipsius (R. A.). Art. Pistis Sophia. Smith and

Wace's Dictionary of Christ. Biog. See Gen. Bibliog.

1887. Amélineau (E.). Essai sur le Gnosticisme égyptien. Especially pt. iii., pp. 106—322. See Gen. Bibliog.

1889. Harnack (A.). Crit. of above. See Gen. Bibliog.

1890. Amélineau (E.). Art. Les Traités gnostiques d' Oxford. Étude critique. Revue de l' Histoire des Religions. Paris. Pp. 1—72.

1891. Schmidt (Carl). Art. Ueber die in koptischer Sprache erhaltenen gnostischen Originalwerke. Sitzungsber. der königl. preuss. Akad. di Wissensch. Berlin. Phil.-hist. Klasse. xi. pp. 215—219.

1891. Harnack (A.). Ueber das gnostische Buch Pistis. Sophia. Leipzig. Text. und Untersuch. Vol vii., pt. 2.

1891. Ryle (H. E.) and James (M. R.). Psalms of the Pharisees, commonly called the Psalms of Solomon. Cambridge. For the five Salomonic Odes quoted in the P.S. See Introd. for full bibliog. of subject.

1891. Amélineau (E.). Notice sur le Papyrus gnostique Bruce. Texte et Traduction. Paris.

1891. Schmidt (C.). Crit. on Amélineau's Notice. Göttingische gelehrte Anzeigen. Göttingen. Nr. xvii., pp. 640—657.

1891. Amélineau (E.). Art. Le Papyrus Bruce. Réponse aux Göttingische gelehrte Anzeigen. Revue de l'Histoire des Religions. Paris. Vol. xxiv., no. 3, pp. 376—380.

1892. Schmidt (C.). Final reply of Schmidt. Gött. gelehr. Anz. Nr. vi., pp. 201—222.

1892. Schmidt (C.). Gnostische Schriften in koptischer

Sprache aus dem Codex brucianus, herausgegeben, übersetzt und bearbeitet. Leipzig. Text. u. Untersuch. Vol. viii., pts. 1, 2.

1894. Preuschen (E.). Crit. on above. Theolog. Litt.-Ztg. Leipzig. Nr. 7.

1894 Schmidt (C.). Reply. Die in dem koptisch-gnostischen Codex brucianus enthaltenen "beiden Bücher Jeû" in ihrem Verhältnis zu der Pistis Sophia. Zeitschr. f. wiss. Theolog. Leipzig. Pt. iv., Nr. xxiv., pp. 555—585.

1895. Amélineau (E.). Pistis Sophia. Ouvrage gnostique de Valentin, traduit du copte en français, avec une Introduction. Paris.

1896. Mead (G. R. S.). Pistis Sophia. A Gnostic Gospel (with Extracts from the Books of the Saviour appended) originally translated from Greek into Coptic, and now for the first time Englished from Schwartze's Latin version of the only known Coptic MS. and checked by Amélineau's French Version, with an Introduction. London.

1896. Schmidt (C.). Art. Ein vorirenaeisches gnostisches Originalwerk in koptisher Sprache. Sitzungsber. der königl. preuss. Akad. der Wissenschaft. zu Berlin. Pp. 837–847.

1898. Schmidt (C.). Review on Amélineau's trans. of P.S. Sonder-Abdruck aus den Göttingisch. gelehr. Anzeigen. Nr. vi.

1901. Liechtenhan (R.). Untersuchungen zur koptisch-gnostischen Literatur. Die Offenbarung im Gnosticismus. Göttingen.

1905. Schmidt (C.). Koptisch-gnostische Schriften. Die Pistis Sophia. Die beiden Bücher des Jeû. Unbekanntes altgnostisches Werk. Leipzig. Vol. 1.

REVIEWS AND ARTICLES IN ENGLISH AND AMERICAN PERIODICALS.

These are taken mostly from Poole's (W. F.) Index to Periodical Literature. Boston. 3rd ed., 1885, with Supplements up to 1898. The British Museum press marks are conveniently given in the tables of abbreviations, etc., of this publication.

1828. Notice on Matter's Histoire (1st ed). The Foreign Quarterly Review. London. Vol. iii., pp. 307—309.

1830. Review on the same. Ibid., vol. v., pp. 569—598.

1830. Art. Gnosticism. The Methodist Magazine. London. Vol. liii., pp. 325 ff.

1831. Art. History of Gnosticism. The Eclectic Review. London. Vol. liv., pp. 373 ff.

1833. Cheever (G. B.). Art. The Philosophy of the Gnostics. The American Biblical Repository. New York. 2 ser. vol. iii., pp. 353 ff.

1833. Cheever (G. B.). Art. The Phil. of the Gnostics. Ibid., vol. vi., pp. 253 ff.

1837. Parker (T.). Art. History of Gnosticism. The Christian Examiner. Boston. Vol. xxiv., pp. 112 ff.

1858. Schaff (P.). Art. Analysis of Gnosticism. The Mercersburg Review. Mercersburg. Vol. x., pp. 520 ff.

1858. Harwood (E.). Art. Gnosticism. The American Church Review. New Haven and New York. Vol. x., pp. 259 ff.

1865. Rev. on King's Gnostics and their Remains. The

Christian Remembrancer. London. Vol. i., pp. 459 ff.

1865. Art. Gnosticism. The Art Journal. London. Vol. xvii. pp. 41 ff.

1867. Clarke (J. C. C.). Art. Gnosticism Outlined. The Baptist Quarterly Review. Philadelphia. Vol. i., pp. 35 ff.

1868. Sears (E. H.). Art. Gnosticism. The Monthly Religious Magazine. Boston. Vol. xli., pp. 101 ff.

1870. Harmon (H. M.). Art. de Groot on Gnostic Testimonies to the N. T. The Methodist Quarterly. New York. Vol. xxx., pp. 485 ff.

1874. Art. Gnosticism. The Dublin Review. Dublin. Vol. lxxvi., pp. 56 ff.

1875. Rev. on Mansel's Gnostic Heresies. The Christian Observer. Vol. lxxv., pp. 438 ff.

1878. Allen (J. H.). Art. Gnosticism. The Unitarian Review. Boston. Vol. x., pp. 543 ff.

1885. Salmon (G.). Art. The Cross-References in the "Philosophumena." Hermathena. Dublin. Vol. v., pp. 389—402.

1887. Rev. on King's Gnostics (2 ed.). The Saturday Review. London. Vol. lxiv., pp. 641 ff.

1887. Lang (J. M.). Art. Gnostic Sects of the Second Century. The British and Foreign Evangelical Review. London. Vol. xxxvi., pp. 226 ff.

1889. Conder (C. R.). Art. The Gnostics. The Asiatic Review. London. Vol. v., pp. 84 ff.

1891. Art. Gnosticism. The London Quarterly. Vol. lxvii., pp. 120 ff.

1895. Stokes (G. T.). Art. Gnosticism and Modern Pantheism. Mind. London. Vol. xx., pp. 320 ff.

1898. Carus (P.). Art. Gnosticism in Relation to Christianity. The Monist. Chicago. Vol. viii., pp. 502—546.

1898. Scott (C. A.) Rev. on Anz's Zur Frage nach dem Ursprung des Gnosticismus.

UNCANONICAL ACTS.

The following may serve as an introduction to the subject. Lipsius' exhaustive work will supply data for a full bibliography.

1851. Tischendorf (C. de). Acta Apostolorum apocrypha. Leipzig.

1871. Wright (W.). Apocryphal Acts of the Apostles. Syriac Text and English Translation. London. 2 vols.

1880. Zahn (T.). Acta Joannis. Erlangen.

1883. Lipsius (R. A.) Die apokryphen Apostelgeschichten und Apostellegenden. Ein Beitrag zur altchristlichen Literaturgeschichte. Braunschweig. 3 vols., 1883, 1884, 1890.

1883. Bonnet (M.). Supplementum Codicis apocryphi. Acta Thomæ. Leipzig.

1891. Lipsius (R. A.) and Bonnet (M.). Acta Apostolorum apocrypha. Leipzig. 2 pts., pt. i. ed. by L., 1891, pt. ii. by B., 1898.

1897. James (M. R.). Apocrypha Anecdota II. Cambridge. Texts and Studies. Vol. v., No. 1.

1897. Bevan (A. A.). The Hymn of the Soul contained in the Syriac Acts of St. Thomas. Cambridge. Texts and Studies. Vol. v., No. 3.

GNOSTIC (?) GEMS AND ABRAXAS-STUDIES.

For works prior to 1828 see Matter's Histoire, 1st ed., vol. ii., pp. 52, 53, where a very fair bibliography is to be found. See also King's Gnostics and their Remains. For more recent researches see:

1891. Dieterich (A.). Abraxas. Studien zur Religionsgeschichte des spätern Altertums. Leipzig.

GNOSTIC WORKS MENTIONED BY ANCIENT WRITERS.

For a list of Gnostic works, fragments of some of which are still extant, but of the majority the titles only, see:

1893. Harnack (A.). Geschichte der altchristlichen Literature bis Eusebius. Leipzig. 2 vols. Gnostische, marcionitische und ebionitische Literatur. Vol. i., pp. 143—231.

THE MOST RECENT TEXTS OF THE HÆRESIOLOGICAL CHURCH FATHERS AND THEIR ENGLISH TRANSLATIONS.

Corpus Hæresiologicum. Oehler (F.). Berlin. 3 vols. 1856, 1859, 1861. Vol. i. continens Scriptores hæresiologicos minores latinos. Philastrius, Augustinus, Prædestinatus, Pseudo-Tertullian, Pseudo-Hieronymus, Isidorus Hispalensis, Paulus, Honorius Augustodunensis, Gennadius Massiliensis. Vols. ii., iii. Epiphanii Panaria.

Justin Martyr. Otto (J. C. T. v.). Jena. 3 vols. 2 ed. 1847—1850. Also in Corpus Apologetarum christianorum Sæculi secundi. 3 vols. 1876—1881.

 Eng. Trans. by Dods (M.) and Reith (G.), in Ante-Nicene Christian Library. Edinburgh. 1867.

Clemens Alexandrinus. Dindorf (G.). Oxford. 4 vols. 1869.

 Eng. Trans. by Wilson (W.), in Ante-N. Ch. Lib. Edin. 2 vols. 1867, 1869.

 (Protrepticus und Paedagogus). Stählin (O.). Leipzig Herausg. v. d. Kirchenväter-Commission der k. Preuss. Akad. d. Wiss.

Irenæus. Stieren (A.). Leipzig. 2 vols. 1848.

 Eng. Trans. by Roberts (A.) and Rambaut (W. H.), in Ante-N. Ch. Lib. Edin. 2 vols. 1868, 1869.

Tertullian. Oehler (F.). Leipzig. 3 vols. 1853, 1854.

 Eng. Trans. by Holmes (P.), in Ante-N. Ch. Lib. Edin. 4 vols., 1868—1870.

 (De Praescriptione Haereticorum). Bindley (T. H.). Oxford. 1893.

 Preuschen (E.). 1892. (Sammlung ausgewählter kirchen und dogmengeschichlicher Quellen-Schriften. Heft iii.).

Hippolytus. (Philos.). Dunker (L.), and Schneidewin (F. G.). Göttingen. 1859. Cruice (P.) Paris. 1860.

 Eng. Trans. by MacMahon (J. H.), in Ante-N. Ch. Lib. Edin. 1868.

Origen. (C. Celsum). Lommatzsch (C. H. E.). Berlin. 3 vols., 1845, 1846. Selwyn (W.). Cambridge. 1873. Bks. i,—iii. only.

	Eng. Trans. by Crombie (F.), in Ante-N. Ch. Lib. Edin. 2 vols., 1869, 1872.
Eusebius.	Dindorf (G.). Leipzig. 4 vols., 1867—1871. Eng. Trans. (Ecc. Hist.) by Crusé (C. F.) in Bohn's Ecclesiastical Library. London. New ed., 1894. (Church Hist., Life of Constantine, etc.) by McGiffert (A. C.) and others, in Select Library of Nicene and Post-Nicene Fathers of the Christian Church. New Series. Oxford. 1890.
Epiphanius.	Dindorf (G). Leipzig. 5 vols., 1859—1863. No Trans. exists in English.
Philastrius.	Marx (F.). Vienna. 1898. No Trans. exists in English.
Theodoret.	Migne (J. P.) Patrologiæ Cursus Completus. Series Græca. Paris. Vols. 80, 84. 1857. No. Trans. exists in English.

Works by G. R. S. MEAD, B.A., M.R.A.S.

Apollonius of Tyana:

THE PHILOSOPHER-REFORMER OF THE FIRST CENTURY A.D.

A critical Study of the only existing Record of his Life, with some Account of the War of Opinion concerning him, and an Introduction on the Religious Associations and Brotherhoods of the Times and the possible Influence of Indian Thought on Greece.

SYNOPSIS OF CONTENTS.

i. Introductory. ii. The Religious Associations and Communities of the First Century. iii. India and Greece. iv. The Apollonius of Early Opinion. v. Texts, Translations and Literature. vi. The Biographer of Apollonius. vii. Early Life. viii. The Travels of Apollonius. ix. The Shrines of the Temples and the Retreats of Religion. x. The Gymnosophists of Upper Egypt. xi. Apollonius and the Rulers of the Empire. xii. Apollonius the Prophet and Wonder-Worker. xiii. His Mode of Life. xiv. Himself and his Circle. xv. From his Sayings and Sermons. xvi. From his Letters. xvii. The Writings of Apollonius. xviii. Bibliographical Notes.

160 *pp. large 8vo. Cloth.* 3s 6d. *net.*

SOME PRESS OPINIONS.

"Mr. Mead is already favourably known to scholars as a well-informed writer on the origins of religion. His particular province of study is that which passes by the name of 'occult'—a word that may be little more than a euphemism for our ignorance. . . . Mr. Mead's work is careful, scholarly, and critical, yet deeply sympathetic with those spiritual ideals of life which are far greater than all the creeds. . . . . Will be found very useful to English readers."—*Bradford Observer.*

"With much that Mr. Mead says about Apollonius we are entirely disposed to agree."
—*Spectator.*

"Mr. Mead's sympathetic monograph is based upon a careful study of the literature of the subject. . . . . Writes with moderation, and has rendered good service by examining Apollonius from a fresh point of view."—*Manchester Guardian.*

"We give a specially cordial welcome to Mr. G. R. S. Mead's 'Apollonius of Tyana. . . . . It is a book which all well-instructed spiritualists will be able to appreciate and understand."—*Light.*

"A charming and enlightening little work, full of knowledge, bright with sympathy, and masterly in style."—*The Coming Day.*

"It is not only interesting, it is fair, and to a great degree scholarly, although it is slight and popular in conception. The spirit and tone are admirable. Mr. Mead neither flouts what he thinks mistaken nor states uncritically what he believes. . . . . He uses his authorities with care and judgment, and gives exact references. Some good suggestions are made in the book."—*Literature.*

"Through this jungle of fable, controversy, and misunderstanding, Mr. Mead has heroically set himself to cut his way to the man as he was. Practically he regards him as a theosophist of the first century, who had been initiated into the loftier orders and commissioned to regenerate the cults at many of the larger sanctuaries. The author has studied the original authorities carefully, and also the work of his predecessors. It is, of course, impossible to say whether his attempt to get back to the real Apollonius has been successful. In most

THE THEOSOPHICAL PUBLISHING SOCIETY, LONDON AND BENARES.

WORKS BY THE SAME AUTHOR.

"respects his account is plausible, and quite possibly may represent the facts. . . . . At any rate, impartial students will be grateful for his sympathetic vindication of Apollonius from the too frequent charge that he was nothing better than a charlatan. He thinks that Apollonius must surely have visited some of the Christian societies, and have met with Paul, if not earlier, at least at Rome in 66. It seems to us very problematical that he should have taken any interest in the Christians, though the probability would be much enhanced if Mr. Mead's view of primitive Christianity could be substantiated."—*The Primitive Methodist Quarterly Review*.

"Students of the religious history of the earlier centuries of the Christian era are already indebted to Mr. Mead for his elucidations of more than one obscure document of that remote age. His account of Apollonius of Tyana will be all the more welcome because, treating its subject without theological or denominational prepossessions, it reveals the ancient philosopher in a new light, which may very well be also a true one. . . . Mr. Mead gives a readable and well-studied account of him, reviewing what little remains known of his life, and inquiring, without controversy, what must have been the character of one who had so real an influence on the religious life of his time. . . . . The book is rich in suggestions of the actualities of the religious life of the ancient world when Christianity was still in its infancy. It is well worthy of the attention of all who are interested in the subject."—*The Scotsman*.

"This little book is an attempt to tell us all that is definitely known of one of the most extraordinary figures in history. . . . It is done in the main with absolute impartiality, and with considerable learning. It is not a satisfactory book, but it is useful and interesting, and, in default of anything better, it may be recommended."—*Saturday Review*.

"The task Mr. Mead has set himself is to recover from Philostratus' highly romantic narrative the few facts which can be really known, and to present to the public a plain and simple story which shall accord with the plain and simple life of the humble Tyanean; and he has achieved no little success. His book is thoroughly readable, the manner of writing most attractive, and his enthusiasm evidently sincere. . . . . Mr. Mead's last work is a thoroughly scholarly one, and he has contributed a very valuable page to philosophical history."—*Chatham and Rochester Observer*.

"Mr. Mead's works are always worth reading. They are characterised by clearness, sanity, and moderation; they are scholarly, and are always conceived in a profoundly religious spirit. The bibliographies are excellent. With Mr. Mead's workmanship we have only one fault to find. In order to give elevation to the utterances of his hero, he not only affects poetical expressions—which is permissible—and poetical inversions of speech—which are not permissible—but he indulges in a whole page of irregular blank verse. Mr. Mead is master of an excellent prose style, and Pegasus is a sorry hack when Pegasus goes lame."—*Journal of the Royal Asiatic Society*.

"This well-written volume affords a critical study of the only existing record of the life of Apollonius of Tyana. . . . . His principles, his mode of teaching, his travels in the east and in the south and west, his mode of life, his sayings, letters, and writings and bibliographical notes, are all set forth in a clear and interesting style."—*Asiatic Quarterly Review*.

"Verfasser will auf Grund der philostratischen Biographie ein Bild vom Leben und Wirken des Apollonius geben. Es fehlt ihm dazu nich an besonnenen Urteil, eben so wenig an der nötigen Belesenheit in der einschlägigen Litteratur. . . . . Verf. hält sich auch, obwohl offenbar selbst Theologe, frei von der theologischen Voreingenommenheit, die bei der Beurteilung des Apollonius so früh und so lange Unheil gestiftet hat."—*Wochenschrift für klassische Philologie*.

Ὁ κ. Mead γράφει λίαν γλαφυρῶς, πραγματεύεται δὲ τὸ θέμα του κριτικώτατα καὶ μετὰ μεγάλης νουνεχείας καὶ δίδει ἡμῖν οὕτω τὴν ἀξιοπιστοτέραν εἰκόνα τοῦ ἀνδρός.—*Erevna*.

THE THEOSOPHICAL PUBLISHING SOCIETY, London and Benares.

WORKS BY THE SAME AUTHOR.

THE GOSPELS AND THE GOSPEL:

A STUDY IN THE MOST RECENT RESULTS OF THE LOWER AND THE HIGHER CRITICISM.

SYNOPSIS OF CONTENTS.

Preamble—A Glimpse at the History of the Evolution of Biblical Criticism—The "Word of God" and the "Lower Criticism"—The Nature of the Tradition of the Gospel Autographs—Autobiographical Traces in the Existing Documents—An Examination of the Earliest Outer Evidence—The Present Position of the Synoptical Problem—The Credibility of the Synoptists—The Johannine Problem—Summary of the Evidence from all Sources—The Life-side of Christianity—The Gospel of the Living Christ.

200 pp. Large octavo. Cloth, 4s. 6d. net.

SOME PRESS NOTICES.

"A clear, intelligent, and interesting account of the history of the development of Biblical criticism . . . . a thoughtful and learned, yet readable book, which well deserves the attention of readers interested in its subject."—*The Scotsman.*

"Mr. Mead begins with a sketch of the recent progress of Biblical criticism. The tone is not altogether what one would wish—the 'Conservatives' were, after all, fighting for what they held to be very precious—but it is substantially true."—*Spectator.*

"Mr. Mead describes his book as 'a study in the most recent results of the higher and the lower criticism.' The description is incomplete rather than inadequate, for the study is made from a neo-Gnostic point of view, and under neo-Gnostic prepossessions. . . . Mr. Mead has shown, in previous volumes, how the fascinating glamour of their writings has attracted him, and, though they are mainly represented by imperfect but suggestive fragments, he has done his best to reconstruct them and to revive, where possible, their lingering vitality. His work, on these lines, has met with due appreciation. . . . . He regards Gnosticism as a suppressed religion which may yet result in an all-embracing creed, which will combine and focus the scattered rays now dispersed abroad among divergent faiths."—*Sheffield Daily Telegraph.*

"In his modest preamble the author describes himself as neither scientist nor theologian, but as 'a friendly spectator, who, as a devoted lover of both science and religion, has no partisan interest to serve, and, as a believer in the blessings of that true tolerance which permits perfect liberty in all matters of opinion and belief, has no desire to dictate to others what their decision should be on any one of the many controversial points touched upon.' Further on he strongly advises the 'disturbed' reader, 'who fears to plunge deeper into the free waters of criticism,' to 'leave the matter alone, and content himself with the creeds and cults of the churches.' We, therefore, cannot complain if in the sequel he puts forth conclusions widely different from those generally held, even in this 'advanced' age, by the average thoughtful student. He claims to treat the subject 'without fear or favour,' and, while disclaiming the 'ultra-rationalism' of the 'extreme school' of criticism, he nevertheless 'feels himself compelled largely to accept the proofs brought forward of the unhistorical nature of much in the Gospel narratives, and also the main positions in all subjects of Gospel criticism which do not involve a mystical or practical religious element.' As a theosophist, he seems to have a peculiar affection, on mystical grounds, for the fourth Gospel, which, however, he sees fit to class with Hermes Trismegistus. It would be far too elaborate a task to attempt to deal with the details of his argument here. Its results claim to be based on Nestle's deservedly popular work. Anyone who wishes to see Nestle theosophically interpreted may well read Mr. Mead's lucid and interesting pages for himself. . . . . There are many other points we should criticise if we had space. But there are many points, on the other hand, which call for hearty commendation; not least, Mr. Mead's crusade against book-worship."—*The Guardian.*

"This work consists of various chapters which have appeared from time to time in a Review devoted to the study of religion from an entirely independent point of view, and perused by a class of readers belonging to many Churches of Christendom, to schools or sects of Brahmanism, Buddhism, Mohammedanism, Zoroastrianism, and others who follow no religion. The author considers that the controversies which have been waged under the term of the 'Higher Criticism' have almost exclusively been that of progressive knowledge of physical facts (natural, historical, and literary) and the conservatism of theological traditional views, and never, at any time, between Science and Religion in their true meaning."—*Asiatic Quarterly Review.*

"While Mr. Mead is thus in general agreement with the extreme left wing in criticism, he is very far from adopting their rationalistic point of view. . . . . As to dates, the author assigns all the Gospels to the reign of Hadrian. The phenomena of the Synoptic

---

THE THEOSOPHICAL PUBLISHING SOCIETY, LONDON AND BENARES.

WORKS BY THE SAME AUTHOR.

Gospels, he thinks, point to concerted effort, and he believes that they were written in Egypt. It is not surprising that he lays much stress on Gnosticism, but he has no wish to revive it. He rather pleads that we should study it with a view to recovering precious truths that have been lost. The book is written in a pleasant style, and we have read it with interest, but we cannot regard it as Mr. Mead's most successful effort."—*The Primitive Methodist Quarterly.*

"This anlysis of the 'Gospels,' however, is preliminary to a vindication of that eterna 'Gospel' which lies beneath all such literature. Mr. Mead contends that this Gospel may be discovered in Gnostic writings which were condemned by the early Christian Church as heresies. He admits freely that the forms of the ancient 'Gnosis' cannot now be revived, but he finds in the popular Evangelical doctrine of the living Christ an adumbration of the ancient wisdom of the condemned Gnostics. But the Christ of Mr. Mead's teaching is one of a sacred brotherhood, including Buddha, Krishna, Zoroaster, and other great enlighteners of the race. These are all living spiritual energies, inspiring and guiding mankind in its toilsome quest for truth and righteousness. Readers will find in Mr. Mead's thoughtful and scholarly pages much that will help in that rational and spiritual reconstruction which is the great religious task of the hour."—*Yorkshire Daily Observer.*

"Ὁ ἐμβριθὴς ἐρευνητὴς τῶν ἀρχῶν τοῦ χριστιανισμοῦ κ. G. R. S. Mead ἐδημοσίευσιν ἄρτι μελέτην περὶ τῆς χριστιανικῆς φιλοσοφίας ἐξόχως διδακτικήν. . . . Ὁ κ. Mead εἶνε εἷς τῶν κορυφαίων σκαπανέων τῆς ἐρευνητικῆς ταύτης ἐργασίας καὶ πᾶν ὅ, τι γράφει κρίνω ἰδιαζούσης προσοχῆς ἄξιον. . . . Ἐμπνεόμενος ὑπὸ τῆς ὑγιοῦς ταύτης ἀρχῆς ὁ κ. Mead συνετέλεσεν ἐσχάτως θαυμάσιον ἔργον."—*Erevna.*

DID JESUS LIVE 100 B.C.?

An Enquiry into the Talmud Jesus Stories, the Toldoth Jeschu, and some Curious Statements of Epiphanius—Being a Contribution to the Study of Christian Origins.

440, xvi. pp. Large octavo. Cloth, 9s. net.

SOME PRESS NOTICES.

"A close and learned investigation. . . . Mr. Mead is a theosophical scholar whose previous works dealing with Gnosticism and Gospel criticism are of some value not only to theosophists, but to theologians."—*The Times.*

"On the examination of these little known tales Mr Mead expends an amount of patience, labour, and learning which the ordinary man . . . would deem ridiculous. Happily, however, the world is not yet peopled exclusively with fat, plump, commonplace people, and those who follow Mr. Mead can be sure of reward in matter which will set them thinking. . . . These researches are contributions to the study of the origins of Christianity, and their uniqueness lies in the fact that very few writers ever enter the fields where Mr. Mead works with such praiseworthy diligence. The ordinary reader trusts too implicitly, in these matters, to his Geikie and his Farrar, and even the student who has the dash of the heretic in him is too easily contented with his Renan. For both these classes of readers Mr. Mead's chapters will open up new fields of thought. The reader will find himself in the midst of those fierce fanaticisms, and weird, occult theosophies which were part of the atmosphere in which infant Christianity grew. Without an adequate acquaintance with these, Christian origins cannot be understood. This knowledge Mr. Mead's readers will obtain if they follow him closely, and their view of the beginnings of Christianity will be correspondingly full and true."—*The Yorkshire Daily Observer.*

"Mr. Mead's previous wanderings in historic by-ways have resulted in much curious lore associated with Gnosticism and the Neo-Platonists, and he seems to have been attracted to this adjacent field as one likely to contain hidden treasure. . . . . For those who desire an introduction to this branch of literature, Mr. Mead has made it easily accessible."—*The Sheffield Daily Telegraph.*

"Written by a professed theosophist, this work is yet entirely free from the taint of dogmatism of any kind. It is indeed a valuable contribution to the literature on the subject, which is as abundant as it is chaotic. The author has collected and reviewed this mass, and has summarised and criticised it until he has shaped it into something of a coherent whole. The Rabbinical and other Hebrew legendary and historical matter dealing with the reputed origin and life of the Messiah is carefully sifted, and the subject is approached with befitting reverence. . . . That the book is most valuable from a suggestive point of view cannot be denied. It merits the attention of all interested in Christian criticism."—*The Scotsman.*

THE THEOSOPHICAL PUBLISHING SOCIETY, LONDON AND BENARES.

WORKS BY THE SAME AUTHOR.

"This book, with its remarkable title, deals in a very critical spirit with the origins of Christianity. . . . Although critical in the highest degree, the author does not dogmatise, and preserves a philosophical calm thought."—*The Chatham and Rochester Observer.*

"The author of this learned work is not propounding a mere theological riddle, nor can he be said to be coming forward wantonly merely to increase the number of puzzles that confront the student of Christian origins. . . . The author has been a very diligent student of the Talmud, and perhaps his lengthened account of that extraordinary body of traditions is one of the best in our language. . . . The argument throughout is marked by great erudition and remarkable modesty."—*The Glasgow Herald.*

"The question is not a fool's question. It is serious, and Mr. Mead takes it seriously."—*The Expository Times.*

"Mr. Mead has done much first-rate work, on untraditional lines, in early Church history, and has propounded theorems of which a good deal more will be heard. He always writes as a scholar, with complete avoidance of infelicities of theological utterance such as too often have handicapped suggestive heterodoxies."—*The Literary World.*

"The materials for the further pursuit of the inquiry are all brought together in this volume, and the author is at very evident pains to hold the balance carefully as between the different authorities whom he quotes. He has read everything of any importance that has been published relating to the subject of which he treats. He is evidently a very widely read man, and is possessed of much critical acumen, as also of all the best qualifications of historical inquiry and original research. The work will, we doubt not, be largely read by Christian theologians."—*The Asiatic Quarterly Review.*

"This is the fifth book by Mr. Mead that we have had the pleasure of bringing before our readers. In our notices of his earlier volumes we have been glad to recognise, whether we agreed with him or not, the learning, the earnestness, the scientific method, and the deep religious spirit by which they have been animated. The title of the present volume will, we anticipate, cause many readers to regard it as a piece of cranky speculation. . . . It is not, however, a work to be dismissed with a mere shrug of the shoulders. . . . Mr. Mead has brought out not simply an interesting but a valuable work, even apart from the special thesis which he investigates."—*The Primitive Methodist Quarterly Review.*

"I would direct the attention of educated scholarly men to a very remarkable book . . . written by G. R. S. Mead. . . . . I invite our educated and serious-minded Protestant clergymen everywhere to read this book and tell me, privately, what they think about it."—Standish O' Grady, in *The All Ireland Review.*

"A much more remarkable collection of apocrypha is the subject of a curious book by Mr. Mead, known to the small public who are interested in such things as learned in the fantasies of Gnosticism. . . . We have not often read a learned book from which we dissent so widely with more genuine interest, and we are bound to recognise the dignified and scholarly fashion in which Mr. Mead puts forward his theses, strange and impossible as some of them seem to us to be.—*The Pilot.*

PISTIS SOPHIA: A Gnostic Gospel.

(With Extracts from the Books of the Saviour appended.) Originally translated from Greek into Coptic, and now for the first time Englished from Schwartze's Latin Version of the only known Coptic MS., and checked by Amélineau's French version. With an Introduction and Bibliography. 394, xliv. pp. large octavo. Cloth. 7s. 6d. net.

(Out of Print. A Revised Edition is contemplated.)

SOME PRESS OPINIONS.

"The 'Pistis Sophia' has long been recognised as one of the most important Gnostic documents we possess, and Mr. Mead deserves the gratitude of students of Church History and of the History of Christian Thought, for his admirable translation and edition of this curious Gospel."—*Glasgow Herald.*

"Mr. Mead has done a service to other than Theosophists by his translation of the 'Pistis Sophia.' This curious work has not till lately received the attention which it deserves. . . . . He has prefixed a short Introduction, which includes an excellent bibliography. Thus, the English reader is now in a position to judge for himself of the scientific value of the only Gnostic treatise of any considerable length which has come down to us."—*Guardian.*

"From a scholar's point of view the work is of value as illustrating the philosophico-mystical tendencies of the second century."—*Record.*

"Mr. Mead deserves thanks for putting in an English dress this curious document from the early ages of Christian philosophy."—*Manchester Guardian.*

THE THEOSOPHICAL PUBLISHING SOCIETY, LONDON AND BENARES